U.S. Immigration and Naturalization Laws and Issues

U.S. IMMIGRATION
AND NATURALIZATION
LAWS AND ISSUES

A Documentary History

Edited by MICHAEL LEMAY
and ELLIOTT ROBERT BARKAN

Primary Documents in American History and Contemporary Issues

GREENWOOD PRESS
Westport, Connecticut • London

Library of Congress Cataloging-in-Publication Data

U.S. immigration and naturalization laws and issues : a documentary
   history / edited by Michael LeMay and Elliott Robert Barkan.
         p.   cm.—(Primary documents in American history and
   contemporary issues, ISSN 1069–5605)
      Includes bibliographical references and index.
      ISBN 0–313–30156–5 (alk. paper)
      1. Emigration and immigration law—United States—History—
   Sources.   I. LeMay, Michael C., 1941– .   II. Barkan, Elliott
   Robert.   III. Series.
   KF4818.I85   1999
   342.73'082—dc21   98–55343

British Library Cataloguing in Publication Data is available.

Library of Congress Catalog Card Number: 98–55343
ISBN: 0–313–30156–5
ISSN: 1069–5605

First published in 1999

Greenwood Press, 88 Post Road West, Westport, CT 06881
An imprint of Greenwood Publishing Group, Inc.
www.greenwood.com

Printed in the United States of America

The paper used in this book complies with the
Permanent Paper Standard issued by the National
Information Standards Organization (Z39.48–1984).

10 9 8 7 6 5 4 3 2 1

We dedicate this volume to our grandparents, Abraham and Lotte Barkan and Henry and Sadie Leder, and Bertha Lenger for having the courage to uproot themselves and settle in a strange new land.

Contents

Series Foreword

This series is designed to meet the research needs of high school and college students by making available in one volume the key primary documents on a given historical or contemporary issue. Documents include speeches and letters, congressional testimony, Supreme Court and lower district court decisions, government reports, position papers, statutes, and occasional news stories.

The purpose of the series is twofold: (1) to provide substantive and background material on an event or issue through the text of pivotal primary documents that shaped policy or law, raised controversy, or influenced the course of events; and (2) to trace the controversial aspects of the event or issue through documents that represent a variety of viewpoints. Documents for each volume have been selected by a recognized specialist in the subject with the advice of a board of other subject specialists, school librarians, and teachers.

To place the subject in historical perspective, the volume editors have prepared an introductory overview and a chronology of events. Documents are organized either topically or chronologically. The documents are full text or, if unusually long, have been excerpted by the volume editors. To facilitate understanding, each document is accompanied by an explanatory introduction. Suggestions for further reading follow the documents or the chapter.

It is the hope of Greenwood Press that this series will enable students and other readers to use primary documents more easily in their research, to exercise critical thinking skills by examining the key documents in American history and public policy, and to critique the variety of viewpoints represented by this selection of documents.

Preface

Immigration to the United States, which has long involved a truly significant mass movement of people, has profoundly shaped the economic, political, social, and cultural development of the nation, and in the process has had a lifelong impact on the immigrants themselves.

According to historian Erika Lee of the University of California at Berkeley (1998), beginning in the late nineteenth-century immigrants were "subjected to the jarring reality of immigration laws which 'sifted' and 'picked' the desirable from the undesirable." Since then, she contends, immigration to and immigrant life within the United States have become increasingly regulated by federal, state, and even local laws. Thus, if one wants to understand our nation's immigration history, it is essential that one examine the ways in which immigration and naturalization laws have shaped those complex processes.

Furthermore, to understand immigration policy fully, one must examine not only the laws passed by the Congress of the United States but also the judicial cases and administrative decisions that have implemented those immigration and naturalization laws. Immigration policy embraces a broad array of laws regulating myriad activities, including immigration with the aim of permanent residence, the admission of refugees and those seeking asylum, naturalization and citizenship policies, the deportation of those adjudged to be here illegally, and the procedures developed by various levels of government that influence such aspects of the immigrant's life as occupational and educational opportunities and access to various health and welfare benefit programs.

This volume presents the primary documents essential to examine and understand the immigration and naturalization policies of the United States from colonial times to the present. It contains the major laws, or key sections of virtually every major law, enacted by the federal government on those subjects. Since some of those laws involved dozens, even hundreds, of pages in the United States Code of Statutes, we have excerpted the key provisions characterizing a particular law. In addition to those essential laws, we have included various presidential proclamations and executive orders as well as several key veto messages, along with significant Supreme Court decisions and several key district court cases. In several instances, congressional statements on the arguments for or against landmark bills are provided for the insight they provide on aspects of some of the most significant laws enacted. We have also included positions taken by political parties, candidates for president, and advocates of various nativist organizations, such as the Ku Klux Klan and the Know Nothing Party. Finally, articles from various foreign language press sources have been selected for the insights gleaned from that perspective.

These primary documents are presented here largely in chronological order, with brief introductory sections for each of the four major parts into which we have grouped these documents. These remarks are intended to provide an overview of various periods of immigration policy and offer a context for a fuller understanding of the primary documents. At the end of the book, a selected bibliography lists important secondary sources of critical scholarship for the various periods and phases of the nation's immigration and naturalization policies, and a glossary defines many important terms.

As this collection of primary documents so richly illustrates, U.S. immigration and naturalization law and policy have involved a complex balancing of several goals and variables that have played key roles in shaping those policies and, indeed, the processes they have been designed to control or regulate. These variables include

- Racial, religious, and gender beliefs, concepts, and prejudices
- Perceived economic needs of the country and the class conflicts involved
- Societal and cultural perceptions of who can and should be allowed entry into the territory and admission into citizenship of the United States, which also concerns the development of a national identity
- Domestic political struggles
- Foreign policy considerations.

These primary documents illustrate, as well, the growth and expansion of the capacity of the federal government to implement policy to control the immigration and naturalization processes, reflecting prevalent, shifting assumptions about whom to allow entry into the sovereign nation. The laws were sometimes a reaction to, and sometimes profoundly shape, the composition and flow of the migration to the United States.

While it is a cliché that the United States is a "nation of nations," it is nonetheless profoundly true that our national legal history reflects our efforts to grapple with that reality positively and negatively. It is essential, then, to analyze both the immigration and the naturalization processes in order to understand our nation's society, culture, and politics. Those processes can shed light on how the nation's quest for control of the immigration and naturalization flow has evolved in response to the nation's needs as well as, at times, to the demands of nativists and xenophobic movements, changing periodic bouts of hyper-nationalism, wartime anxieties, and humanitarian concerns about refugees.

A NOTE ABOUT THE DOCUMENTS

Nearly all of the legislation covering the years 1798 through 1970 were excerpted from the Immigration and Naturalization Service (INS) manual for INS naturalization examiners and other officers: *Laws Applicable to Immigration and Nationality*, compiled by Carl B. Hyatt and edited by Edwina Austin Avery (Washington, D.C.: Government Printing Office, 1953), with supplementary materials up to 1970. Except where an act was given a title in the legislation itself (such as the Nationality Act of 1940 and the Immigration and Nationality Act [of 1952], Avery put subtitles identifying the subjects of the particular acts to facilitate their use by INS staff. It is those subtitles that we have used where legislated ones were not apparent. Thus, the acts, named by the date signed into law—or approved by Congressional override of a presidential veto—("Act of June 29, 1906") are followed either by the official title or by the subtitle appearing in the INS manual (Act of June 29, 1906: Basic Naturalization Act of 1906 Providing for the Naturalization of Aliens throughout the United States and Establishing the Bureau of Immigration and Naturalization). In addition, many of the laws have acquired commonly used names, such the Chinese Exclusion Act, the Scott Act, the Johnson-Reed Act, and the McCarran-Walter Act. In those instances the informal title is quoted within parentheses, as follows: Act of June 27, 1952: The Immigration and Nationality Act ("McCarran-Walter Act"). Where no titles, subtitles, or commonly-used titles readily exist, we have simply put a parenthetical word or phrase following the name of the act to indicate the general topic area, for example: Act of March 3, 1813 (Re: Naturalization). The Index lists both the commonly used titles of legislation and the actual act. Finally, due to the complexity of Avery's arrangement of the laws, in a number of cases small segments of laws that were subsequent amendments (modifying the original language) have been included here as part of the original legislation. However, in order to insure the greatest accuracy, anywhere that this was done the passage is so identified and the law that amended the original is fully indicated.

[See Erika Lee, "Immigrants and Immigration Law: A State of the Field Assessment." Paper presented at the American Historical Association Meeting, Seattle, Washington, January 1988, and published in the *Journal of American Ethnic History* (Summer 1999).]

Acknowledgments

The editors of any such volume examining a topic as rich and complex as this one owe a debt to many scholars who have over the years compiled a body of literature on that topic. First and foremost we acknowledge our enormous debt of gratitude to Marion Smith, historian for the Immigration and Naturalization Service (INS), who provided us with an invaluable copy of the INS manual of immigration and naturalization law covering INS policies through 1970. We gratefully acknowledge our debt to those scholars who wrote the numerous sources cited in the bibliography of this volume. We also gratefully acknowledge the support provided by the Foundation of the California State University in San Bernardino, which awarded a mini-grant that enabled the editors to spend two summers collecting the key documents contained herein. We note also our gratitude to our respective department secretaries, Mrs. Debbi Fox in Political Science and Ms. Stacy Poffek in History, who assisted us in numerous duplicating jobs and in preparing the manuscript for production.

We thank Ms. Abbake Amaira a student assistant, for the help she provided in duplicating many of the documents included in this volume. A special note of thanks goes to Kevin V. Dunphy, who provided us with the text of *In Re Rodriguez*.

We thank Mrs. Barbara Rader, Executive Editor of the School and Public Library Reference Division of Greenwood Publishing, who first asked us to consider editing this volume, and Ms. Emily Birch, who served as this volume's acquisitions editor. We also are grateful to the immigration scholars and public librarians who agreed to critique the manuscript and offer their suggestions to improve it.

Introduction

Immigration policy is a topic of substantive and perennial interest to many Americans. Obviously, the influx of millions has had a profound impact on the nation's economy, culture, and politics. Although it is a cliché, it is nonetheless true that the United States is a nation of nations. To understand the process of immigration to the United States, one needs to grasp the laws concerning immigration and naturalization. The magnitude of the problems associated with the complex process of permanent immigration has led to many and varied laws, the most important of which are presented in this volume.

Scholars consider immigration policy a type of intermestic policy, an inherent interweaving of international and domestic policy. Immigration law performs an essential gatekeeping function, determining at any given time who shall or shall not be allowed entry into the United States.

This reference volume, which chronologically traces the major laws regulating both immigration and naturalization, provides a historical overview of U.S. immigration and naturalization policies. Those policies inevitably blend several essential elements: economic interest, foreign policy, racial values, and a sense of national identity—who should be allowed to be "an American." Since 1860 the relationship of these elements, as embodied in immigration and naturalization laws, has changed as the nation has responded to various situations and concerns. Periods of economic recession or depression as well as social unrest and cultural shift, such as the Cold War period after the Korean War and the civil rights movement of the 1960s, have given rise to fundamental changes in immigration law. As the flow of immigration changed, in terms of the race or national origin of the tens of thousands pouring into the nation annually, concern for our ability to assimilate and even the desirability of absorbing these new "strangers in our midst" has led to other changes in law designed to manage the size and composition of that flow.

The devices used by sponsors of immigration law enacted to control the influx changed dramatically at times, often in response to the advocacy of particular interest groups promoting or opposing such modifications. A recurrent theme in the history of immigration law is whether or not each wave of immigrants can, or should, be assimilated into the nation's culture. Methods used to control immigration have included "excluded categories"—groups deemed to have undesirable physical or mental characteristics—literacy tests, the imposition of a quota system, the development of an elaborate system of preferences, labor certification, refugee, asylee, and parole status, and employer sanctions. Administrative rules, regulations, and procedures as applications of the law were likewise used to bar or slow down immigration, as well as to influence the rates of naturalization. A long-term view of immigration policy shows these various elements of immigration law sometimes working in harmony with one another, reinforcing each other, and at other times working in conflict with each other. Contending forces have sought to influence immigration policy by stressing the different elements (LeMay 1987, xiv).

The history of immigration and naturalization law since the late nineteenth century reflects a continuing struggle for control of the immigration process. Competing forces have attempted to achieve a politically acceptable consensus about procedural justice in the matter of regulating the influx across the nation's borders. Ultimately, the disparities in power among those competing groups is the key to understanding immigration policy (Kritz 1983, 363). The interplay among them is central to the periodic reviews and revisions in policy and procedure designed to arrive at a consensus as to how open or closed the nation's borders would be at any particular time.

For convenience, this book is divided into four major parts or periods. The era of unrestricted entry, in Part I, was, in terms of immigration, the classic period, marked by few restrictions or controls on the admission of newcomers; citizenship, however, was restricted in 1790 to "white persons." From early colonial law [see Documents 1–5] to the early 1880s, national and even state laws [see Documents 15–18] addressing the issue of immigration focused on individual immigrants. While few if any restrictions on admissions were imposed, the naturalization law, by limiting eligibility to whites, reflected a racial-group bias. Indeed, during this period, immigration law sometimes provided incentives to attract immigrants [Documents 24, 25]. Bars against entry were typically limited to a few "lunatics, idiots, the lame or infirm, paupers or indigents" who were likely to become public charges, or criminals and contract laborers [Documents 34, 35].

Europe, China, and Japan were undergoing massive and radical social and economic changes requiring societal reorganization to cope with the problems. In Europe, the old agricultural order changed from the feudal system's communal and subsistence farming to individually owned farms oriented to supplying an urban market economy. These forces led to the creation of a large mass of landless peasants from the British Isles to Russia. The industrial revolution, starting first in England and moving gradually across the European continent, added new strains to the social order as old employment patterns disintegrated. Displaced artisans and farm workers alike often went through a step migration process—moving from a more rural setting in their homeland to an urban place for some months or even a few years and then finally immigrating to the United States. In China and Japan, a similar step migration pattern was evident. As population pressures added to economic disruptions, religious and political persecution often followed. Various governments in Europe and Asia began to encourage emigration. When famine was added to these "push" factors, those migrating numbered in the millions. Push factors accounted for why tens of millions left Europe, but it was various "pull" factors that drew many of them to the United States, in particular, and others to South America, Australia, or Canada. Many first came as "sojourners," intending to settle temporarily in the United States and then return to their homelands. Prior to the 1920s quota system era, this pattern was more often associated with Greek, Italian, Eastern European, French Canadian, Chinese, and Japanese immigrants. Many came attracted by the greater economic opportunities afforded by the expanding American territory and economy.

The view that America should be a place of asylum and opportunity to those millions leaving Europe shaped the early phase of American immigration policy. Official policy was to keep the gates open to all, and little opposition to this policy was voiced at first. When the nation took its first census, in 1790, it recorded a population of 3,227,000, most of whom were descendants of seventeenth- and eighteenth-century arrivals or recent immigrants themselves. Nearly 75 percent were of British origin, about 8 percent were of German origin, and the remainder were of Dutch, French, or Spanish origin and, of course, African origin, the black slaves. Less than 1 percent were Native Americans. This population occupied a land that was vast, sparsely settled, and rich in soil and natural resources. The population density in 1790 was only 4.5 persons per square mile (Select Commission of Immigration and Refugee Policy 1981, 165). There was an obvious need for labor to build the cities and clear the land on the frontier for farms. Additional population was desired to strengthen the nation's defenses against the Indians or to avoid coming under control of various European colonial powers. The sentiment prevailing among most U.S. citizens at the time was that the nation was a brave and bold experiment in freedom which they felt should be shared by any and all who desired to be free, regardless of their former nationality.

The future first president, George Washington, summed up this prevailing view when he stated, "The bosom of America is open to receive not only the opulent and respectable stranger, but the oppressed and persecuted of all Nations and Religions; whom we shall welcome to a participation of all our rights and privileges, if by decency and propriety of conduct they appear to merit the enjoyment" [Document 6].

The United States offered religious freedom to immigrants fleeing religious persecution. Its politically open society drew those escaping political oppression. The abundance of its land and the nearly boundless economic opportunity it offered drew those compelled to flee the economic deprivation and often near-starvation conditions in their homelands and those simply seeking a more open society that offered far better opportunities for economic advancement. Open lands attracted Europeans whose homelands were experiencing acute overpopulation.

The nation's burgeoning cities needed unskilled laborers. Though many immigrants arrived expecting to find the streets "paved with gold," they ironically found the streets unpaved and discovered they were to do the paving! Rapid industrialization was fed by the cheap labor afforded by immigration. The first wave of immigrants entering during the open-door era were largely from northwestern Europe.

In the 1790s Congress began passing laws regulating naturalization. Although the first act confined citizenship to white persons, it was very liberal in requiring only two years of residency and the renunciation of former allegiances [Document 7]. Turmoil in Europe in the mid-1790s, however, raised anew fears about colonial foreign influence, and Congress responded with more stringent naturalization and immigration laws. It now required five years of residency and a renunciation of titles of nobility as well as allegiances [Document 8]. In 1798 Congress, then under control of the Federalist party, raised the period of residency to fourteen years [Document 9] and pushed through the Alien Act, allowing the president to deport any alien considered to be a threat to the nation [Document 10].

The Alien Act was permitted to expire when the Jeffersonian Democratic Republicans replaced the Federalists in power. In 1802 Congress reestablished the five-year provision of the 1795 act [Documents 11–13]. In 1819 Congress passed a law requiring a manifest of all entering ship passengers, including sex, occupation, age, and nation of origin [Document 14].

The wave of Catholic immigrants during the 1830s and 1840s set off a dramatic antiforeign reaction. Immigrants were easy scapegoats to blame for the problems facing a rapidly changing society as it began its initial stages of urbanization and industrialization. Immigration policy was alleged to be allowing the importation of crime, poverty, and drunkenness. Anti-immigration groups, such as the Order of the Star Spangled Banner and the Know-Nothing political party, advocated restrictive immigration and naturalization laws [Documents 20, 21, and 23].

The need for labor, however, prevailed over nativist sentiment in determining public law. The discovery of gold in California in 1848 drew a vast population to the nation's west coast. The Mexican–American War and the Treaty of Guadalupe Hildago [Document 19] added new territory and new population, including Mexicans as new citizens by treaty right. The post–Civil War period generated a nearly insatiable need for immigrants. The transcontinental railroad building boom opened up vast lands to settlement. Massive numbers of immigrant workers were needed to mine coal and ore and to work in the mills and factories that had been spurred to new levels by Civil War–generated production. The Fourteenth Amendment guaranteed citizenship to all persons born in the United States [Document 26]. Congress enacted laws ensuring citizenship for the former slaves and easier naturalization for those who served in military or naval services or the merchant marine. The Gold Rush, railroad building, and other post–Civil War developments drew tens of thousands of Chinese to the West Coast. Meanwhile, the composition of immigrants from Europe began to change, with increasing numbers from South, Central, and Eastern Europe. By the late 1880s, they were beginning to outnumber those from northwestern Europe. These changes in the immigration flow, coupled with economic recessions and a depression during the 1870s, created new political pressures for restriction. The ban on the immigration of convicts and prostitutes was passed in 1875 [Document 28]. Despite President Hayes's veto of a Chinese Exclusion Act [Document 30], the 1880s ushered in a new phase in immigration policy.

Part II contains documents from the next era, one characterized by both limited and unlimited immigration, roughly from 1880 to 1920. The European immigrants arriving during this era were known as the "new" immigrants. A staggering 23.5 million immigrants flooded into the United States, predominantly from South, Central, and Eastern Europe and from Asia. These new immigrants were even more visibly different from the "native stock," which set off a renewed xenophobic reaction that culminated in increasingly restrictive immigration laws directed at specific groups of immigrants deemed undesirable (first Chinese and then Asians more generally). Ironically, at the very time that the Statue of Liberty was being erected, symbolizing the nation as being open to all the "poor and oppressed of the world, the huddled masses yearning to be free," the new immigrants were engendering fear and dislike among segments of the native stock. Their more alien characteristics—

coloring, physique, customs, and languages—aroused new fears that these strangers would be unable to assimilate. Racist fervor had led to the first blatantly restrictionist immigration law, the Chinese Exclusion Act of 1882 [Document 33]. From laws banning the Chinese to those excluding other Asians, and finally to the imposition of literacy tests, immigration and naturalization law was, for the first time, intentionally restrictionist. The door was no longer wide open.

Pseudo-scientific arguments by nativist groups that the new immigrants were racially inferior and more likely to become criminals or diseased were given somewhat popular credence in books and articles written by historians, sociologists, and biologists. Such arguments undercut the earlier prevailing tradition of a welcome to "all the poor and oppressed." Restrictive immigration laws also reflected four historical trends in the 1880s and 1890s: (1) the burgeoning cities and rapid industrialization, which led to visibly corrupt urban political machines, some of which targeted the immigrant ethnic voters; (2) the official census report declaring the American frontier closed; (3) the tendency among the new immigrants, who were crowding into the cities, to maintain their culture and traditions more visibly than did the old immigrants; and (4) greater religious divergence from Protestantism among the new immigrants who, unlike the Northern Europeans, were overwhelmingly Catholic, Jewish, or Orthodox (Greek, Russian, etc.) or not Judeo-Christian at all (Asians). Greater numbers of these new immigrants also came as sojourners, intending to return to their homelands after a few years in America. The sojourner mentality reduced their incentive to acquire the language and customs of their temporary home.

The general Immigration Act of 1882 [Document 34] barred the immigration of "lunatics, idiots, convicts, and those liable to become public charges." Those suffering from "loathsome or contagious diseases" and persons convicted of crimes involving "moral turpitude" were denied entry. The law also provided for the medical inspection of all new arrivals.

The Chinese Exclusion Act was revised several times to close loopholes and made stricter so that, by 1900, it was approaching the total exclusion of laborers and their spouses. U.S. immigration officials used administrative rules to implement these various acts, with harsh measures designed to suppress illegal entries. Between 1901 and 1910, for example, deportations of Chinese averaged 560 per year (Lai, Lim, and Yung 1980, 12). On the West Coast, where anti-Chinese sentiment reached its zenith, immigrants were rigorously examined. Many came through Angel Island, the port of entry in San Francisco Bay for most of the 175,000 Chinese immigrants who entered the United States between 1910 and 1940. Customs officials there carefully examined immigration papers searching for "paper sons and daughters" and for those entering under false pretenses, and they performed cursory medical examinations. The station became the holding place for deportees. Many of the Chinese wrote poems about their ordeals on the wooden barrack walls [Document 71].

At ports of entry, inspectors suspected all Chinese of being illegal until they could prove their identities, which were verified after vigorous cross-examinations. These intensive, detailed interrogations were intended to exclude rather than admit. The Chinese viewed the exclusion laws and regulations as discriminatory and grossly unfair. They referred to those laws as *keli*, or tyrannical laws (Lai, Lim, and Yung 1980, 14). All arriving immigrants, on both coasts, were given these medical exams. Immigration laws classified certain ailments as "loathsome" or "dangerously contagious" and were grounds for exclusion; for example, persons with trachoma (conjunctivitis) were excluded in 1903; those with uncinariasis (hookworm) and filariasis (parasites) in 1910; and those with clonorchiasis (liver fluke) in 1917 (1980, 15).

At the Angel Island station, those who passed the medical barriers were detained awaiting hearings on their applications to enter. Men and women were separated and lived in sparsely furnished communal rooms with rows of double- and triple-tier bunks. Privacy was minimal and the dorm rooms were guarded. At any one time 200 to 300 males and up to 50 females were housed on Angel Island awaiting their hearings or deportation, often for quite lengthy confinements. Several interviews of detainees are presented in Document 70.

Despite the few general restrictions, the number of immigrants continued to rise, arousing nativist groups to seek new devices to restrict immigration, such as literacy tests [Document 63]. The first literacy bill was introduced into Congress in 1895, where it was quickly passed by both houses but vetoed by President Cleveland [Document 48]. In 1906 legislation was introduced that included both a literacy test for admission and an English language test for naturalization [Document 56]. Nativist groups were joined by labor unions in advocating this new policy. Unions were increasingly wary of the economic threat to their wage scales and working conditions implicit in unrestricted immigration. Business leaders opposed the new law. They wanted to avoid any limitation of new and cheaper labor sources. However, the English language was accepted as a requirement for citizenship [Document 56]. Congress created a joint Congressional/Presidential Commission to study the impact of immigration. Begun in 1909, the Dillingham Commission, named after its chair, Senator William Dillingham, operated under the pseudoscientific, racist theories prevalent at the time. Its report recommended a literacy test and other restrictionist legislation [Document 61].

The war in Europe generated economic growth and labor demands in the United States, both of which ran counter to restrictive policy. Although Congress passed a literacy law in 1912, it was vetoed by President Taft. In 1915, after it was passed once more, President Wilson vetoed it [Document 62]. Following entry of the United States into World War I in 1917, Congress enacted another literacy bill and overrode yet another veto. The 1917 law [Document 63] finally made literacy an admission requirement. It codified a list of aliens to be excluded and banned all immigration from an "Asiatic barred zone." The xenophobic reactions during the war years contributed to a significant restrictionist movement and specifically to anti-German activity. The decade also witnessed an "Americanization" movement to educate the foreign born about U.S. language and customs. Between 1919 and 1921, twenty states passed laws creating such Americanization programs (LeMay 1987, 12). When industry joined the movement to restrict immigration, a new phase of immigration policy began—one that involved a quota system approach.

During the third era—that of restrictions, refugees, and reforms, from 1920 to 1965—national immigration law was governed by an elaborate quota system. The quota laws dramatically reduced immigration from more than 23.5 million in the forty-year period of the previous era (1880–1920) to fewer than 6 million in the forty-five years of this period. In 1921 Congress enacted, and President Harding signed into law, a measure implementing the concept of quotas based on the immigrants' country of origin (originally proposed by Senator William Dillingham) [Document 73]. In 1924 this approach was expanded in the Johnson-Reed Act [Document 79]. In 1929 those quotas were fixed based on these percentages of Eastern Hemisphere nationalities in the entire U.S. population in 1920 [Document 89]. This national-origins quota system, implemented in 1929, remained in place until 1965. In 1925 Congress also created the border patrol to halt illegal immigration; an estimated 500,000 had entered during the 1920s (Chiswick 1982, 13) [Document 81]. These quota laws reduced the size of the wave and intentionally shifted the source of immigration from South, Central, and Eastern European nations to northwestern European ones. Approximately 60 percent of this new distribution came from northwestern Europe, and some 35 percent, outside the quotas, from the Western Hemisphere.

The quota system, coupled with the economic impact of the Great Depression during the 1930s, dramatically reduced overall immigration, although there continued to be no restrictions placed on the open immigration from the Western Hemisphere. It was not until the 1940s that any pressure was felt to modify the strict restrictionist nature of the law. A slight relaxation was made during World War II. In a foreign policy–induced response to the wartime alliance with China, Congress repealed the sixty-year ban on Chinese immigration [Document 107]. The need for the labor of aliens after the United States entered the war also led to the enactment of the "bracero" program [Documents 108, 117]. This temporary work program imported labor, mostly from Mexico, to fill wartime needs. When news of Nazi atrocities became widespread at the end of the war, President Truman issued a directive that resulted in the admission of some 40,000 war refugees [Document 111]. Congress enacted a law that allowed 120,000 alien wives, husbands, and children of members of the armed forces to immigrate to the United States separate from the quota system [Document 112].

In the postwar years, the executive branch began to play a more active role in all policy making, including a more prominent role in shaping immigration policy. President Truman initiated the nation's first refugee law, the Displaced Persons Act of 1948 [Document 114], which had been advocated by such groups as the American Jewish Committee and the Citizens Committee on Displaced Persons and supported by the American Federation of Labor. Its most outspoken opponent was the American Legion. Congress passed the law in 1948. It permitted the admission of more than 400,000 displaced persons through the end of 1951 by "mortgaging" their entry against their homelands' future quotas.

Foreign policy considerations brought on by the Cold War era saw additional refugee measures enacted by the Congress [Documents 123, 128, 130]. In 1956 and 1957 Congress passed legislation allowing Hungarian "refugees-escapees," displaced by their failed revolution, to enter. They had initially been "paroled" by President Eisenhower. "Parole" established a category for refugees from Communist-dominated countries or countries in the Middle East. In 1960 Congress passed a temporary program for refugees and displaced persons from World War II who were still in UN refugee camps. Such special refugee-related acts [Documents 127 and 129] did not alter the national origin quota approach but rather weakened it by erasing mortgages and by passing on the parolees, allowing favored treatment under special circumstances largely because of the Cold War inspired, anti-Communist atmosphere.

Meanwhile, in 1952, the Immigration and Nationality Act, better known as the McCarran-Walter Act, had been passed [Document 118]. This act consolidated previous immigration statutes into a single law, retaining the basic national-origin quota system but also introducing the idea of "preferences" for certain skilled laborers and for relatives of U.S. citizens and permanent resident aliens. It set a numerical limit of 150,000 on immigration from the Eastern Hemisphere and retained the unlimited number for the Western Hemisphere. The act included a small quota for Asian immigrants not covered by specific national quota limits and removed all racial, gender, and nationality barriers to citizenship. Congress overrode President Truman's veto of the bill. His veto message, although unsuccessful, provides an articulate case against the quota system [Document 119].

In 1953 the president appointed a special commission to study immigration and naturalization policy. It recommended a more liberalized approach. In 1962 Congress enacted the Migration and Refugee Assistance Act to aid the president in these matters. Some of the commission's recommendations were finally enacted in the Immigration and Nationality Act of 1965, which ended the national-origins quota system and ushered in a new era of immigration policy.

Part IV contains documents and laws enacted during the recent period, the era of globalization (1965 to 1996). Immigration law shifted during this period from the quota system to a more elaborate preference system. In part, the law reflected changing national values on race—rejecting the open racism of the quota system—and the civil rights era, much as the McCarran-Walter Act had reflected the Cold War era. In part, the new law also reflected foreign policy considerations—allowing for refugees fleeing from Communist countries but largely closing admission to "economic refugees" who were simply fleeing their impoverished native economies attracted by the economic opportunities afforded by the world's largest economy. The healthy and expanding economy of the 1960s eased fears of job competition, and even organized labor favored a more liberal approach. The new law in 1965 set an overall limit of 160,000, including a maximum of 20,000 persons per country for all nations outside the Western Hemisphere, and placed a limit of 120,000 on Western Hemisphere nations but without limits for individual nations. Its seven-category preference system gave first priority to reuniting families and a high preference to certain desired occupational skills [Document 132].

The ending of the open-door policy for Western Hemisphere nations was a compromise necessary to pass the law. Ending the bracero program in 1964 and closing the door to open immigration from the Western Hemisphere soon led to an increasing backlog of applicants from Latin America and renewed problems of illegal aliens entering from those countries. In 1968 continuing problems of coping with large refugee flows led President Johnson to issue a proclamation in which the United States agreed to adhere to the United Nations Protocol on the Status of Refugees [Document 136].

The nation continued to struggle, as well, with the difficult issue of coping with a renewed and large-scale influx of illegal aliens. Congress reacted to such pressures by passing, in 1976, an amendment to the 1965 law that set immigration limits for both hemispheres using the 20,000 per country limit. It set a worldwide limit of 290,000 but retained the seven-category preference system [Document 138].

Mass refugee movements linked to our foreign policy concerns led to further special "parole" programs to handle Chinese, Cuban, Vietnamese, and Soviet refugees. Such special cases, however, could still not keep up with the pressures of would-be immigrants to enter. Existing authority became increasingly inadequate to handle what was becoming a recurring "special" situation. Concern over the refugee question led the Congress to enact the Refugee Act of 1980 [Document 139]. It was intended to correct deficiencies in existing policy by providing an ongoing mechanism for the admission and aid of refugees. Enactment of the Refugee Act clearly indicated the need and the willingness of Congress to reexamine immigration policy.

The 1970s was a decade of "stagflation," an economy troubled by both high inflation and high unemployment. These conditions, coupled with a dramatic shift in the flow of immigration from northwestern Europe to Latin America and Asia and the renewed inflow of illegal immigration resulting from the ending of the bracero program, led to calls for a major revision in immigration law. In 1984 alone the Immigration and Naturalization Service (INS) apprehended over 1.2 million undocumented aliens, an astonishing 34 percent increase over two years. The upshot was rather broad support for a new policy and a bipartisan effort to enact one. It became increasingly clear that the United States was not adequately controlling its more than 5,000 miles of border. The combined legal immigration rate and the estimated undocumented rate, which exceeded the peak years of the early 1900s, represented about half of the increase of the total population added to the United States. Once again, a special bipartisan commission was established to study immigration policy—the Select Commission on Immigration and Refugee Policy (SCIRP). Its recommendations became the foundation for several immigration reform acts passed in the following two decades [Document 141].

Since 1985 immigration law has focused largely on ways to "demagnetize" the draw of the U.S. economy that attracts millions of illegal— that is, undocumented—aliens. Most recently, laws were passed to impose employer sanctions [Document 144], increase the total numbers of legal immigrants [Document 145], and withhold various welfare, medical, and even educational benefits from illegal aliens and even from legal resident aliens [Documents 146, 148, 149].

However, as fears of immigrants receded and many groups made known the severely punitive effects of the medical welfare provisions concerning legal alien residents, some of those cuts in aid were gradually restored [Document 150].

The combination of changing global conditions and the legislative reforms have contributed to a profound shift in the sources of immigration. The more than 20 million immigrants who have entered during this period have mostly come from dramatically different places than they did during the previous era. Nearly half of the total wave came from Western Hemisphere nations, and about 34 percent came from Asian nations. European nations supplied approximately 15 percent of the total.

Significant Dates in Immigration and Naturalization Law

1700–1740	Various colonies pass immigration related "province laws."
1740	British Naturalization Law enacted to systematize naturalization procedures and encourage immigration to the American colonies. It set a pattern followed by the colonies and later the United States government after independence.
1789	United States Constitution adopted. Article I, Section 8 empowers the Congress "To establish an uniform Rule of Naturalization."
1790	Among its first actions, the Congress established a uniform rule of naturalization, imposing a two-year residency for aliens who are "free white persons" of good character.
1802	Congress revises the Naturalization Act of 1790, specifying a five-year length of residency and renunciation of allegiance and fidelity to foreign powers.
1813	Congress reaffirms the five-year period for naturalization in the Five-Year Residence Act.
1819	Congress passes an act requiring ship masters to deliver a manifest enumerating all aliens transported for immigration and requiring the Secretary of State to annually inform Congress of the number of immigrants who were admitted.
1848	Treaty of Guadalupe Hidalgo signed guaranteeing U.S. citizenship to Mexicans remaining in the territory ceded by Mexico to the United States.
1855	Castle Garden becomes New York's principal point of entry.
1861–1865	Civil War
1862	Congress enacts the Homestead Act, granting up to 160 acres of free land to settlers who develop the land and remain on it for five years, spurring much immigration.

1867–1877   Reconstruction Era.

1868   The Fourteenth Amendment to the United States Constitution is ratified guaranteeing that all persons born or naturalized in the United States and subject to its jurisdiction are citizens of the United States and that no state may abridge their rights without due process nor deny them equal protection of the law. It insured the citizenship rights of the former slaves and thereby changed the "free white persons" phrase on citizenship to include blacks.

1870   Congress formally enacts a law granting citizenship to persons of African descent.

1882   Congress enacts the Chinese Exclusion Act, prohibiting the immigration of Chinese laborers for ten years (later reenacted and extended in 1892 and 1904) and denying Chinese eligibility for United States citizenship.

               Congress passes an act to regulate immigrations specifying some restrictions on immigration (convicts, persons likely to become public charges, etc.).

1885   Congress passes an act making it unlawful for laborers to immigrate to the United States under a contract with an employer here who in any manner prepays passage to bring the laborer to the United States.

1886   The U.S. Supreme Court decides the case of *Yick Wo v. Hopkins*, which overturns a San Francisco ordinance against Chinese laundry workers as clearly discriminatory and unconstitutional under the Fourteenth Amendment protections prohibiting state and local governments from depriving any person (even non-citizens) of life, liberty, or property without due process.

1888   Congress expands the Chinese Exclusion Act by rescinding reentry permits for Chinese laborers and prohibits their return (Scott Act).

1889   The U.S. Supreme Court decides the case of *Chae Chan Ping v. United States*, which upholds the Congress' right to repeal (and thereby ex-post-facto exclude) the certificate of reentry as contained in the 1888 Act.

1891   Congress passes a law expanding on the classes of individuals excluded from admission, forbids the soliciting of immigrants, and creates the position of superintendent of immigration.

1892   The Ellis Island reception station is opened and becomes the nation's leading immigration port of entry.

1894   Congress extends the Chinese Exclusion Act and establishes the Bureau of Immigration within the Treasury Department.

1896   Congress decides *Plessy v. Ferguson*, establishing the legal princi-
                ple of "separate-but-equal" and giving a constitutional basis to
                legal segregation based on race.

1897   A federal district court in West Texas renders its decision in *In Re
                Rodriguez*, affirming the citizenship rights of Mexicans in the
                United States on the basis of the Treaty of Guadalupe Hidalgo
                (1848) and notwithstanding that such persons may not be consid-
                ered "white."

1898   The U.S. Supreme Court rules in *Wong Kim Ark v. United States*
                that a native-born person of Asian descent is indeed a citizen of
                the United States despite the fact that his or her parents may have
                been resident aliens ineligible for naturalization.

                Spanish-American War, wherein the United States establishes con-
                trol over Guam, Puerto Rico, the Philippines and Cuba. The
                United States also annexes Hawaii.

1903   Congress passes a law moving immigration to the Department of
                Commerce and Labor.

1906   Congress enacts the Basic Naturalization Law, which codifies a
                uniform law for the naturalization process that, with some amend-
                ments and supplements, forms the basic law for naturalization
                thereafter.

1907   Congress adds important regulations regarding issuing of pass-
                ports and the expatriation and marriage of American women to
                foreigners. The act continued to stir controversy until Section 3 of
                the act was repealed in 1922.

                The president of the United States issues the executive order for
                the Gentleman's Agreement with Japan by which Japan would
                restrict the immigration of laborers from Japan and Korea (then
                under Japanese jurisdiction). Picture brides are permitted to mi-
                grate.

1910   Congress enacts The White-Slave Traffic Act, forbidding the im-
                portation of any woman or girl for the purpose of prostitution or
                similar immoral purposes.

1911   The Dillingham Commission issues its report. Its recommenda-
                tions lay the foundation for what becomes the Quota Acts of the
                1920s.

1914–1918   World War I. United States enters April 1917.

1915   The Americanization/100 Percentism campaign begins as both a
                government and private business undertaking. After the war, its
                perceived failure contributed to the disillusionment that set the
                stage for the quota acts of the 1920s.

1917   Congress enacts the Immigration Law that includes a literacy test
            for all immigrants and a provision barring immigration from a
            specified area—the Asiatic barred zone.

            The Departments of State and Labor issue a joint order requiring
            passports from all aliens seeking to enter the United States and
            requiring the issuing of visas from an American consular officer
            in the country of origin rather than allowing a person to come
            and enter the United States and seek permission to enter only
            when arriving at the shores or port of entry.
            Puerto Ricans are granted U.S. citizenship.

1918   Congress grants the president sweeping powers to exclude the
            entrance or departure of aliens during time of war. Similar pres-
            idential promulgations are used in virtually all periods of war
            thereafter.

1919   Congress enacts a law granting honorably-discharged Native
            Americans citizenship for their services during World War I.

            The summer "Red Scare" following the Bolshevik revolution
            leads to the deportation of certain specified "radical" aliens
            deemed a threat to security.

1921   Congress passes the First Quota Act, establishing the quota prin-
            ciple based on 3 percent of the foreign-born population in 1910.

1922   Congress passes the Cable Act assuring that the right of any
            woman to become a naturalized citizen of the United States shall
            not be abridged because of her sex or because she is a married
            woman, unless she was wed to an alien ineligible for citizenship.
            The latter provision was later repealed.

            The Supreme Court decides the case of *Ozawa v. United States*,
            upholding the constitutionality of restricting Japanese aliens from
            becoming naturalized citizens on the grounds that they were not
            Caucasian.

1923   The Supreme Court decides *United States v. Bhagat Singh Thind*,
            ruling that a white person meant those persons who appeared and
            would commonly be viewed as white. Thus, East Asian Indians,
            although Caucasian, were not "white" and were therefore ineli-
            gible for naturalization.

1924   Congress enacts the Immigration Act, known as the Johnson-Reed
            Act, establishing national origin quotas based on 2 percent of the
            census of the 1890 foreign-born population. The new system dra-
            matically shifted the flow of Eastern Hemisphere immigration
            from Southern, Central, and Eastern Europe to those from north-
            western European nations. The act also barred the admission of
            most Asians, who had been classified as "aliens ineligible for cit-
            izenship."

1924	Congress passes an act granting citizenship to those Native Americans who had not already received it by allotments under the 1887 Dawes Act or by military service during World War I.
1925	Congress establishes the Border Patrol.
1929	President Hoover proclaims the new and permanent quotas, basing the national origin quotas on the proportion of Eastern Hemisphere nationalities in the total population as determined by the 1920 census, with the total to be admitted lowered to just over 150,000.
1929–1939	The Great Depression significantly depresses world-wide migration and slows U.S. immigration flows dramatically.
1940	Congress declares the third Sunday of May to be celebrated as Citizenship Day.
	Congress enacts the Registration Law requiring non-citizens to annually register their address. This process remained in effect until 1980.
	Congress passes the Nationality Act of 1940 codifying and consolidating all previous nationality law dealing with the naturalization process.
1941	The president issues a proclamation to control persons entering or leaving the United States based on Congressional passage of the First War Powers Act.
1942	The president issues Executive Order 9066, leading to the evacuation, relocation, and internment of Japanese and Japanese Americans into relocation camps.
1943	The U.S. Supreme Court rules, in *Hirabayashi v. United States*, that the executive orders establishing curfews and evacuation programs were constitutional based upon "military necessities."
	Congress, in recognition of the alliance with China in the war against Japan, repeals the Chinese Exclusion Acts and authorizes a small quota and the naturalization rights of Chinese residents. In 1944 the president officially adds a quota of 105 to the immigration provisions.
1944	The U.S. Supreme Court decides *Korematsu v. United States*, again upholding the constitutionality of the executive orders excluding Japanese American citizens from remaining in certain "excluded zones."
	The Court also rules, in *Ex Parte Mitsuye Endo*, that the internment program was an unconstitutional violation of the habeas corpus rights of American citizens, namely the Nisei.
1945	Congress enacts the War Brides Act.

1946   The U.S. Supreme Court rules, in *Girouard v. United States*, that an applicant may be admitted to naturalization despite his or her conscientious objector status.

            Congress passes a law allowing for the naturalization of Filipinos and Asian Indians.

1948   Congress enacts the Displaced Persons Act, beginning a process of modifying the quota law by enacting exceptions to enable a greater number of immigrants to come to the United States.

1949   Congress passes the Agricultural Act which includes a provision to recruit temporary farm workers from Mexico—the Bracero program.

1952   Congress enacts the Immigration and Nationality Act (The McCarran-Walter Act), which recodifies immigration and naturalization law, maintains the quota system, sets up a quota for the Asia-Pacific triangle, and removes all racial and national origin barriers to U.S. citizenship.

1953   The President's Commission on Immigration and Naturalization issues its report, *Whom Shall We Welcome?* It offers a stinging rebuke of the 1952 act, calls for an end of the quota system, is highly critical of naturalization laws and procedures, and its recommendations become the basis for many of the reforms and amendments to the 1952 act passed in 1965 and thereafter.

            Congress enacts the Refugee Relief Act in response to Cold War foreign policy considerations. It contributes to the growing awareness in Congress that the quotas were too rigid. It allows for "non-quota" immigration based on "refugee" status rather than the national origin quotas.

1954   Ellis Island closes as the nation's largest and primary immigrant receiving and processing station.

1956   President Dwight D. Eisenhower establishes a "parole" system for Hungarian freedom fighters. Two years later, Congress endorses the procedure in an act to admit Hungarian refugees.

1959   Congress amends the Immigration and Nationality Act of 1952 to provide for unmarried sons and daughters of U.S. citizens to enter as non-quota immigrants.

1960   Congress passes an act to assist the resettlement of refugees from communist countries who had been paroled by the Attorney General (mostly Cubans).

1965   Congress enacts the Immigration and Nationality Act, amending the 1952 act by ending the quota system and establishing a preference system stressing family reunification and meeting certain job skill goals, standardizing admission procedures, and setting per country limits of 20,000 for Eastern Hemisphere nations, with a total of 170,000. The first ceiling on Western Hemisphere immigration—120,000—is also legislated.

1967   The U.S. Supreme Court renders its decision in *Afroyim v. Rusk* that a citizen who held dual citizenship with Israel did not lose his citizenship by the act of voting in an Israeli election. It establishes in strong language how limited the government is in "taking away" citizenship once granted by birthright or by naturalization.

1968   President Lyndon Johnson issues a proclamation regarding the UN protocols on the Status of Refugees, basically endorsing the U.S. commitment to the multilateral protocols.

1975   Fall of Vietnam, along with Cambodia and Laos, precipitates a massive flight of refugees to the United States and other countries.

1976   Congress amends the 1965 Immigration and Nationality Act by extending per country limits of visa applicants on a first-come, first-served basis to Western Hemisphere nations as regulated by the preference system.

1980   Congress passes the Refugee Act to systematize refugee policy and incorporate the UN definition of a refugee, initially allowing for 50,000 persons annually who had a "well-founded fear of persecution" on account of race, religion, nationality, or membership in a social or political movement to enter as refugees. It also provides for the first time for the admission of asylum seekers (set at 5,000).

1981   The Select Commission on Immigration and Refugee Policy issues its final report. Its recommendations form the basis for subsequent reforms of immigration law, especially those enacted by Immigration Reform and Control Act (IRCA) in 1986.

1983   The U.S. Supreme Court decides in *INS v. Chadha et al.* that the House of Representative's use of the "legislative veto" to overturn certain INS deportation proceedings, rules and regulations was unconstitutional.

1986   Congress passes the Immigration Reform and Control Act (IRCA), establishing "employer sanctions" for employers who knowingly hire illegal aliens and setting up an amnesty program granting legalization to over one and one-half million illegal aliens and over one million special agricultural workers then in the country.

1990   Congress passes a major reform of the laws concerning legal im-
            migration, setting new ceilings for worldwide immigration, re-
            defining the preference system for family reunification and
            employment, and establishing a new category of preference called
            "diversity immigrants." It set up a Commission on Legal Immi-
            gration Reform. It enacted special provisions concerned with Cen-
            tral American refugees, Filipino veterans, and persons seeking to
            leave Hong Kong. Significant changes were also introduced with
            respect to naturalization procedures.

1996   The Personal Responsibility and Work Opportunity Act cuts off
            SSI benefits and food stamps for non-citizens who had not worked
            for at least ten years. Most cuts were later restored for those al-
            ready in the United States on 8/22/96.

            Congress enacts the Illegal Immigration Reform and Immigrant
            Responsibility Act. It authorizes expansion of the Border Patrol
            and INS agents and procedures to investigate and prosecute var-
            ious aspects of immigration smuggling, authorizes a border fence
            in San Diego, cracks down on document fraud and on illegal vot-
            ing, reforms some detention and deportation procedures, estab-
            lishes an employment verification program, and strictly limits
            public benefits to both legal and illegal immigrants. It also limits
            the ability of the INS to use parole of detainees to facilitate mass
            immigration.

Part I

The Era of Unrestricted Entry and Unrestricted Admission—Colonial Period to 1880

Colonial immigration laws were designed primarily to promote immigration, reflecting the colonies' desire to encourage more people to settle in the new land. They did, however, enact several laws to regulate and restrict immigration in some aspects. They set precedents that were followed in subsequent national legislation. Colonial Americans, who viewed strangers as legitimate objects of suspicion, cautiously allowed settlers but were wary of those of religious difference (i.e., Catholics/Jesuits) or those who might become public charges. The influx of Germans and Quakers in the early 1700s led to specific provincial immigration laws. Documents 1 and 2 exemplify the approach first taken by the colonies—to require masters of ships to provide lists of the settlers and to provide a bond in case such persons became public charges. The first document, enacted nine years after the two Massachusetts Bay colonies unified into one province, demonstrates their economic concerns. Lame, impotent, or infirm persons were prohibited from entering without providing security that the town into which they settled would not be charged with their support.

DOCUMENT 1: Province Laws—Massachusetts (March 12, 1700)

Be it enacted by the Lieutenant-Governor, Council and Representatives in General Court assembled, and by the authority of the same, [Sect. 1.] That every master of ship or other vessel arriving in any port within this province, from any other country, land, island, colony or plantation, at the time of entering his ship or vessel with the receiver of impost for the time being, shall deliver to such receiver a perfect list or certificate in his hand of the Christian sir names of all passengers, as well servants as others, brought in such ship or vessel, and their circumstances so far as he knows, on pain of forfeiting the sum of five pounds, to the use of the poor of the town or place where such passengers shall be landed or sent on shore, for every passenger that he shall omit to enter his or her name in such list or certificate, upon conviction thereof before his majesty's justices in the court of general sessions of the peace within the same county where the offense is committed. And every justice of the peace is hereby empowered, upon complaint made by the selectmen of such town or some of them, to convene such master before him, and to require and take sufficient security of him to appear and answer for his said offence in manner as above said, such complainants also giving bond to prosecute their complaint. And be it further enacted

[Sect. 2] That when it shall happen any passenger so brought to be impotent, lame or otherwise infirm, or likely to be a charge to the place, if such person shall refuse to give security, or cannot procure sufficient surety or sureties to become bound for his saving the town from such charge, in such case the master of the ship or vessel in which such person shall be and hereby is obliged and required to carry or send him or her out of this province again within the space of two months next after their arrival, or otherwise to give sufficient security as aforesaid to indemnify and keep the town free from all charge for the relief and support of such impotent, lame or infirm person, upon demand thereof made by the selectmen, unless such person was, before, an inhabitant of this province, or that such impotence, lameness or other infirmity befell or happened to him or her during the passage; and in such case, if they be servants, their masters shall provide for them, and others shall be relieved at the charge of the province. And the justices of the general sessions of the peace are hereby impowered to enjoyn [sic] and order the performance of what is hereinbefore required of such master accordingly.

[Sect. 5] Nor shall any town be obliged to be at charge for the relief and support of any person residing in such town (in case he or she shall stand in need), that are not approved as aforesaid, unless such person or persons have continued their residence there by the space of twelve months next before, and have not been warned in manner as the law directs, to depart and leave the town, any law, usage or custom to the contrary notwithstanding.

[Sect. 6] And if any person orderly warned to depart from any town whereof he or she is not an inhabitant, and being sent, by warrant from a justice of the peace, unto the town whereto such person properly belongs, or to the place of his or her last abode, shall presume to return back, and obtrude himself or herself upon the town so sent from by residing there, every person so offending shall be proceeded against as a vagabond.

Source: Acts and Resolves, Public and Private, of the Province of Massachusetts Bay, 1692–1786. Vol. 1 of 21 vols. (Boston: Wright and Potter, 1869), Chap. 23, 244–53.

* * *

This first major provincial law was amended in 1722 to increase the bond to secure that no immigrant would become a public charge and specifying the requirement of masters of ships to submit their list to town selectmen or the town treasurer.

DOCUMENT 2: Province Laws—Massachusetts (June 29, 1722)

[Sect. 2] That the master of every coasting vessel, wood-sloop, fishing vessel, or others coming from any port of this government, or any of the neighboring governments, into Boston, or any other port or harbour, within this province, shall, within twenty-four hours after his arrival, deliver to the receiver of impost, where such officers are, and, where none are, to the selectmen of treasurer of the town, a perfect list or certificate of the Christian and sir names of all passengers brought in such vessel (which are not settled inhabitants of this province), and their circumstances so far as he knows; on pain of forfeiting the sum of one hundred pounds, for the use of the poor of the town or place where such passengers shall be landed or sent on shoar. And be it further enacted by the authority aforesaid,

[Sect. 3] That in case any such passengers, strangers, servants or others shall, after their arrival, travel to or into other towns or places within this province, and shall be warned out and sent by authority from place to place, until they come to the place of their last abode, as the law in such cases provides, it shall and may be lawful for all such strangers, servants and others to be carried to the town where they first arrived, and where the selectmen or town treasurer have taken bond as aforesaid, where they shall be accounted inhabitants; unless they have resided for by the space of twelve months in any other place or town, and not regularly of and legally warned out, as the law provides.

[Sect. 4] And in case any master of any ship or vessel, bringing into this province passengers, servants or others shall neglect or refuse to give bond, as aforesaid, within five days after his arrival, every such master of a ship or vessel shall forfeit and pay the sum of two hundred pounds; and the forfeitures herein mentioned to be recovered by bill, plaint or information, by the selectmen, or the major part of them, or the town treasurer of such town where the ship or vessel arrives, in any of his majesties courts of record within this province; any law, usage or custom to the contrary notwithstanding.

Source: Acts and Resolves, Public and Private, of the Province of Massachusetts Bay, 1692–1786. Vol. 2 of 21 vols. (Boston: Wright and Potter, 1874), Chap. 5, 244–45.

* * *

Document 3 illustrates the colonists' concern about religious minorities. It provides incentives for Protestant settlers to enter the colony and encourages French-speaking Protestants to settle in the province. It provides for naturalization after one year of residence in the province.

DOCUMENT 3: Province Laws—Massachusetts (April 2, 1731)

. . . Be it enacted by His Excellency the Governour, Council and Representatives in General Court assembled, and by the authority of the same,

[Sect. 1] That from and after the publication of this act, all Protestants of foreign nations, that have inhabited or resided within this province for the space of one year, are hereby declared to be naturalized, to all intents, constructions and purposes whatsoever, within this province; and from henceforth, and at all times hereafter, shall be entitled to have and enjoy all the rights, liberties and privileges within this province, and no otherwise, which his majesty's natural-born subjects in the said province ought to have and enjoy, as fully, to all intents and purposes whatsoever, as if they had been born within the said province. Provided, always, And it is hereby enacted,

[Sect. 2] That all foreign Protestants that shall have the benefit of this act, shall take the oaths by law appointed to be taken instead of the oaths of allegiance and supremacy, subscribe the test or declaration, and take, repeat and subscribe the abjuration oath, in presence of the governour and council of this province, which shall be made of record in the council books, and for which each person so swearing and subscribing shall pay to the secretary of the province five shillings, and he shall demand no more. And be it further enacted by the authority aforesaid,

[Sect. 3] That if any foreign Protestant having so sworn and subscribed as aforesaid, shall and do demand a certificate of his being entered upon record in manner aforesaid, the secretary of this province, for the time being, is hereby directed and required to grant the same under his hand, for which he may demand two shillings and sixpence, and no more; which certificate shall at all times be sufficient proof that such person is naturalized by this act, and as effectual as if the record aforesaid were actually produced by them or any of them.

Source: Acts and Resolves, Public and Private, of the Province of Massachusetts Bay, 1692–1786. Vol. 2 of 21 vols. (Boston: Wright and Potter, 1874), Chap. 9, 586–87.

* * *

In 1740 the British Parliament passed an act which came to be known as the Plantation Act—meaning the colonies—that sought to regularize the naturalization process. As such, it was also intended to encourage immigration to the American colonies. Under British law at the time, aliens could not engage in British commerce without severe penalties. This aspect was not rigorously enforced in the colonies, but nonetheless such British law made it advantageous for immigrants of the colonies to become naturalized citizens. In England itself, the naturalization process required a profession of Christian faith and proof that an individual had taken the Sacrament in a Protestant church. As noted in this law for the colonies, exception was made for Quakers and Jews but specifically not for Roman Catholics (referred to in the law as Papists). This law, although British, is included as a document in this collection since it governed all the English colonies until Independence, and furthermore, as the reader will see, it was the model upon which the first U.S. naturalization act, with respect to time, oath of allegiance, process of swearing before a judge, and the like, was clearly based.

DOCUMENT 4: The Plantation Act: The British Naturalization Act of 1740

An Act for naturalizing such foreign Protestants, and others herein mentioned, as are settled or shall settle, in any of his Majesty's Colonies in America. Anno 13 Geo. II [1740], Cap. VII.

Whereas the Increase of People is a Means of advancing the Wealth and Strength of any Nation or Country; And whereas many Foreigners and Strangers from the Lenity of our Government, the Purity of our Religion, the benefits of our Laws, the Advantages of our Trade, and the Security of our Property, might be induced to come and settle in some of His Majesty's Colonies in America, if they were made Partakers of the Advantages and Privileges which the natural born Subjects of this Realm do enjoy, Be it therefore enacted by the King's Most Excellent Majesty, by and with the Advice and Consent of the Lords Spiritual and Temporal, and Commons, in this present Parliament assembled, and by the Authority of the same That from and after the first Day of June in the Year of our Lord One thousand seven hundred and forty, all persons born out of the Legiance of His Majesty, His Heirs or Successors, who have inhabited and resided, or shall inhabit or reside for the Space of seven Years or more, in any of His Majesty's Colonies in America, and shall not have been absent out of said Colonies for a longer Space than two Months at any one time during the said seven Years, and shall take and subscribe the Oaths, and make, repeat and subscribe the Declaration appointed by an act made in the first Year of the Reign of His late Majesty King George the First, Intituled, An act for the further Security of His Majesty's Person and Government, and the Succession of the Crown in the Heirs of the late Princess Sophia, being Protestants; and for extinguishing the Hopes of the pretended Prince of Wales, his open and secret Abettors; or, being of the People called Quakers, shall make and subscribe the Declaration of Fidelity, and take and affirm the Effect of the Abjuration Oath, appointed and prescribed by an Act made in the eighth Year of the Reign of His said late Majesty, intituled, An Act for granting the People called Quakers, such Forms of Affirmation or Declaration, as may remove the Difficulties which many of them lie under; and also make and subscribe the Profession of his Christian Belief; appointed and subscribed by an Act made in the First Year of the Reign of their late Majesties King William and Queen Mary, intituled, An Act exempting Their Majesties Protestant Subjects from the Penalties of certain Laws; before the Chief Judge, or other Judge of the Colony wherein such Persons respectively have so inhabited and resided, or shall so inhabit and reside, shall be deemed, adjudged, and taken to be His Majesty's natural born Subjects of this Kingdom, to all Intents, Constructions and Purposes, as if they and every one of them had been or were born within this Kingdom; which said Oath or Affirmation and Subscription of said Declaration is hereby enabled and impowered to administer and take; and the taking and subscribing of every such Oath or Affirmation, and the making, repeating and subscribing of every such Declaration, shall be before such Chief Judge or other Judge, in open Court, between the Hours of nine and twelve in the Forenoon; and shall be entered in the same Court, and also in the Secretary's Office of the Colony wherein such Person shall so inhabit and reside; and every Chief Judge or other Judges of every respective Colony, before whom such Oaths or Affirmation shall be taken and every such Declaration shall be made, repeated and subscribed as aforesaid, is hereby required to make a due and proper entry thereof in a Book to be kept for that Purpose in said Court; for the doing of whereof two Shillings and no more shall be paid at each respective place, under the Penalty and Forfeiture of ten Pounds of lawful Money of Great Britain for every Neglect or Omission; and in like manner every Secretary of the Colony wherein any Person shall so take the said Oaths or Affirmation, and make, repeat and subscribe the said Declarations respectively, as aforesaid, is hereby required to make a due and proper Entry thereof in a Book to be kept for that Purpose in his Office, upon Notification thereof to him by the Chief Judge or other Judges of the same Colony, under the like Penalty and Forfeiture for every such Neglect or Omission.

II. Provided always and be it enacted by the Authority aforesaid, That no Person, of what Quality, Condition or Place soever, other than and except such of the People called Quakers as shall qualify themselves, and be naturalized by the ways and means hereinbefore mentioned, or such who profess the Jewish Religion, shall be naturalized by virtue of this Act, unless such persons shall have received the Sacrament of the Lord's Supper in some Protestant and Reformed Congregation within this Kingdom of Great Britain, or within some of the said Colonies in America, within three Months next before his taking and subscribing the said Oaths, and making, repeating and subscribing the said Declaration; and shall, at the time of his taking and subscribing the said Oaths, and making, repeating, and subscribing the said Declaration, produce a Certificate signed by the Person administering the said Sacrament, and attested by two credible Witnesses, whereof an Entry shall be made in the Secretary's Office of the Colony, wherein such Person shall so inhabit and reside, as also in the Court where the said Oaths shall be so taken as aforesaid, without any Fee or Reward.

III. And whereas, the following Words are contained in the latter Part of the Oath of Adjuration, videlicet (upon the true Faith of a Christian); and whereas the People professing the Jewish Religion may thereby be prevented from receiving the benefit of this Act; Be it further enacted by the Authority aforesaid, That whenever any Person professing the Jewish Religion shall present himself to take the said Oath of Abjuration in pursuance of this Act, the said Words (upon the true Faith of a Christian) shall be omitted out of the Oath in administering the same to such Person, professing the Jewish Religion, without the words aforesaid, and the other Oaths appointed by the said Act in like manner as Jews were permitted to take the Oath of Abjuration, by an Act made in the tenth Year of Reign of His late Majesty King George the First, intituled, An Act for explaining and amending an Act of the last Session of Parliament, intituled, An Act to oblige all Persons, being Papists, in that part of Great Britain called Scotland, and all persons in Great Britain, refusing or neglecting to take the Oaths appointed for the Security of His Majesty's Person and Government, by several Acts herein mentioned, to register their Names and real Estates; and for enlarging the time for taking the said Oaths, and making such Registers, and for allowing further time for the Inrolment of Deeds or Wills made by Papists, which have been omitted to be inrolled pursuant to an Act of the third Year of His Majesty's Reign; and also for giving Relief to Protestant Lessees shall be deemed a sufficient taking of the said Oaths, in order to intitle such Person to the Benefit of being naturalized by virtue of this Act.

IV. And be it further enacted by the Authority aforesaid, That a Testimonial or Certificate under the Seal of any of the said Colonies, of any Persons having resided and inhabited for the Space of seven Years or more as aforesaid within the said Colonies or some of them, to be specified in such Certificate, together with the particular time of Residence in each of such respective Colonies (whereof the Colony under the Seal of which such Certificate shall be given to be one) and of his having taken and subscribed the said Oaths, and of his having made, repeated and subscribed the said Declaration, and in case of a Quaker of his having made and subscribed the Declaration of Filelity, and of his having taken and affirmed the Effect of the Abjuration Oath as aforesaid, and in case of a Person professing the Jewish religion, of his having taken the Oath of Abjuration as aforesaid, within the same Colony, under the Seal whereof such Certificate shall be given as aforesaid, shall be deemed and taken to be sufficient Testimony and Proof thereof, and of his being a natural born Subject of Great Britain, to all Intents and Purposes whatsoever, and as such shall be allowed in every Court within the Kingdoms of Great Britain and Ireland, and also in the said Colonies in America. (Extended, 20 G. 2, c. 44, Sec. 1.)

VI. And be it further enacted by the Authority aforesaid, That every Secretary of the said respective Colonies for the time being, shall and is hereby directed and required at the End of every Year, to be computed from the said first Day of June in the Year of Our Lord One thousand seven hundred and forty, to transmit and send over to the Office of the Commissioners for Trade and Plantations kept in the City of London or Westminster, a true and perfect List of the Names of all and every Person or Persons who have in that Year intitled themselves to the Benefit of this Act, under the Penalty and Forfeiture of fifty Pounds of lawful Money of Great Britain for every Neglect or Omission; All which said lists to [sic] transmitted and sent over, shall, from Year to Year, be duly and regularly entered by the said Commissioners, in a Book or Books to be had and kept for that Purpose in the said Office, for publick View and Inspection as Occasion shall require.

Source: "Publications of the American Jewish Historical Society" 1 (1892): 94–98, in Jonathan D. Sarna and David G. Dalin, *Religion and State in the American Jewish Experience* (Notre Dame, Ind.: University of Notre Dame Press, 1997).

* * *

Document 5 illustrates the specific concern regarding the poor, sick, impotent, or infirm who might become public charges—a theme often seen in U.S. immigration law.

DOCUMENT 5: Province Laws—Massachusetts (June 8, 1756)

An Act to Prevent Charges Arising by Sick, Lame or Otherwise Infirm Persons Not Belonging To This Province, Being Landed and Left Within the Same.

Be it enacted by the Lieutenant-Governour, Council and House of Representatives,

That from and after the first day of July next, no master or commander of any ship or vessel whatsoever, coming into, abiding in or going forth of any port, habour or place within this province, shall cause or suffer to be landed or put on shoar [sic] within the same, any sick or otherwise impotent and infirm person, not being an inhabitant of this province, either belonging to or brought in such ship or vessel, unless the consent of the selectmen of the town where such sick or infirm person shall be landing be first had and obtained thereof, the same to be signified in writing, under their hands; nor unless security be first given, if demanded, to the satisfaction of such selectmen, for indemnifying and keeping such town free from any charge that may arise for the support or relief of the person so landed or left within the province; on pain of forfeiting, to the use of such town, the sum of one hundred pounds for every sick or infirm person so landed, to be recovered by the treasurer of such town, either by action, bill, plaint or information in any of his majesty's courts of record wherein no essoign [*sic*] protection or wager of law shall be allowed.

Source: Acts and Resolves, Public and Private, of the Province of Massachusetts Bay, 1692–1786. Vol. 3 of 21 vols. (Boston: Albert Wright, 1878), Chap. 4, 982.

* * *

In 1783, just before resigning his commission as commander in chief of the Continental Army, General George Washington, in a letter to the "Volunteer Association of the Kingdom of Ireland Lately Arrived in the City of New York," thanked them for their hospitality to American prisoners of war and proclaimed the idea of the new American nation as an asylum for the oppressed.

DOCUMENT 6: Letter of General George Washington on America as Asylum (December 2, 1783)

It was not an uninteresting consideration, to learn, that the Kingdom of Ireland, by a bold and manly conduct had obtained the redress of many of its grievances; and it is much to be wished that the blessings of equal Liberty and unrestrained Commerce may yet prevail ..., in the mean time, you may be assured, Gentlemen, that the Hospitality and Benificence of your Countrymen, to our Brethren who have been Prisoners of War, are neither unknown, or unregarded [*sic*].

The bosom of America is open to receive not only the Opulent and respected Stranger, but the oppressed and persecuted of all Nations and Religions; whom we shall welcome to a participation of all our rights and privileges, if by decency and propriety of conduct they appear to merit the enjoyment. New York, December 2, 1783.

Source: Moses Rischin, ed., *Immigration and the American Tradition* (Indianapolis: Bobbs-Merrill, 1976), 43.

* * *

Soon after gaining independence and adopting the new Constitution the newly formed Congress turned its attention to the question of immigration. Among its very first actions was to adopt a uniform rule of naturalization. This law, using the phrase "being a free white person," illustrates the racial bias or orientation explicit throughout much of the history of U.S. immigration and naturalization law.

DOCUMENT 7: Act of March 26, 1790: An Act to Establish a Uniform Rule of Naturalization

Section 1: Be it enacted by the Senate and House of Representatives of the United States of America in Congress assembled, That any alien, being a free white person, who shall have resided within the limits and under the jurisdiction of the United States for the term of two years, may be admitted to become a citizen thereof, on application to any common court of record, in any one of the states wherein he shall have resided for the term of one year at least, and making proof to the satisfaction of such court, that he is a person of good character, and taking the oath of affirmation prescribed by law, to support the constitution of the United States, which oath or affirmation such court shall administer; and the clerk of such court shall record such application, and the proceedings thereon; and thereupon such person shall be considered as a citizen of the United States. And the children of such persons so naturalized, dwelling within the United States, being under the age of twenty-one years at the time of such naturalization, shall also be considered as citizens of the United States. And the children of citizens of the United States, that may be born beyond sea, or out of the limits of the United States, shall be considered as natural born citizens; Provided, That the right of citizenship shall not descend to persons whose fathers have never been resident in the United States; Provided also, That no person heretofore proscribed by any state, shall be admitted a citizen as aforesaid, except by an act of the legislature in the state in which such person was proscribed.

Source: 1 Stat. 103.

* * *

The extemely generous condition of the 1790 law, requiring only two years of residence, was amended in 1795, changing the minimum time to five years and requiring the renunciation of hereditary titles of nobility, as shown in Document 8.

DOCUMENT 8: Act of January 29, 1795: An Act to Establish a Uniform Rule of Naturalization; and to Repeal the Act Heretofore Passed on That Subject

---

For carrying into complete effect, the power given by the constitution, to establish a uniform rule of naturalization throughout the United States:

Section 1: Be it enacted by the Senate and the House of Representatives of the United States of America in Congress assembled, That any alien, being a free white person, may be admitted a citizen of the United States, or any of them, on the following conditions, and not otherwise—

... He shall at the time of his application to be admitted, declare on oath or affirmation, before some one of the courts aforesaid, that he has resided within the United States, five years at least, and within the state or territory, where such court is at the time held, one year at least; that he will support the constitution of the United States; and that he doth absolutely and entirely renounce and abjure all allegiance and fidelity to every foreign prince, potentate, state or sovereignty whatever, and particularly by name, the prince, potentate, state or sovereignty whereof he was before a citizen or subject; which proceedings shall be recorded by the clerk of the court.

... The court admitting such alien, shall be satisfied that he has resided within the limits and under the jurisdiction of the United States five years; and it shall further appear to their satisfaction, that during that time, he has behaved as a man of good moral character, attached to the principles of the constitution of the United States, and well disposed in the good order and happiness of the same.

... In case the alien applying to be admitted to citizenship shall have borne any hereditary title, or been of any of the orders of nobility, in the kingdom or state from which he came, he shall, in addition to the above requisites, make an express renunciation of his title or order of nobility, in the court to which his application shall be made; which renunciation shall be recorded in the said court ...

Section 4. And be it further enacted, That the act intituled "An act to establish an uniform rule of naturalization," passed the twenty-sixth day of March, one thousand seven hundred and ninety, be, and the same is hereby repealed.

Source: Act of January 29, 1795 (1 Stat. 414).

* * *

In 1798 concern for immigration influenced the Congress to pass a much more restrictive naturalization law—changing the time of residency from five to fourteen years, assessing fees, and stipulating in much greater detail the process for naturalization including a fee for surety of peace and stipulating penalties for various failures to comply with the law. Document summarizes the main provisions of this new naturalization law.

DOCUMENT 9: Act of June 18, 1798 (Amends Naturalization Act of 1795)

An Act supplementary to and to amend the act, intituled [sic] "An act to establish an uniform rule of naturalization, and to repeal the act heretofore passed on that subject."

Section 1. Be it enacted by the Senate and House of Representatives of the United States of America in Congress assembled, That no alien shall be admitted to become a citizen of the United States, or of any state, unless in the manner prescribed by this act, intituled "An act to establish an uniform rule of naturalization; and to repeal the act heretofore passed on that subject," he shall have declared his intention to become a citizen of the United States, five years, at least, before his admission, and shall, at the time of his application to be admitted, declare and prove, to the satisfaction of the court having jurisdiction in the case, that he has resided within the United States fourteen years, at least, and within the state or territory where, or for which such court is at the time held, five years, at least, beside conforming to the other declarations, renunciations and proofs, by the said act required, any thing therein to the contrary notwithstanding. Provided, that any alien who was residing within the limits and under the jurisdiction of the United States, before the twenty-ninth of January, one thousand seven hundred and ninety-five, may, within one year after the passing of this act—and any alien who shall have made the declaration of his intention to become a citizen of the United States, in conformity to the provisions of the act . . . may within four years after having made the declaration aforesaid, be admitted to become a citizen, in the manner prescribed by the said act, upon his making proof that he has resided five years, at least, within the limits, and under the jurisdiction of the United States; And Provided, also, that no alien who shall be a native, denizen or subject of any nation or state with whom the United States shall be at war, at the time of his application, shall be then admitted to become a citizen of the United States.

Sec. 2. [Stipulates that the clerk of the courts send the Secretary of State such declarations of intention to become a citizen and stipulates a few of two dollars be paid to defray the costs of such certificate, as well as a fine of ten dollars for refusal or forfeiture to pay the two dollar fee].

. . .

Sec. 4. *An be it further enacted,* That all white persons, aliens . . . who, after the passing of this act, shall continue to reside in any port or place within the territory of the United States, shall be reported, if free, and of age of twenty-one years, by themselves, or being under the age of twenty-one years, or holden in service, by their parent, guardian, master or mistress in whose care they shall be, to the clerk of the district court of the district, if living within ten miles of the port or place, in which their residence or arrival shall be, and otherwise, to the collect or such port or place, or some other officer or person there, or nearest thereto, who shall be authorized by the President of the United States to register aliens . . . [such reports of registration to be recorded and a fee of fifty cents charged for such registration and certification; and the clerks of the courts etc. to file such with the Secretary of State monthly thereafter all lists of registered aliens.].

Sec. 5. [Assesses a penalty of two dollars for any alien failing to register with any justice of the peace for surety of the peace.]

Sec. 6. *An be it further enacted,* That in respect to every alien, who shall come to reside within the United States after the passing of this act, the time of registry of such alien shall be taken to be the time when the term of residence within the limits and under the jurisdiction of the United States shall have commenced . . . and a certificate of such registry shall be required, in proof of the terms of residence, by the court to whom such application shall and may be made.

Sec. 7. *And be it further enacted,* That all and singular penalties established by this act, shall and may be recovered in the name, and to judge, justice, or court, having jurisdiction in such case, and to the amount of such penalty, respectively.

Source: Nationality Act of June 18, 1798 (1 Stat. 566).

* * *

Responding to those same fears, Congress enacted the famous "Alien and Sedition" Acts of 1798, presented here in Document 10. Although never enforced, they illustrate the degree of xenophobia existing in the nation at the turn of the century. It required oaths of allegiance from aliens residing in the nation and granted the president extraordinary power to remove aliens deemed to be "seditious." It expired after the two-year limitation of the law and was not reenacted. It provided the precedent whereby Congress would later enact laws controlling immigration and grant rather sweeping enforcement powers to the executive branch concerning immigration matters.

DOCUMENT 10: Act of June 25, 1798 ("Alien Act of 1798")

Be it enacted by the Senate and the House of Representatives of the United States of America in Congress assembled, That it shall be lawful for the President of the United States at any time during the continuance of this act, to order all such aliens as he shall judge dangerous to the peace and safety of the United States, or shall have reasonable grounds to suspect are concerned in any treasonable or secret machinations against the government thereof, to depart out of the territory of the United States within such time as shall be expressed in such order, which order shall be served to the alien by delivering a copy thereof, or leaving the same at his usual abode, and returned to the office of the Secretary of State, by the marshal or other person to whom the same shall be directed. And in case any alien, so ordered to depart, shall be found at large within the United States after the time limited in such order for his departure, and not having obtained a license from the President to reside therein, or having obtained such license shall not have conformed thereto, every such alien shall, on conviction thereof, be imprisoned for a term not exceeding three years, and shall never after be admitted to become a citizen of the United States. Provided always, and be it further enacted, that if any alien so ordered to depart shall prove to the satisfaction of the President, by evidence to be taken before such person or persons as the President shall direct, who are for that purpose hereby authorized to administer oaths, that no injury or danger to the United States will arise from suffering such alien to reside therein, the President may grant a license to such alien to remain within the United States for such time as he shall judge proper, and at such place as he may designate. And the President may also require of such alien to enter into a bond to the United States, in such penal sum as he may direct, with one or more sufficient sureties to the satisfaction of the person authorized by the President to take the same, conditioned for the good behavior of such alien during his residence in the United States, and not violating his license, which license the President may revoke, whenever he shall think proper.

Sec. 2. *And be it further enacted,* That it shall be lawful for the President of the United States, whenever he may deem it necessary for the public safety, to order to be removed out of the territory thereof, any alien who may or shall be in prison in pursuance of this act; and to cause to be arrested and sent out of the United States such of those aliens as shall have been ordered to depart therefrom and shall not have obtained a license as aforesaid, in all cases where, in the opinion of the President, public safety requires a speedy removal. And if any alien so removed or sent out of the United States by the President shall voluntarily return thereto, such alien on conviction thereof, shall be imprisoned so long as, in the opinion of the President, the public safety may require. . . .

Sec. 4. *And be it further enacted*, That the circuit and district courts of the United States, shall respectively have cognizance of all crimes and offenses against this act. And all marshals and other officers of the United States are required to execute all precepts and orders of the President of the United States issued in pursuance or by virtue of this act.

Sec. 5. *And be it further enacted*, That it shall be lawful for any alien who may be ordered to be removed from the United States, by virtue of this act, to take with him such part of his goods, chattels, or other property, as he may find convenient; and all property left in the United States by any alien, who may be removed, as aforesaid, shall be, and remain subject to his order and disposal, in the same manner as if this act had not been passed.

Sec. 6. *And be it further enacted*, That this act shall continue and be in force for . . . two years.

Source: The Alien Act of June 25, 1798 (1 Stat. 570).

* * *

In 1802 the Congress enacted a series of laws about naturalization specifying who could be naturalized, the length of residency required, and the process of naturalization.

DOCUMENT 11: Acts of April 14, 1802 (Re: Naturalization)

Children of Persons Naturalized under Certain Laws to Be Citizens

Sec. 2172. The children of persons who have been duly naturalized under any law of the United States, or who, previous to the passing of any law on that subject, by the Government of the United States, may have become citizens of any one of the States, under the laws thereof, being under the age of twenty-one years at the time of the naturalization of their parents, shall, if dwelling in the United States, be considered as citizens thereof; and the children of persons who now are, or have been, citizens of the United States, shall, though born out of the limits and jurisdiction of the United States, be considered as citizens thereof; but no person heretofore proscribed by any State, or who has been legally convicted of having joined the army of Great Britain during the Revolutionary War, shall be admitted to become a citizen without the consent of the legislature of the State in which such person was proscribed.

Alien Enemies Not Admitted to Citizenship [Amendment Added]

Sec. 2171. No alien who is a native citizen or subject, or a denizen of any country, state, or sovereignty with which the United States are at war, at the time of his application, shall then be admitted to become a citizen of the United States; but persons resident within the United States, or the Territories thereof, on the eighteenth day of June, in the year one thousand eight hundred and twelve, who had before that day made a declaration, according to law, of their intention to become citizens of the United States, or who were on that day entitled to become citizens without making such declaration, may be admitted to become citizens thereof, notwithstanding they were enemy aliens at the time and in the manner prescribed by the laws heretofore passed; . . .

Citizenship of Children Born Abroad of Citizen Fathers
[Amendment Added]

Sec. 1993.* Any child hereafter born out of the limits and jurisdiction of the United States, whose father or mother or both at the time of the birth of the child is a citizen of the United States, whose father or mother or both at the time of the birth of the child is a citizen of the United States, is declared to be a citizen of the United States; but the rights of citizenship shall not descend to any such child unless the citizen father or citizen mother, as the case may be, has resided in the United States previous to the birth of such child. In cases where one of the parents is an alien, the right of citizenship shall not descend unless the child comes to the United States and resides therein for at least five years continuously immediately previous to his eighteenth birthday, and unless, within six months after the child's twenty-first birthday, he or she shall take an oath of allegiance to the United States of America as prescribed by the Bureau of Naturalization. (34 Stat. 596)

[Aliens, How Naturalized]

Sec. 2165. An alien may be admitted to become a citizen of the United States in the following manner, and not otherwise: (40 Stat. 545; 48 Stat. 797; 54 Stat. 1173)

First, He shall declare on oath, before a circuit or district court of the

*As amended by Act of May 24, 1834 (48 Stat. 797).

United States, or a district or supreme court of the Territories, or a court of record of any of the States having common-law jurisdiction, and a seal and clerk, two years, at least, prior to his admission, that it is bona fide his intention to become a citizen of the United States, and to renounce forever all allegiance and fidelity to any foreign prince, potentate, state, or sovereignty, and particularly, by name, to the prince, potentate, state, or sovereignty of which the alien may be at the time a citizen.

Second. He shall, at the time of his application to be admitted, declare on oath, before one of the courts above specified, that he will support the Constitution of the United States, and that he absolutely and entirely renounces and abjures all allegiance and fidelity to every foreign prince, potentate, state, or sovereignty; and particularly, by name, to the prince, potentate, state, or sovereignty of which he was before a citizen or subject; which proceedings shall be recorded by the clerk of the court.

Third. It shall be made to appear to the satisfaction of the court admitting such alien that he was resided within the United States five years at least, and within the State or Territory where such court is at the time held, one year at least; and that during that time he has behaved as a man of good moral character, attached to the principles of the Constitution of the United States, and well disposed to the good order and happiness of the same; but the oath of the applicant shall in no case be allowed to prove his residence.

Fourth. In case the alien applying to be admitted to citizenship has borne any hereditary title, or been of any of the orders of nobility in the kingdom or state from which he came he shall, in addition to the above requisites, make an express renunciation of his title or order of nobility in the court to which his application is made, and his renunciation shall be recorded in the court.

Fifth. Any alien who was residing within the limits and jurisdiction of the United States before the twenty-ninth day of January, one thousand seven hundred and ninety five, may be admitted to become a citizen, on due proof made to one of the courts specified above, that he has resided two years, at least, within the jurisdiction of the United States, and one year, at least, immediately preceding his application, within the State or Territory where such court is at the time held.

Source: Acts of April 14, 1802 (54 Stat. 1172).

* * *

In 1804 Congress passed a law allowing for the naturalization of the wife or children of an alien who died while in the process of naturalization but before his process was completed.

DOCUMENT 12: Act of March 26, 1804 (Re: Naturalization)

Widow and Children of Declarant

Sec. 2168. When any alien, who has complied with the first condition specified in section twenty-one hundred and sixty five, dies before he is actually naturalized, the widow and the children of any such alien shall be considered as citizens of the United States, and shall be entitled to all rights and privileges as such, upon taking the oaths proscribed [*sic*] by law.

Source: 34 Stat. 603.

* * *

In 1813 Congress reaffirmed the five-year residency requirement for the naturalization process.

DOCUMENT 13: Act of March 3, 1813 (Re: Naturalization)

Sec. 2170. No alien shall be admitted to become a citizen who has not for the continued term of five years next preceding his admission resided within the United States.

Source: Five-Year Residence Act of March 3, 1813 (45 Stat. 1514).

* * *

Consistent with the precedent established by colonial provincial law, the first purposive law enacted by the Congress concerning immigration to the United States called for captains or masters of ships to provide a list of names and the particulars concerning all passengers delivered to the United States. It established for the first time the collection of data on immigration and immigrants to the United States and marks the beginning of formal immigration law.

DOCUMENT 14: Act of March 2, 1819 (Re: Immigration)

Be it enacted by the Senate and the House of Representatives of the United States of America in Congress assembled. . . .

Sec. 4. *And be it further enacted,* That the captain or master of any ship or vessel arriving in the United States or any of the territories thereof, from any foreign place whatever, at the same time that he delivers a manifest of all cargo, and, if there be no cargo, then at the time of making a report or entry of the ship or vessel, pursuant to the existing laws of the United States, shall also deliver and report, to the collector of the district in which such ship or vessel shall arrive, a list or manifest of all passengers taken on board of the said ship or vessel at any foreign port or place; in which list or manifest it shall be the duty of the said master to designate, particularly, the age, sex, and occupation, of the said passengers, respectively, the country to which they severally belong, and that of which it is their intention to become inhabitants; and shall further set forth whether any, and what number, have died on the voyage; which report and manifest shall be sworn to by the said master, in the same manner as is directed by the existing laws of the United States, in relation to the manifest of the cargo, and that the refusal or neglect of the master aforesaid, to comply with the provisions of this section, shall incur the same penalties, disabilities, and forfeitures, as are at present provided for a refusal or neglect to report and deliver a manifest of the cargo aforesaid.

Sec. 5. *And be it further enacted,* That each and every collector of the customs, to whom such manifest or list of passengers as aforesaid shall be delivered, shall, quarter yearly, return copies thereof to the Secretary of State of the United States, by whom statements of the same shall be laid before Congress at each and every session.

Source: Manifest of Immigrants Act of March 2, 1819 (3 Stat. 489).

* * *

Before the United States became fully engaged in regulating immigration, the government of several states passed laws designed to regulate the immigration flow in order to protect those states from financial responsibility for immigrants. The two most important immigration-receiving states at that time were New York and Massachusetts, the ports of New York City and Boston, respectively. Documents 15 and

17 cite two such statutes enacted by the Commonwealth of Massachusetts, and Document 18 is a similar law enacted in New York. These acts reflect the practice of requiring ship masters to declare immigrants, establish fees and persons for processing immigration, and place certain restrictions on individuals who might immigrate into the state (lunatics and paupers).

DOCUMENT 15: An Act to Prevent the Introduction of Paupers, from Foreign Ports or Places—Commonwealth of Massachusetts (February 25, 1820)

Be it enacted by the Senate and House of Representatives, in General Court assembled, and by the authority of the same, That when any ship or vessel, having any passengers on board, who have not settlement within this Commonwealth, shall arrive at any port or harbor within the Commonwealth, the master of such ship or vessel shall, before such passengers come on shore, leave a list of their names and places of residence with the Selectmen or Overseers of the Poor of the town where such passengers shall be landed; and if, in the opinion of said Selectmen or Overseers of the Poor, any such passenger may be liable to become chargeable for their support to the Commonwealth, the master of such ship or vessel shall, within five days after his arrival, as aforesaid, and on being notified by the Selectmen to that effect, enter into bonds with sufficient surities, to the satisfaction of said Selectmen, in a sum not exceeding five hundred dollars for each passenger, to indemnify and save harmless such town, as well as the Commonwealth, from all manner of charge and expense, which may arise from such passengers, for and during the term of three years; and if the master of such ship or vessel shall land any such passengers, without entering their names and giving bonds as aforesaid, he shall forfeit and pay the sum of two hundred dollars for each passenger so landed, to be recovered by action of debt, by any person who shall sue for the same; one moiety thereof to the prosecutor; provided, this act shall not take effect until the first day of May next, and that nothing in this act shall be construed to extend to the master of the ship or vessel, in any voyage on which such ship or vessel may now be employed. [Approved by the Governor, February 25th, 1820. Chap. CCXC.]

Source: Laws of the Commonwealth of Massachusetts, 1818–1822. Vol. 8 (Boston: Russell and Gardner, 1822), Chap. CCXC, 428–29.

* * *

Congress amended the naturalization process in 1824 by enacting provisions to deal with alien minors—persons immigrating before the age of 21—who came to the United States unaccompanied by a parent. These provisions allowed for naturalization to proceed after the individual had attained 21 years of age as long as he or she had resided within the United States for five years or more, and counted the years since the time of their arrival rather than making them wait and reside for five years after attaining age 21.

DOCUMENT 16: Act of May 26, 1824 (Re: Naturalization)

Sec. 2167. Any alien, being under the age of twenty-one years, who has resided in the United States three years next preceding his arriving at that age, and who has continued to reside therein to the time he may make application to be admitted a citizen thereof, may, after he arrives at the age of twenty-one years, and after he has resided five years within the United States, including the three years of his minority, be admitted a citizen of the United States, without having made the declaration required in the first condition of section twenty-one hundred and sixty-five; but such alien shall make the declaration required therein at the time of his admission; and shall further declare, on oath, and prove to the satisfaction of the court, that, for two years next preceding, it has been his bona-fide intention to become a citizen of the United States; and he shall in all other respects comply with the laws in regard to naturalization.

Source: 934 Stat. 603.

DOCUMENT 17: Alien Passengers Act—Commonwealth of Massachusetts (April 20, 1837)

Be it enacted by the Senate and House of Representatives, in General Court assembled . . . :

Sec. 1. When any vessel shall arrive at any port or harbor within this State, from any port or place without the same, with alien passengers on board, the officer or officers whom the mayor and aldermen of the city, or the selectmen of the town where it is proposed to land such passengers, are hereby authorized and required to appoint, shall go on board such vessel and examine into the condition of said passengers.

Sec. 2. If, on such examination, there shall be found among said passengers, any lunatic, idiot, maimed, aged or infirm persons, incompetent in the opinion of the officer so examining, to maintain themselves, or who have been paupers in any other country, no such alien passenger shall be permitted to land, until the master, owner, consignee or agent of such vessel shall have given such city or town, a bond in the sum of one thousand dollars, with good and sufficient surety, that no such lunatic or indigent passenger shall become a city, town, or state charge, within ten years.

Sec. 3. No alien passengers, other than those spoken of in the preceding section shall be permitted to land until the master, owner, consignee or agent of such vessel shall pay to the regularly appointed boarding officer, the sum of two dollars for each passenger so landing; and the money so collected shall be paid into the treasury of the city or town, to be appropriated as the city or town may direct for the support of foreign paupers. . . .

Sec. 5. The provisions of this act shall not apply to any vessel coming on shore in distress, or to any alien passenger taken from any wreck where life is in danger.

This act shall take effect from and after passage of the same.

Source: Laws of the Commonwealth of Massachusetts, 1837 (Boston: Dutton and Wentworth, 1837), Chap. CCXXXVIII, 270–71.

DOCUMENT 18: An Act Concerning Passengers in Vessels Coming to the City of New York (May 5, 1847)

1. Within twenty-four hours after arrival of any ship or vessel at the port of New York, from any of the United States, other than this state, or from any country out of the United States, the master or commander of such ship or vessel, shall make a report in writing, on oath or affirmation, to the mayor of the city of New York, or in case of his absence or other inability to serve, to the person discharging the duties of his office, which report shall state the name, place of birth, last legal residence, age and occupation of every person or passenger arriving in such ship or vessel, on her last voyage to said port, not being a citizen of the United States, and who shall have, within the last preceding twelve months arrived from any country out of the United States, at any place within the United States, and who shall not have paid the commutation money mentioned under the provisions of the act entitled "An act concerning passengers in vessels coming to the port of New York," passed

February 11, 1824: The said report shall contain a like statement of all such persons or passengers as aforesaid, as shall have been landed, or been suffered to land from any such ship or vessel, at any place during such last voyage, or who shall have been put on board, or been suffered to go on board any other ship, vessel or boat, with the intention of proceeding to or through the said city of New York: The said report shall further specify whether any of said passengers so reported are lunatic, idiot, deaf and dumb, blind or infirm, and if so, whether they are accompanied by relatives who are likely to be able to support them; and shall further specify particularly, the names, last place of residence, and ages of all passengers who may have died during said last voyage of such vessel: In case any such master or commander shall omit or neglect to report as aforesaid, any such person or passenger, with the particulars aforesaid, or shall make any false report or statement in respect to any person or passenger, in all or any of the particulars herein before specified, such master or commander shall forfeit the sum of seventy-five dollars for every such passenger, in regard to whom any such omission or neglect shall have occurred, or any such false report or statement shall be made, for which the owner or owners of every such ship or vessel, shall also be liable, jointly and severally, and which may be sued for and recovered as hereinafter provided.

2. It shall be the duty of said mayor, or other person discharging the duties of his office as aforesaid, by an endorsement to be made on the said report, to require the master or commander of such ship or vessel, to pay to the chamberlain of the city of New York, the sum of one dollar, for every person or passenger reported by such master or commander as aforesaid, which sum shall be paid as aforesaid, within three days after the arrival of such ship or vessel at the said port of New York.

3. It is the duty of the commissioners of emigration hereinafter named, to examine into the condition of passengers arriving at the port of New York in any such ship or vessel, and for that purpose, all or any of the said commissioners, and such other person or persons as they shall appoint, shall be authorized to go on board, and through any such ship or vessel; and if on such examination, there shall be found among such passengers, any lunatic, idiot, deaf and dumb, blind or infirm persons, not members of emigrating families, and who, from attending circumstances, are likely to become permanently a public charge, they shall report the same to the said mayor particularly, and thereupon the said mayor, or the person discharging the duties of his office as aforesaid, shall, instead of the commutation money aforesaid, require, in the endorsement to be made as aforesaid, or in any subsequent endorsement or endorsements thereon, that the master or commander of such ship or vessel, with two sufficient sureties, shall execute a joint and several bond to the people of this state, in a penalty of three hundred dollars for every

such passenger, conditioned to indemnify and save harmless, each and every city, town or county within this state, from any cost or charge, which any such city, town or county shall incur, for the maintenance or support of the person or persons named in such bond, or any of them, within five years from the date of such bond. The sureties to the said bonds shall be required to justify before, and to the satisfaction of the officer making such endorsement, and by their oath or affirmation, shall satisfy such officer, that they are, respectively, residents of the state of New York, and worth double the amount of the penalty of such bond, over and above all debts, liabilities, and all property exempt from execution. . . .

19. This act shall take effect immediately.

Source: Laws of the State of New York, 1847. Vol. I (Albany: Charles Van Benthuysen, 1847), Chap. 195, 182–88.

* * *

In 1848 the United States ended its war with Mexico with the signing of the Treaty of Guadalupe Hidalgo. By this treaty Mexico ceded to the United States most of its northern territory that today comprises all or parts of the following states: California, New Mexico, Arizona, Nevada, Utah, and Colorado. The treaty contained a provision (Article 8) regarding the admission to U.S. citizenship of Mexicans remaining in those territories ceded to the United States and not declaring their wish to remain citizens of Mexico.

DOCUMENT 19: Treaty of Guadalupe Hidalgo, Article VIII (1848)

Mexicans now established in territories previously belonging to Mexico, and which remain for the future within the limits of the United States as defined by the present treaty, shall be free to continue where they now reside, or to remove at any time to the Mexican republic, retaining the property which they possess in the said territories, or disposing thereof, and removing the proceeds wherever they please, without their being subjected on this account, to any contribution, tax, or charge whatever.

Those who shall prefer to remain in the said territories, may either retain the title and rights of Mexican citizens, or acquire those of citizens of the United States. But they shall be under the obligation to make their election within one year from the date of the exchange of ratifications of this treaty, and those who shall remain in the said territories after the expiration of that year, without having declared their intention to retain the character of Mexicans, shall be considered to have elected to become citizens of the United States.

Source: National Archives, Washington, D.C.

* * *

The Know-Nothing party was formed out of a secret nativist association called the Order of the Star Spangled Banner in 1854. The following article, written by an elder, J. R. Graves, published in his *Tennessee Baptist* under the heading "Know Nothing," vividly describes the anti-Catholic, anti-immigrant bias of the new political party.

DOCUMENT 20: Article on Know-Nothing Party (1854)

Nothing is more evident than that our political parties have become sadly, deplorably corrupt. . . . Congress has become a most shameful and disgraceful scene of drunkenness, riot, and caucusing for the Presidency, and the minor offices of the government. The foreign element is increasing in fearful ratio. Nearly one million per annum of foreign Catholics and German infidels—who, though opposed in all else, are agreed in the subversion of our free institutions—are pouring in upon us, and the tide is increasing. These foreigners have already commenced their warfare upon the use of the Bible in our public schools—against our free school system—against our Sabbath—against our laws. They boldly threaten to overthrow our constitution, through profligacy of our politicians; and we see our candidates for political preferment pandering more and more to the Catholic and foreign influence. We see from the last census that the majority of the civil and municipal offices of this government are today in the hands of Catholics and foreigners: an overwhelming majority of our army and navy are foreign Catholics. They hear the editors of Catholic papers, who are endorsed by their Archbishops, threatening in these words: "If Catholics ever gain an immense numerical majority, religious freedom in this country is at end." So say our enemies. So we believe. [Elder Graves then proceeded to list what he called the sixteen cardinal principles of the new party, and predicted a great future for Americanism.]

Source: S. Darrell Overdyke, *The Know-Nothing Party in the South* (Gloucester, Mass.: Peter Smith Publisher, Inc., 1968), 67.

* * *

By 1855 many states, including Illinois, had strong Know-Nothing movements, and the party appeared to hold the balance of power. Abraham Lincoln, in a letter to his fellow Kentuckian, Joshua F. Speed, clearly stated his abhorrence both of slavery and of nativism. Document 21, in which Lincoln states that he is not a Know-Nothing, cites a portion of a letter that addresses his position on nativism.

DOCUMENT 21: Letter of Abraham Lincoln to Joshua F. Speed, August 24, 1855 (Re: Know Nothings)

... I am not a Know Nothing. That is certain. How could I be? How can anyone who abhors the oppression of negroes, be in favor of degrading a class of white people? Our progress in degeneracy appears to me to me pretty rapid. As a nation, we began by declaring that "all men are created equal." We now practically read it "all men are created equal, except negroes." When the Know-Nothings get control, it will read "all men are created equal, except negroes, and foreigners, and Catholics." When it comes to this I should prefer emigrating to some country where they make no pretense of loving liberty—to Russia, for instance, where despotism can be taken pure, and without the base alloy of hypocracy.
Springfield, August 24, 1855   A. Lincoln

Source: Roy P. Basler, ed., Marion Pratt and Lloyd Dunlap, asst. eds., *The Collected Works of Abraham Lincoln*, 8 vols. (New Brunswick: Rutgers University Press, 1953).

* * *

Citizenship was granted to women married to citizens, with the exception of prostitutes, by the Act of 1855.

DOCUMENT 22: Act of February 10, 1855: Citizenship of Married Women

Sec. 1994. Any woman who is now or may hereafter be married to a citizen of the United States, and who might herself be lawfully naturalized, shall be deemed a citizen. That the marriage to an American citizen of a female of the sexually immoral classes the exclusion or deportation of which is prescribed by this Act shall not vest such a female with United States citizenship if the marriage of such alien female shall be solemnized after her arrest or after the commission of acts which make her liable to deportation under this act.

Source: 39 Stat. 889.

* * *

In 1855 national politics was sharply divided over the growing anti-slavery movement and the various political parties' positions on immigration. Former President Millard Fillmore, who had served as president as a Whig, was nominated to run on the American party ticket—the Know-Nothing party—which was staunchly antiforeign. Although Fillmore accepted the nomination primarily to use the election to advocate saving the Union, he did voice their antiforeign sentiment on several occasions. Document 23 presents a speech he gave at Newburgh, New York, on June 26, 1856, in which he enunciated the principles of the American party.

DOCUMENT 23: Millard Fillmore's Speech, June 26, 1856, on the American Party Principles

Fellow-citizens of Newburgh: Accept my cordial thanks for this hearty greeting. My friend has introduced me as the standard-bearer of the American party, and a friend of the Union. For the former position I am indebted to the partiality of my friends, who have without my solicitation made me your standard-bearer in the contest for President, which has just commenced; but I confess to you that I am proud of the distinction, for I am an American with an American heart. I confess that I am a devoted and unalterable friend of the Union. As an American, occupying the position I do before my countrymen, I have no hostility to foreigners. I trust I am their friend. Having witnessed their deplorable condition in the old country, God forbid that I should add to their suffering by refusing them asylum in this. I would open wide the gates and invite the oppressed of every land to our happy country, excluding only the pauper and criminal. I would be tolerant to men of all creeds, but would exact from all faithful allegiance to our republican institutions.

While I did this, I would, for the sake of those who seek an asylum on our shores, as well as for our own sake, declare as a general rule, that Americans should govern America. I regret to say that men who come fresh from the monarchies of the old world, are prepared neither by education, habits of thought, or knowledge of our institutions, to govern America. . . .

I feel, fellow-citizens, that I need hardly allude to the importance of maintaining this Union. I see the national flag floating from yonder height, which marks the consecrated spot of Washington's headquarters. There was performed an act of moral heroism before which the bravest deeds of Alexander pale, and with which the greatest achievements of Bonaparte are not to be compared. It was there, on that sacred spot, now shaded by the flag of a free republic, that Washington refused a crown. It was there that the officers of the army, after independence had been achieved, made him the offer of a crown, which he indignantly spurned.

Source: Millard Fillmore Papers, vol. II (New York: Krause Reprint, 1970), 16–17.

* * *

Certainly among the most important incentives attracting immigrants to the United States was its abundant land, granted through the famous Homestead Act of 1862. Document 24 provides a summary of the act.

DOCUMENT 24: Act of May 20, 1862: To Secure Homesteads

Be it enacted . . . , That any person who is the head of a family, or who has arrived at the age of twenty-one years, and is a citizen of the United States, or who shall have filed his declaration of intention to become such, as required by the naturalization laws of the United States, and who has never borne arms against the United States Government or given aid and comfort to its enemies, shall, from and after the first of January, eighteen hundred and sixty-three, be entitled to enter one quarter section or a less quantity of unappropriated public lands, upon which said person may have filed a preemption claim, or which may, at the time the application is made, be subject to preemption at one dollar and twenty-five cents, or less, per acre; or eighty acres or less of such unappropriated lands, at two dollars and fifty cents per acre, to be located in a body, in conformity to the legal subdivisions of the public lands, and after the same shall have been surveyed; Provided, That any person owning and residing on land may, under the provisions of this act, enter other land lying contiguous to his or her said land, which shall not, with the land so already owned and occupied, exceed in the aggregate one hundred and sixty acres . . .

Approved.

Source: (Chap. LXXV, Thirty-Seventh Congress, Session II, Ch. 75, 1862), 392–93.

* * *

An act of July 1862 granted naturalization to honorably discharged soldiers. This became an important inducement to recruit aliens to serve in the Union Army during the Civil War.

DOCUMENT 25: Act of July 17, 1862: Honorably Discharged Soldiers (Re: Naturalization)

Sec. 2166. Any alien, of the age of twenty-one years and upward, who has enlisted, or may enlist, in the armies of the United States, either the regular or the volunteer forces, and has been, or may be hereafter, honorably discharged, shall be admitted to become a citizen of the United States, upon his petition, without any previous declaration of his intention to become such; and he shall not be required to prove more than one year's residence within the United States previous to his application to become such citizen; and the court admitting such alien shall, in addition to proof of residence and good moral character, as now provided by law, be satisfied by competent proof of such person's having been honorably discharged from the service of the United States.

Source: 40 Stat. S46.

* * *

After the Civil War, a series of amendments and citizenship-related acts were passed by the Congress. Document 26 presents two relevant sections of the Fourteenth Amendment to the United States Constitution (ratified in July 1868). They are especially important not only for their impact on the citizenship status of the former slaves but also because of the "due process" and "equal protection of the law" clauses, which have had an enormous impact on subsequent laws relating to citizenship and naturalization rights.

DOCUMENT 26: Fourteenth Amendment to the U.S. Constitution (July 9, 1868)

Section 1. All persons born or naturalized in the United States, and subject to the jurisdiction thereof, are citizens of the United States and of the State wherein they reside. No State shall make or enforce any law which shall abridge the privileges and immunities of citizens of the United States; nor shall any State deprive any person of life, liberty, or property, without due process of law; nor deny to any person within its jurisdiction the equal protection of the laws.

Section 2. Representatives shall be apportioned among the several States according to their respective numbers, counting whole number of persons in each State, excluding Indians not taxed. But when the right to vote at any election for the choice of electors for President and Vice President of the United States, Representatives in Congress, the Executive and judicial officers of the State, or the members of the Legislature thereof, is denied to any of the male inhabitants of such State, being twenty-one years of age, and citizens of the United States, or in any way abridged, except for participation in rebellion, or other crime, the basis of representation therein shall be reduced in the proportion which the number of such male citizens shall bear to the whole number of male citizens twenty-one years of age in such State.

Source: Fourteenth Amendment (July 9, 1868).

* * *

The following article, published in 1941 on the occasion of the tearing down of the Castle Garden immigration reception station, which, prior to Ellis Island, was the busiest of the nation's major immigrant receiving and processing stations, is included for its description of the role of Castle Garden during the second half of the nineteenth century.

DOCUMENT 27: Article on the Castle Garden Immigrant Reception Station, New York City

More than 7,000,000 immigrants entered America through its doors in 35 years. Castle Garden, the gateway to America for millions of immigrants during the last half of the nineteenth century, is soon to be torn down. . . .

Castle Garden's greatest fame, and its existence as a symbol to millions in America and abroad as the "nation's gateway," began in 1855. In that year the State Emigration Commission took it over. Construction workers tore out the entertainment booths and built offices for examining physicians, police, ticket agents, post office clerks, custom officials, immigration officers, baggage agents, a letter-writing service, a labor exchange and bathrooms.

On August 3, 1855, the first group of immigrants were examined at Castle Garden. From that date until 1890, a period of thirty-five years and eight months, 7,690,606 immigrants passed through its doors, about three-quarters of all the immigrants who entered the country during that time . . .

The labor exchange established in Castle Garden was a great success. In the first six months of 1868 it placed 7,111 male and 5,840 female workers in jobs before they had left the immigration station. Farm and railroad labor and domestic help was most in demand. Farm hands were offered from $6 to $19 a month. Fashionable women frequently journeyed to Castle Garden to pick out their own domestic help. In 1869 more than 12,000 girls, mostly Irish, were placed in jobs, almost the moment they landed, as domestic servants, cooks and laundresses. But the flow of immigration was not enough for America's industrial appetite. Employers complained they could use ten times as many workers.

During the Civil War, recruiting officers of the Union Army erected two huge tents adjacent to the immigration station and sought to enlist the newly arrived immigrants into the army by offering bounties if they could not persuade them to sign up by arguments in their own language. Many of them did and helped to make up the 400,000 aliens and foreign-born from twenty different countries who fought on the Northern side. . . .

In 1880 the first contingent of the Salvation Army arrived with drums and tambourines. In 1883 about 2,800 Mormons who had been converted to the faith in Europe passed through the Castle Garden station on their way to Utah and the Mormon colony. Scarcely a day passed during which a steamship or vessel in full sail did not arrive with its cargo of expectant humans.

When Grover Cleveland became Governor of New York one of the first problems he attacked was the conditions at Castle Garden which were subject to much criticism. Due to bad administration, many of the old practices of exploiting the immigrants had crept back and the station was again gaining an unsavory reputation. In his first message, on January 1, 1883, the Governor called for reforms at Castle Garden. A State investigation led to improvement in 1887.

In 1890, however, immigration through the port of New York was taken out of the hands of State authorities and placed under the jurisdiction of the United States Commissioner of Immigration. All other immigration stations in the country passed to federal control eight years before. The federal government began immediate steps to expand immigration facilities in New York City, then as now the largest port receiving immigrants. Castle Garden was closed and in December, 1890, it was converted into an aquarium which it has been ever since. A year later all immigrants were routed through Ellis Island in New York Harbor.

Source: Foreign Language Information Service, New York, Index No. 4939, February 24, 1941.

* * *

By the 1870s concern over immigration from China and Japan was coming to a head. In California particularly and on the West Coast more generally, the Chinese Exclusion League was vigorously advocating restrictions. In 1875 the first federal anti-Chinese legislation, aimed at the immigration of women from China and Japan "for immoral purposes," was enacted. More restrictive legislation followed.

DOCUMENT 28: Act of March 3, 1875 (Re: Exclusion of Certain Asian Women and Other Matters—"The Page Law")

Be it enacted . . . , That in determining whether the immigration of any subject of China, Japan, or any Oriental country, to the United States, is free and voluntary, as provided by section two thousand one hundred and sixty-two of the Revised Code, title "Immigration," it shall be the duty of the consul-general or consul of the United States residing at the port from which it is proposed to convey such subjects, in any vessel enrolled or licensed in the United States, or any port within the same, before delivering to the masters of any such vessels the permit or certificate provided for in such section, to ascertain whether such immigrant has entered into a contract or agreement for a term of service within the United States, for lewd and immoral purposes; and if there be such contract or agreement, the said consul-general or consul shall not deliver the required permit or certificate.

Sec. 2. That if any citizen of the United States, or other person amenable to the laws of the United States, shall take, or cause to be taken or transported, to or from the United States any subject of China, Japan, or any Oriental country, without their free and voluntary consent, for the purpose of holding them to a term of service, such citizen or other person shall be liable to be indicted therefor, and, on conviction of such offense, shall be punished by a fine not to exceed two thousand dollars and be imprisoned not exceeding one year; and all contracts and agreements for a term of service of such persons in the United States, whether made in advance or in pursuance of such illegal importation, and whether such importation shall have been in American or other vessels, are hereby declared void.

Sec. 3. That the importation into the United States of women for the purposes of prostitution is hereby forbidden; and all contracts and agreements in relation thereto, made in advance or in pursuance of such illegal importation and purposes are hereby declared void; and whoever shall knowingly and willfully import, or cause any importation of, women to the United States for purposes of prostitution, or shall knowingly and willfully hold, or attempt to hold, any woman to such purposes, in pursuance of such illegal importation and contract or agreement, shall be deemed guilty of a felony, and on conviction thereof, shall be imprisoned not exceeding five years and pay a fine not exceeding five thousand dollars. . . .

Source: 18 Stat. 477, 8 U.S.C.

* * *

On the West Coast, especially California, anti-Chinese sentiment was virulent. A new political party, called the Workingmen's party, was led by Denis Kearney. A sample of his rhetoric and the views of the party are evident in a speech he gave in 1877, which was quoted in the San Francisco *Daily Bulletin*.

DOCUMENT 29: Denis Kearney's Workingmen's Party Speech (December 28, 1877)

We intend to try and vote the Chinamen out, to frighten him out, and if this won't do, to kill him out, and when the blow comes, we won't leave a fragment for the thieves to pick up. We are going to arm ourselves to the teeth, and if these land-grabbers and thieves go outside the Constitution, we will go outside the Constitution, too, and woe be to them. You must be prepared. The heathen slaves must leave this coast, if it cost 10,000 lives. We want to frighten capital and thereby starve the white men so that they will be exasperated and do their duty. This is the last chance the white slaves will ever have to gain their liberty. . . . We have the numbers to win at the ballot box, but you will be cheated out of the result, and all history shows that oppressed labor has always to get its right at the point of the sword. If the Republican robber and the Democratic thief cheat you at the election, as I know they will, shoot them down like rats. You must be ready with your bullets. We will go to Sacramento and surround the Legislature with bayonets and compel them to enact such laws as we wish.

Source: Neil L. Shumsky, *The Evolution of Political Protest and the Workingmen's Party of California* (Columbia: Ohio State University Press, 1991), 178.

* * *

Part 1 closes with Document 30, which contains the message of President Rutherford B. Hayes vetoing the first anti-Chinese immigration law. He did so primarily on the grounds of foreign policy considerations related to its potential impact on the Burlingame Treaty with China.

DOCUMENT 30: President Rutherford B. Hayes' Veto Message of the Chinese Laborer Exclusion Bill (March 1, 1879)

After a very careful consideration of House bill 2423, entitled "An act to restrict the immigration of Chinese to the United States," I herewith return it to the House of Representatives, in which it originated, with my objections to its passage.

The bill, as it was sent to the Senate from the House of Representatives, was confined to the object named in its title, which is that of "An act to restrict the immigration of Chinese to the United States." The only means adopted to secure the proposed object was the limitation on the number of Chinese passengers which might be brought to this country in any one vessel to fifteen; and as this number is not fixed in any proportion to the size or tonnage of the vessel or by any consideration of the safety or accommodation of these passengers the simple purpose and effect of the enactment was to repress this immigration to an extent falling but little short of its absolute exclusion.

The bill, as amended in the Senate and now presented to me, includes an independent and additional provision which aims at and in terms requires the abrogation by this Government of Articles V and VI of the treaty with China commonly called the Burlingame treaty, through the action of the Executive enjoined by this provision of the act.

The Burlingame treaty, of which the ratifications were exchanged at Peking November 23, 1869, recites as the occasion and motive of its negotiation between the two Governments, that "since the conclusion of the treaty between the United States of America and the Ta Tsing Empire (China) of the 18th of June, 1858, circumstances have arisen showing the necessity of additional articles thereto," and proceeds to an agreement as to said additional articles. These negotiations, therefore, ending by the signature of the additional articles July 28, 1868, had for their object the completion of our treaty rights and obligations toward the Government of China by the incorporation of these new articles as thenceforth parts of the principal treaty to which they are made supplemental. Upon the settled rule of interpretation applicable to such supplemental negotiations the text of the principle [sic] treaty and of the these "additional articles thereto" constitute one treaty from the conclusion of the new negotiations, in all parts of equal and concurrent force and obligation between the two Governments, and to all intents and purposes as if embraced in one instrument.

The principle [sic] treaty, of which the ratifications were exchanged August 16, 1859, recites that "the United States of America and the Ta Tsing Empire, desiring to maintain firm, lasting, and sincere friendship, have resolved in a manner clear and positive, by means of a treaty or general convention of peace, amity, and commerce, the rules which shall in future be mutually observed in the intercourse of their respective countries," and proceeds in its thirty articles to lay out a careful and comprehensive system for the commercial relations of our people with China. The main substance of all the provisions of this treaty is to define and secure the rights of our people in respect to access to, residence and protection in, and trade with China. The actual provisions in our favor in these respects were framed to be, and have been found to be, adequate and appropriate to the interests of our commerce; and by the concluding article we receive an important guaranty that—

Should at any time the Ta Tsing Empire grant to any nation, or the merchants or citizens of any nation, any right, privilege, or favor, connected either by navigation, commerce, political or other intercourse, which is not conferred by this treaty, such right, privilege and favor shall at once freely inure to the benefit of the United States, its public officers, merchants, and citizens.

Against this body of stipulations in our favor and this permanent engagement of equality in respect of all future concessions to foreign nations the general promise of permanent peace and good offices on our part seems to be the only equivalent. For this the first article [is] as follows:

There shall be, as there have always been, peace and friendship between the United States of America and the Ta Tsing Empire, and between their people respectively. They shall not insult or oppress each other for any trifling cause, so as to produce an estrangement between them; and if any other nation should act unjustly or oppressively, the United States will exert their good offices, on being informed of the case, to bring about an amicable arrangement of the question, thus showing their friendly feelings.

At the date of the negotiation of this treaty our Pacific possessions had attracted a considerable Chinese emigration, and the advantages and the inconveniences felt or feared therefrom had become more or less manifest; but they dictated no stipulations on the subject to be incorporated in the treaty. The principle [sic] feature of the Burlingame treaty was its attention to and its treatment of the Chinese immigration and the Chinese forming, or as they should form, a part of our population. Up to this time our uncovenanted hospitality to immigration, our fearless liberality of citizenship, our equal and comprehensive justice to all inhabitants, whether they abjured their foreign nationality or not, our civil freedom, and our religious toleration had made all comers welcome, and under these protections the Chinese in considerable number had made their lodgement upon our soil.

The Burlingame treaty undertakes to deal with this situation, and its fifth and sixth articles embrace its most important provisions in this regard and the main stipulation in which the Chinese Government has secured an obligatory protection of its subjects within our territory. . . .

An examination of these two articles in the light of the experience then influential in suggesting their "necessity" will show that the fifth article was framed in hostility to what seemed the principal mischief to be guarded against, to wit, the introduction of Chinese laborers by methods which should have the character of a forced and servile importation, and not of a voluntary emigration of freemen seeking our shores upon motives and in a manner consonant with the system of our institutions and approved by the experience of the nation. Unquestionably the adhesion of the Government of China to these liberal principles of freedom in emigration, with which we were so familiar and with which we were so well satisfied, was a great advance toward opening that Empire to our civilization and religion, and gave promise in the future of greater and greater practical results in the diffusion throughout that great population of our arts and industries, our manufactures, our material improvements, and the sentiments of government and religion which seem to us so important to the welfare of mankind. The first clause of this article secures this acceptance by China of the American doctrines of free migration to and fro among the peoples and races of the earth.

The second clause, however, in its reprobation of "any other than an entirely voluntary emigration" by both the high contracting parties, and in the reciprocal obligations whereby we secured the solemn and unqualified engagement on the part of the Government of China "to pass laws making it a penal offense for a citizen of the United States or Chinese subjects to take Chinese subjects either to the United States or to any other foreign country without their free and voluntary consent," constitutes the great force and value of this article. Its importance both in principle and in its practical service toward our protection against servile importation in the guise of immigration cannot be over-estimated. It commits the Chinese Government to active and efficient measures to suppress this iniquitous system, where those measures are most necessary and can be most effectual. It gives to this Government the footing of a treaty right to such measures and opportunity of insisting upon their adoption and of complaint and resentment at their neglect. The fifth article, therefore, if it fall short of what the pressure of the later experience of our Pacific States may urge upon the attention of this Government as essential to the public welfare, seems to be in the right direction and to contain important advantages which once relinquished can not be easily recovered.

The second topic of interest the two Governments under the actual condition of things which prompted the Burlingame treaty was adequate protection, under the solemn and definite guarantees of a treaty, of the Chinese already in this country and those who should seek our shores. This was the object, and forms the subject of the sixth article, by whose reciprocal engagement the citizens and subjects of the two Governments, respectively, visiting or residing in the country of the other are secured the same privileges, immunities, or exemptions enjoyed by the citizens or subjects of the most favored nations. The treaty of 1858, to which these articles are made supplemental, provides for a great amount of privilege and protection, both of person and property, to American citizens in China, but it is upon this sixth article that the main body of the treaty rights and securities of the Chinese already in this country depends. Its abrogation, were the rest of the treaty left in force, would leave them to such treatment as we should voluntarily accord them by our law and customs. Any treaty obligation would be wanting to restrain our liberty of action toward them, or to measure or sustain the right of the Chinese Government to complaint or redress on their behalf.

The lapse of ten years since the negotiation of the Burlingame treaty has exhibited to the notice of the Chinese Government, as well as to our own people, the working of this experiment of immigration in great numbers of Chinese laborers to this country, and their maintenance here of all the traits of race, religion, manners, and customs, habitations, mode of life, segregation here, and the keeping up of the ties of their original home, which stamp them as strangers and sojourners, and not as incorporated elements of our national life and growth. This experience may naturally suggest the reconsideration of the subjects as dealt with by the Burlingame treaty, and may properly become the occasion of more direct and circumspect recognition, in renewed negotiations, of the difficulties surrounding this political and social problem. It may well be that the apprehension of the Chinese Government is no less than our own, the simple provisions of the Burlingame treaty may need to be replaced by more careful methods, securing the Chinese and ourselves against the larger and more rapid infusion of this foreign race than our system of industry and society can take up and assimilate with ease and safety. This ancient Government, ruling a polite and sensitive people, distinguished by a high sense of national pride, may properly desire an adjustment of their relations with us which would in all things confirm and in no degree endanger the permanent peace and amity and the growing commerce and prosperity which it has been the object and the effect of our existing treaties to cherish and perpetuate.

I regard the very grave discontents of the people of the Pacific States with the present working of the Chinese immigration, and their still graver apprehensions therefrom in the future, as deserving the most serious attention of the people of the whole country and a solicitous interest on the part of the Congress and the Executive. If this were not my own judgment, the passage of this bill by both Houses of Congress would impress upon me the seriousness of the situation, when a majority of the representatives of the people of the whole country had thought fit to justify so serious a measure of relief.

The authority of Congress to terminate a treaty with a foreign power by expressing the will of the nation no longer to adhere to it is as free from controversy under our Constitution as is the further proposition that the power of making new treaties or modifying existing treaties is not lodged by the Constitution in Congress, but in the President, by and with the advice and consent of the Senate, as shown by the concurrence of two-thirds of that body. A denunciation of a treaty by any government is confessedly justifiable only upon some reason both of the highest justice and the highest necessity. The action of Congress in the matter of the French treaties in 1798, if it be regarded as an abrogation by this nation of a subsisting treaty, strongly illustrates the character and the degree of justification which was then thought suitable to such a proceeding. . . .

I am convinced that, whatever the urgency might in any quarter or by any interest be supposed to require an instant suppression of further immigration from China, no reason can require the immediate withdrawal of our treaty protection of the Chinese already in this country, and no circumstances can tolerate an exposure of our citizens in China, merchants or missionaries, to the consequences of so sudden an abrogation of their treaty protection. Fortunately, however, the actual recession in the flow of emigration from China to the Pacific Coast, shown by trustworthy statistics, relieves us from any apprehension that the treatment of the subject in the proper course of diplomatic negotiations will introduce any new features of discontent or disturbance among the communities directly affected. Were such delay fraught with more inconveniences than have ever been suggested by the interests most in earnest in promoting this legislation, I can not but regard the summary disturbance of our existing treaties with China as greatly more inconvenient to much wider and more permanent interests of the country.

Source: Messages and Papers of the Presidents. Vol. 9 (New York: Bureau of National Literature, Inc., 1879): 4466–4472.

Part II

Limited Naturalization, Unlimited Immigration— 1880 to 1920

Although immigrants from South, Central and Eastern European nations had arrived in the United States as early as colonial times, their numbers and influence were comparatively small until after 1880. Indeed, 1896 represents the turning point year when their numbers exceeded those from northwestern Europe for the first time. These newcomers were often quite different in their culture and physical features from previous Europeans and, of course, from the majority society. In addition, they arrived in sufficient numbers to preserve much of their cultural and social identities by living in ethnic enclaves in the burgeoning cities of the United States. These factors sparked prejudice and discrimination against them. In addition to the millions of Catholics arriving, many of the newcomers were Greek or Russian Orthodox, or Jews: the Jewish population rose from around 270,000 in 1877 to over 4 million by 1927 (Dinnerstein and Reimers 1975, 37–38).

As was true in the earlier era, several push and pull factors were at work in this vast migration, during which some 27 million immigrants left Europe to come to the United States. Among the push factors were the growing urbanization and industrialization sweeping across Europe that brought about severe political, social, and economic dislocations. Often these newcomers were fleeing sometimes extreme conditions in their homelands that were aggravated by high birthrates, over-population, and cholera and malaria epidemics. These developments resulted in political unrest and often repression. In coping with such pressures, European governments found emigration an expedient policy and openly encouraged the waves of immigration bound for the United States and other parts of the Americas.

In Czarist Russia unrest fed anti-Semitism. Jews became society's scapegoats. Government-sponsored pogroms—brutal campaigns of beatings, lootings, and killings—began in 1881, with the assassination of Czar Alexander II, and continued thereafter for thirty years.

Pull factors also contributed to the flow. Transatlantic travel by steamship greatly facilitated the journey. Letters from friends and relatives induced many to come. The promise of the "golden opportunity" afforded by the United States was a beacon that drew millions. On arrival, however, most found themselves trapped in teeming urban centers. The tenement slum dwellers of New York's East Side constituted the world's most densely populated urban district—about 290,000 persons per square mile. The great influx contributed to a virtual explosion of cities. Chicago, for example, grew from less than 5,000 in 1848 to more than 1,690,000 in 1900. By 1920 the new immigrants comprised 44 percent of the population of New York City, 41 percent of Cleveland, 39 percent of Newark, and 24 percent of Boston, Buffalo, Detroit, Philadelphia, and Pittsburgh (LeMay 1987, 39).

The effects of this new and massive wave of immigration and of its changing composition were significant and were quickly felt. A movement to restrict immigration was under way by 1870, and it had achieved a considerable degree of success by the mid-1880s. Its first target was the Chinese, subsequently South and Eastern Europeans. Anti-Chinese sentiment had begun in California as early as the 1850s. Violence against them in the gold-mine fields had often gone unpunished after 1854, when, in *People v. Hall*, a Know-Nothing judge serving on California's Supreme Court ruled that the Chinese were forbidden to testify against white men (McClain 1994, 21). The California legislature imposed various legal barriers: a foreign miners tax, denial of entry into public schools, and a prohibition against marrying whites. By 1865 calls for banning their immigration had begun. In 1867 the Democratic party swept state offices in California, running on an anti-Chinese platform. The economic Panic of 1873 and subsequent depression fanned fears of the so-called Yellow Peril. The Workingmen's party, which crystallized in late 1877, was successful in Oakland, Sacramento, and San Francisco. It called for an end to all Chinese immigration. The Order of Caucasians, the People's Protective Alliance, the Teamsters, and the Workingmen's party joined organized labor in a campaign for their total restriction. Sinophobia was so strong in California that in 1879 its constitution was amended to place legal restrictions on them. The Chinese Exclusion League, and later the Asian Exclusion League, agitated for national laws prohibiting their immigration.

The movement to pass legislation in Congress, however, met with opposition from the executive branch. A Chinese Exclusion Act passed in 1879 was vetoed by President Rutherford B. Hayes on the grounds that it violated, as it so clearly did, the Burlingame Treaty. This forced negotiations to amend that treaty [Document 31]. It was ratified in 1881 and formally proclaimed by President Chester A. Arthur in October 1881. Immediately after, Congress passed a bill suspending all Chinese immigration for twenty years. President Arthur vetoed that bill [Document 32]. Congress then passed a second bill, in May 1882, which became known as the Chinese Exclusion Act [Document 33]. It stopped virtually all Chinese labor immigration for ten years. Its impact was immediate and dramatic. Chinese immigration dropped from 40,000 in 1882 to 8,031 in 1883 and a mere 23 by 1885. Nonlaboring classes of Chinese people (merchants, businessmen, spouses, and minor children) continued to come to the United States. Between 1891 and 1900, nearly 15,000 such nonlabor Chinese were admitted. Congress also expressly prohibited their naturalization in 1882.

Restrictionists unsatisfied with a limited ban on one aspect of immigration pushed for more sweeping laws. In August 1882 Congress passed the first general immigration law with an avowedly (though limited) restrictionist goal [Document 34]. It excluded "any convict, lunatic, idiot, or any person unable to take care of himself or herself without becoming a public charge." The public charge clause became an administrative tool to restrict immigration during periods of economic recession and depression. It designated the secretary of the treasury responsible for its administration. Congress also imposed a tax of 50 cents per head on immigrants. Its enforcement, however, was left to state boards or officers designated by the secretary of the treasury. In 1885 Congress passed the prohibition of Contract Labor Law [Document 35].

Ironically, the Statue of Liberty was dedicated in October 1886 just when the anti-immigration mood increased sharply. The mood of that movement contrasted dramatically with the sentiment inscribed on her base, from the poem, "The New Colossus," by Emma Lazarus:

Not like the brazen giant of Greek fame,
With conquering limbs astride from land to land;
Here at our sea-washed, sunset gates shall stand
A mighty woman with a torch, whose flame
Is the imprisoned lightning, and her name
Mother of Exiles. From her beacon-hand
Glows world-wide welcome; her mild eyes command
The air-bridged harbor that twin cities frame.
"Keep, ancient lands, your storied pomp!" cries she
With silent lips. "Give me your tired, your poor

Your huddled masses yearning to breathe free,
The wretched refuse of your teeming shore.
Send these, the homeless, tempest-tossed to me.
I lift my lamp beside the golden door!" (Vecoli and Lintelman 1984, 99)

Increasing labor strife in the early 1880s, the officially declared closing of the frontier in the census report for 1890, and the severe panic and depression experienced during the 1890s all contributed to a growing xenophobia. Congress amended the Chinese Exclusion Act in 1884 by adding some provisions and requiring a "re-entry certificate"—that era's version of a green card—before Chinese sailed to China if they planned to reenter the United States. The practice was fairly common among Chinese resident aliens, who returned to China for brides (miscegenation laws forbade their marrying white woman here) or to bury family members with their ancestors. In 1888 another amendment to the Chinese Exclusion Act [Document 38] not only reaffirmed the ban of the original act, but also extended that ban to returning Chinese immigrant laborers [Document 39]. This amendment resulted in a case that challenged the act as to the status of Chinese immigrants as permanent resident aliens: *Chae Chan Ping v. United States* [Document 40]. Chae Chan Ping was a laborer who had resided in San Francisco for twelve years. When he returned to China in 1887, he had a reentry certificate in his possession as required by the law of 1884. When he attempted to return a year later, after passage of the Scott Act, as it was commonly known, he was barred. The U.S. Supreme Court upheld the lower court's ruling of the legality of the Scott Act. Its majority opinion, which alluded to the Yellow Peril theme, reflected the racism of the period. Despite the ex post facto nature of the Scott Act, and despite the obvious lack of due process afforded thousands of Chinese laborers affected by the act (many of whom as long-standing resident aliens had significant property investments here which were essentially being taken from them without due process), the Court ruled in favor of Congress' right and power to make such immigration laws as it saw fit.

In 1891 Congress created the position of superintendent of immigration [Document 41] and prohibited the immigration of "paupers, polygamists, and those with contagious diseases." It placed the supervision of immigration wholly under federal authority. Congress also established a Bureau of Immigration within the Treasury Department. By 1892 Ellis Island had opened, replacing Castle Garden as the nation's major reception depot.

The continued large-scale inflow of immigrants led restrictionists to propose another device to limit immigration. In 1892 Senator Henry Cabot Lodge, one of the leading restrictionists in the Senate, advocated use of a literacy test to bar immigrants, and a congressional committee first recommended use of such a test in 1894. In 1894 Congress enhanced the authority of the Treasury Department, making its decisions final, subject only to appeal to the secretary (rather than to courts) [Document 45]. That year also saw the formation of the Immigration Restriction League which for the next twenty-five years spearheaded the restrictionist movement. In 1896 Congress passed an immigrant literacy bill, but it was vetoed by President Grover Cleveland [Document 48].

In 1896 a significant U.S. Supreme Court decision was handed down. In *Plessy v. Ferguson* [Document 46], the Court ruled that a segregation law of Louisiana was not an unconstitutional infringement of the equal protection clause of the Fourteenth Amendment. The Court established the doctrine of "separate-but-equal" treatment. This case gave a constitutional blessing to all Jim Crow laws, which soon segregated the races in virtually all aspects of life. It was significant, also, in that states along the West Coast, such as California, passed enabling legislation for local school district to segregate Asian schoolchildren from "white" schools.

In 1898, however, the the U.S. Supreme Court rendered an important decision concerning the rights of natural-born citizens of Asian descent. In *Wong Kim Ark v. United States* [Document 49], the court ruled that Wong Kim Ark, whose parents were Chinese immigrants who could not become naturalized citizens, was indeed a native-born citizen. Having been born in the United States, he retained that status regardless of his parents' status. Since he was a native-born citizen, he could not be barred from returning to the United States after visiting China. This set an important precedent for all native-born children of Asian immigrants.

The creation of a federal immigration bureau was important because the Supreme Court deferred to those administrative officers all the powers granted Congress over immigration matters. By the mid-1890s these officers could and did operate with a fairly wide latitude, and their actions gradually reflected the growing racist ideas of the period. In Document 50, an immigration official, writing in 1917 but reflecting the attitudes of officers from a decade earlier as well, illustrates the administrative powers of immigration officers in the inspection process and their racist ideas and norms.

A growing trend in Japanese immigration also fueled the restrictionist movement's drive to ban Asian immigration. Japanese immigrants first came to Hawaii in 1868. In 1870 there were only 56 on the mainland; but, by 1890, their number exceeded 24,000. There were just over 72,000 by the 1910 census; 110,000 by 1920. They were highly literate and quickly successful. California reacted by passing an Alien Land Law in 1913, which prohibited persons ineligible for citizenship (Chinese, Japanese, and others) from owning agricultural land or leasing it for more than three years (Sowell 1978, 77–78). This influx of Japanese instigated Supreme Court cases concerning the power of immigration officials to allow or refuse entry; for example, *Nishimura Ekiu v. United States* [Document 42]. The Court ruled that immigration officials had such power. It also ruled on a case concerning the power of the federal government to *expel* an alien: *Fong Yue Ting v. United States.* The Supreme Court ruled such matters were civil, not criminal, and thus operated under far fewer due process restrictions. Immigration policy was viewed as a matter of *sovereignty* not commerce, and thus the due process protections had no application.

The Immigration Bureau became increasingly important in the process of admission or denial. Boards of Special Inquiry, established in 1893, heard tens of thousands of cases annually. The bureau used the special inquiry process to detain hundreds of immigrants by invoking the "pauper" clause. Its inspectors were hired on the basis of a political spoils system, and throughout the 1890s inspections were badly administered and politically corrupt. The money-exchange service, baggage handling, and food concessions were a source of wealth and an inducement to corruption. The flood of immigrants taxed the system at Ellis Island. After 1902 reforms under President Theodore Roosevelt tightened administrative procedures, and Ellis Island was highly praised for its administration (Pitkin 1975, 42).

By the 1900s the restrictionist movement pushed for the exclusion of Japanese as well as Chinese, advocated the extension of exclusion to other groups, and stressed the need to adopt a literacy test. Restrictionist forces attempted to pass a literacy bill in 1898, 1902, and 1906; all of them were defeated. Pro-business groups desired a more open-door policy as a means to ensure the continued supply of cheap labor. The National Association of Manufacturers and the National Union of Manufacturers helped defeat the literacy bills. They and a coalition of Southern senators helped maintain President Cleveland's veto in 1896.

Between 1903 and 1906 several important immigration laws were passed. One moved the immigration service from the Treasury to the newly created Department of Commerce and Labor [Document 53] and extended the excluded groups to include epileptics, prostitutes, and professional beggars. A second immigration law, also in 1903, codified the immigration laws and extended the excluded class of immigrants to anarchists [Document 54]. At the same time, Congress not only took the novel step of barring the admission of persons because of their political beliefs but it also denied such persons the right to be naturalized because of their political views, another first [Document 55]. These two measures were inspired no doubt by the 1901 assassination of President William McKinley by the avowed anarchist Leon Czolgosz (Bennet 1963, 24). Still another major piece of legislation in 1906 also codified all existing naturalization laws into a single comprehensive statute [Document 56]. Congress also strengthened the organizational structure and administrative authority of the immigration service by giving a commissioner general of immigration greater control over bureau personnel and the activities involved in the machinery of enforcement.

The decade of 1900–1910 saw the largest ever wave of immigrants—8,795,386 persons. This renewed massive inflow, coming with the economic Panic of 1907 and its subsequent economic depression, fueled demands for increased restrictions. In 1905 the Japanese and Korean Exclusion League, formed in California, claimed a membership of over 100,000 in that state. It was renamed the Asiatic Exclusion League in 1907, composed by then of 231 affiliated groups. San Francisco passed ordinances segregating Japanese students in its schools. President Roosevelt issued an executive order in 1907 barring Japanese entry into the United States from a bordering country or U.S. Territory (that is, Canada and Mexico, and Hawaii, respectively). The 1907 Act "To Regulate the Immigration of Aliens into the United States" [Document 57], raised the immigrant head tax to four dollars (it had previously been raised to one and then two dollars) and authorized the president to enter into agreements to regulate immigration, thus setting the stage for the Gentleman's Agreement. It added more stringent enforcement machinery. The sheer volume of immigration taxed the ability of the service to process it. In 1905 Ellis Island, alone, processed 821,169 aliens; each inspector examined between 400 and 500 immigrants per day.

The Gentleman's Agreement resulted in a dramatic change. During the first full year of its implementation, the number of Japanese immigrants dropped from 30,824 in 1907, to 16,418 in 1908, to 3,275 in 1909, and fewer than 3,000 in 1910 (Ringer 1983, 705). Congress again passed a literacy bill in 1909, which again was vetoed, this time by President William Taft.

In 1910 Congress amended the 1907 law to remove all limitations on the deportation of alien prostitutes [Document 60]. From 1907 to 1911 a special immigration commission, the Dillingham Commission, met and studied immigration policy. It was heavily stacked in favor of the restrictionist point of view. Its massive report, including forty-two volumes, which was issued in 1911, called for the adoption of a literacy test. It accepted the Darwinian theories taken up by the Immigration Restriction League [Document 61]. Congress passed another immigrant literacy bill in 1913, which was also vetoed by President Taft. It enacted a law moving the immigration service to the newly established Department of Labor. The act retained the division of the service into two bureaus, the Bureau of Immigration, headed by the commissioner-general of immigration, and the Bureau of Naturalization, headed by a commissioner. Placed under the immediate direction of the secretary of labor, the staff of the immigration service was promptly reduced.

World War I resulted in a reduction in the concerns about immigration; the numbers dropped off by some 75 percent. In 1915 a literacy bill was passed but vetoed by President Woodrow Wilson [Document 62]. He labeled it a test of opportunity, not a test of intelligence. The Russian Bolshevik revolution, however, aroused anew fears of radicalism in the United States. The American Legion, the National Grange, and the American Federation of Labor all supported a literacy test bill. In 1917 Congress again passed a major immigration bill containing a literacy test provision [Document 63], this time sustaining it over President Wilson's veto. The law also doubled the head tax from four to eight dollars and added alcoholics, vagrants, and those suffering from psychopathic inferiority to the list of excluded classes. It established an Asiatic Barred Zone, which virtually excluded all Asian immigration. That year the Congress also granted citizenship to Puerto Ricans [Document 64].

Postwar years are commonly times of reaction, and the years after World War I fit that pattern. Radicals of all types were fiercely persecuted; Wobblies, socialists, anarchists, and anyone suspected of holding such views were tarred and feathered, jailed, and sometimes even lynched. The Red Scare of 1919 led to the arrest of thousands and the deportation of hundreds of aliens. The Ku Klux Klan grew alarmingly, taking on an anti-Catholic, anti-Semitic, and antiforeign outlook. "100 Percent Americanism" became the order of the day. The Klan joined forces with the Immigration Restriction League, the American Protective League, and True Americans and launched an incendiary period of anti-Catholicism. Racist ideas of these groups and the pseudo-science of eugenics, which supposedly proved that certain races were endowed with hereditary superiority or inferiority, provided the basis for the quota system that ushered in a new era of immigration policy in the 1920s.

President Hayes's veto of the first attempt to ban Chinese immigration led to the renegotiation of the Burlingame Treaty. The amended treaty, concluded in 1880 and ratified by the Senate in 1881, was proclaimed by President Arthur on October 5, 1881.

DOCUMENT 31: Treaty Between the United States and China Concerning Immigration (October 5, 1881)

... Whenever in the opinion of the Government of the United States the coming of Chinese laborers to the United States, or their residence therein, affects or threatens to affect the interests of that country, or to endanger the good order of the said country or any locality within the territory thereof, the Government of China agrees that the Government of the United States may regulate, limit, or suspend such coming or residence, but may not absolutely prohibit it. The limitation or suspension shall be reasonable, and apply only to Chinese who may go to the United States as laborers, other classes not being included in the limitations. Legislation taken in regard to Chinese laborers will be of such a character only as is necessary to enforce the regulation, limitation, or suspension of immigration, and immigrants shall not be subject to personal maltreatment or abuse.

Article II

Chinese subjects, whether proceeding to the United States as teachers, students, merchants, or from curiosity, together with their body and household servants, and Chinese laborers who are now in the United States shall be allowed to go and come of their own free will and accord, and shall be accorded all the rights, privileges, immunities, and exemptions which are accorded to citizens and subjects of the most favored nation.

Article III

If Chinese laborers, or Chinese of any other class, now either permanently or temporarily residing in the territory of the United States, meet with ill treatment at the hands of any other persons, the Government of the United States will exert all its powers to devise measures for their protection and to secure to them the same rights, privileges, immunities, and exemptions as may be enjoyed by the citizens or subjects of the most favored nation, and to which they are entitled by treaty.

Article IV

The high contracting powers having agreed upon the foregoing articles, whenever the Government of the United States shall adopt legislative measures in accordance therewith, such measures will be communicated to the Government of China. If the measures as enacted are found to work hardship upon the subjects of China, the Chinese minister at Washington may bring the matter to the notice of the Secretary of State of the United States, who will consider the subject with him; and the Chinese Foreign Office may also bring the matter to the notice of the United States minister at Peking and consider the subject with him, to the end that mutual and unqualified benefit may result.

Source: 22 Stat. L., 826: 1037–39.

* * *

Congress immediately passed a law to execute certain stipulations, which in fact did prohibit Chinese immigration for twenty years. President Arthur promptly vetoed the bill, sending to the Congress a veto message explaining his reasons.

DOCUMENT 32: President Chester A. Arthur's Veto Message of the Chinese Laborer Exclusion Bill (April 4, 1882)

After careful consideration of Senate bill No. 71, entitled "An act to execute certain treating stipulations relating to Chinese," I herewith return it to the Senate, in which it originated, with my objections to its passage.

A nation is justified in repudiating its treaty obligations only when they are in conflict with great paramount interests. Even then all possible and reasonable means of modifying or changing those obligations should be exhausted before resorting to the supreme right of refusal to comply with them. These rules have governed the United States in their past intercourse with other powers as one of the family of nations. I am persuaded that if Congress can feel that this act violates the faith of the nation as pledged to China it will concur with me in rejecting this particular mode which shall meet the expectations of the people of the United States without coming into conflict with the rights of China.

The present treaty relations between that power and the United States spring from an antagonism which arose between our paramount domestic interests and our previous relations.

The treaty commonly known as the Burlingame treaty conferred upon Chinese subjects the right of voluntary emigration to the United States for the purposes of curiosity or trade or as permanent residents, and was in all respects reciprocal as to citizens of the United States in China. It gave to the voluntary emigrant coming to the United States the right to travel there or to reside there, with all the privileges, immunities, or exemptions enjoyed by the citizens or subjects of the most favored nation.

Under the operation of this treaty it was found that the institutions of the United States and the character of its people and their means of obtaining a livelihood might be seriously affected by the unrestricted introduction of Chinese labor . . .

[However,] The examination which I have made of the treaty and of the declarations which its negotiators have left on record of the meaning of its language leaves no doubt in my mind that neither contracting party in concluding the treaty of 1880 contemplated the passage of an act prohibiting immigration for twenty years, which is nearly a generation, or thought that such a period would be a reasonable suspension or limitation, or intended to change the provisions of the Burlingame treaty to that extent. I regard this provision of the act as a breach of our national faith, and being unable to bring myself in harmony with the views of the Congress on this vital point the honor of the country constrains me to return the act with this objection to its passage.

Source: Messages and Papers of the Presidents. Vol. 10 (New York: Bureau of National Literature, Inc., April 4 1882): 4699–4705

* * *

In May 1882 Congress passed a new immigration act which came to be known as the Chinese Exclusion Act. The act does not use the term exclusion but does use the term suspension, and, in response to the president's veto message, it sets the time period at ten years rather than twenty.

DOCUMENT 33: Act of May 6, 1882: To Execute Certain Treaty Stipulations Relating to Chinese ("Chinese Exclusion Act")

Whereas, in the opinion of the Government of the United States the coming of Chinese laborers to this country endangers the good order of certain localities within the territory thereof: Therefore, *Be it enacted by the Senate and the House of Representatives of the United States of America in Congress assembled,* That from and after the expiration of ninety days next after the passage of this act, and until the expiration of ten years next after the passage of this act, the coming of Chinese laborers to the United States be, and the same is hereby, suspended; and during such suspension it shall not be lawful for any Chinese laborer to come, or having so come after the expiration of said ninety days, to remain within the United States.

Sec. 2. That the master of any vessel who shall knowingly bring within the United States on such vessel, and land or permit to be landed, any Chinese laborer, from any foreign port or place, shall be deemed guilty of a misdemeanor, and on conviction thereof shall be punished by a fine of not more than five hundred dollars for each and every such Chinese laborer so brought, and may also be imprisoned for a term not exceeding one year.

Sec. 3. That the two foregoing sections shall not apply to Chinese laborers who were in the United States on the seventeenth day of November, eighteen hundred and eighty, or who shall come into the same before the expiration of the ninety days next after passage of this act . . . nor shall the foregoing sections apply to the case of any master whose vessel is bound to a port not within the United States, [and which] shall come within the jurisdiction of the United States by reason of being in distress or in stress of weather, or touching at any port of the United States on its voyage to any foreign port or place; Provided, That all Chinese laborers brought on such vessel shall depart with the vessel on leaving port.

Sec. 4. That for the purpose of properly identifying Chinese laborers who were in the United States . . . or shall come into the same before the expiration of ninety days next after the passage of this act, and in order to furnish them with the proper evidence of their right to go from and to come to the United States of their own free will and accord, as provided by the treaty of the United States and China . . . the collector of customs of the district from which any such Chinese laborer shall depart from the United States shall, in person or by deputy, go on board each vessel having on board any such Chinese laborer and cleared or about to sail from his district for a foreign port, and on such vessel make a list of all such Chinese laborers, which shall be entered in registry-books to be kept for that purpose, in which shall be stated the name, age, occupation, last place of residence, physical marks or peculiarities, and all facts necessary for the identification of each of such Chinese laborers, which books shall be kept in the custom-house; and every such Chinese laborer so departing from the United States shall be entitled to, and shall receive free of any charge or cost upon application thereof, from the collector or his deputy, at the time such a list is taken, a certificate, signed by the collector or his deputy and attested by his seal of office, in such form as the Secretary of the Treasury shall prescribe, which certificate shall contain a statement of the name, age, occupation, last place of residence, personal description, and facts of identification of the Chinese laborer to whom the certificate is issued, corresponding with the said list and registry in all particulars. . . . The certificate herein provided for shall entitle the Chinese laborer to whom the same is issued to return to and re-enter the United States upon producing and delivering the same to the collector of customs of the district at which the Chinese laborer shall re-enter; and upon delivery of such certificate by such Chinese laborer to the collector of customs at the time of re-entry in the United States, said collector shall cause the same to be filed in the custom-house and duly canceled.

Sec. 5. That any Chinese laborer mentioned in section four . . . and desiring to depart from the United States by land, shall have the right to demand and receive, free of charge or cost, a certificate of identification similar to that provided for in section four. . . .

Sec. 6. That in order to the faithful execution of articles one and two of the treaty in this act before mentioned, every Chinese person other than a laborer who may be entitled by said treaty to come within the United States, and who shall be about to come to the United States, shall be identified as so entitled by the Chinese government in each case, such identity to be evidenced by a certificate issued under the authority of said government, which certificate shall be in the English language . . . stating such right to come, and which certificate shall state the name, title, or official rank, if any, the age, height, and all physical peculiarities, former and present occupation or profession, and place of residence in China of the person to whom the certificate is issued. . . . Such certificate shall be prima-facie evidence of the fact set forth therein. . . .

Sec. 7. That any person who shall knowingly and falsely alter or substitute any name for the name written in such certificate or forge any such certificate, or knowingly utter any forged or fraudulent certificate, or falsely personate any person named in any such certificate, shall be deemed guilty of a misdemeanor; and upon conviction thereof shall be fined in sum not exceeding one thousand dollars, and imprisoned in a penitentiary for a term of not more than five years.

Sec. 8. That the master of any vessel arriving in the United States from any foreign port or place shall, at the same time he delivers a manifest of the cargo, . . . deliver and report to the collector of customs of the district in which such vessel shall have arrived a separate list of all Chinese passengers on board the vessel at that time. Such list shall show the names of such passengers . . . and such list shall be sworn to by the master in the manner required by law in relation to the manifest of the cargo. Any willful refusal or neglect of any such master to comply with the provisions of this section shall incur the same penalties and forfeiture as are provided for a refusal or neglect to report and deliver a manifest of cargo.

Sec. 9. That before any Chinese passengers are landed from any such vessel, the collector, or his deputy, shall proceed to examine such passengers, comparing the certificates with the list and with the passengers; and no passenger shall be allowed to land in the United States from such vessel in violation of law.

Sec. 10. That every vessel whose master shall knowingly violate any of the provisions of this act shall be deemed forfeited to the United States, and shall be liable to seizure and condemnation in any district of the United States into which such vessel may enter or in which she may be found.

Sec. 11. That any person who shall knowingly bring into or cause to be brought into the United States by land, or who shall knowingly aid and abet the same, or aid and abet the landing in the United States from any vessel of any Chinese person not lawfully entitled to enter the United States, shall be deemed guilty of a misdemeanor, and shall, on conviction thereof, be fined in a sum not exceeding one thousand dollars, and imprisoned for a term not exceeding one year.

Sec. 12. That no Chinese person shall be permitted to enter the United States by land without producing the certificate in this act required of Chinese persons seeking to land from a vessel. And any Chinese person found unlawfully within the United States shall be caused to be removed therefrom to the country from whence he came ... after being brought before some justice, judge, or commissioner of a court of the United States and found to be one not lawfully entitled to be or remain in the United States.

Sec. 13. That this act shall not apply to diplomatic and other officers of the Chinese Government traveling upon the business of that government ... and shall exempt them and their body and household servants from the provisions of this act as to other Chinese persons.

Sec. 14. That hereafter no State court or court of the United States shall admit Chinese to citizenship; and all laws in conflict with this act are hereby repealed.

Sec. 15. That the words "Chinese laborers," wherever used in this act, shall be construed to mean both skilled and unskilled laborers and Chinese employed in mining.

Source: 22 Stat. 58; 8 U.S.C.

* * *

In 1882 Congress passed a law that levied a fifty cent head tax on all immigrants, charged the Secretary of the Treasury to establish contracts with each state's commissioner of immigration, and banned the immigration of criminals.

DOCUMENT 34: Act of August 3, 1882: Regulation of Immigration

Be it enacted by the Senate and House of Representatives of the United States of America in Congress assembled, That there shall be levied, collected, and paid a duty of fifty cents for each and every passenger not a citizen of the United States who shall come by steam or sail vessel from a foreign port to any port within the United States. The said duty shall be paid to the collector of customs of the port to which such passenger shall come, or if there be no collector at such port, then to the collector of customs nearest thereto, by the master, owner, agent, or consignee of every such vessel, within twenty-four hours after the entry thereof into such port. The money thus collected shall be paid into the United States Treasury, and shall constitute a fund to be called the immigrant fund, and shall be used, under the direction of the Secretary of the Treasury, to defray the expenses of carrying this act into effect. The duty imposed by this section shall be a lien upon the vessels which shall bring such passengers to the United States against the owner or owners of such vessels; and the payment of such duty may be enforced by any legal or equitable remedy. *Provided,* That no greater sum shall be expended for the purposes hereinbefore mentioned, at any port, than shall have been collected at such port.

Sec. 2. That the Secretary of the Treasury is hereby charged with the duty of executing the provisions of this act with the supervision over the business of immigration to the United States, and for that purpose he shall have the power to enter into contracts with such State commissions, board or officers as may be designated for that purpose by the governor of any State to take charge of the local affairs of immigration in the ports within said State, and to provide for the support and relief of such immigrants, therein landing as may fall into distress or need public aid . . . and [they] shall be authorized to go on board of and through any such ship or vessel; and if on such examination there shall be found among such passengers any convict, lunatic, idiot or person unable to take care of himself or herself without becoming a public charge, they shall report the same in writing to the collector of such port, and such persons shall not be permitted to land. . . .

Sec. 4. That all foreign convicts except those convicted of political offenses, upon arrival, shall be sent back to the nations to which they belong and from whence they came. . . . The Secretary of the Treasury shall prescribe regulations for the return of the aforesaid persons to the countries from whence they came and shall furnish instructions to the

board, commission, or persons charged with the execution of the provisions of this section as to the mode of procedure in respect thereto,
and may change such instructions from time to time. The expense of
such return of the aforesaid persons not permitted to land shall be borne
by the owners of the vessels in which they came.

Sec. 5. This act shall take effect immediately.

Source: 22 Stat. 214; 8 U.S.C.

* * *

Congress passed what became known as the Foran Act in 1885. This
law prohibited the immigration of contract labor and imposed fines on
the masters of vessels bringing such immigrants to the United States or
the employers of any such laborer imported under a contract.

DOCUMENT 35: Act of February 26, 1885: Prohibition of Contract Labor ("Foran Act")

*Be it enacted by the Senate and House of Representative of the United States
of America in Congress assembled*, That from and after the passage of this
act it shall be unlawful for any person, company, partnership, or corporation, in any manner whatsoever, to prepay the transportation, or in
any way assist or encourage the importation or migration of any alien
or aliens, any foreigner or foreigners, into the United States, its Territories, or the District of Columbia, under contract or agreement, [*sic*] parol
from or special, express or implied, made previous to the importation or
migration of such alien or aliens, foreigner or foreigners, to perform labor
or service of any kind in the United States, its Territories, or the District
of Columbia.

Sec. 2. That all contracts or agreements, express or implied, parol, or
special, which may hereafter be made by and between any person, company, partnership, or corporation, and any foreigner or foreigners, alien
or aliens, to perform labor or service or having reference to the performance of labor or service by any person in the United States, its Territories,
or the District of Columbia previous to the migration or importation of
the person or persons whose labor or service is contracted for into the
United States, shall be utterly void and of no effect.

Sec. 3. That for every violation of any of the provisions of section one
of this act the person, partnership, company, or corporation violating the
same, by knowingly assisting, encouraging or soliciting the migration or
importation of any alien or aliens, foreigner or foreigners, into the United

States . . . shall forfeit and pay for every such offense the sum of one thousand dollars. . . .

Sec. 4. That the master of any vessel who knowingly brings within the United States on any such vessel and land, or permit to be landed, from any foreign port or place, any alien laborer, mechanic, or artisan, who, previous to embarkation on such vessel, had entered into contract or agreement, parol or special, express or implied, to perform labor or service in the United States, shall be deemed guilty of a misdemeanor, and on the conviction thereof, shall be punished by a fine of not more than five hundred dollars for each and every such alien laborer, mechanic, or artisan so brought as aforesaid, and may also be imprisoned for a term not exceeding six months.

Sec. 5. That nothing in this act shall be so construed as to prevent any citizen or subject of any foreign country temporarily residing in the United States, either in private or official capacity, from engaging, under contract or otherwise, persons not residents or citizens of the United States to act as private secretaries, servants, or domestics for such foreigner temporarily residing in the United States as aforesaid; nor shall this act be construed so as to prevent any person, or persons, partnership, or corporation from engaging, under contract or agreement, skilled workmen in foreign countries to perform labor in the United States in or upon any new industry not at present established in the United States; Provided, That the skilled labor for that purpose cannot be otherwise obtained; nor shall the provisions of this act apply to professional actors, artists, lecturers, or singers, nor to persons employed strictly as the personal or domestic servants, nor to ministers of any recognized religious denomination, nor persons belonging to any recognized profession, nor professors for colleges and seminaries; Provided, That nothing in this act shall be construed as prohibiting any individual from assisting any member of his family to migrate from any foreign country to the United States for the purpose of settlement here. . . .

Source: 23 Stat. 332; 8 U.S.C.

* * *

In an attempt to discourage Chinese immigration, the city of San Francisco passed municipal ordinances discriminating against Chinese laundry workers. These ordinances were first challenged to the California Supreme Court, which upheld them. They were then taken to the U.S. Supreme Court. In *Yick Wo v. Hopkins* (1886), the Court overturned the California court, finding that the laundry ordinance was clearly discriminatory. Document 36 presents a summary of the majority opinion in the case, written by Justice Matthews.

DOCUMENT 36: *Yick Wo v. Hopkins* (May 10, 1886)

In the case of the petitioner, brought here by writ or error to the Supreme Court of California, our jurisdiction is limited to the question whether the plaintiff in error has been denied a right in violation of the Constitution, laws, or treaties of the United States. The question whether his imprisonment is illegal, under the Constitution and laws of the state, is not open to us. And although that question might have been considered in the circuit court in the application made to it, and by this court on appeal from its order, yet judicial propriety is best consulted by accepting the judgment of the state court upon the points involved in that inquiry. . . .

Class legislation discriminating against some and favoring others is prohibited, but legislation which, in carrying out a public purpose, is limited in its application, if within the sphere of its operation it affects alike all persons similarly situated, is not within the amendment. . . .

It appears that both petitioners have complied with every requisite, deemed by the law or by the public officers, charged with its administration necessary for the protection of neighboring property from fire, or as a precaution against injury to the public health. No reason whatever, except the will of the supervisors, is assigned why they should not be permitted to carry on, in the accustomed manner, their harmless and useful occupation, on which they depend for a livelihood. And while this consent of the supervisors is withheld from them and from two hundred others who have also petitioned, all of whom happen to be Chinese subjects, eighty others, not Chinese subjects, are permitted to carry on the same business under similar conditions. The fact of this discrimination is admitted. No reason for it is shown, and the conclusion cannot be resisted, that no reason for it exists except hostility to the race and nationality to which the petitioners belong, and which in the eye of the law is not justified. The discrimination is therefore illegal, and the public administration which enforces it is a denial of the equal protection of the laws and a violation of the Fourteenth Amendment to the Constitution. The imprisonment of the petitioners is therefore illegal, and they must be discharged.

To this end, the judgment of the Supreme Court of California in the case of Yick Wo, and that of the Circuit Court of the United States for the District of California in the case of Wo Lee, are severally reversed, and the cases remanded, each to the proper court, with directions to discharge the petitioners from custody and imprisonment.

Source: 118 U.S. 220 (1885).

* * *

In 1887 Congress amended the Contract Labor Act of 1885 by extending it and increasing the authority of the secretary of the treasury to implement and enforce the act.

DOCUMENT 37: Act of February 23, 1887: Amendment to the Act to Prohibit Contract Labor

Be it enacted by the Senate and House of Representatives of the United States of America in Congress assembled, That an act to prohibit the importation and immigration of foreigners and aliens under contract or agreement to perform labor in the United States, its Territories, and the District of Columbia. . . . be amended by adding the following:

Sec. 6. That the Secretary of the Treasury is hereby charged with the duty of executing the provisions of this act, and for that purpose he shall have the power to enter into contracts with such State Commission, board, or officers as may be designated for that purpose by the Governor of any State to take charge of the local affairs of immigration in the ports of said State, under the rule and regulations to be prescribed by said Secretary; and it shall be the duty of such State Commission, board, or officers so designated to examine into the condition of passengers arriving at the ports within such State in any ship or vessel, and for that purpose all or any such commissioners or officers, or such other person or persons as they shall appoint, shall be authorized to go on board of and through any such ship or vessel; and if in any such examination there shall be found among such passengers any person included in the prohibition in this act, they shall report the same in writing to the collector of such port, and such person shall not be permitted to land.

Sec. 7. That the Secretary of the Treasury shall establish such regulations and rules, and issue from time to time such instructions, not inconsistent with the law, as he shall deem best calculated for carrying out the provisions of this act; and he shall prescribe all forms of bonds, entries, and other papers to be used under and in the enforcement of the various provisions of this act.

Sec. 8. That all persons included in the prohibition in this act, upon arrival, shall be sent back to the nations to which they belong and from whence they came. The Secretary of the Treasury may designate the State board of charities of any State in which such board shall exist by law, or any commission in any State, or any person or persons in any State, whose duty it shall be to execute the provisions of this section and shall be entitled to reasonable compensation thereof to be fixed by regulation prescribed by the Secretary of the Treasury. . . .

Sec. 9. That all acts and parts of acts inconsistent with this act are hereby repealed.

Sec. 10. That this act shall take effect at the expiration of thirty days after its passage.

Source: 24 Stat. 414; 8 U.S.C.

* * *

In 1888 Congress amended the Chinese Exclusion Act. This law, commonly known as the Scott Act, extended the ban on Chinese laborers and rescinded the right of Chinese immigrants to return to the United States unless they had obtained certificates of reentry in advance.

DOCUMENT 38: Act of September 13, 1888: Immigration of Chinese Laborers Prohibited ("Scott Act")

Be it enacted by the Senate and the House of Representatives of the United States of America in Congress assembled, That from and after the date of the exchange of ratifications of the pending treaty between the United States of America and His Imperial Majesty the Emperor of China, signed on the twelfth day of March, anno Domini eighteen hundred and eighty-eight, it shall be unlawful for any Chinese person, whether a subject of China or any other power, to enter the United States except as hereinafter provided.

Sec. 2. That Chinese officials, teachers, students, merchants, or travelers for pleasure or curiosity, shall be permitted to enter the United States, but in order to entitle themselves to do so, they shall first obtain the permission of the Chinese Government, or other Government of which they may at the time be citizens or subjects. Such permission and also their personal identity shall in such case be evidenced by a certificate to be made out by the diplomatic representative of the United States in that country, or of the consular representative of the United States at the port or place from which there person therein named comes. The certificate shall contain a full description of such person, of his age, height, and general physical features, and shall state his former and present occupation or profession and place of residence, and shall be made out in duplicate. One copy shall be delivered open to the person named and described, and the other copy shall be sealed up and delivered by the diplomatic or consular officer as aforesaid to the captain of the vessel on which the person named in the certificate sets sail for the United States, together with the sealed certificate, which shall be addressed to the collector of customs at the port where such person is to land. . . . And any captain who lands or attempts to land a Chinese person in the United States, without having in his possession a sealed certificate, as required in this section, shall be liable to the penalties prescribed in section nine of this act.

Sec. 3. That the provisions of this act shall apply to all persons of the Chinese race, whether subjects of China or other foreign power, excepting Chinese diplomatic or consular officers and their attendants; and the words "Chinese laborers," whenever used in this act, shall be construed to mean both skilled and unskilled laborers and Chinese employed in mining.

Sec. 4. That the master of any vessel arriving in the United States from any foreign port or place with any Chinese passengers on board shall, when he delivers his manifest of cargo, and if there be no cargo, when he makes legal entry of this vessel, and before landing or permitting to land any Chinese person (unless a diplomatic or consular officer, or attendant of such officer) deliver to the collector of customs of the district in which the vessel shall have arrived the sealed certificates and letters as aforesaid, and a separate list of all Chinese persons taken on board of his vessel at any foreign port or place, and of all such persons on board at the time of the arrival as aforesaid. Such list shall show the names of such persons and other particulars as shown by their open certificates, or other evidences required by this Act, and such list shall be sworn to by the master in the manner required by law in relation to the manifest of the cargo.

The master of any vessel as aforesaid shall not permit any Chinese diplomatic or consular officer or attendant of such officer to land without having first been informed by the collector of customs of the official character of such officer or attendant. Any refusal or willful neglect of the master of any vessel to comply with the provisions of this section shall incur the same penalties and forfeitures as are provided for a refusal or neglect to report and deliver a manifest of the cargo.

Sec. 5. That from and hereafter the passage of this act, no Chinese laborer in the United States shall be permitted, after having left, to return thereto, except under the conditions stated in the following sections.

Sec. 6. That no Chinese laborer within the purview of the preceding section shall be permitted to return to the United States unless he has a lawful wife, child, or parent in the United States, or property therein of the value of one thousand dollars, or debts of like amount due him and pending settlement. The marriage to such wife must have taken place at least one year prior to the application of the laborer for a permit to return to the United States, and must have been followed by the continuous cohabitation of the parties as man and wife.

If the right to return be claimed on the ground of property or of debts, it must appear that the property is bona fide and not colorably acquired for the purpose of evading this act, or that the debts are unascertained and unsettled, and not promissory notes or other similar acknowledgments of ascertained liability.

Sec. 7. That a Chinese person claiming the right to be permitted to leave the United States and return thereto on any of the grounds stated in the foregoing section, shall apply to the collector of customs of the district from which he wishes to depart at least one month prior to the time of his departure, and shall make an oath before the said collector a full statement descriptive of his family, or property, or debts, as the case may be, and shall furnish to the said collector such proofs of the facts entitling him to return as shall be required by the rules and regulations prescribed from time to time by the Secretary of the Treasury, and for any false swearing in relation thereto he shall incur the penalties of perjury. He shall also permit the collector to take a full description of his person, which description the collector shall retain and mark with a number. And if the collector, after hearing the proofs and investigating all the circumstances of the case, shall decide to issue a certificate of return, he shall at such time and place as he may designate, sign and give to the person applying a certificate containing the number of the description last aforesaid, which shall be the sole evidence given to such person of his right to return. If the last named certificate be transferred, it shall become void, and the person to whom it was given shall forfeit his right to return to the United States. The right of return under said certificate shall be limited to one year; but it may be extended for an additional period, not to exceed a year, in cases where, by reason of sickness or other cause of disability beyond his control, the holder thereof shall be rendered unable sooner to return, which facts shall be fully reported to and investigated by the consular representative of the United States at the port or place from which such laborer departs for the United States, and certified by such representatives of the United States to the satisfaction of the collector of customs at the port where such Chinese person shall seek to land in the United States, such certificate to be delivered by said representative to the master of the vessel on which he departs for the United States. And no Chinese laborer shall be permitted to re-enter the United States without producing to the proper officer of the customs of the port of such entry the return certificate herein required. A Chinese laborer possessing a certificate under this section shall be admitted to the United States only at the port from which he departed therefrom, and no Chinese person, except Chinese diplomatic or consular officers, and their attendants, shall be permitted to enter the United States except at the ports of San Francisco, Portland, Oregon, Boston, New York, New Orleans, Port Townsend, or such other ports as may be designated by the Secretary of the Treasury. . . .

[Sec. 9 through 12 are essentially unchanged from previous law.]

Sec. 13. That any Chinese person, or persons of Chinese descent, found unlawfully in the United States, or its Territories, may be arrested upon a warrant issued upon a complaint, under oath, filed by any party on behalf of the United States, by any justice, judge, or commissioner of any United States court, returnable before any justice, judge, or commissioner of a United States court, or before any United States court, and when convicted, upon a hearing, and found and adjudged to be one not lawfully entitled to be or remain in the United States, such person shall be removed from the United States to the country from whence he came. . . . And in all such cases the person who brought or aided in bringing such person into the United States shall be liable to the Government of the United States for all necessary expenses incurred in such investigation and removal; and all peace officers of the several States and Territories of the United States are hereby invested with the same authority in reference to carrying out the provisions of this act, as a marshal or deputy marshal of the United States, and shall be entitled to like compensation, to be audited and paid by the same officers.

Sec. 14. That the preceding sections shall not apply to Chinese diplomatic or consular officers or their attendants, who shall be admitted to the United States under special instructions of the Treasury Department, without production of other evidence than that of personal identity.

Sec. 15. That the act entitled "An act to amend said act approved July fifth, eighteen hundred and eighty-four" is hereby repealed to take effect upon the ratification of the pending treaty as provided in section one of this act.

Source: 25 Stat. 476; 8 U.S.C., 261–99.

* * *

In October 1888, Congress passed another act barring Chinese laborers, rescinding, ex post facto, the validity of any certificates of reentry previously granted.

DOCUMENT 39: Act of October 1, 1888: Exclusion of Chinese Laborers (Rescinding Reentry)

Be it enacted by the Senate and House of Representatives of the United States of America in Congress assembled, That from and after the passage of this act, it shall be unlawful for any Chinese laborer who shall at any time heretofore have been, or who may now or hereafter be, a resident within the United States, and shall not have returned before the passage of this act, to return to, or remain in, the United States.

Sec. 2. That no certificates of identity provided for in the fourth and fifth sections of the act to which this is a supplement shall hereafter be issued; and every certificate heretofore issued in pursuance thereof, is hereby declared void and of no effect, and the Chinese laborer claiming admission by virtue thereof shall not be permitted to enter the United States.

Sec. 3. That all duties prescribed, liabilities, penalties, and forfeitures imposed, and the powers conferred by the second, tenth, eleventh, and twelfth, sections of the act to which this is a supplement are hereby extended and made applicable to the provisions of this act.

Sec. 4. That all such part or parts of the acts to which this is a supplement as are inconsistent herewith are hereby repealed.

Source: 25 Stat. 540; 8 U.S.C. 270.

* * *

The act of 1888, with its ex post facto repeal of a certificate of reentry, was challenged in the courts. In *Chae Chan Ping v. United States,* 1889, the U.S. Supreme Court ruled against the plaintiff in the case, rejecting his argument of due process and of treaty rights, and found for the government. It based its decision on the concept of sovereignty. The racial attitudes of the justices—in reference to the "vast hordes" and "different races who will not assimilate with us"—is evident in the arguments of the majority. A summary of the majority opinion in the case is presented in Document 40.

DOCUMENT 40: *Chae Chan Ping v. United States* (May 13, 1889)

To preserve its independence, and give security against foreign aggression and encroachment, it is the highest duty of every nation, and to attain these ends nearly all other considerations are to be subordinated. It matters not in what form such aggression and encroachment come, whether from a foreign nation acting in its national character or from vast hordes of its people crowding in upon us. The Government, possessing the powers which are to be exercised for its protection and security, is clothed with authority to determine the occasion on which the powers shall be called forth; and its determination, so far as the subjects affected are concerned, are necessarily conclusive upon all the departments and officers. If, therefore, the Government of the United States, through its legislative department, considers the presence of foreigners of a different race in this country, who will not assimilate with us, to be dangerous to its peace and security, their exclusion is not to be stayed because at the time there are no actual hostilities with the nation of which the foreigners are subjects. The existence of war would render the necessity of the proceeding only more obvious and pressing. The same necessity, in a less pressing degree, may arise when war does not exist, and the same authority which adjudges the necessity in one case must also determine it in another. In both cases its determination is conclusive upon the judiciary. If the Government of the country of which the foreigners excluded are subject is dissatisfied with this action, it can make complaint to the executive head of our Government, or resort to any other measure which, in its judgment, its interests or dignity may demand; and there lies its only remedy.

The power of the Government to exclude foreigners from the country, whenever in its judgment, the public interests require such exclusion, has been asserted in repeated instances, and never denied by the executive or legislative departments. . . .

The power of exclusion of foreigners being an incident of sovereignty belonging to the Government of the United States, as a part of those sovereign powers delegated by the Constitution, the right to its exercise at any time when, in the judgment of the Government, the interests of the country require it, cannot be granted away or restrained on behalf of any one. The powers of Government are delegated in trust to the United States, and are incapable of transfer to any other parties. They cannot be abandoned or surrendered. Nor can their exercise be hampered, when needed for the public good, by any considerations of private interest. The exercise of these public trusts is not the subject of barter or contract. What ever license, therefore, Chinese laborers may have obtained previous to the Act of October 1, 1888, to return to the United States after their departure, is held at the will of the Government, revocable at any time, at its pleasure. Whether a proper consideration by our Government of its previous laws, or a proper respect for the nation whose subjects are affected by its action, ought to have qualified its inhibition and made applicable only to persons departing from the country after passage of the Act, are not questions for judicial determination. If there be any ground of complaint on the part of China, it must be made to the political department of our Government, which is alone competent to act upon the subject. The rights and interests created by a treaty, which have become so vested that its expiration or abrogation will not destroy or impair them, are such as are connected with and lie in property capable of sale and transfer, or other disposition, not such as are personal and untransferable in their character. . . . It is enough, however, to say that it is entirely different from the Act before us, and the validity of its provisions was never brought to the test of judicial decision in the courts of the United States. Order affirmed.

Source: 130 U.S. 581–611 (1889).

* * *

In 1891 the Congress passed an immigration act that expanded the classes of individuals excluded from admission, forbade the advertisement for and soliciting of immigrants, increased the penalties for landing an illegal alien, created the position of superintendent of immigration, and generally strengthened or specified the enforcement processes. Some regard this act as the crucial one whereby the federal government established its decisive role in immigration affairs.

DOCUMENT 41: Act of March 3, 1891 (Re: Immigration and the Superintendent of Immigration)

Be it enacted by the Senate and House of Representatives of the United States of America in Congress assembled, That the following classes of aliens be excluded from admission to the United States, in accordance with the existing acts regulating immigration, other than those concerning Chinese laborers: All idiots, insane persons, paupers or persons likely to become public charges, persons suffering from a loathsome or a dangerous contagious disease, persons who have been convicted of a felony or other infamous crime or misdemeanor involving moral turpitude, polygamists, and also any person whose ticket or passage is paid for with the money of another or who is assisted by others to come, unless it is affirmatively and satisfactorily shown on special inquiry that such person does not belong to one of the foregoing excluded classes, or to the class of contract laborers excluded by the act of February twenty-sixth, eighteen hundred and eighty-five, but this section shall not be held to include persons living in the United States from sending for a relative or friend who is not of the excluded classes under such regulations as the Secretary of the Treasury may prescribe; Provided, That nothing in this act shall be construed to apply to or exclude persons convicted of a political offense, notwithstanding said political offense may be designated as a "felony, crime, infamous crime, or misdemeanor, involving moral turpitude" by the laws of the land whence he came or by the court convicting.

Sec. 2. That no suit or proceeding for violations of said act of February twenty-sixth, eighteen hundred and eighty-five, prohibiting the importation or migration of foreigners under contract or agreement to perform labor, shall be settled, compromised, or discontinued without the consent of the court of record with reasons therefor.

Sec. 3. That it shall be deemed a violation of said act . . . to assist or encourage the importation or migration of any alien by promise of employment through advertisements printed and published in any foreign country; and any alien coming to this country in consequence of such an advertisement shall be treated as coming under a contract as contemplated by such act; and the penalties by said act shall be applicable in such a case: Provided, This section shall not apply to States and Bureaus of States advertising the inducements they offer for immigration. . . .

Sec. 4. That no steamship or transportation company or owners of vessels shall directly, or through agents, either by writing, printing, or oral representation, solicit, invite or encourage the immigration of any alien into the United States except by ordinary commercial letters, circulars, advertisements, or oral representations, stating the sailings of their vessel and the terms and facilities of transportation therein; and for a violation of this provision any such steamship or transport company, and any such owners of vessels, and the agents by them employed, shall be subject to the penalties imposed by the third section of said act of February twenty-sixth, eighteen hundred and eighty-five, for violations of the provisions of the first section of said act.

Sec. 5. That section five of said act . . . shall be, and hereby is, amended by adding to the second proviso in said section the words "nor to min-

isters of any religious denomination, nor persons belonging to any recognized profession, nor professors for colleges and seminaries," and by
excluding from the second proviso of said section the words "or any
relative or personal friend."

Sec. 6. That any person who shall bring into or land in the United
States by vessel or otherwise, or who shall aid to bring into or land in
the United States by vessel or otherwise, any alien not lawfully entitled
to enter the United States shall be deemed guilty of a misdemeanor, and
shall, on conviction, be punished by a fine not exceeding one thousand
dollars, or by imprisonment for a term not exceeding one year, or by
both such fine and imprisonment.

Sec. 7. That the office of superintendent of immigration is hereby created and established, and the President, by and with the advice and
consent of the Senate, is authorized and directed to appoint such officer,
whose salary shall be four thousand dollars per annum, payable
monthly. The superintendent of immigration shall be an officer in the
Treasury Department, under the control and supervision of the Secretary
of the Treasury, to whom he shall make annual reports in writing of the
transactions of his office, together with such special reports, in writing,
as the Secretary of the Treasury shall require. The Secretary shall provide
the superintendent suitable furnished office in the city of Washington,
and with such books of record and facilities for the discharge of the
duties of his office as may be necessary. He shall have a chief clerk, at
a salary of two thousand dollars per annum, and two first-class clerks.

Sec. 8. That upon arrival by water at any place within the United States
of any alien immigrants it shall be the duty of the commanding officer
and the agents of the steam or sailing vessel by which they came to
report the name, nationality, last residence, and destination of every such
alien, before any of them are landed, to the proper inspection officers,
who shall thereupon go or send competent assistants on board such vessel and there inspect all such aliens, or the inspection officer may order
a temporary removal of such aliens for examination at a designated time
and place, and then and there detain them until a thorough inspection
is made. But such removal shall not be considered a landing during the
pendency of such examination. The medical examination shall be made
by surgeons of the Marine Hospital Service. In cases where the services
of the Marine Hospital Surgeon can not be obtained without causing
unreasonable delay, the inspector may cause an alien to be examined by
a civil surgeon and the Secretary of the Treasury shall fix the compensation for such examination. The inspection officers and their assistants
shall have the power to administer oaths, and take and consider testimony touching on the right of any such alien to enter the United States,
all of which shall be entered on record. During such inspection after
temporary removal the superintendent shall cause such aliens to be

properly housed, fed, and cared for, and also, in his discretion, such as are delayed in proceeding to their destination after inspection. All decisions made by the inspection officers or their assistants touching on the right of any alien to land, when adverse to such right, shall be final unless appeal be taken to the superintendent of immigration, whose action shall be subject to review by the Secretary of the Treasury. It shall be the duty of the aforesaid officers and agents of such vessel to adopt due precautions to prevent the landing of any alien immigrant at any time or place other than that designated by the inspection officer, and any such officer or agent in charge of such vessel who shall knowingly or negligently land or permit to land any alien immigrant at any place or time other than that designated by the inspection officers, shall be deemed guilty of a misdemeanor punished by a fine not exceeding one thousand dollars, or by imprisonment not exceeding one year, or by both such fine and imprisonment.

That the Secretary of the Treasury may prescribe rules for inspection along the borders of Canada, British Columbia, and Mexico so as not to obstruct or unnecessarily delay, impede, or annoy passengers in ordinary travel between said countries; Provided, That not exceeding one inspector shall be appointed for each customs district, and whose salary shall not exceed twelve hundred dollars per year. . . .

Sec. 10. That all aliens who may unlawfully come to the United States shall, if practicable, be immediately sent back on the vessel by which they were brought in. The cost of their maintenance while on land, as well as the expense of the return of such aliens, shall be borne by the owner or owners of the vessel on which such aliens came; and if any master, agent, consignee, or owner of such vessel shall refuse to receive back on board the vessel any such aliens, or shall neglect to detain them thereon, or shall refuse or neglect to return them to the port from whence they came, or to pay the cost of their maintenance while on land, such master, agent, consignee, or owner shall be deemed guilty of a misdemeanor, and shall be punished by a fine not less than three hundred dollars for each and every offense; and any such vessel shall not have clearance from any port of the United States while any such fine is unpaid.

Sec. 11. That any alien who shall come into the United States in violation of law may be returned as by law provided . . . at the expense of the person or persons, vessel, transportation company, or corporation bringing such alien to the United States, and if that can not be done, then at the expense of the United States; and any alien who becomes a public charge within one year after his arrival in the United States from causes existing prior to his landing therein shall be deemed to have come in violation of law and shall be returned as aforesaid.

Sec. 12. That nothing contained in this act shall be construed to affect any prosecution or other proceeding, criminal or civil, begun under existing act or any acts hereby amended, but such prosecution or other proceedings . . . , shall proceed as if this act had not been passed.

Source: 26 Stat. 1084; U.S.C. 101.

* * *

The Immigration Act of 1891 was soon challenged in the courts. The U.S. Supreme Court ruled that the law was constitutional in *Nishimura Ekiu v. United States*, 1892. Excerpts of the majority opinion in the case, which follow, stress the sovereignty issue and the power of Congress both to set immigration policy and to delegate such powers to service officers.

DOCUMENT 42: *Nishimura Ekiu v. United States* (January 18, 1892)

. . .

The supervision of the admission of aliens into the United States may be intrusted by Congress either to the Department of State, having the general management of foreign relations, or to the Department of the Treasury, charged with the enforcement of laws regulating foreign commerce; and Congress has often passed acts forbidding the immigration of particular classes of foreigners, and has committed the execution of these acts to the Secretary of the Treasury, to collectors of customs, and to inspectors acting under their authority. . . .

An alien immigrant, prevented from landing by such officer claiming authority to do so under an Act of Congress, and thereby restrained of his liberty, is doubtless entitled to a writ of habeas corpus to ascertain whether the restraint is lawful. . . .

It is not within the province of the judiciary to order that foreigners who have never been naturalized, nor acquired any domicile or residence within the United States, nor even been admitted to the country pursuant to law, shall be permitted to enter, in opposition to the constitutional and lawful measures of the legislative and executive branches of the national government. As to such persons, the decision of the executive administrative officers, acting within powers expressly conferred by Congress, are due process of law. . . .

The doings of Thornley, the state commissioner of immigration, in examining and detaining the petitioner, and in reporting to the collector, appear to have been under that Act and would be justified under the second section thereof . . . Putting her in the mission house, as a more suitable place than the steamship, pending the decision of the question of her right to land, and keeping her there, by agreement between her attorney and the attorney for the United States, until final judgment upon the writ of habeas corpus, left her in the same position, so far as regarded her right to land in the United States, as if she never had been removed from the steamship.

Before the hearing upon the writ of habeas corpus, Hatch was appointed by the Secretary of the Treasury inspector of immigration at the port of San Francisco, and after making the inspection and examination required by the Act of 1891, refused to allow petitioner to land, and made a report to the collector of customs, stating facts which tended to show, and which the inspector decided did show, that she was a "person likely to become a public charge," and so within one of the classes of aliens "excluded from admission into the United States" by the first section of that Act. And Hatch intervened in the proceedings on the writ of habeas corpus, setting up his decision in bar of the writ.

A writ of habeas corpus is not like an action to recover damages for an unlawful arrest or commitment, but its object is to ascertain whether the prisoner can lawfully be detailed [sic] in custody; and if sufficient ground for his detention by the government is shown, he is not to be discharged for defects in the original arrest or commitment. . . . The case must therefore turn on the validity and effect of the action of Hatch as inspector of immigration. . . .

The decision of the inspector of immigration being in conformity with the Act of 1891, there can be no doubt that it was final and conclusive against the petitioner's right to land in the United States. The words of section 8 are clear to that effect, and were manifestly intended to prevent the question of an alien immigrant's right to land, when once decided adversely by an inspector, acting within the jurisdiction conferred upon him, from being impeached or reviewed, in the courts or otherwise, save only by appeal to the inspector's official superiors, and in accordance with the provisions of the Act. . . .

The result is that the Act of 1891 is constitutional and valid; the inspector of immigration was duly appointed; his decision against the petitioner's right to land in the United States was within the authority conferred upon him by that Act; no appeal having been taken to the superintendent of immigration, that decision was final and conclusive; the petitioner not unlawfully restrained of her liberty; and the order of the circuit court is affirmed.

Source: 142 U.S. 651 (January 18, 1892).

*   *   *

In 1892 the Congress amended the Chinese Exclusion Act by extending it another ten years and by increasing some of the penalties and generally tightening its procedures.

DOCUMENT 43: Act of May 5, 1892: Chinese Exclusion Extended 10 Years ("Geary Act")

Be it enacted by the Senate and House of Representatives . . . , That all laws now in force prohibiting and regulating the coming to this country of Chinese persons and persons of Chinese descent are hereby continued in force for a period of ten years from the passage of this act.

Sec. 4. That any such Chinese person or person of Chinese descent convicted and adjudged to be not lawfully entitled to be or to remain in the United States shall be imprisoned at hard labor for a period of not exceeding one year and thereafter removed from the United States, as hereinbefore provided [this section was subsequently declared unconstitutional].

Sec. 5. That after passage of this act on an application to any judge or court of the United States in the first instance for a writ of habeas corpus, by a Chinese person seeking to land in the United States, to whom that privilege has been denied, no bail shall be allowed, and such application shall be heard and determined promptly without unnecessary delay.

Sec. 6. And it shall be the duty of all Chinese laborers in the United States at the time of the passage of the act, and who were entitled to remain in the United States, to apply to the collector of internal revenue of their respective districts, within one year after passage of this act, for a certificate of residence, and any Chinese laborer, within the limits of the United States, who shall neglect, fail, or refuse to comply with the provisions of this act, or who, after one year from the passage hereof, shall be found within the jurisdiction of the United States without such certificate of residence, shall be deemed and adjudged to be unlawfully in the United States, and may be arrested by any United States customs offical, collector of internal revenue or his deputies, United States marshal or his deputies, and taken before a United States judge, whose duty it shall be to order that he be deported from the United States, as hereinbefore provided, unless he shall clearly establish to the satisfaction of said judge that by reason of accident, sickness, or other unavoidable cause he has been unable to procure his certificate, and to the satisfaction of the court, and by at least one credible white witness, that he was a resident of the United States at the time of the passage of this act; and if, upon the hearing, it shall appear that he is so entitled to a certificate, it shall be granted upon his paying the cost. Should it appear that said Chinaman had procured a certificate which has been lost or destroyed, he shall be detained and judgment suspended a reasonable time to enable him to procure a duplicate from the officer granting it; and in such cases the cost of said arrest and trial shall be in the discretion of the court. And any Chinese person, other than a Chinese laborer, having a right to be and remain in the United States, and desiring such certificate as evidence of such right, may apply for and receive the same without charge.

Sec. 7. That immediately after passage of this act, the Secretary of the Treasury shall make such rules and regulations as may be necessary for the efficient execution of this act, and shall prescribe the necessary forms and furnish the necessary blanks to enable collectors of internal revenue to issue the certificates required hereby, and make such provisions that certificates may be procured in localities convenient to the applicants, such certificates to be issued without charge to the applicant, and shall contain the name, age, local residence and occupation of the applicant, and such other description of the applicant as shall be prescribed by the Secretary of the Treasury, and a duplicate thereof shall be filed in the office of the collector of internal revenue for the district within which such Chinaman makes application.

Sec. 8. That any person who shall knowingly and falsely alter or substitute any name for the name written in such certificate or forge such certificate, or knowingly utter any forged or fraudulent certificate, or falsely personate any person name in such certificate, shall be guilty of a misdemeanor, and upon conviction thereof shall be fined in a sum not exceeding one thousand dollars or imprisoned in the penitentiary for a term of not more than five years.

Sec. 9. The Secretary of the Treasury may authorize the payment of such compensation in the nature of fees to the collectors of internal revenue, for services performed under the provisions of this act in addition to the salaries now allowed by law, as he shall deem necessary, not exceeding the sum of one dollar for each certificate issued.

Source: 27 Stat. 25; 8 U.S.C.

* * *

In 1893 Congress again amended the Chinese Exclusion Act, extending its period of exclusion and somewhat increasing the restrictions imposed.

DOCUMENT 44: Act of November 3, 1893 (Re: Amending the Chinese Exclusion Act)

Be it enacted by the Senate and House of Representatives of the United States of America in Congress assembled, That Section six of an act entitled "An act to prohibit the coming of Chinese persons into the United States," approved May fifth, eighteen hundred and ninety-two, is hereby amended so as to read as follows:

Sec. 6. And it shall be the duty of all Chinese laborers within the limits of the United States who were entitled to remain in the United States . . . to apply to the collector of internal revenue of their respective districts within six months after passage of this act for a certificate of residence; and any Chinese laborer within the limits of the United States who shall neglect, fail, or refuse to comply with the provisions of this act and the act to which this is an amendment, or who, after the expiration of said six months, shall be found within the jurisdiction of the United States without such certificate of residence, shall be deemed and adjudged to be unlawfully within the United States, and may be arrested by any United States customs official, collector of internal revenue or his deputies, United States marshal or his deputies, and taken before a United States judge, whose duty it shall be to order that he be deported from the United States, as provided in this act . . . unless he shall establish clearly to the satisfaction of said judge that by reason of accident, sickness, or other unavoidable cause he was unable to procure his certificate, and to the satisfaction of said United States judge, and by at least one credible witness other than Chinese, that he was a resident of the United States. . . . Should it appear that said Chinaman had procured a certificate which has been lost or destroyed, he shall be detained and judgment suspended a reasonable time to enable him to procure a duplicate from the officer granting it, and in such case the costs of said arrest and trial shall be in the discretion of the court; and any Chinese person, other than a Chinese laborer, having a right to be in the United States, desiring such a certificate as evidence of such right, may apply for and receive the same without charge; and that no proceedings for a violation of the provisions of said section six of said act . . . shall hereafter be instituted, and that all proceedings for said violation now pending are hereby discontinued: Provided, That no Chinese person heretofore convicted in any court of the States or Territories or of the United States of a felony shall be permitted to register under the provisions of this act, but all such persons who are now subject to deportation for failure or refusal to comply with the act . . . shall be deported from the United States as in said act and as in this act provided, upon any appropriate proceedings now pending or which may be hereafter instituted.

Sec. 2. The words "laborer" or "laborers," wherever used in this act, or in the act to which it is an amendment, shall be construed to mean both skilled and unskilled manual laborers, including Chinese employed in mining, fishing, huckstering, peddling, laundrymen, or those engaged in taking, drying, or otherwise preserving shell or other fish for home consumption or exportation.

The term "merchant," as employed herein and in the acts of which this is amendatory, shall have the following meaning and none other: A merchant is a person engaged in buying and selling merchandise, at a fixed place of business, which business is conducted in his name, and who during the time he claims to be engaged as a merchant, does not engage in the performance of any manual labor, except such as is necessary in the conduct of his business as merchant.

Where the application is made by a Chinaman for entrance into the United States on the ground that he was formerly engaged in this country as a merchant, he shall establish by the testimony of two credible witnesses other than Chinese the fact that he conducted such business before his departure from the United States, and that during such year he was not engaged in the performance of any manual labor, except such as was necessary in the conduct of his business as a merchant, and in default of such proof he shall be refused a landing.

Such order of deportation shall be executed by the United States marshal of the district within which such order is made, and he shall execute the same with all convenient dispatch; and pending the execution of such order such Chinese person shall remain in the custody of the United States Marshal, and shall not be admitted to bail.

The certificate herein provided for shall contain the photograph of the applicant, together with his name, local residence and occupation, and a copy of such certificate, with a duplicate of such photograph attached, shall be filed in the office of the United States Collector of Internal Revenue of the district in which such Chinaman makes application.

Source: 28 Stat. 7.

* * *

In 1894 the Congress again amended the Exclusion Act and established a Bureau of Immigration.

DOCUMENT 45: Act of August 18, 1894 (Re: Chinese Exclusion and Establishing a Bureau of Immigration)

Enforcement of the Chinese Exclusion Act: To prevent unlawful entry of Chinese into the United States, by the appointment of suitable officers to enforce the laws in relation thereto, and for expenses of returning to China all Chinese persons found to be unlawfully in the United States, including the cost of imprisonment and actual expense of conveyance of Chinese persons to the frontier or seaboard for deportation, and for enforcing the provisions of the Act of May fifth, eighteen hundred and ninety-two, . . . fifty thousand dollars.

In every case where an alien is excluded from admission into the United States under any law or treaty now existing or hereafter made, the decision of the appropriate immigration or custom officers, if adverse to the admission of such alien, shall be final, unless reversed on appeal to the Secretary of the Treasury.

Bureau of Immigration: That head money from alien passengers on and after the first day of October next, collected under the Act of August third, eighteen hundred and eighty-two, to regulate immigration, shall be one dollar in lieu of the fifty cents provided in said Act, and such head money and all other receipts which shall be collected on or after July first, eighteen hundred and ninety-five, in connection with immigration shall be covered into the Treasury; and the Secretary of the Treasury shall report to the next regular session of Congress a plan for the organization of the service in connection with immigration and make detailed estimates of the employees necessary for such service, and the compensation and other expenses.

The commissioners of immigration at the several ports shall be appointed by the President, by and with the advice and consent of the Senate, to hold their offices for the term of four years, unless sooner removed, and until their successors are appointed; and nominations for such offices shall be made to the Senate by the President as soon as practicable after passage of this Act.

Source: 28 Stat. 390; 8 U.S.C. 174.

* * *

In 1896 the U.S. Supreme Court issued another watershed decision in the case of *Plessy v. Ferguson*. The issue in this case was whether a state law segregating accommodations of interstate train travel was unconstitutional in as much as it denied "equal protection under the law" as guaranteed by the Fourteenth Amendment. The Court ruled, under a self-proclaimed doctrine of "separate-but-equal," that the law did not abridge or deny the plaintiff, Homer Plessy, equal protection of the law. The case underscored a racial interpretation of the law that gave a constitutional approval to de jure segregation laws in the South (which came to be known as Jim Crow laws). This doctrine, which lasted until the Court overturned *Plessy* in 1954, was very important in restricting the rights of all citizens of color in the United States—blacks, Asians, Hispanics, American Indians—by allowing state governments to pass laws segregating them from white schools, places of public accommodation, and so on. Document 46 presents a summary of the *Plessy* decision.

DOCUMENT 46: *Plessy v. Ferguson* (May 18, 1896)

Mr. Justice Brown delivered the opinion of the court: This case turns upon the constitutionality of an act of the general assembly of the state of Louisiana, passed in 1890, providing for separate railway carriages for the white and colored races. Acts 1890, No. 111, p. 152. The 1st section of the statute enacts "that all railway companies carrying passengers in their coaches in this state shall provide equal but separate accommodations for the white and colored races, by providing two or more passenger coaches for each passenger train, or by dividing the passenger coaches by a partition so as to secure separate accommodations: Provided, That this section shall not be construed to apply to street railroads. No person or persons shall be permitted to occupy seats in coaches other than the ones assigned to them, on account of the race they belong to. . . ."

The information filed in the criminal district court charged in substance that Plessy, being a passenger between two stations within the state of Louisiana, was assigned by officers of the company to a coach used for the race to which he belonged, but he insisted upon going into a coach used by the race to which he did not belong. Neither in the information nor pleas was his particular race or color averred.

The petition for the writ of prohibition averred that petitioner was seven eighths Caucasian and one eighth African blood; that the mixture of colored blood was not discernible in him, and that he was entitled to every right, privilege, and immunity assured to citizens of the United States of the white race; and that, upon such theory, he took possession of a vacant seat in a coach where passengers of the white race were accommodated, and was ordered by the conductor to vacate said coach and to take a seat in another assigned to persons of the colored race, and having refused to comply with such demand he was forcibly ejected with the aid of a police officer, and imprisoned in the parish jail, to answer a charge of having violated the above act.

The constitutionality of this act is attacked upon the ground that it conflicts with the 13th Amendment of the Constitution, abolishing slavery, and the 14th Amendment, which prohibits certain restrictive legislation on the part of the states. . . .

We consider the underlying fallacy of the plaintiff's argument to consist in the assumption that the enforced separation of the two races stamps the colored race with a badge of inferiority. If this be so, it is not by reason of anything found in the act, but solely because the colored race choses to put that construction upon it. The argument necessarily assumes that if, as has been more than once the case, and is not unlikely to be so again, the colored race should become the dominant power in the state legislature, and should enact a law in precisely similar terms, it would thereby relegate the white race to an inferior position. We imagine that the white race, at least, would not acquiesce in this assumption. The argument also assumes that social prejudice may be overcome by legislation, and that equal rights cannot be secured to the negro except by an enforced commingling of the two races. We cannot accept this position. If the two races are to meet on terms of social equality, it must be the result of natural affinities, a mutual appreciation of each other's merits and a voluntary consent of individuals . . . Legislation is powerless to eradicate racial instincts or to abolish distinctions based upon physical differences, and the attempt to do so can only result in accentuating the difficulties of the present situation. If the civil and political rights of both races be equal, one cannot be inferior to the other civilly or politically. If one race be inferior to the other socially, the Constitution of the United States cannot put them upon the same plane.

It is true that the question of the proportion of colored blood necessary to constitute a colored person, as distinguished from a white person, is one upon which there is a difference of opinion in the different states, some holding that any visible admixture of black blood stamps the person as belonging to the colored race . . . and still others that it depends upon the predominance of white blood must only be in the proportion of three fourths . . . But these are questions to be determined under the laws of each state and are not properly the issue in this case. Under the allegation of his petition it may undoubtedly become a question of importance whether, under the laws of Louisiana, the petitioner belongs to the white or colored race.

The judgement of the court below is therefore affirmed.

Source: 163 U.S. 537.

* * *

In 1897 a federal district court in West Texas dealt with the issue of citizenship of Mexican Americans based on the right established by the Treaty of Guadalupe Hidalgo. Notwithstanding the conventional wisdom that citizenship was limited to whites, blacks, and some Native Americans, this decision affirmed that Mexicans, largely a mixed-race people, were also eligible for naturalization. The following presents the summary judgment in the case of *In Re Rodriguez*.

DOCUMENT 47: *In Re Rodriguez,* **District Court, W.D. Texas (May 3, 1897)**

. . .

When all the foregoing laws, treaties, and constitutional provisions are considered, which either affirmatively confer the rights of citizenship upon Mexicans, or tacitly recognize in them the right of individual naturalization, the conclusion forces itself upon the mind that citizens of Mexico are eligible to American citizenship, and may be individually naturalized . . .

After careful and patient investigation of the question discussed, the court is of the opinion that, whatever may be the status of the applicant viewed solely from the standpoint of the ethnologist, he is embraced within the spirit and intent of our laws upon naturalization, and his application should be granted if he is shown by the testimony to be a man attached to the principles of the constitution, and well disposed to the good order and happiness of the same . . . In the judgment of the court, the applicant possesses the requisite qualifications for citizenship, and his application will therefore be granted.

Source: District Court, W.D. Texas (81 F. 337, May 3, 1897).

* * *

In 1896 President Grover Cleveland vetoed the first of what was to become several attempts by the Congress to enact a literacy law as a means to control immigration. President Cleveland's veto message stresses the dramatic shift in immigration policy entailed by the new device, rejecting the need for or wisdom of such a change and objecting to the unclear and untested nature of implementing such a device to screen and exclude immigrants. His veto was the first of several presidential veto messages concerning the literacy device.

DOCUMENT 48: President Grover Cleveland's Veto Message of the Immigrant Literacy Test Bill (March 2, 1897)

To the House of Representatives: I hereby return without approval House bill No. 7864, entitled "An act to amend the immigration laws of the United States."

By the first section of this bill it is proposed to amend section 1 of the act of March 3, 1891, relating to immigration by adding to the classes of aliens thereby excluded from admission to the United States the following:

"All persons physically capable and over 16 years of age who can not read and write the English language or some other language, but a person not so able to read and write who is over 50 years of age and is the parent or grandparent of a qualified immigrant over 21 years of age and capable of supporting such parent or grandparent may accompany such immigrant, or such parent or grandparent may be sent for and come to join the family of a child or grandchild over 21 years of age similarly qualified and capable, and a wife or minor child not so able to read and write may accompany or be sent for and come and join her husband or parent similarly qualified and capable."

A radical departure from our national policy relating to immigration is here presented. Heretofore we have welcomed all who came to us from other lands except those whose moral or physical conditions or history threatened danger to our national welfare and safety. Relying upon zealous watchfulness of our people to prevent injury to our political and social fabric, we have encouraged those coming from foreign countries to cast their lot with us and join in the development of our vast domains, securing in return a share in the blessings of American citizenship.

A century of stupendous growth, largely due to the assimilation and thrift of millions of sturdy and patriotic adopted citizens, attests the success of this generous and free-handed policy which, while guarding the people's interests, exacts from our immigrants only physical and moral soundness and a willingness and ability to work.

A contemplation of the grand results of this policy cannot fail to arouse a sentiment in its defense, for however it might have been regarded as an original proposition and viewed as an experiment its accomplishments are such that if it is to be uprooted at this late day its disadvantages should be plainly apparent and the substitute adopted should be just and adequate, free from uncertainties, and guarded against difficult or oppressive administration.

It is not claimed, I believe, that the time has come for the further restriction of immigration on the grounds that an excess of population overcrowds our land.

It is said, however, that the quality of recent immigration is undesirable. The time is quite within recent memory when the same thing was said of immigrants who, with their descendants, are now numbered among our best citizens.

It is said that too many immigrants settle in our cities, thus dangerously increasing their idle and vicious population.

The claim is also made that the influx of foreign laborers deprives of the opportunity to work those who are better entitled than they to the privilege of earning their livelihood by daily toil. An unfortunate condition is certainly presented when any who are willing to labor are unemployed, but so far as this condition now exists among our people it must be conceded to be as a result of a phenomenal business depression and the stagnation of all enterprises in which labor is a factor. . . .

It is proposed by the bill under consideration to meet the alleged difficulties of the situation by establishing an educational test by which the right of a foreigner to make his home with us shall be determined. . . .

The best reason that could be given for this radical restriction of immigration is the necessity of protecting our population against degeneration and saving our national peace and quiet from imported turbulence and disorder.

I can not believe that we would be protected against those evils by limiting immigration to those who can read and write in any language twenty-five words of our Constitution. In my opinion, it is infinitely more safe to admit a hundred thousand immigrants who, though unable to read and write, seek among us only a home and opportunity to work than to admit one of those unruly agitators and enemies of governmental control who can not only read and write, but delight in arousing by inflammatory speech the illiterate and peacefully inclined to discontent and tumult. Violence and disorder do not originate with illiterate laborers. They are, rather, the victims of the educated agitator. The ability to read and write, as required by this bill, in and of itself affords, in my opinion, a misleading test of contended industry and supplies unsatisfactory evidence of desirable citizenship or a proper apprehension of the benefits of our institutions. If any particular element of our illiterate immigration is to be feared for causes other than illiteracy, these causes should be dealt with directly, instead of making illiteracy the pretext for exclusion, to the detriment of other illiterate immigrants against whom the real cause of complaint can not be alleged.

The provision intended to rid that part of the proposed legislation already referred to from obvious hardship appears to me to be indefinite and inadequate. . . .

A careful examination of this bill has convinced me that for the reasons given and others not specifically stated its provisions are unnecessarily harsh and oppressive, and that its defects in construction would cause vexation and its operation would result in harm to our citizens.

Source: Messages and Papers of the Presidents. Vol. 13 (New York: Bureau of National Literature, Inc., 1897): 6189–93.

* * *

In 1898 the U.S. Supreme Court rendered its decision in *Wong Kim Ark v. United States* in which it ruled that a native-born person of Asian (in this case, Chinese) descent was indeed a citizen of the United States despite the fact that his or her parents may have been resident aliens not eligible for naturalization. This case affirmed an important precedent that all persons born in the United States—no matter their race—were, in fact, native-born citizens of the United States.

DOCUMENT 49: *Wong Kim Ark v. United States* (March 28, 1898)

Mr. Justice Gray delivered the opinion of the court:

The facts in this case as agreed by the parties are as follows: Wong Kim Ark was born in 1873 in the City of San Francisco, in the state of California and United States of America, and was and is a laborer. His father and mother were persons of Chinese descent, and subjects of the Emperor of China; they were at the time of his birth domiciled residents of the United States, having previously established and still enjoying a permanent domicile and residence at San Francisco; they continued to reside and remain in the United States until 1890, when they departed for China; and during all the time of their residence in the United States they were engaged in business and were never employed in any diplomatic or official capacity under the Emperor of China. Wong Kim Ark, ever since his birth, has had but one residence, to wit, in California, within the United States, and has there resided, claiming to be a citizen of the United States, and has never lost or acquired another residence, and neither he nor his parents acting for him, ever renounced his allegiance to the United States, or did or committed any act or thing to exclude him therefrom. In 1890, (when he was about seventeen years of age) he departed for China on a temporary visit and with the intention of returning to the United States and did return thereto by sea in the same year, and was permitted by the collector of customs to enter the United States, upon the sole ground that he was a native born citizen of the United States. After such return, he remained in the United States, claiming to be a citizen thereof, until 1894 when he (being about twenty-one years of age, but whether a little above or a little under that age does not appear) again departed for China on a temporary visit with the intention of returning to the United States; and he did return thereto by sea in August, 1895, and applied to the collector of customs for permission to land; and was denied such permission, upon the sole ground that he was not a citizen of the United States.

It is conceded that, if he is a citizen of the United States, the acts of Congress known as the Chinese exclusion acts, prohibiting persons of the Chinese race, and especially Chinese laborers, from coming to the United States, do not and cannot apply to him.

The question presented by the record is whether a child born in the United States, of parents of Chinese descent, who at the time of his birth are subjects of the Emperor of China, but have a permanent domicile and residence in the United States, and are there carrying on business, and are not employed in any diplomatic or official capacity under the Emperor of China, becomes at the time of his birth a citizen of the United States, by virtue of the first clause of the 14th Amendment of the Constitution: "All persons born or naturalized in the United States, and subject to the jurisdiction thereof, are citizens of the United States and of the state wherein they reside."

. . .

The fact, therefore, that acts of Congress or treaties have not permitted Chinese persons born out of this country to become citizens by naturalization cannot exclude Chinese persons born in this country from the operation of the broad and clear words of the Constitution, "All persons born in the United States, and subject to the jurisdiction thereof, are citizens of the United States."

VII. Upon the facts agreed in this case, the American citizenship which Wong Kim Ark has acquired by birth within the United States has not been lost or taken away by anything happening since his birth. . . . The evident intention, and the necessary effect, of the submission of this case to the decision of the court upon the facts agreed by the parties, were to present for determination the single question, stated at the beginning of this opinion, namely, whether a child born in the United States, of parents of Chinese descent, who, at the time of this birth, are subjects of the Emperor of China, but have a permanent domicile and residence in the United States, and are there carrying on business, and are not employed in any diplomatic, or official capacity under the Emperor of China, becomes at the time of his birth a citizen of the United States. For the reasons above stated, this court is of the opinion that the question must be answered in the affirmative. Order affirmed.

Source: 169 U.S. 649 (March 28, 1898).

* * *

The 1891 Chinese Exclusion Act, and the Court's affirmation of its constitutionality, gave immigration inspectors wide latitude in enforcing the act, especially in deciding whether an individual fell within an excluded class on the basis of their assessment of the "public charge" issue, or that an existing medical condition justified exclusion. The attitude of the inspectors of immigration influenced those assessments and examinations. Document 50 presents a speech made by an immigration inspector reflecting the norms of behavior of those officials during the late 1890s and early 1900s.

DOCUMENT 50: An Immigration Examination Officer's Speech

The average immigrant remains at Ellis Island for two or three hours, during which time he undergoes an examination by the Public Health Service in order to determine his mental and physical condition, and by the Immigration Service in order to find out whether he is otherwise admissible.

Line Inspection

Upon entering the examination plant of the Public Health Service, the immigrants are guided by an attendant into different inspection lines. . . . The alien after passing the scrutiny of the first medical officer passes on to the end of the line where he is quickly inspected again by the second examiner. This examiner is known in service parlance as "the eye man." He stands at the end of the line with his back to the window and faces this approaching alien. This position affords good light, which is so essential for eye examinations. The approaching alien is scrutinized by the eye man immediately in front of whom the alien comes to a standstill. The officer will frequently ask a question or two so as to ascertain the condition of the immigrant's mentality. He may pick up a symptom, mental or physical, that has been overlooked by the first examiner.

He looks carefully at the eyeball in order to detect signs of defect and disease of that organ and then quickly everts the upper lids in search of conjunctivitus and trachoma. Corneal opacities, nystagmus, squint, bulging eyes, the wearing of eye glasses, clumsiness, and other signs on the part of the alien, will be sufficient cause for him to be chalk-marked "Vision." He will then be taken out of the line by an attendant and his vision will be carefully examined. If the alien passes the line without receiving a chalk mark, he has successfully passed the medical inspection and off he goes to the upper hall, there to undergo another examination to see that he is not an anarchist, bigamist, pauper, criminal, or otherwise unfit.

In the medical inspection which is conducted by the first officer or one who occupies the proximal position, attention is paid to each passing alien. The alien's manner of entering the line, his conversation, style of dress, any peculiarity or unusual incident in regard to him are all observed. Knowledge of racial characteristics in physique, costume, and behavior are important in the primary sifting process. Every effort is made to detect signs and symptoms of mental disease and defect. Any suggestion, no matter how trivial, that would point to abnormal mentality is sufficient cause to defer the immigrant to a thorough examination.

The following signs and symptoms occurring in immigrants at the line inspection might suggest active or maniacal psychosis: striking peculiarities in dress, talkativeness, witticism, facetiousness, detailing, apparent shrewdness, keenness, excitement, impatience in word or manner, impudence, unruliness, flightiness, nervousness, restlessness, egotism, smiling, facial expression of mirth, laughing eroticism, boisterous conduct, meddling with the affairs of others, and uncommon activity.

Psychosis of a depressive nature would be indicated by: slow speech, low voice, trembling articulation, sad faces, tearful eyes, perplexity, difficulty in thinking, delayed responses, psycho motor retardation.

Alcoholism, paresis, and organic dementia may exhibit any of the following signs: surliness, apparent intoxication, confusion, aimlessness, dullness, stupidity, expressionless face, ataxia, stuttering and tremulous speech, great amount of calmness, jovial air, self-confident smile, talkativeness, fabrications, grandiousness, sulleness, fussiness, excessive friendliness, defective memory, misstatement of age, disorientation, difficulty in computation, pupil symptoms, and other physical signs. Various kinds of demential, mental deficiency, or epilepsy would be suggested by: stigmata of degeneration, facial scars, acne from rashes, stupidity, confusion, inattention, lack of comprehension, facial expression of earnestness or preoccupation, inability to add simple digits, general untidiness, forgetfulness, verbigeration, neologisms, talking to one's self, incoherent talk, impulsive or stereotyped actions, constrained bearing, suspicious attitude, refusing to be examined, objecting to have eyelids turned, nonresponse to questions, evidence of negativism, silly laughing, hallucinating, awkward manner, biting nails, unnatural actions, mannerisms and other eccentricities.

Source: "Foreign Language Information Services" Interpreter Release E. F. S. no. 46, November 1, 1923.

* * *

Congress enacted several laws dealing with the Territory of Hawaii. In them Congress first annexed the Territory of Hawaii; then granted citizenship status to Hawaiians, exempting them from some of the steps in the naturalization process; and applied the contract labor and Chinese labor exclusion provisions of immigration law to Hawaii. These three acts are presented in Document 51.

DOCUMENT 51: Act of July 7, 1898: Annexation of Hawaiian Islands, and Acts of April 30, 1900: Regarding the Territory of Hawaii

---

Act of July 7, 1898: Annexation of the Hawaiian Islands

Whereas the Government of the Republic of Hawaii having, in due form, signified its consent, in the manner provided by its constitution, to cede absolutely and without reserve to the United States of America all rights of sovereignty of whatsoever kind in and over the Hawaiian Islands and their dependencies. . . . Therefore,

Resolved by the Senate and House of Representatives of the United States of America in Congress assembled, That said cession is accepted, ratified, and confirmed, and that the said Hawaiian Islands and their dependencies be, and they are hereby, annexed as a part of the territory of the United States and are subject to the sovereign dominion thereof, and that all and singular the property and rights hereinbefore mentioned are vested in the United States of America. . . . Until legislation shall be enacted extending the United States customs laws and regulations to the Hawaiian Islands the existing customs relations of the Hawaiian Islands with the United States and other countries will remain unchanged.

There shall be no further immigration of Chinese into the Hawaiian Islands, except upon such conditions as are now or may hereafter be allowed by the laws of the United States; and no Chinese, by reason of anything herein contained, shall be allowed to enter the United States from the Hawaiian Islands. . . .

Source: 30 Stat. 750; 48 U.S.C. 491.

Act of April 30, 1900: Citizenship of Hawaiians

Sec. 4. That all persons who were citizens of the Republic of Hawaii on August twelfth, eighteen hundred and ninety eight, are hereby declared to be citizens of the United States and citizens of the Territory of Hawaii.

And all citizens of the United States resident in the Hawaiian Islands who were resident there on or since August twelfth, eighteen hundred and ninety-eight, and all the citizens of the United States who hereafter reside in the Territory of Hawaii for one year shall be citizens of the Territory of Hawaii.

Source: 31 Stat. 141; 48 U.S.C. 494.

Act of April 30, 1900: Contract Labor Laws Applicable to Territory of Hawaii

Sec. 10. That the Act approved February twenty-sixth, eighteen hundred and eighty-five, "to prohibit the importation and migration of foreigners and laborers and aliens under contract or agreement to perform labor in the United States, its Territories, and the District of Columbia," and the Acts amendatory thereof and supplemental thereto, be, and the same are hereby, extended to and made applicable to the Territory of Hawaii.

Sec. 101. That Chinese in the Hawaiian Islands when this Act takes effect may within one year thereafter obtain certificates of residence as required by "An Act to prohibit the coming of Chinese persons into the United States," approved May fifth, eighteen hundred and ninety-two, as amended . . . and until the expiration of said year shall not be deemed to be unlawfully in the United States if found therein without such certificates: Provided, however, That no Chinese laborer, whether he shall hold such certificates or not, shall be allowed to enter any State, Territory, or District of the United States from the Hawaiian Islands.

Source: 31 Stat. 143; 48 U.S.C. 504.

Act of April 30, 1900: Residence in Hawaiian Islands and Exemption from Declaration of Intention and Renunciation of Allegiance in Certain Cases

Sec. 100. That for the purposes of naturalization under the laws of the United States, residence in the Hawaiian Islands prior to the taking effect of this Act shall be deemed equivalent to residence in the United States and in the Territory of Hawaii, and the requirement of previous declaration of intention to become a citizen of the United States and to renounce former allegiance shall not apply to persons who have resided on said islands at least five years prior to the taking effect of this Act; but all other provisions of the laws of the United States relating to naturalization shall, so far as applicable, apply to persons in the said islands.

All records relating to naturalization, all declarations of intention to become citizens of the United States, and all certificates of naturalization filed, recorded, or issued prior to the taking effect of the naturalization Act of June twenty-ninth, nineteen hundred and six, in or from any circuit court of the Territory of Hawaii, shall for all purposes be deemed to be and to have been made, filed, recorded, or issued by a court with jurisdiction to naturalize aliens, but shall not be by this Act further validated or legalized.*

Source: 31 Stat. 161; 8 U.S.C. 385.

* * *

In April 1902 Congress reenacted and extended the Chinese Exclusion Act, which remained in effect until its repeal in 1943.

DOCUMENT 52: Act of April 29, 1902: Chinese Immigration Prohibited

Be it enacted by the Senate and the House of Representatives of the United States of America in Congress assembled, That all laws now in force prohibiting and regulating the coming of Chinese persons, and persons of Chinese descent, into the United States, and the residence of such persons therein, including sections five, six, seven, eight, nine, ten, eleven, thirteen, and fourteen of the Act entitled, "An Act to prohibit the coming of Chinese laborers into the United States," approved September thirteenth, eighteen hundred and eighty-eight, be, and the same are hereby, re-enacted, extended, and continued so far as they are not inconsistent with treaty obligations, until otherwise provided by law, and said laws shall also apply to the island territory under the jurisdiction of the United States, from such island territory to the mainland territory of the United States, whether in such island territory at the time of cession or not, and from one portion of the island territory of the United

*Paragraph added by Act of May 27, 1910 (36 Stat. 448; 8 U.S.C. 385).

States to another portion of said island territory: Provided, however, That said laws shall not apply to the transit of Chinese laborers from one island to another island of the same group; and any islands within the jurisdiction of any State or the District of Alaska shall be considered a part of the mainland under this section.

Sec. 2. That the Secretary of the Treasury is hereby authorized and empowered to make and prescribe, and from time to time to change, such rules and regulations not inconsistent with the laws of the land as he may deem necessary and proper to execute the provisions of this Act and of the Acts hereby extended and continued and of the treaty of December eighth, eighteen hundred and ninety-four, between the United States and China, with the approval of the President to appoint such agents as he may deem necessary for the efficient execution of said treaty and said Act.

Sec. 4. That it shall be the duty of every Chinese laborer other than a citizen, rightfully in, and entitled to remain in any of the insular territory of the United States (Hawaii excepted) at the time of the passage of this Act, to obtain within one year thereafter a certifcate of residence in the insular territory wherein he resides, which certificate shall entitle him to residence therein, and upon failure to obtain such certificate as herein provided he shall be deported from such insular territory; and the Philippine Commission is authorized and required to make all regulations and provisions necessary for the enforcement of this section in the Philippine Islands, including the form and substance of the certificate of residence so that the same shall clearly and sufficiently identify the holder thereof and enable officials to prevent fraud in the transfer of the same: Provided however, That if said Philippine Commission shall find that it is impossible to complete the registration herein provided for within one year from the passage of this Act, said Commission is hereby authorized and empowered to extend the time of such registration for a further period not exceeding one year.

Source: 32 Stat. 176; U.S.C.

* * *

In 1903 Congress moved immigration policy control from the Treasury to the newly established Department of Commerce and Labor.

DOCUMENT 53: Act of February 14, 1903: Department of Commerce and Labor Act to Control Immigration

Sec. 7. That the jurisdiction, supervision and control now possessed and exercised by the Department of the Treasury over the fur seal, salmon and other fisheries in Alaska and over the immigration of aliens to the United States, its waters, territories and any place subject to the jurisdiction thereof, are hereby transferred and vested in the Department of Commerce and Labor: Provided, That nothing contained in this Act shall be construed to alter the method of collecting and accounting for the head-tax prescribed in section one of the Act entitled "An Act to regulate immigration," approved August third, eighteen hundred and eighty-two. . . .

Source: 32 Stat. 825; 8 U.S.C.

* * *

In March 1903, as part of its major codification of immigration laws, Congress increased the head tax on the immigration of aliens and also prohibited entry to and the naturalization of anarchists—the first such ban on the entry or the naturalization of persons based upon their political or ideological beliefs. This legislation also provided (in Sec. 12) for the extensive recording of detailed data on all immigrants arriving in the United States. The major immigration provisions are excerpted in Document 54 and the naturalization ban is contained in Document 55.

DOCUMENT 54: Act of March 3, 1903 (Re: Codification of Immigration Laws)

Be it enacted . . . , That there shall be levied, collected, and paid a duty of two dollars for each and every passenger not a citizen of the United States or the Dominion of Canada, Newfoundland, or the Republic of Cuba, or the Republic of Mexico, who shall come by steam, sail, or other vessel from any foreign port within the United States, or by any railway or other mode of transportation, from foreign contiguous territory to the United States. The said duty shall be paid to the collector of customs of the port or customs district to which said alien passenger shall come, or, if there be no collector at such port or district, then to the collector nearest thereto, by the master, agent, owner, or consignee of every such vessel or transportation line. . . .

Sec. 2. That the following classes of aliens shall be excluded from admission into the United States: All idiots, insane persons, epileptics, and persons who have been insane within five years previous; persons who have had two or more attacks of insanity at any time previously; paupers; persons likely to become a public charge; professional beggars; persons afflicted with a loathsome or with a dangerous contagious disease; persons who have been convicted of a felony or other crime or misdemeanor involving moral turpitude; polygamists, anarchists, or persons who believe in or advocate the overthrow by force or violence the Government of the United States or of all government or of all forms of law, or the assassination of public officials; prostitutes, and persons who procure or attempt to bring in prostitutes or women for the purpose of prostitution; those who have been, within one year from the date of the application for admission to the United States, deported as being under offers, solicitations, promises, or agreements to perform labor or service of some kind therein; and also any person whose ticket or passage is paid for with the money of another, or who is assisted by others to come, unless it is affirmatively and satisfactorily shown that such person does not belong to one of the foregoing excluded classes; but this section shall not be held to prevent persons living in the United States from sending for a relative or friend who is not of the foregoing excluded classes: Provided, That nothing in this Act shall exclude persons convicted of an offense purely political, not involving moral turpitude: And provided further, That skilled labor may be imported, if labor of like kind unemployed can not be found in this country: And provided further, That the provisions of this law applicable to contract labor shall not be held to exclude professional actors, artists, lecturers, singers, ministers of any religious denomination, professors for colleges or seminaries, persons belonging to any recognized learned profession, or persons employed strictly as personal or domestic servants. . . .

Sec. 12. That upon arrival of any alien by water at any port within the United States it shall be the duty of the master or commanding officer of the steamer, sailing or other vessel, having said alien on board to deliver to the immigration officers at the port of arrival lists or manifests made at the time and place of embarkation of such alien on board such steamer or vessel, which shall, in answer to the questions at the top of said lists, state as to each alien the full name, age, and sex; whether married or single; the calling or occupation; whether able to read or write; the nationality; the race; the last residence; the seaport for landing in the United States; the final destination, if any, beyond the port of landing; whether having a ticket through to such final destination; whether the alien has paid his own passage, or whether it has been paid by any other person or corporation, society, municipality, or government, and if so, by whom; whether in possession of fifty dollars, and if less, how much; whether going to join a relative or friend, and if so, what relative or friend and his name and complete address; whether ever before in the United States, and if so, when and where; whether ever in prison or almshouse or an institution or hospital for the care and treatment of the insane or supported by charity; whether a polygamist; whether an anarchist, whether coming for any reason of any offer, solicitation, promise, or agreement, expressed or implied, to perform labor in the United States, and what is the alien's condition of health mental and physical, and whether deformed or crippled, and if so, for how long and from what cause.

Source: 32 Stat. 1213; 8 U.S.C.

DOCUMENT 55: Act of March 3, 1903: Naturalization of Anarchists Forbidden . . .

Sec. 39. That no person who believes in or who is opposed to all organized government, or who is a member of or affiliated with any organization entertaining and teaching such disbelief in or opposition to all organized government, or who advocates or teaches the duty, necessity, or propriety of the unlawful assaulting or killing of any officers, either of specific individuals or of officers generally, of the Government of the United States or of any other government, because of his or their official character, or who has violated the provisions of this Act, shall be naturalized or be made a citizen of the United States. All courts and tribunals and all judges and officers thereof having jurisdiction of naturalization proceedings or duties to perform in regard thereto shall, on the final application for naturalization, make careful inquiry into such matters, and before issuing the final order or certificate of naturalization cause to be entered of record the affidavit of the applicant and of his witnesses so far as applicable, reciting and affirming the truth of every material requisite for naturalization. All final orders and certificates of naturalization hereafter made shall show on their face specifically that said affidavits were duly made and recorded, and all orders and certificates that fail to show such facts shall be null and void.

That any person who purposely procures naturalization in violation of the provisions of this section shall be fined not more than five thousand dollars, or shall be imprisoned not less than one nor more than ten years, or both, and the court in which such conviction is had shall thereupon adjudge and declare the order or decree and all certificates admitting such person to citizenship null and void. Jurisdiction is hereby conferred on the courts having jurisdiction of the trial of such offense to make such adjudication.

That any person who knowingly aids, advises, or encourages any such person to apply for or to secure naturalization or to file the preliminary papers declaring an intent to become a citizen of the United States, or who in any naturalization proceeding knowingly procures or gives false testimony as to any material fact, or who knowingly makes an affidavit false as to any material fact required to be proved in such proceeding, shall be fined not more than five thousand dollars, or imprisoned not less than one nor more than ten years, or both.

The foregoing provisions concerning naturalization shall not be enforced until ninety days after the approval hereof.

Source: 32 Stat. 1222.

* * *

In 1906 Congress enacted a comprehensive naturalization act that formed the basic law for the naturalization process thereafter, with some amendments and supplements. Excerpts of the act, which runs more than forty pages in the code of statutes, are presented in Document 56.

DOCUMENT 56: Act of June 29, 1906: Basic Naturalization Act of 1906, Providing for the Naturalization of Aliens Throughout the United States and Establishing the Bureau of Immigration and Naturalization

---

Be it enacted by the Senate and House of Representatives of the United States of America in Congress assembled, That the designation of the Bureau of Immigration in the Department of Commerce and Labor is hereby changed to the "Bureau of Immigration and Naturalization," which said Bureau, under the direction and control of the Secretary of Commerce and Labor, in addition to the duties now provided by law, shall have charge of all matters concerning the naturalization of aliens.

That it shall be the duty of said (Bureau) Service to provide, for use at the various immigration stations throughout the United States, books of record, wherein the commissioners of immigration shall cause a registry to be made in the case of each alien arriving in the United States, from and after passage of this Act of the name, age, occupation, personal description (including height, complexion, color of hair and eyes), the place of birth, the last residence, the intended place of residence in the United States, and the date of arrival of said alien, and if he entered through a port, the name of the vessel in which he comes. And it shall be the duty of said commissioners of immigration to cause to be granted to such alien a certificate of such registry, with the particulars thereof. . . .

Sec. 3. That the exclusive jurisdiction to naturalize aliens as citizens of the United States is hereby conferred upon the following specified courts: United States circuit and district courts now existing, or which may hereafter be established by the Congress in any State, United States district courts for the Territories of Arizona, New Mexico, Oklahoma, Hawaii, and Alaska, the supreme court for the District of Columbia, and the United States courts for the Indian Territory; also all courts of record in any State or Territory now existing, or which may hereafter be created, having a seal, a clerk, and jurisdiction in actions at law or equity, or law and equity, in which the amount in controversy is unlimited.... The courts herein specified shall, upon the requisition of the clerks of such courts, be furnished from time to time by the Immigration and Naturalization Service with such blank forms as may be required in the naturalization of aliens, and all certificates of naturalization shall be consecutively numbered and printed on safety paper by said Service.

Sec. 4. That an alien may be admitted to become a citizen of the United States in the following manner and not otherwise;

First. *He shall declare on oath before the clerk of any court authorized by this Act to naturalize citizens, or his authorized deputy, in the district within which such alien resides, two years at least prior to his admission, and after he has reached the age of eighteen years, that it is bona fide his intention to become a citizen of the United States, and to renounce forever all allegiance and fidelity to any foreign prince, potentate, state, or sovereignty, and particularly, by name, to the prince, potentate, state or sovereignty of which the alien may be at the same time a citizen or subject. And such declaration shall set forth the name, age, occupation, personal description, place of birth, last foreign residence and allegiance, the date of arrival, the name of the vessel, if any, in which he came to the United States, and the present place of residence in the United States of said alien. No declaration of intention or petition for naturalization shall be made outside of the office of the clerk of court.

Second. Not less than two years nor more than seven years after he has made such declaration of intention he shall make and file, in duplicate, a petition in writing, signed by the applicant in his own handwriting and duly verified, in which petition such applicant shall state his full name, his place of residence (by street and number if possible), his occupation, and if possible, the date and place of his birth; the place from which he emigrated, and the date and place of his arrival in the United States, and, if he entered through a port, the name of the vessel on which he arrived; the time and place when and the place and the name of the court where he declared his intention to become a citizen of the United States; if he is married he shall state the name of his wife and, if possible, the country of her nativity and her place of residence at the time of filing of his petition; and if he has children, the name, date, and place of birth and place of residence of each child living at the time of the filing of his

*As amended by Act of June 20, 1939 (53 Stat. 843), following amendment by Act of March 4, 1929 (45 Stat. 1545).

petition: Provided, That if he has filed his declaration before the passage of this Act [of June 29, 1906] he shall not be required to sign the petition in his own handwriting.

*The petition shall set forth that he is not a disbeliever in or opposed to organized government or a member of or affiliated with any organization or body of persons teaching disbelief in or opposed to organized government, a polygamist or believer in the practice of polygamy, and that it is his intention to become a citizen of the United States and to renounce absolutely and forever all allegiance and fidelity to any foreign prince, potentate, state, or sovereignty, and that it is his intention to reside permanently within the United States, whether or not he has been denied admission as a citizen of the United States, and if denied, the ground or grounds of such denial, the court or courts in which such decision was rendered, and that the cause of such denial has since been cured or removed and every fact material to his naturalization and required to be proved upon the final hearing of his application.

**As to each period of residence at any place in the county where the petitioner resides at the time of filing of his petition, there shall be included in the petition the affidavits of at least two credible witnesses, citizens of the United States, stating that each has personally known the petitioner to have been a resident at such place for such period, and that the petitioner is and during all such period has been a person of good moral character.

At the time of his petition there shall be filed with the clerk of the court a certificate from the Department of Justice . . . stating the date, place, and manner of his arrival in the United States, and the declaration of intention of such petitioner, which certificate and declaration shall be attached to and made a part of said petition. . . .

*Third. He shall, before he is admitted to citizenship, declare on oath, in open court, that he will support the Constitution of the United States, and that he absolutely and entirely renounces and abjures all allegiance and fidelity to any foreign prince, potentate, state, or sovereignty of which he was before a citizen or subject; and he will support and defend the Constitution and laws of the United States against all enemies, foreign and domestic, and bear true faith and allegiance to the same.

***Fourth. No alien shall be admitted to citizenship unless (1) immediately preceding the date of his petition the alien has resided continuously within the United States for at least five years and within the county where the petitioner resided at the time of his filing his petition for at least six months, (2) he has resided continuously within the United States from the date of his petition up to the time of his admission to citizen-

---

*As amended by Act of June 20, 1939 (53 Stat. 843).
**As amended by Act of March 2, 1929 (45 Stat. 1512).
***As amended by Act of June 29, 1948 (52 Stat. 1247).

ship, and (3) during all the periods referred to in this subdivision he has behaved as a person of good moral character . . . [R]esidence shall be proved by the oral testimony of at least two credible witnesses, citizens of the United States, in addition to the affidavits required by this Act to be included in the petition. . . .

Absence from the United States for a continuous period of more than six months and less than one year during the period for which continuous residence is required for admission to citizenship, immediately preceding the date of filing the petition for naturalization, or during the period between the date of filing the petition, and the date of final hearing, shall be presumed to break the continuity of such residence. . . .

Fifth. In case the alien applying to be admitted to citizenship has borne any hereditary title, or has been of any of the orders of nobility in the kingdom or state from which he came, he shall, in addition to the above requisites, make an express renunciation of his title or order of nobility in the court in which his application is made, and his renunciation shall be recorded in the court. . . . [Several sections were added when this law was amended by the May 9, 1918, law—see Document 63.]

Sec. 8. That no alien shall hereafter be naturalized or admitted as a citizen of the United States who cannot speak the English language: Provided, That this requirement shall not apply to aliens who are physically unable to comply therewith if they are otherwise qualified to become citizens. . . .

Sec. 11. That the United States shall have the right to appear before any court or courts exercising jurisdiction in naturalization proceedings for the purpose of cross-examining the petitioner and witnesses produced in support of his petition concerning any matter touching or in any way affecting his right to admission to citizenship, and shall have the right to call witnesses, produce evidence, and be heard in opposition to the granting of any petition of naturalization proceedings. (34 Stat. 599; 8 U.S.C. 399). . . .

Sec. 15. That it shall be the duty of the United States district attorneys for the respective districts, upon affidavit showing good cause therefor, to institute proceedings in any court having jurisdiction to naturalize aliens in the judicial district in which the naturalized citizen may reside at the time of the bringing of the suit, for the purpose of setting aside and canceling the certificate of citizenship on the ground of fraud or on the ground that such certificate of citizenship was illegally procured. . . .

Sec. 16. That every person who falsely makes, forges, counterfeits, or causes or procures to be falsely made, forged or counterfeited, or knowingly aids or assists in falsely making, forging or counterfeiting any certificate of citizenship, with intent to use the same, or with the intent that the same may be used by some other person or persons, shall be guilty of a felony, and a person convicted of such offense shall be punished by imprisonment for not more than ten years, or by a fine of not more than ten thousand dollars, or by both such fine and imprisonment. . . .

Sec. 18. That it is hereby made a felony for any clerk or other person to issue or be a party to the issuance of a certificate of citizenship contrary to the provisions of this Act . . . and upon conviction thereof such clerk or person shall be punished by imprisonment for not more than five years and by a fine of not more than five thousand dollars, in the discretion of the court (34 Stat. 602; 8 U.S.C. 410). . . .

Sec. 23. That any person who knowingly procures naturalization in violation of the provisions of this Act shall be fined not more than five thousand dollars, or shall be imprisoned not more than five years, or both, and upon conviction the court in which the conviction is had shall thereupon adjudge and declare the final order admitting such person to citizenship void. (34 Stat. 603; 8 U.S.C 414). . . .

Source: 34 Stat. 596.

* * *

In 1907 Congress amended the immigration act, increasing the head tax and adding to the excluded classes of individuals but essentially restating the comprehensive act of June 6, 1906. This act also established what became known as the Dillingham Commission.

DOCUMENT 57: Act of February 20, 1907: To Regulate the Immigration of Aliens into the United States

Be it enacted by the Senate and House of Representatives of the United States of America in Congress assembled, That there shall be levied, collected, and paid a tax of four dollars for every alien entering the United States. The said tax shall be paid to the collector at such port or customs district to which said alien shall come, or, if there be no collector at such port or district, then to the collector nearest thereto, by the master, agent, owner or consignee of the vessel, transportation line, or other conveyance or vehicle bringing such alien to the United States. . . .

[The law, in section 2, elaborates the classes of excluded individuals for health, mental and physical, and for moral turpitude characteristics. The fines and penalties were increased. Thirty sections essentially repeat the comprehensive act of March 3, 1903 (Document 54)].

Sec. 33. That for the purpose of this Act the term "United States" as used in the title as well as in the various sections of this Act shall be construed to mean the United States and any waters, territory, or other place subject to the jurisdiction thereof, except the Isthmian Canal Zone: *Provided,* That if any alien shall leave the canal zone and attempt to enter any other place under the jurisdiction of the United States, nothing contained in this Act shall be construed as permitting him to enter under any other than those applicable to all aliens. . . .

Sec. 35. That the deportation of aliens arrested, within the United States after entry and found to be illegally therein, provided for in this Act, shall be to the trans-Atlantic or trans-Pacific ports from which said aliens embarked for the United States; or, if such embarkation was for foreign contiguous territory, to the foreign port at which said aliens embarked for such territory.

Sec. 36. That all aliens who shall enter the United States except at the seaports thereof, or at such place or places as the Secretary of Commerce and Labor may from time to time designate, shall be adjudged to have entered the country unlawfully and shall be deported as provided in sections twenty and twenty-one of this Act. . . .

Sec. 39. That a commission is hereby created, consisting of three Senators, to be appointed by the Speaker of the House, and three persons, to be appointed by the President of the United States. Said commission shall make full inquiry, examination, and investigation by sub-committee or otherwise into the subject of immigration. . . . Said commission shall make a report to the Congress of the conclusions reached by it and make such recommendations as in its judgments may seem proper. . . .

Sec. 40. Authority is hereby given under the Commissioner-General of Immigration to establish . . . a division of information in the Bureau of Immigration and Naturalization . . . It shall be the duty of said division to promote a beneficial distribution of aliens admitted into the United States among the several States and Territories desiring immigration. Correspondence shall be had with the proper officials of the States and Territories, and said division shall gather from all available sources useful information regarding the resources, products, and physical characteristics of each State and Territory, and shall publish such information in different languages and distribute the publication among all admitted aliens who may ask for such information at the immigration stations of the United States and to such other persons who may desire the same. . . . [The act then rather elaborately specifies the square footage that must be allotted to passengers, including deck space.]

Sec. 43. That the Act of March third, nineteen hundred and three, being an Act to regulate the immigration of aliens into the United States, except section thirty-four thereof . . . is hereby repealed.

Source: 34 Stat. 898; U.S.C.

* * *

In 1907 Congress added important regulations regarding the issuing of passports, expatriation, and the marriage of American women to foreigners; among other related matters. This act continued to stir controversy until 1922, when Section 3 of the act was repealed by the Act of September 22, 1922 (42 Stat. 1021).

DOCUMENT 58: Act of March 2, 1907: The Expatriation Act (Re: Passports, Expatriation, and Citizenship of Women and Children)

Be it enacted by the Senate and House of Representatives of the United States of America in Congress assembled, That the Secretary of State shall be authorized, in his discretion, to issue passports to persons not citizens of the United States as follows: Where any such person has made a declaration to become such a citizen as provided by the law and has resided in the United States for three years, a passport may be issued to him entitling him to the protection of the Government in any foreign country: *Provided,* That such passport shall not be valid for more than six months and shall not be renewed, and that such passport shall not entitle the holder to the protection of this Government in the country of which he was a citizen prior to making such declaration of intent.

Sec. 2. That any American citizen shall be deemed to have expatriated himself when he has been naturalized in any foreign state in conformity with its laws, or when he has taken an oath of allegiance to any foreign power.

When any naturalized citizen shall have resided for two years in the foreign state from which he came, or for five years in any other foreign state, it shall be presumed that he has ceased to be an American citizen, and the place of his general abode shall be deemed his place of residence during said years. . . . *And provided also,* That no American citizen shall be allowed to expatriate himself when this country is at war.

Sec. 3. That any American woman who marries a foreigner shall take the nationality of her husband. At the termination of her marital relation she may resume her American citizenship, if abroad, by registering as an American citizen within one year with a consul of the United States, or by returning to reside in the United States, or, if residing in the United States at the termination of the marital relation, by continuing to reside therein.

Sec. 4. That any foreign woman who acquires American citizenship by marriage to an American shall be assumed to retain the same after the termination of the marital relation if she continues to reside in the United States, unless she makes formal renunciation thereof before a court having jurisdiction to naturalize citizens, or if she resides abroad she may retain her citizenship by registering as such before a United States consul within one year after the termination of such marital relation.

Sec. 5. *That a child born without the United States of alien parents shall be deemed a citizen of the United States by virtue of naturalization of or resumption of American citizenship by the father or the mother: *Provided,* That such naturalization or resumption shall take place during the minority of such child: *And provided further,* That the citizenship of such minor child shall begin five years after the time such minor child begins to reside permanently in the United States.

Sec. 6. That all children born outside the limits of the United States who are citizens thereof in accordance with the provisions of section nineteen hundred and ninety-three of the Revised Statutes of the United States and who continue to reside outside the United States shall, in order to receive the protection of this Government, be required upon reaching the age of eighteen years to record at an American consulate their intention to become residents and remain citizens of the United States, and shall be further required to take the oath of allegiance to the United States upon attaining their majority.

Sec. 7. That duplicates of any evidence, registration, or other acts required by this Act shall be filed with the Department of State for record.

Source: 34 Stat. 1228; 8 U.S.C. 17.

* * *

In March 1907 the president of the United States issued an executive order that implemented the "Gentleman's Agreement" between the United States and Japan to control the immigration of persons from Japan and Korea (then under Japanese jurisdiction).

DOCUMENT 59: Executive Order No. 589, March 14, 1907: Entrance of Japanese and Korean Laborers into the United States ("Gentleman's Agreement")

Whereas, by the act entitled "An Act to regulate the immigration of aliens into the United States," approved February 20, 1907, whenever the President is satisfied that passports issued by any foreign Government to its citizens to go to any country other than the United States or to the Canal Zone, are being used for the purpose of enabling the holders to come to the continental territory of the United States from such country or from such insular possession or from the Canal Zone;

*Amended by Act of May 24, 1934 (48 Stat. 797).

AND WHEREAS, upon sufficient evidence produced before me by the Department of Commerce and Labor, I am satisfied that passports issued by the Government of Japan to citizens of that country or Korea and who are laborers, skilled or unskilled, to go to Mexico, to Canada and to Hawaii, are being used for the purpose of enabling the holders thereof to come to the continental territory of the United States to the detriment of labor conditions therein;

I hereby order that such citizens of Japan or Korea, to wit: Japanese and Korean laborers, skilled and unskilled, who have received passports to go to Mexico, Canada, or Hawaii, and come therefrom, be refused permission to enter the continental territory of the United States.

It is further ordered that the Secretary of Commerce and Labor be, and he hereby is, directed to take, through the Bureau of Immigration and Naturalization, such measures and to make and enforce such rules and regulations as may be necessary to carry this order into effect.

Source: Executive Order No. 589, March 14, 1907.

* * *

In 1910 Congress attempted to crack down on the practice of bringing in women immigrants for the purpose of prostitution by enacting the White-Slave Traffic Act.

DOCUMENT 60: Act of June 25, 1910: The White-Slave Traffic Act

Sec. 1. That the term "interstate commerce" as used in this Act, shall include transportation from any State or Territory or the District of Columbia to any other State or Territory or the District of Columbia, and the term "foreign commerce," as used in this Act, shall include transportation from any State or Territory or the District of Columbia to any foreign country and from any foreign country to any State or Territory or the District of Columbia.

Sec. 2. That any person who shall knowingly transport or cause to be transported, or aid or assist in obtaining transportation for, or in transporting, in interstate or foreign commerce, or in any Territory or in the District of Columbia, any woman or girl for the purpose of prostitution or debauchery, or for any other immoral purpose, or with the intent and purpose to induce, entice, or compel such woman or girl to become a prostitute or to give herself up to debauchery, or to engage in any other immoral practice; or who shall knowingly procure or obtain, or cause to be procured or obtained, or aid or assist in procuring or obtaining, any ticket or tickets, or any form of transportation or evidence of the right thereto, to be used by any woman or girl in interstate or foreign commerce, or in any Territory or the District of Columbia, in going to any place for the purpose of prostitution or debauchery, or for any other immoral purpose, or with the intent or purpose on the part of such person to induce, entice, or compel her to give herself up to the practice of prostitution, or to give herself up to debauchery, or any other immoral purpose, whereby such woman or girl shall be transported in interstate or foreign commerce, or in any Territory or the District of Columbia, shall be deemed guilty of a felony, and upon conviction thereof shall be punished by a fine not exceeding five thousand dollars, or by imprisonment of not more than five years, or by both such fine and imprisonment, in the discretion of the court....

Sec. 3. That any person who shall knowingly persuade, induce, entice, or coerce, or cause to be persuaded, induced, enticed, or coerced, or aid or assist in persuading, inducing, enticing, or coercing any woman or girl to go from one place to another in interstate or foreign commerce ... for the purpose of prostitution or debauchery, or for any other immoral purpose ... shall be deemed guilty of a felony and on conviction thereof, shall be punished by a fine of not more than five thousand dollars, or by imprisonment for a term not exceeding five years, or by both such fine and imprisonment, in the discretion of the court....

Sec. 6. That for the purpose of regulating and preventing the transportation in foreign commerce of alien women and girls for the purpose of prostitution and debauchery, and in pursuance of and for the purpose of carrying out the terms of the agreement or project of arrangement for the suppression of the white-slavery traffic ... the Commissioner of Immigration and Naturalization is hereby designated as the authority of the United States to receive and centralize information concerning the procuration of alien women and girls with a view to their debauchery, and to exercise supervision over such alien women and girls....

Every person who shall keep, maintain, control, support, or harbor in any house or place for the purpose of prostitution, or for any other immoral purpose, any alien woman or girl within three years after she shall have entered the United States from any country ... shall be deemed guilty of a felony, and on conviction thereof shall be punished by a fine of not more than ten thousand dollars, or by imprisonment for a term of not exceeding ten years, or by both such fine and imprisonment, in the discretion of the court.

Source: 36 Stat. 825; U.S.C. 397–404.

* * *

Congress established a special commission, named the Dillingham Commission after its chairman, U.S. Senator William P. Dillingham, in 1907 to study immigration matters. This commission, which embraced many of the racial attitudes prevalent among the pro-restriction forces, compiled a monumental volume, known as the *Dictionary of Races*. This massive, multivolume report, issued in 1911, provided recommendations that became the basis of much subsequent legislation, including the literacy act and ultimately the quota acts of the next decade.

DOCUMENT 61: Summary Recommendations of the Dillingham Commission Report, 1911

As a result of the investigation the Commission is unanimously of the opinion that in framing legislation emphasis should be laid upon the following principles:

1. While the American people, as in the past, welcome the oppressed of other lands, care should be taken that immigration be such both in quality and quantity as not to make too difficult the process of assimilation.

2. Since the existing law and further legislation recommended in this report deal with the physical and morally unfit, further general legislation concerning the admission of aliens should be based primarily upon economic or business considerations touching the prosperity and economic well-being of our people.

3. The development of business may be brought about by means which lower the standard of living of the wage earners. A slow expansion of industry which would permit the adaption and assimilation of the incoming labor supply is preferable to a very rapid industrial expansion which results in the immigration of laborers of low standards and efficiency, who imperil the American standard of wages and conditions of employment.

The Commission agrees that:

1. To protect the United States more effectively against the immigration of criminal and certain other debarred classes—

(a) Aliens convicted of serious crimes within a period of five years after admission should be deported in accordance with the provisions of House bill 20980, Sixty-first Congress, second session.

(b) Under the provisions of section 39 of the immigration act of February 20, 1907, the President should appoint commissioners to make arrangements with such countries as have adequate police records to supply emigrants with copies of such records, and that thereafter immigrants from such countries should be admitted to the United States only upon the production of proper certificates showing an absence of convictions for excludable crimes.

(c) So far as practicable the immigration laws should be so amended as to be made applicable to alien seamen.

(d) Any alien who becomes a public charge within three years after his arrival in this country should be subject to deportation in the discretion of the Secretary of Commerce and Labor.

2. Sufficient appropriation should be regularly made to enforce vigorously the provisions of the law previously recommended by the Commission and enacted by Congress regarding the importation of women for immoral purposes.

3. As the new statute relative to steerage conditions took effect so recently as January 1, 1909, and as the most modern steerage fully complies with all that is demanded under the law, the Commission's only recommendation in this connection is that a statute be immediately enacted providing for the placing of Government officials, both men and women, on vessels carrying third class or steerage passengers for the enforcement of the law and the protection of the immigrants. The system inaugurated by the Commission of sending investigators in the steerage in the guise of immigrants should be continued at intervals by the Bureau of Immigration.

4. To strengthen the certainty of just and humane decisions of doubtful cases at ports of entry it is recommended—

That section 25 of the immigration act of 1907 be amended to provide that boards of special inquiry should be appointed by the Secretary of Commerce and Labor, and that they should be composed of men whose ability and training qualify them for the performance of judicial functions; that the provisions compelling their hearings to be separate and apart from the public should be repealed, and that the office of an additional Assistant Secretary of Commerce and Labor to assist in reviewing such appeal be created.

5. To protect the immigrant against exploitation; to discourage sending savings abroad; to encourage permanent residence and naturalization; and to secure better distribution of alien immigrants throughout the country—

(a) The States should enact laws strictly regulating immigrant banks.

(b) Proper State legislation should be enacted for the regulation of employment agencies.

(c) Since numerous aliens make it their business to keep immigrants from influences that may tend toward their assimilation and naturalization as American citizens with the purposes of using their funds, and of encouraging investment of their savings abroad and their return to their home land, aliens who attempt to persuade immigrants not to become American citizens should be made subject to deportation.

(d) Since the distribution of the thrifty immigrant to sections of the country where he may secure a permanent residence to the best advantage, and especially where he may invest his savings in farms or engage in agricultural pursuits, is most desirable, the Division of Information, in the Bureau of Immigration and Naturalization, should be so conducted as to cooperate with States desiring immigrant settlers; and information concerning the opportunities for settlement should be brought to the attention of immigrants in industrial centers who have been here for some time and who might be thus induced to invest their savings in this country and become permanent agricultural settlers. The division might also secure and furnish to all laborers alike information showing opportunities for permanent employment in various sections of the country, together with the economic conditions of such places.

6. One of the provisions of section 2 of the act of 1907 reads as follows: And provided further, That skilled labor may be imported if labor of like kind unemployed can not be found in this country. Instances occasionally arise, especially in the establishment of new industries in the United States, where labor of the kind desired, unemployed, cannot be found in this country and it becomes necessary to import such labor. Under the law the Secretary of Commerce and Labor has no authority to determine the question of the necessity for importing such labor in advance of the importation, and it is recommended that an amendment to the law be adopted by adding to the clause cited above a provision to the effect that the question of the necessity of importing such skilled labor in any particular instance may be determined by the Secretary of Commerce and Labor upon the application of any person interested prior to any action in that direction by such person; such determination by the Secretary of Commerce and Labor to be reached after a full hearing and an investigation into the facts of the case.

7. The general policy adopted by Congress in 1882 of excluding Chinese laborers should be continued. The question of Japanese and Korean immigration should be permitted to stand without further legislation so long as the present method of restriction proves effective.

An understanding should be reached with the British Government whereby East Indian laborers would be effectively prevented from coming to the United States.

8. The investigations of the Commission show an oversupply of unskilled labor in basic industries to an extent which indicates an oversupply of unskilled labor in the industries of the country as a whole, a condition which demands legislation restricting the further admission of such unskilled labor.

It is desirable in making the restriction that—

(a) A sufficient number be debarred to produce a marked effect upon the present supply of unskilled labor.

(b) As far as possible, the aliens excluded should be those who come to this country with no intention to become American citizens or even to maintain a permanent residence here, but merely to save enough, by the adoption, if necessary, of low standards of living, to return permanently to their home country. Such persons are usually men unaccompanied by wives or children.

(c) As far as possible the aliens excluded should also be those who, by reason of their personal qualities or habits, would least readily be assimilated or would make the least desirable citizens.

The following methods of restricting immigration have been suggested:

(a) The exclusion of those unable to read or write in some language.

(b) The limitation of the number of each race arriving each year to a certain number of the average of that race arriving during a given period of years.

(c) The exclusion of unskilled laborers unaccompanied by wives or families.

(d) The limitation of the number of immigrants arriving annually at any port.

(e) The material increase in the amount of money required to be in the possession of the immigrant at the port of arrival.

(f) The material increase of the head tax.

(g) The levy of the head tax so as to make a marked discrimination in favor of men with families.

All these methods would be effective in one way or another in securing the restrictions in a greater or lesser degree. A majority of the Commission favor the reading and writing test as the most feasible single method of restricting undesirable immigration.

The Commission as a whole recommends restrictions as demanded by economic, moral, and social considerations, furnishes in its report reasons for such restriction, and points out methods by which Congress can attain the desired result if its judgment coincides with that of the Commission.

Source: Reports of the Immigration Commission, vol. 1 (New York: Arno Press, 1970), 45–48.

* * *

Congress enacted an immigrant literacy provision on several occasions: 1896, 1913, 1915, and 1917, all of which were vetoed respectively, by Presidents Cleveland, Taft, and Wilson. President Wilson's veto message of 1915 succinctly summarizes presidential opposition to the literacy bill: it went against the American tradition of free immigration. Document 62 gives that veto message virtually in full.

DOCUMENT 62: President Woodrow Wilson's Veto Message of the Immigrant Literacy Bill (January 28, 1915)

It is with unaffected regret that I find myself constrained by clear conviction to return this bill (H.R. 6060, "An act to regulate the immigration of aliens to and the residence of aliens in the United States") without my signature. Not only do I feel it to be a very serious matter to exercise the power of veto in any case, because it involves opposing the single judgment of the President to the judgment of the majority of both the Houses of the Congress, a step which no man who realizes his own liability to error can take without great hesitation, but also because this particular bill is in so many important respects admirable, well conceived, and desirable. Its enactment into law would undoubtedly enhance the efficiency and improve the methods of handling the important branch of the public service to which it relates. But candor and a sense of duty with regard to the responsibility so clearly imposed upon me by the Constitution in matters of legislation leave me no choice but to dissent. . . . In two particulars of vital consequence this bill embodies a radical departure from the traditional and long-established policy of this country, a policy in which our people have conceived the very character of their Government to be expressed, the very mission and spirit of the Nation in respect to its relations to the peoples of the world outside their borders. It seeks to all but close entirely the gates of asylum which have always been open to those who could find nowhere else the right and opportunity of constitutional agitation for what they conceived to be the natural and inalienable rights of men; and it excludes those to whom the opportunities of elementary education have been denied, without regard to their character, their purposes, or their natural capacity.

Restrictions like these, adopted earlier in our history as a Nation, would very materially have altered the course and cooled the humane ardors of our politics. The right of political asylum has brought to this country many a man of noble character and elevated purpose who was marked as an outlaw in his own less fortunate land, and who has yet become an ornament to our citizenship and to our public councils. The children and the compatriots of these illustrious Americans must stand amazed to see the representatives of their Nation now resolved, in the fullness of our national strength and at the maturity of our great institutions, to risk turning such men back from our shores without test of quality or purpose. It is difficult for me to believe that the full effect of this feature of the bill was realized when it was framed and adopted, and it is impossible for me to assent to it in the form in which it is here cast.

The literacy test and the tests and restrictions which accompany it constitute an even more radical change in the policy of the Nation. Hitherto we have generously kept our doors open to all who were not unfitted by reason of disease or incapacity for self-support or such personal records and antecedents as were likely to make them a menace to our peace and order or to the wholesome and essential relationships of life. In this bill it is proposed to turn away from tests of character and of quality and impose tests which exclude and restrict; for the new tests here embodied are not tests of quality or of character or of personal fitness, but tests of opportunity. Those who come seeking opportunity are not admitted unless they have already had one of the chief opportunities they seek, the opportunity of education. The object of such provisions is restriction, not selection.

If the people of this country have made up their minds to limit the number of immigrants by arbitrary tests and so reverse the policy of all the generations of Americans that have gone before them, it is their right to do so. I am their servant and have no license to stand in their way. But I do not believe that they have. I respectfully submit that no one can quote their mandate to that effect. Has any political party ever avowed a policy of restriction in this fundamental matter, gone to the country on it, and been commissioned to control its legislation? Does this bill rest upon the conscious and universal assent and desire of the American people? I doubt it. It is because I doubt it that I make bold to dissent from it. I am willing to abide by the verdict, but not until it has been rendered. Let the platforms of parties speak out upon this policy and the people pronounce their wish. The matter is too fundamental to be settled otherwise.

I have no pride of opinion in this question. I am not foolish enough to profess to know the wishes and ideals of America better than the body of her chosen representatives knows them. I only want instruction direct from those whose fortunes, with ours and all men's, are involved.

Source: U.S. Congress, House of Representatives, *Congressional Record*, 63rd Congress, 3rd sess., January 28, 1915, vol. 52, pp. 2481–82.

* * *

In February 1917, overriding President Woodrow Wilson's veto, Congress enacted another comprehensive immigration law. The omnibus Immigration Act consists of sixty pages in the Code of Statutes. Most of the law reenacts the comprehensive acts of 1903 and 1907. The Immigration Act of 1917 is excerpted, citing those provisions that pertain especially to the literacy aspect of the law and to an Asiatic Barred Zone. The historian Roger Daniels (1990) identifies this law as "the first significant general restriction of immigration ever passed." With it, he adds, immigration policy had become "restricted in seven major ways. Admission was denied to Asians . . . ; criminals; persons who failed to meet certain moral standards; persons with various diseases; paupers; assorted radicals; and illiterates (278–279)."

DOCUMENT 63: Act of February 5, 1917: Immigration Act of 1917, Regulating the Immigration of Aliens to and Residence of Aliens in the United States

Sec. 1. That the word "alien" wherever used in this Act shall include any person not a native-born or naturalized citizen of the United States; but this definition shall not be held to include Indians of the United States not taxed or citizens of the islands under the jurisdiction of the United States. That the term "United States" as used in the title as well as in the various sections of this Act shall be construed to mean the United States, and any waters, territory, or other place subject to the jurisdiction thereof, except the Isthmian Canal Zone. . . .

Sec. 2. That there shall be levied, collected, and paid a tax of $8 for every alien, including alien seamen regularly admitted as provided in this Act, entering the United States. . . .

Sec. 3. That the following classes of aliens shall be excluded from admission into the United States: All idiots, imbeciles, feeble-minded persons, epileptics, insane persons . . . persons with chronic alcoholism; paupers; professional beggars; vagrants; persons afflicted with tuberculosis in any form or a loathsome or dangerous contagious disease; persons not comprehended within any of the foregoing excluded classes who are found to be and are certified by the examining surgeon as being mentally or physically defective, such physical defect being of a nature which may affect the ability of such alien to earn a living; *persons who have departed from the jurisdiction of the United States for the purpose of evading or avoiding training or service in the armed forces of the United States during time of war or during a period declared by the President to be a period of national emergency; persons who have been convicted . . . of a felony or other crime or misdemeanor involving moral turpitude; polygamists, or persons who practice polygamy or believe in and advocate the practice of polygamy; anarchists, or persons who ad-

---

*Clause added by Act of September 29, 1944 (58 Stat. 746; 8 U.S.C. 136).

vocate the overthrow by force or violence of the Government of the United States, or of all forms of law . . . or who advocate the assassination of public officials, or who advocate and teach the unlawful destruction of property. . . ; prostitutes, or persons coming to the United States for the purpose of prostitution or immoral purposes. . . ; persons hereinafter called contract laborers. . . ; persons likely to become public charges. . . ; persons whose ticket or passage is paid for with the money of another; persons whose ticket or passage is paid for by any corporation, association, society, municipality, or foreign government, either directly or indirectly; stowaways. . . ; all children under sixteen years of age unaccompanied by or not coming to one or both of their parents . . . unless otherwise provided for by existing treaties, persons who are natives of islands not possessed by the United States adjacent to the continent of Asia, situate [sic] south of the twentieth parallel latitude north, west of the one hundred and sixtieth meridian of longitude east from Greenwich, and north of the tenth parallel of latitude south, or who are natives of any country, province, or dependency situate on the Continent of Asia west of the one hundred and tenth meridian of longitude east from Greenwich and east of the fiftieth meridian of longitude east from Greenwich and south of the fiftieth parallel of latitude north, except that portion of said territory situate between the fiftieth and sixty-fourth and thirty-eighth parallels of latitude north, and no alien now in any way excluded from, or prevented from entering the United States shall be admitted to the United States. . . .

That after three months from the passage of this Act in addition to the aliens who are by law now excluded from admission into the United States, the following persons shall also be excluded:

All aliens over sixteen years of age, physically capable of reading, who cannot read the English language, or some other language or dialect, including Hebrew or Yiddish: *Provided*, That any admissible alien, or any alien heretofore or hereafter legally admitted, or any citizen of the United States, may bring in or send for his father or grandfather over fifty-five years of age, his wife, his mother, his grandmother, or his unmarried or widowed daughter, if otherwise admissible, whether such relative can read or not; and such relative shall be permitted to enter. That for the purpose of ascertaining whether aliens can read the immigrant inspectors shall be furnished with slips of uniform size, prepared under the direction of the Attorney General, each containing not less than thirty nor more than forty words in ordinary use, printed in plainly legible type in some one of the various languages or dialects of immigrants. Each alien may designate the particular language or dialect in which he desires the examination to be made, and shall be required to read the words printed on the slip in such language or dialect. . . .

Provided, That nothing in this Act shall exclude, if otherwise admissible, persons convicted, or who admit to the commission, or who teach or advocate the commission, of an offense purely political. . . .

Provided further, That skilled labor, if otherwise admissible, may be imported if labor of the kind unemployed can not be found in this country, and the question of the necessity of importing such skilled labor in any particular instance may be determined by the Attorney General upon the application of any person interested, such application to be made before such importation, and such determination by the Attorney General to be reached after a full hearing and an investigation into the facts of the case. . . .

It shall also be unlawful for any person to bring to any port of the United States any alien who is excluded by the provisions of section 3 of this Act because unable to read, or who is excluded by the terms of section 3 of this Act as a native of that portion of the Continent of Asia and the islands adjacent thereto described in said section. . . .

Sec. 27. That for the preservation of the peace and in order that arrests may be made for crimes under the laws of the States and Territories of the United States where the various immigration stations are located, the officers in charge of such stations, as occasion may require, shall admit therein the proper State and municipal officers charged with the enforcement of such laws, and for the purpose of this section the jurisdiction of such officers and of the local courts shall extend over such stations. . . .

Sec. 29. That the President of the United States is authorized, in the name of the Government of the United States, to call, in his discretion, an international conference, to assemble at such point as may be agreed upon, or to send special commissioners to any foreign country, for the purpose of regulating by international agreement, subject to the advice and consent of the Senate of the United States, the immigration of aliens to the United States; of providing for the mental, moral, and physical examination of such aliens by American consuls or other officers of the United States Government at the ports of embarkation, or elsewhere; of securing the assistance of foreign Governments in their own territories to prevent the evasion of the laws of the United States governing immigration to the United States; of entering into such international agreements as may be proper to prevent the immigration of aliens who, under the laws of the United States, are or may be excluded from entering the United States, and of regulating any matters pertaining to such immigration. . . .

Sec. 37. That the word "person" as used in this Act shall be construed to import both plural and singular, as the case may be, and shall include corporations, companies, and associations. When construing and enforcing the provisions of this Act, the act, omission, or failure of any director, officer, agent, or employee of any corporation, company, or association acting within the scope of his employment or office shall in every case be deemed to be the act, omission, or failure of such corporation, company, or association, as well as that of the person acting for or in behalf of such corporation, company, or association.

Sec. 38. That this Act, except as otherwise provided in section three, shall take effect and be enforced on and after May first, nineteen hundred and seventeen . . . Provided, That this Act shall not be construed to repeal, alter, or amend existing laws relating to the immigration or exclusion of Chinese persons or persons of Chinese descent, except as provided in section nineteen hereof. . . .

Source: 39 Stat. 874; 8 U.S.C.

* * *

In March 1917 Congress granted citizenship to Puerto Ricans.

DOCUMENT 64: Act of March 2, 1917: An Act to Provide a Civil Government for Puerto Rico and for Other Purposes (including U.S. Citizenship)

Sec. 5. That all citizens of Puerto Rico,* as defined by section seven of the Act of April twelfth, nineteen hundred, "temporarily to provide revenues and a civil government for Puerto Rico, and for other purposes," and all natives of Puerto Rico, who were temporarily absent from that island on April eleventh, eighteen hundred and ninety-nine, and have since returned and are permanently residing in that island, and are not citizens of any foreign country, are hereby declared, and shall be deemed and held to be, citizens of the United States: Provided, That any person hereinbefore described may retain his present political status by making a declaration, under oath, of his decision to do so within six months of the taking effect of this Act before a district court in which he resides, the declaration to be in form as follows:

"I,_____, being duly sworn, hereby declare my intention not to become a citizen of the United States as provided in the Act of Congress conferring United States citizenship upon citizens of Puerto Rico and certain natives permanently residing in said island." . . .

[It continues for several subsections specifying how persons of Puerto Rican citizenship become citizens of the United States, closing as follows:]

After making such declaration and submitting such proofs, such persons shall be admitted to take the oath of allegiance before the court, and

*Spelling changed from Porto Rico to Puerto Rico by Act of May 17, 1932 (47 Stat. 148).

thereupon shall be considered a citizen of the United States. [The act then stipulates, in a number of subsections, their qualifications to vote and the processes for naturalization. The act closes as follows:]

Sec. 58. That all laws or parts of laws applicable to Puerto Rico not in conflict with any of the provisions of this Act, including laws relating to tariffs, customs, duties on importations into Puerto Rico prescribed by the Act of Congress . . . approved April twelfth, nineteen hundred, are hereby continued in effect, and all laws and parts of laws inconsistent with the provisions of this Act are hereby repealed.

Source: 39 Stat. 951; 48 U.S.C. 733 a-1.

* * *

In 1917 a joint order of the departments of State and of Labor was issued requiring passports and certain other information from all aliens seeking to enter the United States during World War I. This act also required the issuing of visas from an American consular officer in the country of origin rather than allowing a person to enter the United States and seek permission to enter having already arrived at the shores or port of entry.

DOCUMENT 65: Joint Order of Department of State and Department of Labor (July 26, 1917)

To Diplomatic and Consular Officers and Immigration Officers of the United States, Steamship and Railway Lines of the United States and Other Countries, Aliens, and All Others Concerned:

After due publication of this order in foreign countries every person leaving a foreign country for the United States (except persons starting from Canada) with the purpose of entering, passing through or touching at a port of the United States shall be required, before he is permitted to enter the United States, to present a valid passport, or other official document in the nature of a passport, satisfactorily establishing his identity and nationality, with a signed and certified photograph of the bearer attached. A wife, or female child, under 21 years of age, or male child under 16 years of age, may be included in the passport of the husband or parent, but a photograph of each must be attached to the passport. Each male child 16 years of age or over must carry a separate passport; *Provided*, That, where it is shown to the satisfaction of the Secretary of Labor that passports are denied to seamen to prevent their coming ashore in American ports for the purposes of reshipment, the Secretary of Labor may authorize the admission of such seamen without the presentation of passports. Each passport of an alien must be visaed by an American consulate, or the diplomatic mission if specially authorized, in the country from which the holder starts his trip to the United States. If the country from which he starts his trip to the United States is not the country to which he owes allegiance, he must also have his passport visaed by a diplomatic or consular officer therein of his own country. Moreover, every alien coming to the United States must have his passport, or document in the nature of a passport, visaed by a consular officer of the United States in the country from which he embarks for the United States or, if he comes by land, from which he enters the United States. The form of such visa should read as follows: "Seen. Number____. The bearer is to depart for the United States of America between (date) and (date)."

[The order then elaborates on the process of the visa and all the information to be recorded as to the person's identity, nationality, and so on, specifying what information is to be kept regarding the mode of travel by land or sea; what the consular officials are to swear to in the document, numbers of copies to be made and where given or filed, and so on.]

No fee shall be collected by diplomatic or consular officers of the United States for or in connection with the execution of such declaration or the visaing of passports.

No American embassy, legation, or consulate shall visa a passport of an alien enemy of the United States to enable him to enter this country unless special authorization of this Government has been previously obtained.

[The order then elaborates on certain provisions to avoid persons who might become public charges or persons from those classes not admitted to the United States for certain physical or mental characteristics.]

Provided, however, That such exclusion shall not be made in the cases of alien seamen arriving in ports of the United States, unless such seamen apply for permanent admission to this country, or unless it is necessary to require such papers in order to ascertain whether alien seamen are enemies of the United States; nor in the cases of aliens entering temporarily from contiguous foreign territory to follow agricultural pursuits, in accordance with the terms of the Department of Labor circular of May 23, 1917, and the supplements thereto. . . . Any alien who enters the United States in violation of this order shall be arrested, in substantial conformity with rule 22 of the Immigration Rules, with a view to his deportation to the country from whence he came, and his detention under proper restrictions until such deportation can be effected.

Signed, Frank L. Polk, Acting Secretary of State, and W. B. Wilson, Secretary of Labor.

Source: Immigration and Nationality Laws, Joint Order Department of State, Department of Labor. July 26, 1917, Washington, D.C.: 1042–1044.

* * *

In addition to the omnibus Immigration Act, Congress also passed a law in 1917 allowing for the repatriation of persons expatriated because of service in an allied foreign armed service during World War I.

DOCUMENT 66: Act of October 5, 1917 (Re: Resumption of Citizenship)

Be it enacted by the Senate and House of Representatives of the United States of America in Congress assembled, That any person, formerly an American citizen, who may be deemed to have expatriated himself under the provisions of the first paragraph of section two of the Act approved March second, nineteen hundred and seven, entitled "An Act in reference to the expatriation of citizens and their protection abroad," by taking, since August first, nineteen hundred and fourteen, an oath of allegiance to any foreign State engaged in war with a country with which the United States is at war, and who took such oath in order to be able to enlist in the armed forces of such foreign State, and who actually enlisted in such armed forces, and who has been or may be duly and honorably discharged from such armed forces, may, upon complying with the provisions of this Act, reassume and acquire the character and privileges of a citizen of the United States: *Provided, however,* That no obligation in the way of pensions or other grants because of service in the army or navy of any other country, or disabilities incident thereto, shall accrue to the U.S.

Any such person who desires so to reacquire and reassume the character and privileges of a citizen of the United States shall, if abroad, present himself before a consular officer of the United States, or, if in the United States, before any court authorized by law to confer American citizenship upon aliens, shall offer satisfactory evidence that he comes within the terms of this Act, and shall take an oath declaring his allegiance to the United States and agreeing to support the Constitution thereof and abjuring and disclaiming allegiance to such foreign State and to every foreign prince, potentate, State, or sovereignty. The consular officer or court officer having jurisdiction shall thereupon issue in triplicate a certificate of American citizenship, giving one copy to the applicant, retaining one copy for his files, and forwarding one copy to the Secretary of Labor. Thereafter such person shall in all respects be deemed to have acquired the character and privileges of a citizen of the United States. The Secretary of State and the Secretary of Labor shall jointly issue regulations for the proper administration of this Act.

Source: 40 Stat. 340.

* * *

World War I also led to congressional action to amend the naturalization laws to reward certain persons with special naturalization provisions, for example, Filipinos, seamen serving in the U.S. merchant marine or on U.S. fishing vessels, or persons whose naturalization process was interrupted by the war, or other persons serving in the United States armed forces.

DOCUMENT 67: Act of May 9, 1918: Naturalization of Persons with Military Service; Citizenship Education; Naturalization of Other Special Classes of Persons; Alien Enemies

Sec. 1. That section four of the Act entitled "An Act to establish a Bureau of Immigration and Naturalization and to provide a uniform rule for the naturalization of aliens throughout the United States," approved June twenty-ninth, nineteen hundred and six, be, and is hereby, amended by adding seven new subdivisions as follows:

Seventh. Any native-born Filipino of the age twenty-one years and upward who has declared his intention to become a citizen of the United States and who has enlisted or may hereafter enlist in the United States Navy or Marine Corps or the Naval Auxiliary Service, and who, after service of not less than three years, may be honorably discharged therefrom, or who may receive an ordinary discharge with recommendation for re-enlistment; or any alien, or any Puerto Rican not a citizen of the United States, of the age twenty-one years and upward, who has enlisted or entered or may hereafter enlist in or enter the armies of the United States, either the regular or the Volunteer Forces, or the National Army, the National Guard or Naval Militia of any State, Territory, or the District of Columbia, or the State Militia in the Federal service, or in the United States Navy or Marine Corps, or in the United States Coast Guard, or who has served for three years on board any vessel of the

United States, or for three years on board of merchant or fishing vessel of the United States ... may on presentation of the required declaration of intention petition for naturalization without proof of the required five years' residence within the United States ...; any alien serving in the military or naval service of the United States during the time this country is engaged in the present war may file his petition for naturalization without making the preliminary declaration of intention and without proof of the required five years' residence within the United States; any alien declarant who has served in the United States Army or Navy, or the Philippine Constabulary, and has been honorably discharged therefrom ... may file his petition for naturalization upon proof of continuous residence within the United States for the three years immediately preceding the petition ... and in these cases only residence in the Philippine Islands and the Panama Canal Zone by aliens may be considered residence in the United States, and the place of military service shall be construed as the place of residence required to be established for purposes of naturalization. ...

During the time when the United States is at war no clerk of a United States court shall charge or collect a naturalization fee from an alien in the military service of the United States for filing his petition or issuing the certificate of naturalization upon admission to citizenship. ... (40 Stat. 544; 8 U.S.C. 403.)

Eighth. That every seaman, being an alien, shall, after his declaration of intention to become a citizen of the United States, and after he shall have served three years upon such merchant or fishing vessel of the United States, be deemed a citizen of the United States for the purpose of serving on board any such merchant or fishing vessel of the United States. ...

Ninth. That for the purpose of carrying on the work of the Immigration and Naturalization Service of sending names of candidates for citizenship to the public schools and otherwise promoting instruction and training in citizenship responsibilities of applicants for naturalization, as provided in this subdivision, authority is hereby given for the reimbursement of the printing and binding ... and for the cost of publishing the citizenship textbook prepared and distributed by the Immigration and Naturalization Service to those candidates for citizenship only who are in attendance upon the public schools ... and to aid the local Army exemption boards and cooperate with the War Department in locating declarants subject to the Army draft and expenses incidental thereto.

Tenth. That any person not an alien enemy who resided uninterruptedly within the United States during the period of five years next preceding July first, nineteen hundred and fourteen, and was on that date otherwise qualified to become a citizen of the United States, except that he had not made the declaration of intention required by the law and who during or prior to that time, because of misinformation regarding his citizenship status erroneously exercised the rights and performed the duties of a citizen of the United States in good faith, may file the petition of naturalization prescribed without making the preliminary declaration of intention required of other aliens, and upon satisfactory proof . . . may be admitted as citizen of the United States upon complying in all respects with the other requirements of the naturalization law.

Eleventh. No alien who is a native, citizen, subject, or denizen of any country, State, or sovereignty with which the United States is at war shall be admitted to become a citizen of the United States unless he made his declaration of intention not less than two nor more than seven years prior to the existence of the state of war. . . .

Twelfth. That any person who, while a citizen of the United States and during the existing war in Europe, entered the military or naval service of any country at war with a country with which the United States is now at war, who shall be deemed to have lost his citizenship by reason of any oath or obligation taken by him for the purpose of entering such service, may resume his citizenship by taking the oath of allegiance to the United States prescribed by the naturalization law and regulations. . . .

Thirteenth. That any person who is serving in the military or naval forces of the United States at the termination of the existing war, and any person who before the termination of the existing war, may have been honorably discharged from the military or naval services of the United States on account of disability incurred in line of duty, shall, if he applies to the proper court for admission as a citizen of the United States, be relieved of the necessity of proving . . . he resided continuously in the United States the time required by law of other aliens . . . but his petition for naturalization shall be supported by the affidavits of two credible witnesses, citizens of the United States, identifying the petitioner as the person named in the certificate of honorable discharge, which said certificate may be accepted as evidence of good moral character required by law, and he shall comply with the other requirements of the naturalization law.

Source: 40 Stat. 542; 8 U.S.C. 388.

* * *

In 1918 the president issued a detailed executive order of fourteen pages in length specifying the rules and regulations to implement a proclamation concerning the exclusion, entrance, and departure of aliens during the war. Document 68 highlights some of those rules and regulations contained in the thirty-six sections that specify how the secretary of state shall implement the departure from or entry into the United States.

DOCUMENT 68: Executive Order No. 2932, August 8, 1918: Rules and Regulations Governing the Issuance of Permits to Enter and Leave the United States

[The executive order in several sections refers to the laws and proclamation that grant the authority to the Secretary of State, then goes on to define all the terms—United States, departure from, enter in, passport, permit, seaman, etc.]

Sec. 9. Limitations Upon and Exceptions to the Application of the Act of May 22, 1918.

The following general limitations upon and exceptions to the application of the Act of May 22, 1918 are authorized and prescribed:

(a) No passports or permits to depart from or enter the United States shall be required of persons other than hostile aliens traveling between ports of the continental United States on vessels making no intermediate calls at foreign or noncontinental ports. Hostile aliens must obtain permits for all departures from, and entries into, the United States.

(b) No passports or permits shall be required of persons other than hostile aliens traveling between points of the continental United States and Canada or Bermuda....

(c) No passports or permits ... shall be required of persons in or attached to the military or naval forces of the United States or of any nation associated with the United States in the prosecution of the war....

Sec. 10 ... (b) Hostile aliens residing in Canada or the United States may secure special permits allowing them to cross the border of the two countries by making application therefore to the Bureau of Immigration and the Department of Labor stationed nearest their place of residence....

(c) Aliens who are seamen on vessels arriving at ports of the United States and who desire to land ... shall apply to an immigration inspector....

(e) Identity cards issued to alien seamen as provided by the foregoing ... shall be retained by them and used from time to time as they land in and sail from the United States....

(g) No permits to depart from or enter the United States shall be required of officials or representatives of foreign countries duly accredited to the United States or a friendly country provided that such persons bear valid passports ... and the Department of State is notified in advance of their intended entry or departure and consents thereto....

Sec. 12. No person registered or enrolled or subject to registry or enrollment for military service in the United States shall depart from the United States without previous consent of the Secretary of War ... [The act then specifies in detail in numerous sections the agents who will grant, accept, and check upon permits to enter or depart and the times and process whereby such permits are to be granted, covering women and minors accompanying their husband or parent.]

Sec. 33. As a restriction additional to those provided by said Joint Order, hostile aliens shall not enter the United States from Canada unless they secure visas in the manner prescribed [herein]. . . .

Sec. 34. An alien's passport duly visaed together with a copy of the declaration required by said Joint Order shall constitute a permit to enter the United States. . . .

Sec. 36. The actual control of persons departing from the United States at all seaboard and lake ports shall be exercised by the representatives of the customs service of the Department of the Treasury, who shall act as control officers for this purpose.

Source: Executive Order No. 2932, August 8, 1918.

* * *

In October 1918 Congress expanded the provision spelled out in the Act of March 3, 1903, dealing with Sections 2 and 38 of that law, and amended section 3 of the Act of February 5, 1917, which added membership in or espousal of communism to the list of excluded classes or those subject to expulsion which previously had stipulated anarchists.

DOCUMENT 69: Act of October 16, 1918: Exclusion and Expulsion of Anarchists and Similar Cases

Be it enacted by the Senate and the House of Representatives . . . , That any alien who is a member of any of the following classes shall be excluded from admission into the United States*:

(1) Aliens who seek to enter . . . to engage in activities which would be prejudicial to the public interest, or would endanger the welfare or safety of the United States:

(2) Aliens who, at any time, shall be or shall have been members of any of the following classes:

(A) Aliens who are anarchists

(B) Aliens who advocate or teach. . . . anarchy,

*As amended by Internal Security Act of September 23, 1950 (64 Stat. 987), following amendment by Act of June 5, 1920 (41 Stat. 1008).

(C) Aliens who are members of or affiliated with (i) the Communist Party of the United States, (ii) any other totalitarian party of the United States, (iii) the Communist Political Association. . . .

(D) Aliens not within any of the other provisions of this paragraph (2) who advocate the economic, international, and governmental doctrines of world communism or the economic and governmental doctrines of any other form of totalitarianism. . . .

(E) Aliens . . . who are members of or affiliated with any organization which is registered or required to be registered under section 7 of the Subversive Activities Control Act. . . .

(F) Aliens who advocate or teach or are affiliated with any organization that advocates or teaches the overthrow by force or violence or other unconstitutional means of the Government of the United States or of all forms of law. . . .

(G) Aliens who write or publish . . . or who knowingly circulate, distribute, print or display. . . . any written or printed matter advocating or teaching opposition to all forms of government, or the overthrow by violence or other unconstitutional means the Government of the United States or all forms of law. . . .

(H) Aliens who are associated with organizations [that do such matters as described in section (G)]. . . .

Sec. 9. Any statute or other authority or provision having the force or effect of law, to the extent that it is inconsistent with any of the provisions of this Act, is hereby expressly declared to be inapplicable to any alien whose case is within the purview of this Act.

Sec. 10. If any portion of this Act, or the application thereof to any person or circumstance, is held invalid, the remaining portions of this Act, or the application of such provisions to other persons or circumstances, shall not be affected thereby.

Source: 40 Stat. 1012; 8 U.S.C. 137.

* * *

After World War I, and in recognition of their outstanding contributions and services during the war, Congress granted citizenship to all Native Americans who served in the war.

DOCUMENT 70: Act of November 6, 1919: Granting Citizenship to Certain Honorably Discharged Indians Who Served During the World War

That every American Indian who served in the Military or Naval Establishments of the United States during the war against the Imperial

German Government, and who has received or who shall hereafter receive an honorable discharge, if not now a citizen and if he so desires, shall, on proof of such discharge and after proper identification before a court of competent jurisdiction, and without other examination except as prescribed by said court, be granted full citizenship with all the privileges pertaining thereto, without in any manner impairing or otherwise affecting the property rights, individual or tribal, of any such Indian or his interest in tribal or other Indian property.

Source: 41 Stat. 350; 8 U.S.C. 3.

* * *

Chinese immigrants detained at Angel Island, in San Francisco Bay, beginning in 1910, left poems on the walls of the wooden barrack buildings used as the detention station. Document 71 presents three of the 135 poems that have so far been translated into English. They give a sense of the desires of the would-be immigrants to come to the "land of the flowery flag," or the "land of the Golden Mountain"—both colloquial terms for the United States. Many also refer to the harsh treatment they experienced.

DOCUMENT 71: Chinese Poems from Detention Barracks, Angel Island Station, San Francisco

Poem 7

Originally, I had intended to come to America last year.
Lack of money delayed me until autumn.
It was on the day that the Weaver Maiden met the Cowherd [Westerner]
That I took passage on the *President Lincoln*.
I ate wind and tasted waves for more than twenty days.
Fortunately, I arrived safely on the American continent.
I thought I could land in a few days.
How was I to know I would become a prisoner suffering in the wooden
     building?
The barbarians' abuse is really difficult to take.
When my family's circumstances stir my emotions, a double stream of
     tears flow.
I only wish I can land in San Francisco soon,
Thus sparing me this additional sorrow here.

Poem 9

I used to admire the land of the Flowery Flag as a country of abundance.
I immediately raised money and started my journey.

For over a month, I have experienced enough winds and waves.
Now on an extended sojourn in jail, I am subject to the ordeals of prison life.
I look up and see Oakland so close by.
I wish to go back to my motherland to carry the farmer's hoe.
Discontent fills my belly and it is difficult for me to sleep.
I just write these few lines to express what is on my mind.

Poem 62

I entered the land of the Flowery Flag by way of Lusong.
Conditions at the border were strict and I was not clever.
In the wooden jail, I was imprisoned for days.
Now I am to be deported back in the steel vessel, *Persia*.
When Ruan Ji reached the end of the road who took pity on his weeping?
In a distant land, Li Ling sadly sighed in vain.
There is nothing that can be done about misfortune caused by tyranny.
Fate is unlucky and times are perverse; therefore, I suffer these ordeals.

Source: Him Mark Lai, Genny Lim and Judy Yung, *Island: Poetry and History of Chinese Immigrants on Angel Island, 1910–1940* (San Francisco: Hoc Doi—Chinese Culture Foundation, 1980), 38, 46, 126.

* * *

Document 72 contains some brief oral interviews of Angel Island detainees, translated into English. Many who came to America were "paper sons"—immigrants who tried to enter the country on false claims of being the offspring of a Chinese merchant, or a Chinese man claiming to be a U.S. citizen. They used "coaching papers" to give them sufficient information to answer the questions asked during their entrance examinations. Since they typically were entering as the minor children of Chinese immigrants already here, they were generally males under the age of twenty-one. Some came as the "wives" of immigrants already here.

DOCUMENT 72: Oral Interviews of Angel Island Detainees

Mr. Wong, age 12, in 1933:

They told me that anyone who comes to Gam Saan [Golden Mountain, or the United States] will make money fast and go home a rich man. Anyone who comes to America is well respected in China. My family pushed me to come. They wanted me to make a better living. They couldn't send my older brother because he was too old to match the age of my uncle's paper son. I studied coaching papers for a whole summer at school. It included many, many generations. I had to remember everyone's name, the birthday, and if they passed away, when. And you had to know the different points of the village, what it looked like. I remember I had a English cap that we picked up in Hong Kong and inside the cap, my father hid some coaching notes, so that once in awhile, I could refresh my memory. But I never had a chance to look at them, because you're among people all the time and you don't trust anyone. There was no private place where I could be alone to study them. One time, they were playing catch with my cap and they didn't understand why I was so upset. I was scared.

Mrs. Chang, age 23, in 1939:

I was forced to come to America, I had never seen my husband before. My mother matched me in marriage so that I could bring the family over later. I had a passport to come when I was 16, but I didn't come until I was 23, when the Japanese attacked. Most of us then came as daughters of citizens or wives of businessmen. Other wives weren't allowed to come. I came as a granddaughter of a citizen. The papers had been purchased for me.

Mr. Tom, age 17, in 1921:

My father was here in the late 1890s. After he died in an accident, my uncle bought a merchant's son's paper for me to come to America. All the papers then were false and cost $100 per year of age. I was actually 17, but the paper said 19. After I got here, I found out that when an elder wishes to bring a younger relative over from China, he must go make contact at such places as Hip Sing Chong and buy papers for the closest age. He pays a deposit and the balance after the immigrant has landed. If he can't land, you just lose the passage cost and get the deposit back. If court fees are needed to land the immigrant, the seller of the papers must foot it. At that time, there were few court battles. Later, when the immigration law became stricter, the applicant and seller shared the court costs fifty-fifty, and the paper was paid for in full regardless of the results. If you're deported, it's your own bad luck.

Coming to the Flowery Flag, I stopped over in Hong Kong for one month and stayed at Wing Chong's, a *gam saan jong* [Golden Mountain firm] run by fellow villagers from Wong Leung Dou. It took me a month, because first, I had to go to the Consulate's for papers, then to the doctor's to be examined for trachoma. Often, they can't see you right there and then, so you have to make an appointment and come back. Then maybe, your eyes aren't okay and you have to correct them. If they're okay, the doctor gives you the necessary papers and you go buy passage tickets next. They might not have seats when you want them, so you end up waiting again. Wing Chong's still operating now, helping people buy passage tickets, handling mail and remittances, helping travellers to get to the Flowery Flag, and putting up guarantees for aliens from America visiting Hong Kong.

Source: Him Mark Lai, Genny Lim, and Judy Yung, *Island: Poetry and History of Chinese Immigrants on Angel Island, 1910–1940* (San Francisco: Hoc Doi—Chinese Culture Foundation, 1980), 44, 49.

Part III

Restrictions, Refugees, and Reform—1920 to 1965

During the 1920s the restrictionist fervor rose to its highest point. A revived Ku Klux Klan grew in membership and influence. It advocated extensive restrictions on immigration [Document 77]. Both the Democratic and Republican party platforms also called for limits on immigration.

The fear that the nation would experience a renewed flood of immigration in response to the postwar economic turmoil in Europe fed a xenophobic demand for increased restrictions. When an economic recession hit in 1920, the House of Representatives voted to end all immigration. The Senate refused to go that far, but clearly Congress was ready to pass significantly more restrictionist immigration laws than before World War I. The restrictionist forces in Congress gained not only in their numbers but also in their influence. Senator William P. Dillingham, for example, who had chaired the Immigration Commission in 1907, was, by 1917, chair of the Immigration Committee in the Senate. Chairing the House Immigration Committee in that Republican-dominated chamber was Albert Johnson of Washington, a leading voice for restrictionist policy.

In 1919, after the so-called Palmer raids, 500 immigrants suspected of being radical anarchists were deported on a ship going to Russia, nicknamed the "Soviet Ark." The Congress rejected joining the League of Nations, and a postwar isolationist mood was easily tapped by the forces advocating restrictions on immigration. The new nationalism was distrustful of Europe, disillusioned with the aftermath of the war and the failure of the Americanization program, committed to isolationism, and disdainful of all things foreign. It echoed through the debates about joining the League of Nations. It rumbled in the "konklaves" of the Klan. It unleashed a torrent of state laws that attempted to exclude aliens from many occupations. Licensing acts barred foreigners from practicing architecture, engineering, chiropractic, pharmacy, surgery, and surveying and from executing wills. They were even barred from operating motor buses (Higham 1955, 271, 301).

Because of the 1920 depression, business interests, which previously had been strong advocates of keeping the immigration doors relatively open to ensure a cheap labor supply, either remained silent or shifted to a restrictionist position. The halls of Congress soon echoed with calls to end the "alien flood," the "barbarian horde," and the "foreign tide."

Restrictionist forces turned to the Dillingham Commission's recommendation for a quota system as the approach to take. Several trends converged to support that strategy. The return to economic prosperity in 1921 reduced the economic issues to a secondary role in the debate over immigration reform, although the American Federation of Labor (AFL) did attack unchecked immigration as the source of cheap labor. A leading sociologist, Henry Pratt Fairchild, advocated a restrictive policy. Restrictionist forces concentrated their attacks on immigrants, using an "ethnic theory" approach. Among the leading voices was Madison Grant, the highly influential author of *The Passing of the Great Race*. Grant's book, first published in 1916 but released in new editions in 1921 and 1923, sold 16,000 copies and inspired newspaper editorials and series articles. He was the leading advocate of the theory that configured within the "white race" a three-tiered hierarchy of Mediterraneans, Alpines, and Nordics. Grant held that Americans were Nordics, the highest, and should regard any mixture with the other two as a destructive process of "mongrelization." (Higham, 1955: 154, 272).

Responding to a resurgence of immigration by early 1921, Congress passed the first immigration quota act in 1921 [Document 73], which reflected the racist theories underlying the restrictionist movement. Yet, Congress was not the only major national institution subscribing to racial theories. In 1922 the U.S. Supreme Court, in *Ozawa v. United States* [Document 75], upheld the constitutionality of a blatantly racist law that made Japanese "aliens ineligible for citizenship" and expanded the scope of that concept the following year in *United States v. Bhagat Singh Thind* (1923) [Document 76]. The Court agreed that "alien race and allegiance" were a legitimate object of legislation and could be made the basis of a permanent classification. Such judicial reasoning allowed state licensing laws to limit aliens from practicing certain occupations.

The percentage quota system became the central piece of all immigration laws passed in the 1920s. The pivotal function of the quota system was to limit immigration and to reconstitute its sources away from Southern, Central, and Eastern European nations toward northwestern European nations.

Passage of the 1921 law, however, hardly settled the matter. The temporary quotas were based on 3 percent of the foreign-born population in 1910, with an overall ceiling of 357,800 placed on immigration from outside the Western Hemisphere. Nonetheless, ships arriving during the first months after passage of the law often carried more than the monthly quota for some countries. Polish, Romanian, and Italian immigrants soon jammed Ellis Island and steamships in the harbors of Boston and New York City. Administrative "exemptions" to the monthly quotas in response to these dire conditions angered the congressional restrictionist forces.

For two years the Congress deadlocked over attempts to set up a permanent quota system. Shifting economic forces during 1923 and 1924 resulted in a shifting battleground over the approach to permanent quotas. Various ethnic groups pushed for or against different quota schemes, depending on how each quota formula affected the number of newcomers from those countries. A "Nordic theory" gained ground. In 1924 President Calvin Coolidge (who had succeeded the deceased Warren G. Harding) gave the restrictionist cause his blessings.

In the House, the Immigration Committee, chaired by Albert Johnson, introduced a new bill in 1924. The Ku Klux Klan launched a massive letter-writing campaign supporting the bill to "preserve" America's racial purity [Document 77]. The AFL also backed the bill. Congressional support from the South and the West, especially from California, concentrated on the Yellow Peril theme. Senator David Reed of Pennsylvania, using a quota system based on 1890 census data, pushed a proposal through the Senate's Immigration Committee and received valuable support from Senator Henry Cabot Lodge of Massachusetts. The Immigration Act of 1924 [Document 79], which became popularly known as the Johnson-Reed Act, passed with comfortable support from members of both parties and virtually every area of the country. It reflected the triumph of the Nordic majority in the country over the southeastern minority.

Perhaps as much as the system of permanent quotas, the requirement of visas was an effective regulating device. Overseas visas issued against a particular country's quota became the most effective means devised to control the use of quotas. It allowed for the administrative screening of immigrants and enabled officials to regulate the flow of newcomers and thereby avoid the chaos in American ports that followed the signing of the 1921 act.

Yet passage of the 1924 Johnson-Reed Act did not end the battles, although it settled the issue of using the national origins system as the basis for the nation's immigration policy. The new legislation lowered the ceiling to approximately 164,700, distributed quotas based on 2% of the foreign-born population in 1890, and barred immigrants entirely who were ineligible for citizenship (e.g. mostly Asians). This was to remain in effect until a special commission had developed a National Origins formula based on the entire population in the 1920 census. The consequences of the 1924 Act were dramatic. European immigration slumped from over 800,000 in 1921 to less than 150,000 by the end of the decade. In 1929, the National Origins Plan was finally accepted by Congress; the ceiling was reduced even further, to about 153,700, and the quotas system became permanently fixed and operational [Document 89].

The decade of the Great Depression resulted in a great slacking off of immigration, both quota and nonquota (for example, from Canada, Mexico, and the Philippines) as the depressed economic conditions and the rigid screening process for visas lessened the incentive to migrate. Indeed, many foreigners returned to their homelands. Unable legislatively to curb Western Hemisphere immigration, the restrictionists shifted their concern to immigration from the Philippines. After several attempts to enact laws limiting Filipino migration, Congress passed a bill granting the Philippines independence in ten years in exchange for their accepting an annual quota of fifty. Only a small number accepted a subsequent offer for a no-cost repatriation to the Philippines. The problem of Filipino restriction had been settled.

With that, the rest of the 1930s was a time of relative inaction. The quota system had its desired effects. Total immigration fell sharply. Immigration from northwestern Europe rose from under 20 percent of the total flow during the 1910–1920 decade to nearly 40 percent of the much smaller flow of the 1930s. Southern and Eastern European immigration fell from nearly 71 percent in the 1910–1920 decade to under 30 percent of the 1930s. However, once the repressive actions of the fascist governments in Germany and Italy began to generate refugee flows, pressure began to build to address the problems created by those seeking to escape. The inflexibility of the quota system began to show in response to this mushrooming refugee issue.

The attack on Pearl Harbor, which brought America into World War II, also ushered in a virtual nightmare experience for Japanese Americans living on the mainland. A total of 112,000 persons of Japanese ancestry, some 70,000 of whom were native-born U.S. citizens, were sent to relocation camps in the interior for what was termed "military necessity" [Document 103]. The relocation camps were, in fact, concentration camps where conditions were often grim and caused great hardships. Men and women, grandparents and infants, young children and young adults, simple gardeners and fishermen, merchants and small businessmen—all were herded behind fifteen-foot-high barbed-wire fences guarded by armed troops stationed around the perimeter in spotlight towers. Residents lived in crude barracks, in which sections a mere eighteen feet by twenty-one feet might house families of up to six or seven persons. A barrack building of ninety feet by twenty feet typically held six families. Executive Order 9102, issued by President Franklin D. Roosevelt on March 18, 1942, established the War Relocation Authority and, along with Executive Order 9066 (February 1942), provided the bases for the detention, relocation, and internment of Japanese resident aliens and Japanese American citizens. These Orders were endorsed by the Act of March 21, 1942 [Document 105]. The constitutionality of various actions taken principally against persons of Japanese ancestry, based in part on notions of racial loyalty and military necessity, was upheld in three Supreme Court cases:

Hirabayashi v. United States (1943) [Document 106], Yasui v. United States (1943), and Korematsu v. United States (1944) [Document 109]. In Ex Parte Mitsuye Endo (1944) [Document 110], however, the Court held that loyal U.S. citizens could not be detained in the camps in violation of their habeas corpus rights and that military necessity was not a valid argument for such action since the camps were operated by a civilian agency. With the Pacific war moving toward victory, the government revoked the West Coast Exclusion Order, and by the summer of 1946, the camps were closed.

Ironically, the wartime experience which so plagued the Japanese Americans helped Chinese Americans. The alliance with China in the war with Japan was a leading factor in Congress' decision to repeal the Chinese Exclusion Act in December 1943, establishing a small quota for Chinese and, of great significance, declaring them eligible for citizenship [Document 107].

The immediate postwar years highlighted several problems with the inflexibility of the quota system. In 1945 Congress passed the War Brides Act [Document 112], allowing up to 150,000 wives and fiancées, some 25,000 children, and several hundred husbands of U.S. citizens serving in the armed forces to be brought in outside the quota system.

It was the problem of refugees and displaced persons that most showed the need for some modification of the quota system. At war's end there were an estimated 8 million displaced persons in Austria, Italy, and Germany, over 1 million of whom were located in displaced-persons camps. President Harry Truman responded first by issuing an executive order in December 1945 [Document 111] admitting some 2,500 that fiscal year. For the next two-and-one-half years, Truman's directive was used to bring in 41,000 persons. About 12 percent of the displaced persons admitted as quota immigrants were relatives of citizens or of resident aliens (Bennett 1963, 89).

In June 1948, Congress passed the Displaced Persons Act [Document 114], which set up a preference category and established a Displaced Persons Commission to administer the act. Among its provisions, it allowed for persons from some countries to immigrate in numbers beyond that county's quotas by "mortgaging" future quotas. Existing health, literacy, and related requirements, however, were not set aside for the displaced persons. President Truman signed the act even though he felt it did not go far enough. Ultimately, the act provided for the admission of 400,000 refugees over a four-year period (Barkan 1996, 75; Bennett 1963, 76–77).

The growing need for agricultural workers led to the Agriculture Labor and Illegal Entry Act of 1948. It established an agreement among the United States, Canada, Mexico, and the British West Indies that allowed migrants to come as temporary farm workers, which essentially repealed the Contract Labor Act of 1917. The new act also strengthened the Border Patrol.

In 1949 Congress amended the Philippine Act of 1946 by extending its benefits to June 1951 and passed another act for the recruitment of agricultural labor in short supply [Document 117]. The following year, Congress declared Guamanians born after April 11, 1899, to be citizens, thus eliminating any immigration restrictions on them. (Congress had extended citizen rights to Asian Indians and Filipinos in 1946). In that same year, 1950, in reaction to a growing fear about communism, Congress enacted the Internal Security Act, which increased the grounds for exclusion and deportation of alleged alien subversives, reflecting the Cold War tenor of the times.

The need for revisions in the quota system, highlighted by the Displaced Persons Act, led to a slight relaxation in the quota system. In 1952 Congress enacted the McCarran-Walter Act, in which it reaffirmed restrictionism and the national origins quota system but established the Asian-Pacific Triangle, allocating small, token quotas to the nations within its boundaries (essentially from Afghanistan to Japan and from Mongolia to Indonesia and the Pacific Islands). The act also included a preference system within the quotas based on family reunification and economic considerations. It repealed the last racial and national-origin barriers to U.S. citizenship, in effect establishing for the first time a uniform standard for the naturalization of all applicants. However, the act did not impose any quotas on Western Hemisphere nations, allowing for the general provisions against persons "likely to become public charges" to limit immigration from that region [Document 118]. President Truman vetoed the bill, objecting to what he termed its unfair racial biased quotas [Document 119]. Congress overrode his veto by 278 to 113 in the House and 57 to 26 in the Senate.

Cold War foreign policy considerations led Congress to enact a "special" refugee act, the Refugee Relief Act of 1953 [Document 123].

Three years later, President Dwight D. Eisenhower "paroled" 5,000 "freedom fighters" of the failed Hungarian revolution. Congress sanctioned this strategy and permitted 30,000 more Hungarian refugees to enter in 1957 and canceled the quotas mortgaged under the Displaced Persons Act.

The Cuban revolution generated another wave of refugees from communism, and the parole option was used again to allow ultimately some of about 800,000 Cuban refugees to enter, making them the largest long-term refugee movement up to that time in the nation's history (Chiswick 1982, 32). President Eisenhower also used the parole status to admit Chinese immigrants from Hong Kong. In all, from the end of World War II to 1980, nearly 1.6 million refugees from all over the world were admitted to the United States (McClellan 1981, 45).

Another method of getting around the quota system was the use of the private bill. Under this procedure, an alien sought exemption to the quota system through private legislation. A member of Congress introduced a bill for his or her relief. Use of this procedure expanded greatly in the 1950s, and while the total number to enter was not large, it illustrated the steps needed to bypass the inflexibility of the quota system.

In 1921 Congress enacted the first law that regulated immigration by imposing a quota based on the national origin of the immigrant. The annual quota for each country was based upon three percent of the foreign-born residents from that country residing in the United States as determined by the 1910 census.

DOCUMENT 73: Act of May 19, 1921: The Quota Act of 1921 (also called "Emergency Quota Act")*

Be it enacted by the Senate and the House of Representatives . . . , That [hereafter the key terms "United States," "alien," and "Immigration Act," are defined].

Sec. 2. (a) That the number of aliens of any nationality who may be admitted under the immigration laws to the United States in any fiscal year shall be limited to 3 per centum of the number of foreign-born persons of such nationality resident in the United States as determined by the United States census of 1910. This provision shall not apply to the following, and they shall not be counted in reckoning any of the percentage limits provided in this Act: (1) Government officials, their families, attendants, servants, and employees; (2) aliens in continuous

---

*Other legislation referred to it as "An Act to limit immigration into the United States."

transit through the United States; (3) aliens lawfully admitted to the United States who later go in transit . . . to another foreign contiguous territory; (4) aliens visiting the United States as tourists or temporarily for business or pleasure; (5) aliens from countries immigration from which is regulated in accordance with treaties or agreements relating solely to immigration; (6) aliens from the so-called Asiatic barred zone . . . (7) aliens who have resided continuously for at least five years immediately preceding the time of their application for admission . . . in the Dominion of Canada, Newfoundland, the Republic of Cuba, the Republic of Mexico, countries of Central and South America, or adjacent islands; or (8) aliens under the age of eighteen who are children of citizens of the United States.

(b) For the purposes of this Act nationality shall be determined by country of birth, treating as separate countries the colonies or dependencies for which separate enumeration was made in the United States census of 1910;

(c) That the Secretary of State, the Secretary of Commerce, and the Attorney General, jointly, shall, as soon as feasible after enactment of this Act, prepare a statement showing the number of persons of the various nationalities resident in the United States as determined by the census of 1910, which statement shall be the population basis for the purposes of this Act. . . .

(d) When the maximum number of aliens from any nationality who may be admitted in any fiscal year under this Act shall have been admitted all other aliens of such nationality, except as otherwise provided for by this Act . . . shall be excluded. . . .

Provided further, That in the enforcement of this Act preference shall be given so far as possible to the wives, parents, brothers, sisters, children under eighteen years of age, and fiancees, (1) of citizens of the United States, (2) of aliens now in the United States who have applied for citizenship in the manner provided by law, or (3) of persons eligible to United States citizenship who served in the military or naval forces of the United States at any time between April 6, 1917 and November 11, 1918 . . . and have been separated from such forces under honorable conditions.

Sec. 3. That the Commissioner of Immigration and Naturalization, with the approval of the Attorney General, shall as soon as feasible after the enactment of this Act, and from time to time hereafter, prescribe rules and regulations necessary to carry the provisions of this Act into effect. He shall, as soon as feasible . . . publish a statement showing the number of aliens of the various nationalities who may be admitted to the United States. . . . Thereafter he shall publish monthly statements during the time this Act remains in force showing the number of aliens of each nationality already admitted under provisions of this Act . . . and the number who may be admitted . . . during the then current fiscal year . . . but when 75 per centum of the maximum number of any nationality . . .

shall have been admitted such statements shall be issued weekly thereafter.... The Attorney General shall also submit such statements to the Secretary of State, who shall transmit the information contained therein to the proper diplomatic and consular officials of the United States, which officials shall make the same available to persons intending to emigrate to the United States and to others who may apply.

Sec. 5.* That this Act shall take effect and be enforced 15 days after its enactment ... and shall continue in force until June 30, 1924 [originally "1922" but extended for two more years], and the number of aliens of any nationality who may be admitted during the remaining period of the current fiscal year, from the date when this Act becomes effective until June 30, shall be limited in proportion to the number admissible during the fiscal year 1922.

Sec. 6.* That it shall be unlawful for any person, including any transportation company other than railway lines entering the United States from foreign contiguous territory, or the owner, master, agent, or consignee of any vessel, to bring to the United States either from a foreign country or any insular possession of the United States any alien not admissible under the terms of this Act or regulations made thereunder.

Source: 42 Stat. 5; 8 U.S.C. 229.

* * *

In 1922, following a campaign conducted by women's groups, Congress passed the Married Woman's Act, which stipulates that the citizenship process for spouses be separated from one another and that the practice of wives automatically acquiring citizenship when their husbands were naturalized be ended. While it retained expatriation for American-born women who wed aliens ineligible for citizenship (e.g., Asians), it otherwise declared that there be no denial or abridgment of an American-born woman's rights because of her sex or marital status.

DOCUMENT 74: Act of September 22, 1922: Married Woman's Act ("Cable Act")

Be it enacted by the Senate and House of Representatives of the United States of America in Congress assembled, That the right of any woman to become a naturalized citizen of the United States shall not be abridged because of her sex or because she is a married woman....

Sec. 2. That a woman who marries a citizen of the United States, after passage of this Act, or any woman whose husband is naturalized after

*As amended May 11, 1922 (42 Stat. 540).

passage of this Act, shall not become a citizen of the United States by reason of such marriage or naturalization; but, if eligible to citizenship, she may be naturalized upon full and complete compliance with all requirements of the naturalization laws with the following exceptions:

(a) No declaration of intention be required.

(b) In lieu of the five-year period of residence within the United States . . . she shall have resided continuously in the United States, Hawaii, Alaska, or Puerto Rico for at least one year immediately preceding the filing of the petition.

Sec 3. That a woman citizen of the United States shall not cease to be a citizen of the United States by reason of her marriage after the passage of this act, unless she makes a formal renunciation of her citizenship before a court having jurisdiction over naturalization of aliens: *Provided*, That any woman citizen who marries an alien ineligible to citizenship shall cease to be a citizen of the United States. If at the termination of the marital status she is a citizen of the United States, she shall retain her citizenship regardless of her residence. If during the continuance of the marital status she resides continuously for two years in a foreign State of which her husband is a citizen or subject, or for five years continuously outside the United States, she shall thereafter be subject to the same presumption as is a naturalized citizen. . . . [refering to Sec. 2 of the Act of March 2, 1907, Doc. 58 above]

(b) Any woman who before this section, as amended, takes effect, lost her United States citizenship by residence abroad after marriage to an alien or by marriage to an alien ineligible to citizenship, may, if she has not acquired any other nationality by affirmative act, be naturalized in the manner prescribed in section 4 of this Act, as amended. Any woman who was a citizen of the United States at birth shall not be denied naturalization under section 4 on account of her race.

Source: 42 Stat. 1021; 8 U.S.C. 367.

* * *

In 1922 the U.S. Supreme Court ruled on a case that challenged the constitutionality of the law that forbade Japanese immigrants to become naturalized citizens. The Court upheld the law, ruling that it was constitutional to restrict them from citizenship.

DOCUMENT 75: *Ozawa v. United States* (November 13, 1922)

It may be true that these two races [Japanese and Chinese] were alone thought of as being excluded, but to say that they were the only ones within the intent of the statute would be to ignore the affirmative form of the legislation. The provision is not that Negroes and Indians shall be *excluded*, but it is, in effect, that only free white persons shall be *included*. The intention was to confer citizenship upon that class of persons whom the fathers knew to be white, and to deny it to all who could not so be classified. It is not enough to say that the framers did not have in mind the brown or yellow races of Asia. It is necessary to go farther and be able to say that, had these particular races been suggested, the language of the act would have been varied so as to include them within its privileges. As said by Chief Justice Marshall . . . in deciding a constitutional construction: "It is enough to say that this particular case was not in the mind of the Convention when the article was framed, nor of the American people when it was adopted. It is necessary to go farther, and to say that, had this particular case been suggested, the language would have been varied as to exclude it, or it would have been made a special exception. The case, being within the words of the rule, must be within its operation likewise, unless there be something in the literal construction so obviously absurd or mischievous, or repugnant to the general spirit of the instrument, as to justify those who expound the Constitution in making it an exception." If it be assumed that the opinion of the framers was only persons who would fall outside the designation "white" were Negroes and Indians, this would go no farther than to demonstrate their lack of sufficient information to enable them to foresee precisely who would be excluded by that term in the subsequent administration of the statute. It is not important, in construing their words, to consider the extent of their ethnological knowledge, or whether they thought that, under the statute, the only persons who would be denied naturalization would be Negroes and Indians. It is sufficient to ascertain whom they intended to include: and, having ascertained that, it follows, as a necessary corollary, that all others are to be excluded.

The question, then, is, Who are comprehended within the phrase "free white persons"? Undoubtedly the word "free" was originally used in recognition of the fact that slavery then existed, and that some white persons occupied that status. The word, however, has long since ceased to have any practical significance and can now be discarded.

. . . The Federal and state courts, in an almost unbroken line, have held that the words "white person" were meant to indicate only a person of what is popularly known as the Caucasian race. . . . With the conclusion reached in these several decisions we see no reason to differ. Moreover, that conclusion has become so well established by judicial and executive concurrence and legislative acquiescence that we should not, at this late date, feel at liberty to disturb it, in the absence of reasons far more cogent than any that have been suggested. . . . The determination that the words "white person" are synonymous with the words "a person of the Caucasian race" simplifies the problem. . . .

The appellant in the case now under consideration, however, is clearly not Caucasian, and therefore belongs entirely outside the zone on the negative side. A large number of Federal and state courts have so decided, and we find no reported case definitely to the contrary. These decisions are sustained by numerous scientific authorities, which we do not deem it necessary to review. We think these decisions are right, and so hold.

The briefs filed on behalf of appellant refer in complimentary terms to the culture and enlightenment of the Japanese people, and with this estimate we have no reason to disagree; but these are matters which cannot enter into our consideration of the question here at issue. We have no function in the matter other than to ascertain the will of the Congress and declare it. Of course, there is not implied—either in the legislation or our interpretation of it—any suggestion of individual unworthiness or racial inferiority. These considerations are in no manner involved.

Source: 260 U.S. 195.

* * *

The Supreme Court ruled further on what constituted a "white" person insofar as that word was understood in terms that admission to naturalization was open only to a "free white person" in 1923. The Court here ruled that in the law "free white person" meant those persons who appeared and would commonly be viewed as "white" and specifically rejected a person of the Caucasian race who, as an East Indian, did not appear to be "white" and therefore was judged ineligible for naturalization. Document 76 summarizes the main points from the majority opinion in that case.

DOCUMENT 76: *United States v. Bhagat Singh Thind* (February 19, 1923)

Mr. Justice Sutherland delivered the opinion of the court:
The cause is here upon a certificate from the circuit court of appeals, requesting instruction of this court in respect to the following questions:
1. Is a high caste Hindu of full Indian blood, born in Amritsar, Punjab, India, a white person within the meaning of #2169, Revised Statutes (Comp. Stat. #4358, 6 Fed. Stat. Anno. 2d ed. P. 944)?
2. Does the Act of February 5, 1917 . . . disqualify from naturalization as citizens those Hindus now barred by that act, who had lawfully entered the United States prior to passage of said act?
. . . No question was made in respect to the individual qualifications

of the appellee. The sole question is whether he falls within the class designated by Congress as eligible. Section #2169, Revised Statutes, provides that the provision of the Naturalization Act "shall apply to aliens being free white persons and to aliens of African nativity and to persons of African descent."

If the applicant is a white person within the meaning of this section he is entitled to naturalization; otherwise not. . . .

In the endeavor to ascertain the meaning of the statute we must not fail to keep in mind that it does not apply the word "Caucasian," but the words "white persons," and these are words of common speech, and not of scientific origin. The word "Caucasian" not only was not employed in the law, but was probably wholly unfamiliar to the original framers of the statute in 1790. When we employ it, we do so as an aid to the ascertainment of the legislative intent, and not as an invariable substitute for the statutory words. . . . But in this country, during the last half century especially, the word by common usage has acquired a popular meaning, not clearly defined, to be sure, but sufficiently so to enable us to say that its popular, as distinguished from its scientific application, is of appreciably narrower scope. It is in the popular sense of the word, therefore, that we employ it as an aid to the construction of the statute, for it would be obviously illogical to convert words from common speech, used in a statute, into words of scientific terminology, when neither the latter nor the science for whose purposes they were coined was within the contemplation of the framers of the statute or of the people for whom it was framed. The words of the statute are to be interpreted in accordance with the understanding of the common man from whose vocabulary they were taken. . . .

. . . . The words of familiar speech, which were used by the original framers of the law, were intended to include only the type of man whom they knew as white. The immigration of that day was almost exclusively from the British Isles and northwestern Europe, whence they and their forebears had come. When they extended the privilege of American citizenship to "any alien being a free white person," it was these immigrants—bone of their bone, flesh of their flesh—and their kind whom they must have had affirmatively in mind. The succeeding years brought immigration from eastern, southern, and middle Europe, among them the Slavs and the dark-eyed, swarthy people of Alpine and Mediterranean stock, and these were received as unquestionably akin to those already here, and readily amalgamated with them. It was the descendants of these and other immigrants of like origin, who constituted the white population of the country when . . . the naturalization test [was reenacted] . . . with like intent and meaning.

What we now hold is that the words "free white persons" are words of common speech, to be interpreted in accordance with the understanding of the common man, synonymous with the word "Caucasian" only as that word is popularly understood. As so understood and used, whatever may be the speculations of the ethnologist, it does not include the body of people to whom the appellee belongs. It is a matter of familiar observation and knowledge that the physical group characteristics of the Hindus render them readily distinguishable from the various groups of persons in this country commonly recognized as white. . . . It is very far from our thought to suggest the slightest question of racial superiority or inferiority. What we suggest is merely racial difference, and it is of such character and extent that the great body of our people instinctively recognize it and reject the thought of assimilation.

It is not without significance in this connection that Congress, by the Act of February 5, 1917, . . . has now excluded from admission to this country all natives of Asia within designated limits of latitude and longitude, including the whole of India. This not only constitutes conclusive evidence of the congressional attitude of opposition to Asiatic immigration generally, but is persuasive of a similar attitude toward Asiatic naturalization as well, since it is not likely that Congress would be willing to accept as citizens a class of persons whom it rejects as immigrants.

It follows that a negative answer must be given to that first question, which disposes of the case and renders an answer to the second question unnecessary, and it will be so certified. Answer to question No. 1, No.

Source: 61 U.S.C. 616 (February 19, 1923).

* * *

The restrictionist movement was not satisfied with the results of the 1921 act in stemming the flow of immigration into the United States. They pushed for greater restrictions and quotas that would further shift the flow coming in toward northwestern European nations of origin. One nativist group that advocated greater restrictions is the Klan. Document 77 contains the statement of the Grand Dragon of South Carolina, issued in 1924, advocating the enactment of the stricter quota system that was passed later that year. His statement touches upon most of the issues and illustrates many of the arguments used by the restrictionist forces at the time and some of the exaggerations, as well.

DOCUMENT 77: The Regulation of Immigration—A Statement by the Grand Dragon of the Ku Klux Klan, South Carolina (1924)

I regard the regulation of immigration as one of the most perplexing and important questions confronting the American people today. There are few questions that deserve the attention of this great organization, which I represent, more than the immigration problem.

The time has now come when the Knights of the Ku Klux Klan should take the leadership in this great fight, to prevent America from becoming the melting pot or dumping ground of the world for the millions of heterogeneous elements who are seeking admission to our shores.

In my opinion a law should be enacted restricting immigration to the United States for a period of at least ten years, while we take an inventory of the human assets and liabilities within our borders, do a bit of house cleaning and set our domestic affairs in better order. We have already enough social and economic problems to study in connection with the 14,000,000 foreign born now in the United States.

America is just awakening to the fact that it is not a nation but a mixture of nationalities, and if this country is to be populated and governed by a class of people who are so different in character, thought and ideals, the inevitable result will be a nation of nationalities chattering all the tongues of Babel.

The immigrants who come to this country form communities by themselves and congregate in the great cities. Paupers, diseased and criminals predominate among those who land upon American soil. They have a very low standard of morals, they are unable to speak our language and a great majority of them are unable to read and write their own language. They come from countries where they have been accustomed to a lower standard of wages and living and, therefore, compete with American labor which is already overcrowded.

We must insist that a law be enacted prohibiting the printing of any newspaper or magazine not printed in the English language, and to require all aliens within our borders to speak English within a limited period of time.

All Should Speak English

There are more than 14,000,000 foreign born in the United States, of whom more than 7,000,000 have never taken out naturalization papers, and who can neither speak nor read our language. We have aliens living in America who have never been naturalized and who never expect to become citizens, editing newspapers and magazines and endeavoring to dictate to the American citizen the policies of his Government. How do we expect to naturalize and make good citizens of those 14,000,000 foreigners who are already in this country unless we require them to speak our language and print their newspapers and magazines in English? We can never have a homogeneous population unless we require every man, woman and child in America to speak the English language. And it will be a most powerful means of stopping the spread of unsound doctrines, the spread of anarchy and Bolshevism.

Unless we safeguard ourselves against the further influx of undesirables there will no longer be an America for Americans. If foreign-language newspapers may be taken as reflecting the sentiments of the foreign born within our gates then our non-Anglo-Saxon citizens are far more interested in forcing their own customs and institutions upon us than in helping us build a superstructure to fit the foundation upon which America rests. . . .

Of the 805,000 admitted to the United States in 1921 more than half, 432,000, were Jews, Italians, Armenians, Greeks, Japanese, Chinese, and Finns, races which generation after generation maintain their own churches, customs, languages, schools, and social affiliations almost as intact as if they had remained in their native countries.

I am afraid that we fail to realize how stupendous, though noiseless, is the pressure of this immigration avalanche. We have heard the great noise made about the Zionist movement, and might be led to think that a large Jewish migration to Palestine was in progress. But the record shows that last year 53,524 Hebrew aliens came to the United States, while 18 left this country for Palestine, where there are only 50,000 Jews all told. . . .

America is saturated with aliens, and some of our great States will soon be populated entirely by aliens, unless a law is enacted restricting immigration to the United States for a period of years. There are today thirteen States with a majority of the population of alien origin. Thirteen other states have more than 35 percent of their population foreign born. Some of our great cities are in even worse condition than those States.

The Japanese Problem

The Japanese question is another great menace that confronts the American people today. And the Knights of the Ku Klux Klan can do no greater service than to take up the fight with those loyal citizens of California in their effort to prevent their State from becoming a little Japan. There are more than 100,000 Japanese in California, who today own and control one-eighth of the entire acreage of irrigated lands in that State.

Two-thirds of the entire Japanese population of continental United States is located in California; that is to say, twice as many Japanese are found in California as in the other forty-seven states combined. They maintain a government of their own, subject to the dictates of a foreign power, and acting in the interests of that power and adverse to those of this country. Something must be done to protect the great West. The remedy calls for an absolute exclusion of all Japanese who may seek to come here in any capacity for permanent residence. This will prevent an element in our population, which, is not only undesirable, but dangerous to American interests.

America has within her borders many of the so-called hyphenated Americans. They call themselves Hungarian-Americans, French-Americans, Irish-Americans, Italian-Americans, Russian-Americans, Polish-Americans and German-Americans. Such a class of people do not deserve the respect of any decent, loyal, patriotic, red-blooded, pure and unadulterated American citizen. There is but one kind of American. One who would not for one moment tolerate any prefix to "America;" one whose every thought and interest places America first, above all other nations on earth; one who acknowledges allegiance to no country but America; and no flag but the Stars and Stripes. Any alien who is not willing to measure up to the standard of true Americanism should be deported. We have no room in this country for any individual or element opposed to America, and who are unwilling to give their undivided allegiance to our country, its institutions, its language and its flag.

Klan Must Fight

The Knights of the Ku Klux Klan should adopt a policy and program for combating the influence of individuals or organizations who are endeavoring to open the gates of our ports to the admission of aliens. Therefore, the Imperial Wizard should appoint an Imperial Immigration and Naturalization Commission to make a thorough study and outline a program. Such a Commission should make an analysis of the Immigration and Naturalization questions, and submit a report to the Imperial Wizard, for his approval, with a definite policy to handle this complex question. Our Government departments have acquired sufficient information to guide this country aright, if it were assembled, analyzed and made available to the public.

America is governed by public opinion and the sources of that opinion concerning the problems of immigration are of vital importance. To deal with so complex a national situation and so profound an international situation requires the public to be intelligently informed before we can have a united public opinion. This can be acquired only by a great movement, such as the Knights of the Ku Klux Klan, which is willing to gather this information and see that the public is properly and correctly informed of the true facts. . . .

The present 3 per cent admission law on the basis of the 1910 census is the first attempt of Congress to restrict immigration. It was passed just at the time when a flood of destitute, restless wanderers and adventurers had an eye on the United States. This law substantially checked the alien flood, but it has not given the relief needed.

Under the existence of the 3 per cent law the northern races who alone amalgamate with us, do not send more than half as many as the law would admit, while all southern European nations exhaust their quotas and howl for more.

The Secretary of Labor, in his annual report for 1922, states that even with the existing restriction laws the United States is still the greatest immigrant-receiving nation on earth. With this in view, the time has come for the Knights of the Ku Klux Klan to begin its work, because the 3 per cent law expires June 30, 1924. When Congress meets again in December, we will be in the midst of a national campaign, and the various hyphenated foreign organizations will be uppermost in the minds of certain politicians. It behooves us that Americans be on guard to guard our gates [he closes with a Klan poem].

Source: Papers Read at the Meeting of Grand Dragons, Knights of the Ku Klux Klan (New York: Arno Press, 1977), 69–74.

*   *   *

The debate to change the quotas as set up in the "emergency" quota act of 1921 to more permanent quotas raged and reached its peak between 1921 and 1924. The vigorous debate in the Congress is reflected in Document 78, which cites the arguments of Congressman William Vaile, a Republican from Colorado, a leading proponent of drastic immigration restriction based on both racial and nationalistic grounds. His comments, summarized from the *Congressional Record*, articulate and vividly define the immigration quota controversy. In Document 87, we present a speech made by Representative John J. O'Conner of New York who articulates the antirestrictionist position.

DOCUMENT 78: "We Prefer to Base Quotas on Established Groups"—A Statement of Congressman William N. Vaile (April 1924)

The present law, our first numerical limitation on immigration, which has been in effect for three years, admits from any country—with certain exceptions not involved in this inquiry—3 per cent of the number of persons born in that country who were resident in the United States by the census of 1910. The total quota is 357,803.

The Johnson bill, now pending, proposes to admit from any country 2 per cent of the number of persons born in such country who were resident in the United States by the census of 1890, and, in addition, 100 from each country. The total proposed quota is 161,184.

Now, people who have come here from Italy, Rumania, Greece, Czechoslovakia, and other countries in southern and eastern Europe claim that this "discriminates" against their countrymen. Why? The answer is a complete refutation of their own argument. The "discrimination" lies in the fact that, as they themselves admit, the bulk of their immigration came after 1890, whereas the great bulk of their immigration from northern and western Europe came before that year.

We would not want any immigration at all unless we could hope that they would become assimilated to our language, customs, and institutions, unless they could blend thoroughly into our body politic. This would be admitted, I suppose, by the most radical opponent of immigration restriction. In fact, it is one of the stock arguments of these gentlemen that, although the immigrant himself may be assimilated slowly, his children, born here, become Americans in thought, action, speech, and character. That statement, often splendidly true, must nevertheless be accepted with many qualifications: but at least it is clear enough that the second generation will be assimilated quicker than the first—whatever may be the effect in many cases of such assimilation upon the United States. It would seem still clearer that the third and subsequent generations will be still more American than their predecessors.

It is also one of the stock arguments of the anti-restrictionists that the immigrant has taken an important part in the building up of the country. Surely his children and grandchildren, both in numbers and in the quality of their work, have taken a still more important part.

Now, it seems rather logical for gentlemen who vaunt the assimilability and the work of alien groups in our population to claim that those who have been for the shortest time in the process of assimilation and in the work of the Republic should have greater or even equal consideration because of this very newness. It would seem if those who came to work at the eleventh hour are to have a penny, then at least those who have "borne the heat and burden of the day" should not be put off with a farthing.

It is a fact, not merely an argument, that this country was created, kept united, and developed—at least for more than a century of existence—almost entirely by people who came here from the countries of northern and western Europe. That people from southern and eastern Europe did not begin to come in large numbers until after 1890 proves that those who came before them had built up a county desirable enough to attract these late comers.

Shall the countries which furnished those earlier arrivals be discriminated against for the very reason, forsooth, that they are represented here by from 2 to 10 generations of American citizens, whereas the others are largely represented by people who have not been here long enough to become citizens at all?

If there is a charge of "discrimination," the charge necessarily involves the idea that the proposed quota varies from some standard which is supposed to be not "discriminatory." What is that standard? From the arguments of those opposed to the bill it would appear that the census of 1910 is now regarded as not "discriminatory," or at least less "discriminatory" than the census of 1890. It will be remembered that the census of 1910 was adopted as a base for emergency legislation, legislation not expected to be permanent, legislation not claimed to be exact, but intended to answer the purpose of an urgently needed restriction of the total volume of immigration. It has answered that purpose fairly well, but with some unnecessary hardships obviated by the present bill. The number admitted under it, however, has been far too great, and it is now proposed to cut the quota by more than one-half.

But it is not the cut which is so bitterly complained of. It is the change in the proportions, and it is interesting to note that those who violently opposed the passage of the 3 per cent law now with equal violence demand the retention of its proportions to the present legislation. But at least we can say that it has not been in operation long enough to have become an established and inviolable principle of distribution if some more equitable basis could be devised.

It is submitted that the Immigration Committee might fairly have determined to disregard the claims of very recently arrived immigrants that they should be figured at all as a basis for the admission of others. Congress might reasonably say, "Your value to the United States may be proved. We hope it will be. But it has not yet been fully proved, and we prefer to base our quotas on groups whose value has been established through several generations. We will therefore endeavor to distribute immigration in proportion to the elements of our population as they existed a generation ago."

But the committee did nothing of the sort, and the use of the 1890 census proposes nothing of the sort. Whatever our inducement to question it, we did accept the new immigration at its full value, and we said, "We will distribute immigration in proportion to the elements of our population as they exist to-day. We will give you full credit for your recent additions to our population on exactly the same basis as we credit the contributions which started nearly a century and a half ago."

It is submitted that this is the very height of liberality to those who with ungrateful clamor are now complaining that they are being discriminated against . . . The countries of northern and western Europe contributed 85.02 per cent of our present white population (1920), and that under the present law they are entitled to only 56.33 per cent of our quota immigration, but under the pending bill they will be entitled to 84.11 per cent of our annual quota immigration. In other words, for the last three years those countries have been having about two-thirds of their share of the immigration, while under the proposed quota they get to within 1 per cent of their exact share.

On the other hand, the countries of southern and eastern Europe have furnished 14.62 per cent of our present—1910—white population, but under the present quota law those countries as a group are getting 44.64 per cent of our immigration. Under the proposed bill they will receive 1.88 per cent, which is about a quarter of 1 per cent more than their "share". . . .

Under the pending bill the British Isles would be entitled to furnish about 38.87 per cent of our new immigration. This is nearly twice what the British Isles can get under our present law, but it is still less than two-thirds of their "share" on the basis of their total contribution to our population. . . . Italy, one of the loudest complainers, is cut a little, because the great bulk of her immigration came very late, not only after 1890 but considerably after that date. She has furnished 3.92 per cent of our present white population. She will only be entitled to send 2.92 per cent of our future immigration. But for the last three years she has been sending 11.75 per cent of our total quota immigration, or nearly three times her "share" on the basis of her contribution to the population of the United States.

Poland, in whose behalf the welkin rings with cries of "unjust discrimination," has been receiving nearly three times her "share." She will be reduced to only a little less than twice her "share." This is doing pretty well for a country whose recently arrived population in one American city alone—Buffalo—outnumbers the native stock by 20,000 people.

Source: U.S. Congress, House of Representatives, *Congressional Record*, 68th Congress, 1st sess., April 1–14, 1924, 65, pt. 6, pp. 5643–45.

* * *

The restrictionist movement succeeded as advocated by the Grand Dragon of South Carolina and Congressman Vaile. In May 1924 Congress enacted the second quota immigration act, this one consolidating prior law into a comprehensive act that runs for thirty-five pages in the code of statutes. Its most salient provisions are excerpted in Document 79. Its percentage of population quota was revised from 3 percent to 2 percent, and the census of population upon which the quotas were based changed from 1910 to 1890. As intended, this new quota system shifted the flow dramatically from Southern, Central, and Eastern European nations to those from northwestern European origin.

DOCUMENT 79: Act of May 26, 1924: The Immigration Act of 1924 ("Johnson-Reed Act")

Sec. 1. That this Act may be cited as the "Immigration Act of 1924."

Sec. 2. (a) A consular officer upon the application of any immigrant . . . may . . . issue to such an immigrant an immigration visa which shall consist of one copy of the application provided for in section 7, visaed by such consular officer. Such visa shall specify (1) the nationality of the immigrant; (2) whether he is a quota immigrant (as defined in section 5) or a non-quota immigrant (as defined in section 4); (3) the date on which the validity of the immigration visa shall expire; and (4) such additional information necessary to the proper enforcement of the immigration laws and the naturalization laws as may be by regulation prescribed.

[The act then goes on to prescribe photographs, notation on the passport of the number of visa, when such visas are not to be issued, the fees for visas.]

[Sections 3, 4, and 5 then define the terms "immigrant," "non-quota immigrant," and "quota immigrant." See these terms as defined in the Glossary.]

*Enumeration of Preferences within quotas: time for giving preferences; percentage of preferences.

Sec. 6. (a) Immigration visas to quota immigrants shall be issued in each fiscal year as follows:

*As amended by Act of May 29, 1928 (45 Stat. 1009). Original provision enumerated unmarried young children, parents and spouses of U.S. citizens and immigrants skilled in agriculture.

(1) Fifty per centum of the quotas of each nationality for such year shall be made available . . . to the following classes of immigrants, without priority of preference as between such classes: (A) Quota immigrants who are the fathers or mothers of citizens of the United States . . . or who are the husbands of citizens of the United States by marriages occurring on or after May 31, 1928 of citizens who are citizens of the United States who are twenty-one years of age or over; and (B) in the case of any nationality the quota of which is three hundred or more, quota immigrants who are skilled in agriculture, and the wives, and the dependent children under the age of eighteen years, of such immigrants skilled in agriculture, if accompanying or following to join them.

(2) The remainder of the quota of each nationality for such year . . . shall be made available in such year for the issuance of immigration visas to quota immigrants of such nationality who are the unmarried children under twenty-one years of age, or the wives, of alien residents of the United States who were lawfully admitted to the United States for permanent residence. . . .

Sec. 7. [Gives an elaborate description of duplicate application of visas and the form of visas, copies to be kept for records, statements required as to membership in classes of aliens excluded, statements as to exemptions from exclusion and the various verifications as to signatures, ages, fees paid, etc.]

Sec. 8. [Covers when a consular official may issue a nonquota immigration visa.]

Sec. 9. [Covers the issuance of nonquota visas and quota visas to relatives.]

Sec. 10. (a) Any alien about to depart temporarily from the United States may make application to the Commissioner of Immigration and Naturalization for a permit to reenter the United States stating the length of his intended absence, and the reasons therefor.
[Subsections (b)–(g) detail the issuance of reentry permits, their fees, effects, and treaty-merchant reentry permits.]

Sec. 11. (a) The annual quota of any nationality shall be 2 per centum of the number of foreign-born individuals of such nationality resident in continental United States as determined by the United States census of 1890, but the minimum quota of any nationality shall be 100.
[Subsections (b)–(g) detail how national origin is determined, presidential proclamation of quotas, monthly issuances of visa limits, and the issue of visas to nonquota immigrants.]

Sec. 12. (a) For the purpose of this Act nationality shall be determined by country of birth, treating as separate countries the colonies, dependencies, or self-governing dominions for which separate enumeration was made in the United States census of 1890 and which was not included in the enumeration for the country to which such colony or dependency belonged. . . .

[Subsection (b) requires the secretaries of state and commerce, with the attorney general, to issue jointly statements as to the numbers of the various nationalities as of the census of 1890. Subsection (c) covers the effects of changes in the political boundaries of foreign countries; (d) and (e) cover the issuance of monthly statements and the proclamation of quotas available.]

Sec. 13. (a) No immigrant shall be admitted . . . unless he (1) has an unexpired immigration visa . . .; (2) is of the nationality specified in the visa; (3) is a nonquota immigrant if specified in the visa as such; (4) is a preference-quota immigrant if specified . . . as such; and (5) is otherwise admissible under the immigration laws. [Subsection 13(b) covers such details as readmission of aliens without visas.]

(c) No alien ineligible to citizenship shall be admitted to the United States unless such alien (1) is admissible as a non-quota immigrant under the provisions of subdivisions (b), (d) or (e) of section 4, or (2) is the wife, or the unmarried child under 18 years of age, of an immigrant admissible . . . , and is accompanying or following to join him, or (3) is not an immigrant as defined in section 3. . . .

(e) No quota immigrant shall be admitted under subdivision (d) if the entire number of immigrant visas which may be issued to quota immigrants of the same nationality for the fiscal year has already been issued. . . .

Sec. 14. [Covers deportation procedures for alien children under age sixteen.]

Sec. 15. [Covers the maintenance of exempt status.]

Sec. 16. [Covers when it is unlawful to bring to the United States by water an alien, including the fines or prison penalties thus engendered.]

Sec. 17. [Covers the commissioner of Immigration and Naturalization's authority to issue rules and regulations to implement the act.]

Sec. 18. If a quota immigrant of any nationality having an immigration visa is excluded from admission to the United States under the immigration laws and deported, or does not apply for admission to the United States before the expiration of the validity of the immigration visa, or if any alien of any nationality having an immigration visa issued to him as a quota immigrant is found not to be a quota immigrant, no additional immigration visa shall be issued in lieu thereof to any other immigrant.

Sec. 19. No alien seaman excluded from admission . . . shall be permitted to land . . . except temporarily for medical treatment, or pursuant to such regulations as the Attorney General may prescribe for the ultimate departure, removal, or deportation of such alien from the United States.

[Subsequent sections and subsections detail the detention of seamen on board vessels, penalties, evidence of failure to detain or deport, deportation procedures, preparation or use of documents and the offenses in connection with forging, counterfeiting, immigration visas or permits, false statements, and so on.]

Sec. 23. Whenever any alien attempts to enter the United States the burden of proof shall be upon the alien to establish that he is not subject to exclusion under any of the provisions of the immigration laws.

[Sections 24 to 32 essentially repeat prior law as to steamship line fines, prevention of alien landings, and so on of the Immigration Act of 1917.]

Source: 43 Stat. 153; 8 U.S.C. 201.

* * *

In June 1924 the U.S. Congress granted citizenship to those Native Americans who had not already received it either by accepting allotments of land under the 1887 Dawes Act or by military service in World War I.

DOCUMENT 80: Act of June 2, 1924 and Act of June 4, 1924 (Re: Citizenship for Non-citizen Indians)

Be it enacted by the Senate and House of Representatives of the United States of America in Congress assembled, That all non-citizen Indians born within the territorial limits of the United States be, and they are hereby, declared to be citizens of the United States: *Provided*, That the granting of such citizenship shall not in any manner impair or otherwise affect the right of any Indian to tribal or other property.

Act of June 4, 1924 (43 Stat. 380)

Disposition of Lands of Eastern Band of Cherokee Indians; Citizenship of Allottees

Sec. 19. That lands allotted under this Act shall not be alienable, either by voluntary or enforced sale by the allottee or their heirs or otherwise, for a period of twenty-five years from and after the date when the deed conveying such land to the allottee is recorded as directed herein: *Provided*, That upon the completion of the allotments and the recording of the deeds as herein directed each allottee shall become a citizen of the United States and a citizen of the particular State wherein he (or she) may reside, with all the rights, privileges, and immunities of such citizens.

Source: 43 Stat. 253; 8 U.S.C. 3; 43 Stat. 380.

* * *

In order to enforce more effectively the immigration laws and to regulate more effectively the control of illegal aliens entering the United States, mostly through its borders with Mexico, the Congress established a Border Patrol in 1925.

DOCUMENT 81: Act of February 27, 1925: Relating to the Border Patrol

Provided, That $1,000,000 of this amount [$5,084,865] shall be available only for coast and land-border patrol: and *Provided further*, Any employee of the Immigration and Naturalization Service authorized to do so by the Commissioner of Immigration and Naturalization with the approval of the Attorney General, shall have the power without warrant (1) to arrest any alien who in his presence or view is entering or attempting to enter the United States in violation of any law or regulation made in pursuance of law regulating the admission, exclusion, or expulsion of aliens, or any alien who is in the United States in violation of any such law or regulation and is likely to escape before a warrant can be obtained for his arrest, but the person arrested shall be taken without unnecessary delay for examination before an officer of the Immigration and Naturalization Service having authority to examine aliens as to their right to enter or to remain in the United States; (2)* within reasonable distance from any external boundary of the United States, to board and search for aliens any vessel within the territorial waters of the United States and any railway car, aircraft, conveyance, or vehicle, and within a distance of twenty-five miles from any such external boundary to have access to private lands, but not dwellings, for the purpose of patrolling the border to prevent the illegal entry of aliens into the United States; and (3) to make arrests for felonies which have been committed and which are cognizable under any law of the United States regulating the admission, exclusion, or expulsion of aliens, if the person making the arrest has reason to believe that the person so arrested is guilty of such felony and if there is likelihood of the person escaping before a warrant can be obtained for his arrest, but the person arrested shall be taken without unnecessary delay before the nearest available commissioner or before any other nearby officer empowered to commit persons charged with such offenses against the laws of the United States; and such employee shall have the power to execute any warrant or other process issued by any law regulating the admission, exclusion, or expulsion of aliens.**

Source: 43 Stat. 1049–1050; 8 U.S.C. 110.

* * *

*Second provision amended by Act of March 20, 1952 (66 Stat. 26).
**The original fourth provision was amended by Act of August 7, 1942 (60 Stat. 865, 8 U.S.C. 110) and then repealed by Act of June 27, 1952 (66 Stat. 279).

The effects of the new quota act of 1924 were immediate and dramatic. An article released by the Foreign Language Information Service in 1925, which assesses the impact of the new law after its first year, addresses its role in assisting immigrants and the foreign-language press in its dealings with foreign-language speakers regarding immigration.

DOCUMENT 82: Foreign Language Information Service Article (1925)

Statistics for the fiscal year ended June 30, 1925, show that the new immigration law has not only checked the amount of immigration, but has had an important effect on its racial character. During the first twelve months that the Immigration Act of 1924 was in operation 294,314 immigrants were admitted to the United States—less than one-half of the 706,896 who entered during the preceding fiscal year. 75.6 per cent of the immigrants admitted belong to the peoples of northern and western Europe. This is a significant increase as compared with a corresponding proportion of 55.7 per cent in 1923–24 and of only 25.7 per cent in 1920–21. On the other hand only 10.8 per cent of the immigrants of the past year belonged to the peoples of southern and eastern Europe and Turkey, a material decrease from the 27.2 per cent which the same peoples contributed to our total immigration in 1923–24, and the 66.7 per cent which they contributed in 1920–21....

During the past year 92,278 aliens left the United States to take up permanent residence abroad. Thus, 19,956 more Italians left the United States than entered it. In the same way, the number of Czechs, Jugoslavs, Greeks, Lithuanians, Hungarians, Poles, Portugese, Rumanians, Spaniards, Chinese and Japanese who left the country considerably exceeded those of the same nationality who entered....

Of the immigrants admitted during the past year, almost exactly one-half, or 145,971, were quota immigrants, and the remainder had non-quota status.... It is true, however, that there were small balances in the quotas for Czechoslovakia (107), France (3), Greece (2), Hungary (106), Italy (1,149), and Jugoslavia (103). These balances are due to the unexpected return of quota numbers at the end of the year, to the failure of foreign governments to give their nationals the necessary passports or to similar reasons. The unfilled quotas are not due to lack of desire to immigrate to the United States. On the contrary, our consuls have reported a demand for passports and immigration visas which under the existing quota allowances could not be filled in 100 years for Hungary,

70 years for Italy and Russia, 50 years for Rumania, and 10 years for Czechoslovakia, Poland, and Greece.

Reaching the Immigrant Through His Newspaper

Since 1917 our immigration laws have admitted only literate immigrants. The newer immigrants can therefore be reached through the newspapers published in foreign languages. Some 1,200 such newspapers and magazines in 40 different languages, are now published in the United States. Reaching as it does the great mass of foreign speaking peoples in the country, the foreign language press is obviously the most important instrument for conveying to them information about American ideas and institutions. Unfortunately few foreign language publications are financially strong enough to employ an efficient staff of writers who could undertake the work of interpreting America to their readers, but the foreign language editors as a class gladly welcome material that will help their readers understand and value the country of their adoption. Their appreciation is clearly evidenced by the steadily increasing use which, irrespective of political or religious affiliation, they have made of the unbiased and informative releases furnished them by the Foreign Language Information Service. During 1924 more than 48,000 reprints of such articles were actually clipped from the 800 papers receiving the releases.

The articles released are derived chiefly from the Federal Government, educational organizations like the National Geographic Society and Science Service, and reference books generally recognized as reliable. They are prepared for publication by a staff of native and foreign-born Americans who possess journalistic experience and who know at first hand both the United States and the needs of the newcomer. Much material can be used as it is released by the government and national organizations. An editorial committee compiles and criticizes articles on topics not covered by such material.

Source: Foreign Language Information Service, FLIS File No. 01211–01212, 1925.

* * *

The increasing use of air travel by the mid-1920s required Congress to address the application of laws relating to foreign commerce to air travel. Some aspects of those applications affected immigration admission procedures. Document 83 presents two sections of a law enacted in 1926.

DOCUMENT 83: Act of May 20, 1926: Air Commerce Act of 1926

Sec. 7. .... (d) The Attorney General is authorized to (1) designate any of the ports of entry for civil aircraft as ports of entry for aliens arriving by aircraft, (2) detail to such ports of entry such officers and employees of the Immigration and Naturalization Service as he may deem necessary, and to confer or impose upon any employee of the United States stationed at such port of entry ... any of the powers, privileges, or duties conferred or imposed upon officers or employees of the Immigration and Naturalization Service, and (3)* by regulation to provide for the application to civil air navigation of the laws and regulations relating to the administration of the customs laws to such extent and upon such conditions as he deems necessary.....

Sec. 11. Any person who (1) violates any provision of subdivision (a) of this section or any entry or clearance regulations made under section 7 (b), or (2) any immigration regulation made under such section, shall be subject to a civil penalty of $500 which may be remitted or mitigated by the Secretary of Commerce, or the Attorney general, respectively, in accordance with such proceedings as the Secretary (or the Attorney General) shall by regulation prescribe....

(c) Any aircraft subject to a lien for any civil penalty imposed under this section may be summarily seized by and placed in the custody of such persons as the appropriate Secretary [or the Attorney General] may by regulation prescribe and a report of the case thereupon transmitted to the United States attorney for the judicial district in which the seizure is made. The United States attorney shall promptly institute proceedings for the enforcement of the lien or notify the Secretary of his failure so to act. The aircraft shall be released from such custody upon (1) payment of the penalty or so much thereof as is not remitted or mitigated, (2) seizure in pursuance of process of any court in proceedings in rem for enforcement of the lien, or notification by the United States attorney of failure to institute such proceedings, or (3) deposit in a bond in such amount and with such sureties as the Secretary may prescribe, conditioned upon the payment of the penalty or so much thereof as is not remitted or mitigated.

Source: 44 Stat. 572; 49 U.S.C. 177(d).

*Amended by Act of July 1, 1944 (58 Stat. 682).

DOCUMENT 84: Act of March 4, 1927: Certain Puerto Rican Citizens Deemed to be Citizens of the United States

Be it enacted by the Senate and the House of Representatives of the United States of America in Congress assembled, That section 3 of an Act entitled "An Act to provide a civil government for Puerto Rico, and for other purposes, approved March 2, 1917, as amended by an Act approved February 3, 1921, be, and the same is hereby, amended to read as follows:

Sec. 2. That a new section is hereby inserted between sections 5 and 6 of the Act entitled "An Act to provide a civil government for Porto Rico, and for other purposes," approved March 2, 1917, as amended, as follows:

Sec. 5a. That all citizens of the United States who have resided or who shall hereafter reside in the island for one year shall be citizens of Porto Rico: *Provided,* That persons born in Porto Rico of alien parents, referred to in the last paragraph of section 5, who did not avail themselves the privilege granted to them of becoming citizens of the United States, shall have a period of one year from the approval of this Act to make the declaration provided for in the aforesaid section: *And provided further,* That persons who elected to retain the political status of citizens of Porto Rico may within one year after the passage of this Act become citizens of the United States upon the same terms and in the same manner as is provided for the naturalization of Porto Ricans born of foreign parents.

Source: 44 Stat. 1418.

* * *

In the 1928 campaign, both of the major political parties adopted positions in support of restrictionist immigration policy. Document 85 excerpts their party-platform planks (their official party positions) on immigration, and Document 86 excerpts speeches of their presidential nominees concerning immigration.

DOCUMENT 85: Political Party Positions on Immigration (1928 Presidential Campaign)

The Democratic Platform on Immigration:

The platform of the Democratic party contains only one short reference to immigration and none to naturalization. . . .

"Laws which limit immigration must be preserved in full force and effect, but the provisions contained in these laws that separate husbands from wives and parents from infant children, are inhumane and not essential to the efficiency of such law."

The Republic Party Platform on Immigration:

"The Republican Party believes that in the interest of both native and foreign-born wage earners, it is necessary to restrict immigration. Unrestricted immigration would result in wide-spread unemployment and in the breakdown of the American standard of living. Where, however, the law works undue hardship by depriving the immigrant of the comfort and society of those bound by close family ties, such modification should be adopted as will afford relief."

"We commend Congress for correcting defects for humanitarian reasons and for providing an effective system of examining prospective immigrants in their home countries."

"Through the saneness and soundness of Republican rule, the American workman is paid a 'real wage' which allows comfort for himself and his dependents and an opportunity and leisure for advancement. It is not surprising that the foreign workman, whose greatest ambition still is to achieve a 'living wage', should look with longing toward America as the goal of his desires."

"The ability to pay such wages and maintain such a standard comes from the wisdom of the prospective legislation which the Republican Party has placed on the national statute books: the tariff which bars cheap foreign-made goods from the American market and provides continuity of employment for our workmen and fair profits for the manufacturers, and the restriction of immigration which not only prevents the glutting of our labor market, but allows to our newer immigrants a greater opportunity to secure a footing in their upward struggle."

The Republican Platform on Naturalization:

"The priceless heritage of American citizenship is our greatest gift to our friends of foreign birth. Only those who will be loyal to our institutions, who are here in conformity with our laws, and who are in sympathy with our national traditions, ideals, and principles, should be naturalized."

Source: Congressional Record Press, as quoted in the Foreign Language Information Service, *Interpreter Release Clip Sheet,* 5, 15, July 5, 1928.

DOCUMENT 86: Presidential Nomination Acceptance Speeches (1928 Presidential Campaign)

Herbert Hoover, Republican Nominee:

The Republican Party has ever been the exponent of protection to all our people from competition with lower standards of living abroad. We have always fought for tariffs designed to establish this protection from imported goods. We also have enacted restrictions upon immigration for the protection of labor from the inflow of workers faster than we can absorb them without breaking down our wage levels.

The Republican principle of an effective control of imported goods and of immigration has contributed greatly to the prosperity of our country. There is no selfishness in this defense of our standards of living. Other countries gain nothing if the high standards of America are sunk and if we are prevented from building a civilization which sets the level of hope for the entire world.

No man will say that any immigration or tariff law is perfect. We welcome our new immigrant citizens and their great contribution to our nation; we seek only to protect them equally with those already here. We shall amend the immigration laws to relieve unnecessary hardships on families. As a member of the commission whose duty it is to determine the quota basis under the national origins law, I have found it is impossible to do so accurately and without hardship. The basis now in effect carries out the essential principle of the law and I favor the repeal of that part of the act calling for a new basis of quotas. [Palo Alto, California, August 11, 1928.]

Alfred E. Smith, Democratic Nominee:

During all of our national life the freedom of entry to the country has been extended to the millions who desired to take advantage of the freedom and the opportunities offered by America. The rugged qualities of our immigrants have helped to develop our country and their children have taken their places high in the annals of American history.

Every race has made its contributions to the betterment of America. While I stand squarely on our platform declaration that the laws which limit immigration must be preserved in full force and effect, I am heartily in favor of removing from the immigration law the harsh provision which separates families, and I am opposed to the principle of restriction based upon the figures of immigrant population contained in a census thirty-eight years old. I believe this is designed to discriminate against certain nationalities and is an unwise policy. It is in no way essential to a continuance of the restriction advocated in our platform. [Albany, New York, August 22, 1928.]

Source: Quoted in the Foreign Language Information Service, *Interpreter Release Clip Sheet*, 5, 16, August 29, 1928.

* * *

In sharp contrast to these statements of support for restrictionism, and of the arguments cited above by the Ku Klux Klan and by Congressman Vaile [Documents 77 and 78, respectively], consider the impassioned statements made by Representative John J. O'Connor, a Democrat from New York, who spoke in opposition to several bills to revise immigration, including the 1929 law in Document 88, which were rushed through the House to the floor where they were passed. Representative O'Connor spoke in opposition to the pervasive spirit of intolerance and bigotry that he believed infused the United States to an alarming extent. Document 87 presents his speech to the House.

DOCUMENT 87: Statement of Congressman John J. O'Connor (February 15, 1929) (Re: Nativist Attitudes)

... Here today I want to discuss [the] spirit [that] I believe pervades our country to an alarming extent, and I want to discuss it without any thought of the past or recent events. I approach it looking to my country's future.

I believe that there are many people in this country today who fear that these United States of ours is the most intolerant, narrow-minded nation on the globe. I am not going to use any bromides about loving my country. That is the gratuitous mouthing of a demagogue. If I think my country is wrong, I propose to criticize it in its own citadel. I will defend it against attack from without, but I reserve the right to criticize it from within. I fear there is a spirit pervading our country today reflected in these immigration bills that is a menace to the country—a spirit of intolerance and bigotry not only to religion but to races.

Take this first bill before us today, the Box bill, relating to immigrants coming over our borders. It represents a spirit of superior intolerance to our neighbors on the north and south.

Oh, I do not like the spirit behind all these measures. There seems to be a spirit of bigotry and intolerance in America directed at the races of the rest of the world that surely is un-American. There are certain people in our country who believe that no other race on the face of the globe can be compared in education, in culture, in respectability to the inhabitants of the United States.

Let me state here, gentlemen, not in order to say anything sensational but to bring the truth forcibly before this body: Take a railroad train and go through the South, through the West, through the North, and in the outlying sections of the country. Look at what we call our own people, who have not had the opportunities of the people of the big cities. You will see American people of the Nordic races, you will see people whose forefathers were here 300 years ago, but you will see them in the lowest state of civilization. Is that the type to which you refer when you speak of the 'American blood' in America? Yes, you will see them in rags and tatters; you will see them unkempt, uncultured, uneducated, and uncouth.

Then I suggest you take an automobile and ride through the so-called foreign sections of the big cities and see these foreign people whom you hate so vehemently. Look at their children going to school in droves, seeking every opportunity for education, eager to acquire and to assimilate all the customs and habits of our country. See them going through the grammar schools, the high schools, to the colleges, from Harvard to Stanford, eager to become a part of America and of its institutions.

Let me make this assertion here, after due consideration, that I believe that the foreigners in this country today on the whole furnish better material for citizenship than many of the so-called American types living in the outlying sections of the country.

Oh, I do not consider that an attack on my country. Every one of these bills is directed at one or a few particular races. Why is that spirit rampant in America? It is daily commented upon in colleges in nearly every issue of the current magazines.

How long can demagogues in all political parties continue to preach this doctrine of saying 'America for Americans only'? It surely must result in damage to our country. It is a spirit of vindictiveness against anybody whose ancestors were not born here 300 years ago. I do not care what its effects is [sic] in elections, but I do care what effect it is going to have on our country in the future.

Where is this doctrine being preached? On the political stumps by demagogues. But, more than that, this doctrine of intolerance of 'American' narrow-mindedness is being preached in the pulpits of our churches, from the rostrums of small communities where people go to learn the thought of their communities. This doctrine is being propagated through the country by what I believe to be an ignorant, uneducated cleric party, and I have no hesitation in saying it.

I further have no hesitation in saying that the preaching of intolerance, and I am talking principally about intolerance to races, are [sic] the most uneducated of any profession in America; that the clergy of America are the least educated of any profession in America, but they have the most powerful influence of any profession in America. They get a smattering of general knowledge, a little ecclesiastical training, but no broad vision, and then they go into a community and try to shape the thought of that community and preach that the Italian, the Jew, the Irish, the German are not fit to live in America. That is the danger to America. The country is flooded I might say with 'Elmer Gantrys' preaching an un-American doctrine. Many Members are as afraid of an immigration bill as they are of a prohibition bill. They fear what will be said about them at home if they take a position in opposition to them. The preachers will attack them.

It is not a bad rule in approaching legislation to 'beware of the Greeks bearing gifts,' to see what spirit is behind the legislation.

These three bills are not needed now, but they will go to credit some man in their districts with having furthered the cause of intolerance. I am as much interested in the question of restrictive immigration as anybody else, but I do not want to see America become so narrow that it feels that these people of the Old World can not furnish something to this country. They have, in fact, furnished a great deal it has today. This smug nationalism is the greatest snobbishness that any nation could wear on its countenance in facing the rest of the world. Much we have in this country today we owe to the immigrants who came here from the Old World. Everyone knows the spirit behind the 1924 immigration law, directed principally at two peoples, the Italians and the Jews. That spirit of the Ku Klux Klan has continued to persist. The same spirit I believe pervades these three bills here today—the sanctimonious, self-opinionated, conceit that nobody else except the natural-born American, whatever he may be, is fitted to enjoy our present-day America.

I am not so much interested for the moment in what happens in immigration legislation. Perhaps immigration should be regulated. Perhaps we should close the door. But I do detest the giving of false economic reasons to disguise intolerance. I regret to see labor deceived and deluded by false economic reasons advanced, when I feel confident that the spirit behind the whole question is mean and contemptible and, worst of all, un-American.

Source: Congressional Record, as cited in the Foreign Language Information Service, *Interpreter Release Clip Sheet,* 6, 4, February 23, 1929.

* * *

In 1929 Congress passed several acts that amended the immigration and naturalization laws. Document 88 presents an amendment to the 1906 act.

DOCUMENT 88: Act of March 2, 1929: Registry Act

Sec. 1. That (a) the registry of aliens at ports of entry required by section 1 of the Act of June 29, 1906, . . . as amended, may be made as to any alien not ineligible to citizenship in whose case there is no record of admission for permanent residence, if such alien shall make a satisfactory showing to the Commissioner of Immigration and Naturalization . . . that he:

(1) Entered the United States prior to June 3, 1921;

(2) Has resided in the United States continuously since such entry;

(3) Is a person of good moral character;

(4) Is not subject to deportation. (45 Stat. 1512–1513; 8 U.S.C. 106a.)

(b) For each such record of registry made as herein authorized the alien shall pay a fee of $20. All fees collected under this section shall be deposited in the Treasury as miscellaneous receipts. . . .

Sec. 3. For the purposes of immigration laws and the naturalization of the alien, in respect of whom a record of registry has been authorized by section 1 of this Act, shall be deemed to have been lawfully admitted to the United States for permanent residence as of the date of his entry. (45 Stat. 1513; 8 U.S.C. 106c.). . . .

Sec. 6. . . . If an individual returns to the country of his allegiance and remains therein for a continuous period of more than six months and less than one year during the period immediately preceding the date of filing the petition for citizenship for which continuous residence is required as a condition precedent to admission to citizenship, the continuity of such residence shall be presumed to be broken, but such presumption may be overcome by the presentation of satisfactory evidence that such individual had a reasonable cause for not returning to the United States prior to the expiration of six months. . . .

Sec. 10. The Commissioner of Immigration and Naturalization is authorized and directed to prepare from the records in the custody of the Immigration and Naturalization Service a report upon those heretofore seeking citizenship to show by nationalities their relation to the numbers of annually arrived aliens and to the prevailing census populations of foreign born, their economic, vocational, and other classification, in statistical form, with analytical comment thereon, and to prepare such report annually thereafter.

Source: 45 Stat. 1512; 8 U.S.C. 106a.

* * *

President Hoover issued a presidential proclamation in 1929 that stipulated the new and permanent quotas for each fiscal year thereafter. Identified as the national origins system, it was based on the proportion of each nationality in the total U.S. population, determined by an analysis of the 1920 census. The overall ceiling for non–Western Hemisphere immigration was lowered to somewhat over 150,000.

DOCUMENT 89: President Herbert Hoover's Proclamation No. 1872, March 22, 1929: On the National Origin Immigration Quotas

Whereas it is provided in the Act of Congress approved May 26, 1924, entitled "An Act to limit the immigration of aliens to the United States, and for other purposes," as amended by Joint Resolution of March 4, 1927 . . . that—

The annual quota of any nationality for the fiscal year beginning July 1, 1929, and for each fiscal year thereafter, shall be a number which bears the same ratio to 150,000 as the number of inhabitants in continental United States in 1920 having that national origin (ascertained as hereinafter provided in this section) bears to the number of inhabitants in continental United States in 1920, but the minimum quota of any nationality shall be 100. Sec. 11 (b)(1924).

And whereas the Secretary of State, the Secretary of Commerce, and the Secretary of Labor have reported to the President that pursuant to the duty imposed and the authority conferred upon them in and by the Act approved May 26, 1924, they jointly have made the determination required by said law and fixed the quota of each respective nationality in accordance therewith to be as hereinafter set forth: . . .

NOW, THEREFORE, I HERBERT HOOVER, President of the United States of America, acting under and by virtue of the power in me vested by the aforesaid Act of Congress, do hereby proclaim and make known that the annual quota of each nationality for the fiscal year beginning July 1, 1929, and for each fiscal year thereafter, has been determined in accordance with the law to be, and shall be, as follows:

Country or Area	Quota	Country or Area	Quota
Afghanistan	100	Japan	100
Albania	100	Latvia	236
Andorra	100	Liberia	100
Arabian peninsula	100	Liechtenstein	100
Armenia	100	Lithuania	386
Australia	100	Luxemburg	100
Austria	1,413	Monaco	100
Belgium	1,304	Morocco	100
Bhutan	100	Muscat (Oman)	100
Bulgaria	100	Naura	100
Cameroon	100	Nepal	100
China	100	Netherlands	3,153
Czechoslovakia	2,874	New Zealand	100
Danzig	100	Norway	2,377
Denmark	1,181	New Guinea	100
Egypt	100	Palestine	100
Estonia	116	Persia	100
Ethiopia	100	Poland	6,524
Finland	569	Portugal	440
France	3,086	Ruanda and Urundi	100
Germany	25,957	Rumania	295
Great Britain and Northern Ireland	65,721	Russia, European and Asiatic	2,784
Greece	307	Samoa	100
Hungary	869	San Marino	100
Iceland	100		
India	100		
Iraq	100		
Irish Free State	17,853		
Italy	5,802		

Source: President's Proclamation 1872 of March 22, 1929. Orders, Proclamations and Treaties: 1092–93.

* * *

In an important Supreme Court case handed down on May 27, 1929, the Court ruled on a question of whether or not a person could be denied naturalization because of his or her political beliefs (in this case, pacifism). In the *United States v. Rosika Schwimmer* the court decided that a woman who refused to swear that she would fight to defend the Constitution of the United States, because of her beliefs in pacifism, could be denied her application for naturalization.

DOCUMENT 90: *United States v. Schwimmer* (May 27, 1929)

Mr. Justice Butler delivered the opinion of the Court:

Respondent filed a petition for naturalization in the District Court for the Northern District of Illinois. The court found her unable, without mental reservation, to take the prescribed oath of allegiance and not attached to the principles of the Constitution of the United States and not well disposed to the good order and happiness of the same, and it denied her application. The Circuit Court of Appeals reversed the decree and directed the District Court to grant respondent's petition.

The Naturalization Act of June 29, 1906, requires: "He [the applicant for naturalization] shall, before he is admitted to citizenship, declare on oath in open court . . . that he will support and defend the Constitution and laws of the United States against all enemies, foreign and domestic, and bear true faith and allegiance to the same . . ." "It shall be made to appear to the satisfaction of the court . . . that during that time [at least 5 years preceding the application] he has behaved as a man of good moral character, attached to the principles of the Constitution of the United States, and well disposed to the good order and happiness of the same. . . ."

Respondent was born in Hungary in 1877 and is a citizen of that country. She came to the United States in August, 1921, to visit and lecture, has resided in Illinois since the latter part of that month, declared her intention to become a citizen the following November, and filed petition for naturalization in September, 1926. . . . On a preliminary form, she stated that she understood the principles of and fully believed in our form of government and that she had read, and in becoming a citizen was willing to take, the oath of allegiance. Question 22 was this: "If necessary, are you willing to take up arms in defense of this country?"

She answered: "I would not take up arms personally."

She testified: "If ... the United States can compel its women citizens to take up arms in defense of the country—something no other civilized government has ever attempted—I would not be able to comply with this requirement of American citizenship. In this case I would recognize the right of the Government to deal with me as it is dealing with its male citizens who for conscientious reasons refuse to take up arms."

The district director of naturalization by letter called her attention to a statement made by her in private correspondence: "I am an uncompromising pacifist ... I have no sense of nationalism, only a cosmic consciousness of belonging to the human family." She answered that the statement in her petition demonstrated that she was an uncompromising pacifist. "Highly as I prize the privilege of American citizenship, I could not compromise my way into it by giving an untrue answer to question 22, though for all practical purposes I might have done so, as even men my age—I was 49 years old last September—are not called to take up arms. ... That "I have no nationalistic feeling" is evident from the fact that I wish to give up the nationality of my birth and to adopt a country which is based on principles and institutions more in harmony with my ideals. My 'cosmic consciousness of belonging to the human family' is shared by all those who believe that all human beings are the children of God."

Except for the eligibility to the Presidency, naturalized citizens stand on the same footing as do native born citizens. All alike owe allegiance to the Government, and the Government owes to them the duty of protection. These are reciprocal obligations and each is a consideration of the other. ... But aliens can acquire such equality only by naturalization according to the uniform rule prescribed by the Congress. They have no natural right to become citizens, but only that which is by statute conferred upon them. ...

That it is the duty of citizens by force of arms to defend our government against all enemies whenever necessary arises is a fundamental principle of the Constitution. ... Whatever tends to lessen the willingness of citizens to discharge their duty to bear arms in the country's defense detracts from the strength and safety of the Government. And their opinions and beliefs as well as their behavior indicating a disposition to hinder in the performance of that duty are subjects of inquiry under the statutory provisions governing naturalization and are of vital importance, for if all or a large number of citizens oppose such defense the "good order and happiness" of the United States can not long endure. ...

The language used by the respondent to describe her attitude in respect to the principles of the Constitution was vague and ambiguous; the burden is upon her to show what she meant and that her pacifism and lack of nationalistic sense did not oppose the principle that it is the duty of citizenship by force of arms when necessary to defend the country against all enemies, and that her opinions and beliefs would not prevent or impair the true faith and allegiance required by the Act. She failed to do so. The District Court was bound by the law to deny her application.

The decree of the Circuit Court of Appeals is reversed. The decree of the District Court is affirmed.

Source: 279 U.S. 644.

* * *

The U.S. government was not the only government concerned with the literacy of the immigrant in the 1920s. New York State, among others in the Northeast, required new voters to prove their ability to read and write English. Document 91 presents an article published by the Foreign Language Information Service describing the test and its effects during a six-year period.

DOCUMENT 91: New York's Literacy Test Law (1929)

In November 1921 New York State amended its constitution so as to require the new voters to prove their ability to read and write English. . . .

Unlike most of the other States which have legislated against the illiterate vote, New York decided not to test the would be voter's ability by requiring him to read from the federal or state constitution, which, it was estimated, might result in about 70 per cent failures. The test finally adopted, the New York Regents' Literacy test, just about represents the reading ability of a normal child in the fifth grade in New York public schools. Even so, it has disenfranchised a considerable number of new voters. For the years 1923 to 1927 inclusive the percentage of failures ranged between 16 and 21 but in 1928 there was a notable decrease, the failure for that year amounting only to 10 percent.

Meanwhile, the number of applicants for literacy certificates has greatly increased each year; especially in the years of Presidential election, 1924 and 1928, has the demand been great. The increase in new women voters is especially notable. In 1923, 78.6 per cent of those applying for certificate of literacy were men and 31.4 women; in 1928, the percentages were 64.28 and 35.72 respectively. The women also made a somewhat better showing in the test. Of the persons to whom certificates were issued in 1923, 75.9 percent were men and 24.1 percent were women; and in 1928 the percentages were 62.48 and 37.52 respectively.

	1923	1924	1925	1926	1927	1928
Total No. Applicants for Certificate of Literacy	33,795	76,280	39,457	43,855	55,276	163,299
Certificates Issued	28,402	64,024	33,956	37,000	48,605	150,194
(A) Number Issued after Literacy Test	19,806	48,886	25,358	28,108	37,002	116,760
(B) Number Issued on School Credentials	8,596	15,136	8,598	8,892	11,603	33,435
Total No. Denied Certificate of Literacy	5,393	12,256	5,501	6,855	6,671	13,104
Percent Denied	21.4	16.1	17.8	19.6	20.66	10.09

Source: Foreign Language Information Service, *Interpreter Release Clip Sheet*, 6, 8, April 24, 1929.

* * *

In 1931 Congress amended the naturalization law to allow the naturalization as citizens of persons who had previously lost their citizenship for residence abroad by becoming naturalized in some other country. This important act [Document 92] also took another step toward remedying the defects of the 1922 act that left American-born women married to aliens ineligible for citizenship still deprived of their own U.S. citizenship and unable to reacquire it. Five years later, some remaining features of the inequity affecting such women were corrected [Document 95]. Even then, American women who were not citizens by birth (e.g., older Hawaiian-born women) experienced problems in the event of the divorce or death of a spouse who was ineligible for citizenship.

DOCUMENT 92: Act of March 3, 1931: Naturalization of Persons Establishing Residence Abroad Prior to January 1, 1917; and Citizenship of Married Women

... Sec. 3. (a) Any person, born in the United States, who had established permanent residence in a foreign country prior to January 1, 1917, and who has heretofore lost his United States citizenship by becoming naturalized under the laws of such foreign country, may, if eligible to citizenship and if, prior to the enactment of this Act, he has been admitted to the United States for permanent residence, be naturalized upon full and complete compliance with all of the requirements of the naturalization laws, with the following exceptions:

(1) The five-year period of residence within the United States shall not be required;

(2) The declaration of intention may be made at any time after admission to the United States, and the petition may be filed at any time after the expiration of six months following the declaration of intention;

(3) If there is attached to the petition, at the time of filing, a certificate from a naturalization examiner stating that the petitioner has appeared before him for examination, the petition may be heard at any time after filing.

(b) After naturalization, such person shall have the same citizenship status as immediately preceding the loss of United States citizenship.

Sec. 4. (a) Section 3 of the Act entitled "An Act relative to the naturalization and citizenship of married women," approved September 22, 1922, as amended, is amended to read as follows:

Sec. (3). (a) A woman citizen of the United States shall not cease to be a citizen of the United States by reason of her marriage after this section, as amended, takes effect, unless she makes a formal renunciation of her citizenship before a court having jurisdiction over naturalization of aliens.

(b) Any woman who before this section, as amended, takes effect, has lost her United States citizenship by residence abroad after marriage to an alien or by marriage to an alien ineligible for citizenship may, if she has not acquired any other nationality by affirmative act, be naturalized in the manner prescribed in section 4 of this act, as amended. Any woman who was a citizen of the United States by birth shall not be denied naturalization under section 4 on account of her race.

(c) No woman shall be entitled to naturalization under section 4 of this Act, as amended, if her United States citizenship originated solely by reason of her marriage to a citizen of the United States or by reason of the acquisition of United States citizenship by her husband.

Source: 46 Stat. 1511; 8 U.S.C. 397.

* * *

In 1934 Congress amended the naturalization law. This Act was passed to clarify the citizenship status of children of U.S. citizens who were born outside the United States, the status of such children upon the naturalization of their parents, and the status of women who were citizens and married to a foreigner. Such women did not lose their citizenship status unless they specifically and formally renounced it.

DOCUMENT 93: Act of May 24, 1934: Citizenship of Children Born Abroad; Renunciation of Citizenship; Naturalization of Spouses of Citizens

Sec. 1. That section 1993 of the Revised Statutes is amended to read as follows:

Sec. 1993. Any child hereafter born out of the limits and jurisdiction of the United States, whose father or mother or both at the time of the birth of such child is a citizen of the United States, is declared to be a citizen of the United States; but the rights of citizenship shall not descend to any such child unless the citizen father or citizen mother, as the case may be, has resided in the United States previous to the birth of such child. In cases where one of the parents is an alien, the right of citizenship shall not descend unless the child comes to the United States and resides therein for at least five years continuously immediately previous to his eighteenth birthday, and unless, within six months after the child's twenty-first birthday, he or she shall take an oath of allegiance to the United States of America as prescribed by the Immigration and Naturalization Service. . . .

Sec. 3. A citizen of the United States may upon marriage to a foreigner make a formal renunciation of his or her United States citizenship before a court having jurisdiction over naturalization of aliens, but no citizen may make such renunciation in time of war, and if war shall be declared within one year after such renunciation then such renunciation shall be void. (48 Stat. 497; 8 U.S.C. 17a.)

Sec. 4. Section 2 of the Act entitled "An Act relative to the naturalization and citizenship of married women," approved September 22, 1922, is amended to read as follows:

Sec. 2. That an alien who marries a citizen of the United States, after passage of this Act, as here amended, or an alien whose husband or wife naturalized after passage of this Act, as here amended, shall not become a citizen of the United States by reason of such marriage or naturalization, but, if eligible for citizenship, he or she may be naturalized upon full and complete compliance with all requirements of the naturalization laws, with the following exceptions:

(a) No declaration of intention shall be required.

(b) In lieu of the five-year period of residence within the United States and the one-year of residence within the State or Territory where the naturalization court is held, he or she shall have resided continuously in the United States, Hawaii, Alaska, or Puerto Rico for at least three years immediately preceding the filing of the petition (48 Stat. 797; 8 U.S.C. 368).

Sec. 5. That a child born without the United States of alien parents shall be deemed a citizen of the United States by virtue of the naturalization of or resumption of American citizenship by the father or mother: Provided, That such naturalization or resumption shall take place during the minority of such child: And provided further, That the citizenship of such minor child shall begin five years after the time such minor child begins to reside permanently in the United States.

Source: 48 Stat. 797.

* * *

In 1935 Congress allowed for the naturalization of alien veterans, including veterans of Allied armies. In addition, Congress now corrected an injustice committed by the courts that denied Asian veterans of World War I the right to citizenship. The original legislation granted any alien who served honorably the right to apply for citizenship. The courts held that other laws, as well as the *Ozawa* (1922) and *Thind* (1923) decisions, precluded that right for aliens otherwise ineligible for citizenship. Following a long campaign conducted by Asian veterans, Congress explicitly accorded them the right of citizenship.

DOCUMENT 94: Acts of June 24, 1935: Naturalization of Alien Veterans, Including Veterans Ineligible to Citizenship

Be it enacted by the Senate and House of Representatives of the United States of America in Congress assembled, That subdivision (a) of section

1 of the Act entitled "An Act to further amend the immigration laws, and for other purposes," approved May 25, 1932 . . . shall, as herein amended, continue in force and effect to include petitions for citizenship filed prior to May 25, 1937, with any court having naturalization jurisdiction: Provided, That for the purposes of this Act clause (1) of subdivision (a) of section 1 of the aforesaid Act . . . is amended by striking out the words "all such period" and in lieu thereof inserting the words "the five years immediately preceding the filing of his petition."

Sec. 2. The provisions of section 1 of this Act are hereby extended to include any alien lawfully admitted to the United States for permanent residence who departed therefrom between August 1, 1914 and April 5, 1917, or who, having been denied entry into the military forces and naval forces of the United States, departed therefrom . . . for the purpose of serving and actually served prior to November 11, 1918, in the military forces of any of the countries allied with the United States in the World War and was subsequently discharged from such service under honorable circumstances . . .

Act of June 24, 1935 (49 Stat. 397)—Naturalization of Alien Veterans Ineligible to Citizenship

Be it enacted by the Senate and House of Representatives of the United States of America in Congress assembled, That notwithstanding the racial limitations contained within section 2169 of the Revised Statutes of the United States, as amended . . . and within section 14 of the Act of May 6, 1882, as amended . . . any alien veteran of the World War heretofore ineligible to citizenship because not a free white person or of African nativity . . . may be naturalized under this Act if he—

(a) Entered the service of the armed forces of the United States prior to November 11, 1918;

(b) Actually rendered service with the armed forces between April 6, 1917, and November 11, 1918;

(c) Received an honorable discharge from such service for any reason other than his alienage;

(d) Resumed his previous permanent residence continuously in the United States or any Territory thereof; and

(e) Has maintained a permanent residence continuously since the date of discharge and is now a permanent resident of the United States or any Territory thereof; upon compliance with all requirements of the naturalization laws, except—

(f) No certificate of arrival and no declaration of intention shall be required;

(g) No additional residence shall be required before the filing of petition for certificate of citizenship; and

(h) The petition for certificate of citizenship shall be filed with a court having naturalization jurisdiction prior to January 1, 1937.

Source: 49 Stat. 395.

* * *

In 1936 Congress restored citizenship to women who previously had lost such status solely by reason of her prior marriage to an alien.

DOCUMENT 95: Act of June 25, 1936: Repatriation of Native-Born Women Who Lost Citizenship by Marriage

Be it enacted by the Senate and House of Representatives of the United States of America in Congress assembled, That hereafter a woman, being a native-born citizen, who has or is believed to have lost her United States citizenship solely by reason of her marriage prior to September 22, 1922, to an alien, and whose marital status with such alien has or shall have terminated* or who has resided continuously in the United States since the date of such marriage, shall be deemed to be a citizen of the United States to the same extent as though her marriage to said alien had taken place on or after September 22, 1922: *Provided*, however, That no such woman shall have or claim any rights as a citizen of the United States until she shall have duly taken the oath of allegiance as prescribed in section 4 of the Act approved June 29, 1906.

Source: 49 Stat. 1917.

* * *

In 1937 Congress granted citizenship status to certain Panama Canal zone residents—the children of U.S. citizens who were born in the zone on or after February 1904 (when the zone became U.S. territory),

*The following fifteen words were added by Act of July 2, 1940 (54 Stat. 715).

or whose Panamanian parents were employed by the U.S. government or by the Panama Railroad company after February 1904.

DOCUMENT 96: Act of August 4, 1937: Citizenship Status of Certain Persons Born in the Canal Zone and the Republic of Panama

Be it enacted by the Senate and House of Representatives of the United States of America in Congress assembled, That any person born in the Canal Zone on or after February 26, 1904, and whether before or after the effective date of this Act, whose father or mother or both at the time of the birth of such person was or is a citizen of the United States, is declared to be a citizen of the United States.

Sec. 2. Any person born in the Republic of Panama on or after February 26, 1904, and whether before or after the effective date of this Act, whose father or mother or both at the time of the birth of such person was or is a citizen of the United States employed by the Government of the United States or by the Panama Railroad Company, is declared to be a citizen of the United States.

Source: 50 Stat. 1917.

* * *

Although not actually directed at naturalized citizens, the following legislation establishing Citizenship Day was used to promote naturalization and American patriotism in general. Citizenship Day became a popular event, especially during the 1940s.

DOCUMENT 97: Act of May 3, 1940: To Dignify and Emphasize the Significance of Citizenship

Whereas some two million young men and women in the United States each year reach the age of twenty-one years; and

Whereas it is desirable that the sovereign citizens of our Nation be prepared for the responsibilities and impressed with the significance of their status in our self-governing Republic:

Therefore be it:

Resolved by the Senate and House of Representatives of the United States of America in Congress assembled, That the third Sunday in May each year be, and hereby is, set aside as Citizenship Day and that the President of the United States is hereby authorized and requested to issue annually a proclamation setting aside that day as a public occasion for the recognition of all who, by coming of age or naturalization, have attained the status of citizenship, and the day shall be designated as "I Am An American Day."

That the civil and educational authorities of States, counties, cities, and towns be, and they are hereby urged to make plans for the proper observance of this day and for the full instruction of future citizens in their responsibilities and opportunities as citizens of the United States and of the States and localities in which they reside.

Nothing herein shall be construed as changing, or attempting to change, the time or mode of any of the many commendable observances of similar nature now being held from time to time, or periodically, but, to the contrary, such practices are hereby praised and encouraged.

Sec. 2. Either at the time of the rendition of the decree of naturalization or at such other time as the judge may fix, the judge or someone designated by him shall address the newly naturalized citizen upon the form and genius of our Government and the privileges and responsibilities of citizenship; it being the intent and purpose of this section to enlist the aid of the judiciary, in cooperation with civil and educational authorities, and patriotic organizations in a continuous effort to dignify and emphasize the significance of citizenship.

Source: 54 Stat. 178.

* * *

In 1940 President Franklin D. Roosevelt issued an executive order concerning documents that would thereafter be required of all aliens entering the United States and ordered the transfer of the Immigration and Naturalization Service to the Department of Justice where it has remained ever since.

DOCUMENT 98: Executive Order No. 8430, June 5, 1940: Documents Required of Aliens Entering the United States and Transfer of the INS (Immigration and Naturalization Service) to the Department of Justice

By virtue of and pursuant to the authority vested in me by the act of May 22, 1918 . . . I hereby prescribe the following regulations pertaining to documents required of aliens entering the United States (which regulations shall be applicable to Chinese and to Philippine citizens who are not citizens of the United States except as otherwise provided by special laws and regulations governing the entrance of such persons):

Part I

1. Non-immigrants must present unexpired passports or official documents of the nature of passports issued by the governments of the countries to which they owe their allegiance or other travel documents showing their origin and identity . . . and valid passport visas, except in the following cases:

(a) A non-immigrant alien coming within a category and domiciled in a country, island, or territory of the Western Hemisphere . . . if passing through the United States or entering the United States temporarily. . . . [Subsections (b) through (d) and sections 2 through 5 restate prior regulations.]

Part II

1. Immigrants must present unexpired passports, or official documents in the nature of passports . . . and valid visas granted by the consular officers of the United States in accordance with the requirements of the Immigration Act of 1924, except in the following cases:

[Subsections (a) through (f) and sections 2 through 4 restate prior regulations.]

Part III

The Executive Secretary of the Panama Canal is hereby authorized to issue passports, visas, transit certificates, limited entry certificates, and immigration visas to aliens coming to the United States from the Canal Zone. The Governor of American Samoa is hereby authorized to issue passport visas . . . to aliens coming to the United States. The Governor of Guam is hereby authorized to issue passport visas . . . to aliens coming to the United States. . . .

Part VII

This order shall take effect immediately and shall supersede and cancel the provisions of Executive Order 8029 of December 27, 1938 entitled "Documents Required of Aliens Entering the United States". . . .

Reorganization Plan No. V—Immigration and Naturalization Service

Sec. 1. Transfer of Immigration and Naturalization Service—The Immigration and Naturalization Service of the Department of Labor (including the Office of the Commissioner of Immigration and Naturalization) and its functions are transferred to the Department of Justice and shall be administered under the direction and supervision of the Attorney General. All functions and powers of the Secretary of Labor relating to the administration of the Immigration and Naturalization Service and its functions or to the administration of the immigration and naturalization laws are transferred to the Attorney General. In the event of disagreement between the head of any department or agency and the Attorney General concerning the interpretation or application of any law pertaining to immigration, naturalization, or nationality, final determination shall be made by the Attorney General. . . .

This order shall take effect immediately and shall supersede the provisions of Executive Order No. 7865 of April 12, 1938 entitled, "Documents Required of Aliens Entering the United States on Airships," or Executive Order No. 7797 of January 26, 1938, entitled, "Documents Required of Bona Fide Alien Seamen Entering the United States."

Source: Executive Order No. 8430 of June 5, 1940. Orders, Proclamations, and Treaties: 1133–1137.

* * *

Concerned about the outbreak of World War II and the number of aliens remaining noncitizens, the government decided that the need for greater security and knowledge of the exact number and whereabouts of such persons necessitated a formal system of registration. It required prompt notification of address changes and would come to include, until 1980, annual registration. Implementation in the 1940s revealed many more aliens present than the government had calculated.

DOCUMENT 99: Act of June 28, 1940: Alien Registration Act of 1940

Be it enacted by the Senate and House of Representatives of the United States of America in Congress assembled, That:

Title I

Interference With the Military or Naval Forces of the United States

Sec. 1. (a) It shall be unlawful for any person, with intent to interfere with, impair, or influence the loyalty, morale, or discipline of the military or naval forces of the United States— . . . .

Title II

Sec. 20. Section 19 of the Immigration Act of February 5, 1917 . . . as amended, is amended by inserting, after "Sec. 19," and by adding to the end of such section the following new subsections:

Additional Deportable Classes of Aliens

(b) Any alien of any of the classes of aliens specified in this subsection in addition to aliens who are deportable under other provisions of the law, shall, upon warrant of the Attorney General, be taken into custody and deported:

(1) Any alien who, at the time within five years after entry, shall have, knowingly and for gain, encouraged, induced, assisted, abetted, or aided any other alien to enter or to try to enter the United States in violation of law.

(2) Any alien who, at any time after entry, shall have more than one occasion, knowingly and for gain, encouraged, induced, assisted, abetted, or aided any other alien or aliens to enter or to try to enter the United States in violation of the law.

(3) Any alien who, at any time after entry, shall have been convicted of possessing or carrying in violation of any law any weapon which shoots or is designed to shoot automatically or semiautomatically more than one shot without manual reloading, by a single function of the trigger, or a weapon commonly called a sawed-off shotgun.

(4) Any alien who, at any time within five years after entry, shall have been convicted of violating the provisions of title I of the Alien Registration Act, 1940. . . .

(5) Any alien who, at any time after entry, shall have been convicted of more than once violating the provisions of title I of the Alien Registration Act of 1940. . . .

(c) In the case of any alien (other than one to whom subsection (d) is applicable) who is deportable under any law of the United States and who has proved good moral character for the preceding five years, the Attorney General may (1) permit such alien to depart the United States to any country of his choice at his own expense, in lieu of deportation, or (2) suspend deportation if such alien is not racially inadmissible or ineligible for naturalization in the United States if he finds such deportation would result in serious economic detriment to a citizen or legally resident alien who is the spouse, parent, or minor child of such deportable alien. . . .

Title III

Sec. 30. No visa shall hereafter be issued to any alien seeking to enter the United States unless said alien has been registered and fingerprinted in duplicate. One copy of the registration and fingerprint record shall be retained by the consul. The second copy shall be attached to the alien's visa and shall be taken up by the examining immigrant inspector at the port of arrival of the alien in the United States and forwarded to the Department of Justice, at Washington, District of Columbia.

Any alien seeking to enter the United States who does not present a visa . . . a reentry permit, or a border-crossing identification card shall be excluded from admission to the United States. . . .

Sec. 31. (a) It shall be the duty of every alien now or hereafter in the United States, who (1) is fourteen years of age or older, (2) has not been registered and fingerprinted under section 30, and (3) remains in the United States for thirty days or longer, to apply for registration and to be fingerprinted before the expiration of such thirty days. . . .

(b) It shall be the duty of every parent or legal guardian of any alien now or hereafter in the United States, who (1) is less than fourteen years of age, (2) has not been registered under section 30, and (3) remains in the United States for thirty days or longer, to apply for the registration of such alien before the expiration of such thirty days. Whenever any alien attains his fourteenth birthday in the United States he shall, within thirty days thereafter, apply in person for registration and to be fingerprinted. . . .

Sec. 33. (b) It shall be the duty of every postmaster, with such assistance as shall be provided by the Commissioner, to register and fingerprint any applicant for registration and fingerprinting under such section, and for such purposes to designate appropriate space in the local post office for such registration and fingerprinting. Every postmaster shall forward promptly to the Department of Justice, at Washington, District of Columbia, the registration and fingerprint record of every alien registered and fingerprinted by him. . . .

Sec. 34 (c) Every person required to apply for the registration of himself or another under this title shall submit under oath the information required for such registration. . . .

Sec. 35.* Any alien required to be registered under this time who is a resident of the United States shall notify the Commissioner in writing of each change of residence and new addresses within five days from the date of such change. Any other alien required to be registered under this title shall notify the Commissioner in writing of his address at the expiration of each three months' period of residence in the United States. In the case of an alien for whom a parent or legal guardian is required to apply for registration, the notices required by this section shall be given by such parent or legal guardian.

Source: 54 Stat. 670; 8 U.S.C. 451–460.

* * *

In October 1940 Congress revised extensively the naturalization act in a new comprehensive law that reenacted and consolidated prior laws dealing with the naturalization process. This statute goes on for 95

---

*As amended by Act of September 22, 1950 (64 Stat. 987).

pages in the statutes, and is very briefly summarized with a few of the changed procedures highlighted.

DOCUMENT 100: Act of October 14, 1940 (Codifying All Previous Naturalization Laws)

Be it enacted by the Senate and House of Representatives of the United States of America in Congress assembled, That the nationality laws of the United States are revised and codified as follows:

[Chapter I, Sec. 101 defines all the major terms used in the act.]

Chapter II—Nationals and Citizens of the United States at Birth

Sec. 201. The following shall be nationals and citizens of the United States at birth:

(a) A person born in the United States, and subject to the jurisdiction thereof;

[Subsections (b) through (i) codify all other cases in which someone not born in the continental United States is nonetheless native born; for example, born in Territories and outlying possessions of parents who are citizens, as variously revised and amended, including sections regarding Puerto Rico, the Panama Canal Zone, and so on.]

[Sec. 204. Covers persons born outside the United States who are nationals but not citizens of the United States at birth—illegitimate children, foundlings, and so on—and makes special provisions for persons born in Guam.]

Chapter III—Nationality Through Naturalization

[The law elaborately codifies all the existing statutes that had established the rules and regulations for naturalization, including which courts have jurisdiction, the forms to be used, and so on in subsections 301 (a) through (d).]

ELIGIBILITY FOR NATURALIZATION

Sec. 302. The right of a person to become a naturalized citizen of the United States shall not be denied or abridged because of sex or because such person is married.

Racial Restrictions Upon Naturalization

Sec. 303. The right to become a naturalized citizen under the provisions of this Act shall extend only to white persons, persons of African nativity or descent, descendants of races indigenous to the Western Hemisphere: *Provided,* That nothing in this section shall prevent the naturalization of native-born Filipinos having the honorable service in the United States Army, Navy, Marine Corps, or Coast Guard as specified in section 324, nor of former citizens of the United States who are otherwise eligible to naturalization under the provisions of section 317.

304. No person except as otherwise provided in this Act shall hereafter be naturalized as a citizen of the United States upon his own petition who cannot speak the English language. This requirement shall not apply to any person physically unable to comply therewith, if otherwise qualified to be naturalized.

Sec. 305. No person shall hereafter be naturalized as a citizen of the United States—

(a) Who advises, advocates, or teaches, or who is a member of or affiliated with any organization, association, society, or group that advises, advocates, or teaches opposition to all organized government; or

(b) Who believes in, advises, advocates, or teaches, or who is a member of or affiliated with any organization, association, society, or group that believes in, advises, advocates, or teaches—

(1) the overthrow by force or violence of the Government of the United States or all forms of law; or (2) the duty, necessity, or propriety of the unlawful assaulting or killing of any officer or officers . . . of the Government of the United States or any other organized government, because of his or their official character; or (3) the unlawful damage, injury, or destruction of property; or (4) sabotage.

(c) Who writes, publishes, or causes to be written or published . . . any written or printed matter advising, advocating, or teaching all opposition to all organized government. . . .

(d) Who is a member of or affiliated with any organization . . . that writes, circulates . . . [etc.] any written or printed matter in the character described in subdivision (c). . . .

The provision of this section shall be applicable to any applicant for naturalization who at any time within a period of ten years immediately preceding the filing of the petition for naturalization is, or has been, found to be within any of the clauses (classes) enumerated in this section, notwithstanding that at the time petition is filed he may not be included in such classes.

Sec. 306. Any person who, at the time during which the United States has been or shall be at war, deserted or shall desert the military or naval forces of the United States, or who, having duly enrolled, departed, or shall depart from the jurisdiction of the district in which enrolled, or went or shall go beyond the limits of the United States, with intent to avoid any draft into the military or naval service, lawfully ordered, shall, upon conviction thereof by a court martial, be ineligible to become a citizen of the United States; and such deserters shall be forever incapable of holding any office or trust or of profit under the United States, or of exercising any rights of citizens thereof.

Sec. 307. (a) No person, except as hereinafter provided in this Act, shall be naturalized unless the petitioner, (1) immediately preceding the date of filing petition . . . has resided continuously in the United States for at least five years and within the State in which the petitioner has resided . . . for at least six months. . . . [The section then provides for when exceptions of continuous residence is allowed.]

Sec. 309. (a) As to each period and place of residence in the State in which the petitioner resides . . . during the entire period of at least six months immediately preceding the date of the filing of the petition, there shall be included in the petition the affidavits of at least two credible witnesses, citizens of the United States, stating that each has personally known the petitioner to have been a resident at such place and for such period, and that the petitioner is and during all such periods has been a person of good moral character, attached to the principles of the Constitution of the United States, and well disposed to the good order and happiness of the United States.

317. (a) A person who was a citizen of the United States and who prior to September 22, 1922, lost United States citizenship by marriage to an alien or by the spouse's loss of United States citizenship, and any person who lost United States citizenship on or after September 22, 1922, by marriage to an alien ineligible to citizenship, may, if no other nationality was acquired by affirmative act other than such marriage, be naturalized upon compliance with all requirements of the naturalization laws. . . .

(b) (1) From and after the effective date of this Act, a woman who was a citizen of the United States at birth, and who has or is believed to have lost her United States citizenship solely by reason of her marriage prior to September 22, 1922, to an alien, and whose marital status with such alien has or shall have terminated, if no other nationality was acquired by affirmative act other than such marriage, shall, from and after the taking of the oath of allegiance prescribed by . . . this Act, be deemed to be a citizen of the United States to the same extent as though her marriage to said alien had taken place on or after September 22, 1922. . . .

(c) A person who shall have been a citizen of the United States and also a national of a foreign state, and who shall have lost his citizenship of the United States under provisions of section 401 (c) of this Act, shall be entitled to the benefits of the provisions of subsection (a) of this section, except that contained in subdivision (2) thereof. Such person, if abroad, may enter the United States as a non-quota immigrant, for the purpose of recovering his citizenship, upon compliance with the provisions of the Immigration Acts of 1917 and 1924. . . .

318. (b). No former citizen of the United States, expatriated through the expatriation of such person's parent or parents, shall be obliged to

comply with the requirements of the immigration laws, if he has not acquired the nationality of another country by any affirmative act other than the expatriation of his parent or parents, and if he has come to or shall come to the United States before reaching the age of twenty-five years. . . .

[The act slightly revises some of the registry and penal provisions and reenacts the procedural and administrative provisions of prior naturalization laws.]

Source: 54 Stat. 1137.

* * *

President Franklin D. Roosevelt issued a proclamation in November 1941 imposing strict controls on persons entering or leaving the country or its territories while the United States was at war.

DOCUMENT 101: President's Proclamation No. 2523, November 14, 1941: Control of Persons Entering and Leaving the United States

. . . I, FRANKLIN D. ROOSEVELT, President of the United States of America, acting under and by virtue of the authority vested in me set forth above, do hereby find and publically proclaim and declare that the interests of the United States require that restrictions and prohibitions, in addition to those otherwise provided by law, shall be imposed upon the departure of persons from and their entry into the United States . . . and I make the following rules, regulations, and orders which shall remain in force and effect until otherwise ordered by me:

(1) After the effective date of the rules and regulations hereinafter authorized, no citizen of the United States or person who owes allegiance to the United States shall depart from or enter, or attempt to depart from or enter, the United States . . . unless he bears a valid passport issued by the Secretary of State . . . or unless he comes within the provisions of such exceptions or fulfills such conditions as may be prescribed in rules and regulations which the Secretary of State is hereby authorized to prescribe in execution of . . . orders herein prescribed. Seamen are included in the classes of persons to whom this paragraph applies.

(2) No alien shall depart from or attempt to depart from the United States unless he is in possession of a valid permit to depart issued by the Secretary of State . . . of such purpose, or unless he is exempted from obtaining a permit, in accordance with the rules and regulations which the

Secretary of State, with the concurrence of the Attorney General, is hereby authorized to prescribe in execution. . . .

[The proclamation, in nine subsections, grants the Attorney General and the Secretary of State or agencies thereunder to prescribe rules and regulations regarding entrance and departure.]

Source: President's Proclamation No. 2523 of November 14, 1941.

* * *

On December 7, 1941, Japan attacked the U.S. Naval base at Pearl Harbor, on Oahu, Hawaii, and Congress declared war. President Roosevelt immediately thereafter issued a series of proclamations concerning the control of enemy aliens, including Japanese, German, and Italian enemy aliens, which are briefly excerpted in Document 102.

DOCUMENT 102: President's Proclamations of December 7, 8, 1941 (Concerning Control of Various Alien Enemies)

Proclamation 2525: Control of Japanese Alien Enemies

. . .

NOW, THEREFORE, I, FRANKLIN D. ROOSEVELT, as President of the United States and Commander in Chief of the Army and Navy of the United States, do hereby make public proclamation to all to whom it may concern that an invasion has been perpetrated upon the territory of the United States by the Empire of Japan.

Conduct To Be Observed by Alien Enemies

And, acting under and by virtue of the authority vested in me by the Constitution of the United States and the said sections of the United States Code, I do hereby further declare and direct the conduct to be observed on the part of the United States on all natives, citizens, denizens or subjects of the Empire of Japan being of the age of fourteen years and upwards who shall be within the United States . . . who for the purpose of this Proclamation and under such sections of the United States Code are termed enemy aliens, shall be as follows:

All alien enemies are enjoined to preserve the peace towards the United States and to refrain from crimes against the public safety, and from violating the laws of the United States and the States and Territories thereof; and to refrain from actual hostility or giving information, aid or comfort to the enemies of the United States or interfering by word or deed with the defense of the United States or the political processes and public opinion thereof; and to comply strictly with the regulations which are hereby or which may be from time to time promulgated by the President.

All alien enemies shall be liable to restraint . . . as prescribed in the regulations duly promulgated by the President.

Duties and Authority of the Attorney General and the Secretary of War

And, pursuant to the authority vested in me, I hereby charge the Attorney General with the duty of executing all regulations hereinafter contained regarding the conduct of alien enemies within continental United States, Puerto Rico, and the Virgin Islands and Alaska, and the Secretary of War with the duty of executing the regulations which are hereinafter set forth and which may be hereafter adopted regarding the conduct of alien enemies in the Canal Zone, the Hawaiian Islands and the Philippine Islands. Each of them is specifically directed to cause the apprehension of such alien enemies as in the judgment of each are subject to apprehension or deportation under such regulations. . . . All such agents, agencies, officers and departments are hereby granted full authority for all acts done by them in the execution of such regulations when acting by direction of the Attorney General or the Secretary of War, as the case may be.

Regulations

And, pursuant to the authority vested in me, I hereby declare and establish the following regulations which I find necessary in the premises and for the public safety:

(1) No alien enemy shall be found within the Canal Zone and no alien enemy shall enter or leave the Hawaiian Islands or the Philippine Islands except under such regulations as the Secretary of War shall from time to time prescribe. Any alien enemy found [therein] in violation of such regulation . . . may be immediately apprehended by authority of the Military Commanders of each such territory . . . and detained until it is determined, under regulations to be prescribed by the Secretary of War, whether any such alien enemy should be permanently interned following which such alien enemy shall either be released, released on bond, or permanently interned, as the case may be.

(2) The exercise of the power to prescribe restricted areas and the power of arrest, detention and internment of alien enemies . . . shall be under the jurisdiction of the Military Commanders of each territory, acting under such regulations as the Secretary of War shall hereafter prescribe.

(3) No alien enemy shall enter or leave Alaska, Puerto Rico, or the Virgin Islands except under such regulation as the Attorney General shall from time to time prescribe. Any alien enemy found [therein] shall be immediately apprehended . . . and detained until it is determined, under the regulations to be prescribed by the Attorney General, whether any such

alien enemy shall either be released, released under bond, or permanently detained, as the case may be.

(4) The Military Commanders in Alaska and Puerto Rico and the Naval Commander in the Virgin Islands shall have the power to prescribe restricted areas.

(5) No enemy alien shall have in his possession or custody or control at any time or place or use or operate any of the following enumerated items: firearms, weapons or implements of war or component parts thereof, ammunition, bombs, explosives or material used in the manufacture of explosives, short-wave radio receiving sets, transmitting sets, signal devices, codes or ciphers, cameras, papers, documents or books in which there may be invisible writing, photograph, sketch, picture, drawing, map or graphic representation of any military or naval installation or equipment ... or device or thing intended to be used in the combat equipment of the land or naval forces of the United States or of any military or naval post, camp or station. All such property ... shall be subject to seizure and forfeiture.

(6) No alien enemy shall undertake any air flight or ascend into the air in any airplane, aircraft or balloon of any sort ... except that travel by an alien enemy in airplane or aircraft may be authorized by the Attorney General ... or the Secretary of War ... under such regulations as they shall prescribe.

(7) Alien enemies deemed dangerous to the public peace or safety of the United States ... are subject to summary apprehension. ... Alien enemies arrested shall be subject to confinement in such place of detention as may be directed by the officers responsible for the execution of these regulations and for the arrest, detention and internment of alien enemies in each case ... and there confined until he shall have received such permit as the Attorney General or the Secretary of War ... shall prescribe.

(8) No alien enemy shall land in, enter, or leave or attempt to land in, enter, or leave the United States, except under the regulations prescribed ... and the regulations promulgated thereunder or any proclamation or regulation promulgated thereafter.

(9) Whenever the Attorney General ... or the Secretary of War ... deems it necessary for the public safety and protection, to exclude alien enemies from a designated area, surrounding any fort, camp, arsenal, airport, landing field, ... etc., then no alien enemy shall be found within such area or the immediate vicinity thereof. Any alien enemy found within such area ... shall be subject to summary apprehension and to be dealt with as herein above prescribed.

(10) With respect to the continental United States, Alaska, Puerto Rico and the Virgin Islands, an alien enemy shall not change his place of abode or occupation or otherwise travel or move from place to place without full compliance with any such regulations as the Attorney Gen-

eral may . . . make and declare . . . as he may deem necessary in the premises and for the public safety.

(11) With respect to the Canal Zone, the Hawaiian Islands and the Philippine Islands, an alien enemy shall not change his place of abode or occupation or otherwise travel or move from place to place without full compliance with any such regulations as the Secretary of War may, from time to time, make and declare . . . as he may deem necessary in the premises and for the public safety.

(12) No alien enemy shall enter or be found in or upon any highway, waterway, airway, railway, railroad, subway, public utility, building, place or thing not open and accessible to the public generally, and not generally used by the public.

(13) No alien enemy shall be a member or an officer of, or affiliated with, any organization, group or assembly hereafter designated by the Attorney General. . . .

Proclamation 2526: Control of German Alien Enemies

[This proclamation repeats the regulations and restrictions as described above in 2525 and simply applies the same to German alien enemies.]

Proclamation 2527: Control of Italian Alien Enemies

[This proclamation repeats the same regulations and restrictions as in 2525 applied to Italians.]

Source: President's Proclamations Nos. 2525–2527 of December 7–8, 1941.

* * *

The entrance of the United States into World War II after the surprise attack on Pearl Harbor naturally elicited a great deal of patriotic fervor among American-born citizens as well as naturalized American citizens who had immigrated to the nation from all over the world and had proudly adopted America as their new homeland. The foreign language press in the United States strongly supported the war effort. Document 103 presents a small sample of press releases from various foreign-language newspapers in the days immediately following the attack on Pearl Harbor that exemplify the patriotic attitudes of various national-origin groups of naturalized American citizens.

DOCUMENT 103: Sample of Foreign Language Newspapers' Reactions to the Outbreak of World War II, 1941

French: *L'Avenir National*, Manchester, New Hampshire, December 8, 1941:

The die is cast . . . it is war! What we have foreseen, foretold and feared has taken place under the most treacherous and enraging circumstances. . . . United in struggle, in battle and in defense, we shall also be united in victory though it may demand great sacrifices and even our blood. Our promises of allegiance and faithfulness to the American flag are not vain words. That flag, now attacked, we shall defend unto death. And we are all under the orders of our chiefs for that battle and the victory which God will surely give to those who fight for justice, order and true liberty.

German: *New Yorker Staats Zeitung und Herod*, New York City, New York, December 12, 1941:

Ever since Adolph Hitler took over Germany in 1933 and proceeded to fasten himself on Europe, it was inevitable that we would either have to accept him, or go to war. Today America accepts his challenge. We will fight until this danger to our way of life is eliminated.

For our readers and for the German-American element, there is no doubt as to where their course lies. It lies in this country of which they are part; to which they have contributed so much, and to which they have given full allegiance at all times.

So we face the struggle ahead of us with strong hearts and the knowledge that our America is worth fighting for, worth dying for. America today fights three enemies—Hitler, Mussolini, and the Japs. Their leadership, their ideology and their methods are similar. They seek to conquer. They will fail.

German: *America Herald*, Winona, Minnesota, December 10, 1941:

As in the World War of 1914–1918, the German-Americans have undoubtedly proved that they are fully aware of their duties as citizens and as part of the American nation toward their American homeland. And they will fulfill their duties in a united front in war even if their country of birth has entered war against America. When the nation is at war there can be no longer any misunderstanding about united duty and the united will of the nation. Every personal consideration must be put aside and every one must stand behind the Government which was chosen by the people and which represents the will of the people.

Italian: *Il Progresso*, New York City, New York, December 12, 1941:

There is only one reality which predominates: we are at war, and a simple, supreme duty guides us—loyalty to America and its government. The American people of Italian origin who are loyal to the United States need have no fear because the Government will protect them in their right and liberty and justice.

Every human sentiment in our hearts for the land which gave us birth cannot distract us from our precise and intelligent duty which is to confirm without the slightest shadow of mental restriction our full loyalty which is the fruit of our appreciation and affection for America of which we are proud citizens and where we have been able to carry on our careers, create our families and where we gave birth to our children who are today as always ready to serve their country.

Hungarian: *Az Ember*, New York City, New York, December 13, 1941:

It is with a painful heart that we say "Farewell" to the happy, peaceful days granted to us in this great and beautiful country. But at the same time we close our ranks behind our President and are awaiting his orders. No people in history were more united in purpose and determination than the people of the United States are today against the yellow wolves of Asia and their Nazi and Italian cohorts.

All of us, native and foreign-born Americans, not only offer, but demand our share in the struggle ahead of us in the heroic defense of our land. We must say a few words about Americans of Hungarian birth, and those unfortunates who have been driven out of their homes by the Fascist epidemic raging in Europe, and who have been given shelter on these shores of American generosity. In firm conviction do we assure American public opinion that Americans of Hungarian birth are as loyal to this land as the native sons of America. We may also affirm the many scores of Hungarian citizens, who are thankful for American hospitality which in many cases saved their very lives, and are equally grateful and loyal to our national purpose. Many thousands of Americans of Hungarian birth in the mines and factories all over the land wish to be in the front lines of national defense.

Japanese: *Doho*, Los Angeles, California, December 9, 1941:

Nothing could be more shameless, cowardly, unwarranted and unjustified than Japan's attack on the United States. We must now fight for the complete defeat of militaristic Japan. To join in the defense of America, to fight against Japan now, is to fight not only to defeat of the dictator clique of Japan, but also for the complete defeat of Hitlerite Germany.

Polish: *Howy Swiat*, New York City, New York, December 11, 1941:

Our mines and factories, our industry and technical efficiency will bring us advantage. The last blow is important, not the first. The knock-out punch will not be delivered by the excited and the angry, but by those who will have enough strength, after a long fight, to strike with their fists and draw the vital blood.

Polish: *Dziennick Zwiazkowy*, Chicago, Illinois, December 8, 1941:

Now the duty of all Americans of Polish descent and of all Poles re-siding in the United States is to make every effort to bring victory to the United States, to defeat the enemy who wants to deprive us and the future generations of all our achievements.

Russian: *Novoye Russkoye Slovo*, New York City, New York, December 9, 1941:

Japan cowardly and treacherously attacked our country, the U.S.— Long live the United States.

The die is cast. At this moment our valiant Navy and Aviation hero-ically defend the existence of our adoptive fatherland, our great and glorious nation, our free country, the United States. Our army is being mobilized. Our whole country is preparing itself for the decisive battle for honor, freedom, national independence and life.

We, Russian people in America, are happy to see that the ways of two great nations are merging into one common way and to know that by defending the United States we are defending Russia and by defending Russia we are defending the United States, while by defending both we are defending the freedom of the whole world.

Slovak: *Katolicky Sokol*, Passaic, New Jersey, December 10, 1941:

We are all Americans and regardless of party ties we stand united and strong and invincible since we have a common and just American cause to serve and support.

It is an accepted fact that a peaceful people, provoked to righteous war, make the most fearsome adversary. That is the position in which Japan will find, to its utter regret, that it has placed the United States and the peaceful and freedom loving people that make America a mecca free from tyranny and oppression. Already we have close to 1000 Sokols in Uncle Sam's armed forces. At the very start of hostilities when the Japs launched their surprise attack Sunday our Sokols were in the midst of the furious battle fighting to maintain freedom and democracy and to keep the Stars and Stripes waving proudly in the blue.

Swedish: *Nordstjernan*, New York City, New York, December 12, 1941:

After these first deceitful horrible blows under the belt Uncle Sam knows, if he had not known before, what a scoundrel he had to deal with. It was an expensive lesson the United States got the first day and it will be more expensive. There is, however, a credit item to set up against the material losses and the lost lives. Japan's deceitful Blitz blow has welded the American people together as nothing else could have done. Americans at last have found themselves. . . . We all knew that the war would drag us in sooner or later. How it is done and the way it happened will be found to have been best. Instead of gradually being dragged in we are now in it completely. We have no choice now. There will be a life and death battle. About the final outcome there is no doubt, despite Uncle Sam's slow awkward start and the gullibility which has caused defeat in the first round. But the battle has just begun and Japan will see that he who reaches for the sword will be killed by the sword. "Japan has started it, we shall finish it," should be our motto. It coincides with Great Britain's in the great battle with Hitler. With grim determination and growing wrath, America confronts its attackers.

Source: Translated into English and published by the Foreign Language Information Service, *Press Releases*, New York City, New York, December 12, 1941: 1–5.

* * *

War time security concerns prompted President Franklin D. Roosevelt to issue another proclamation, in January 1942, requiring that all enemy aliens residing in the United States or its territories obtain a certificate of identification from the Attorney General of the United States and to carry such certificates on their persons at all times.

DOCUMENT 104: President's Proclamation No. 2537, January 14, 1942: Certificates of Identification Required of Alien Enemies

. . .

NOW, THEREFORE, I, FRANKLIN D. ROOSEVELT, President of the United States, acting under and by virtue of the authority vested in me . . . do hereby prescribe and proclaim the following regulations . . . to those prescribed by the aforesaid proclamation of December 7, 1941, and December 8, 1941:

All alien enemies within the continental United States, Puerto Rico, and the Virgin Islands are hereby required, at such times and places and in such manner as may be fixed by the Attorney General of the United States, to apply for and acquire certificates of identification; and the Attorney General is hereby authorized and directed to provide, as speedily as may be practicable, for the receiving of such applications and for the issuance of appropriate identification certificates, and to make such rules and regulations as he may deem necessary for effecting such identifications; and all alien enemies and all persons are hereby required to comply with such rules and regulations . . . [E]very alien enemy within the limits of the continental United States, Puerto Rico, or the Virgin Islands shall at all times have his identification card on his person.

Source: President's Proclamation No. 2537 of January 14, 1942.

* * *

A few months after the attack on Pearl Harbor, President Roosevelt issued an executive order that led to the evacuation and internment into what were called "relocation camps" of all Japanese resident aliens and Japanese American citizens, including some 70,000 native-born citizens of Japanese ancestry, for what was called military necessity. This executive order represents one of the darkest stains on the civil rights and civil liberties record of the United States. Congress quickly passed legislation endorsing the policy of the executive order. The order, in its entirety, and the subsequent Congressional act are presented below in Document 105.

DOCUMENT 105: Executive Order No. 9066, February 19, 1942, Establishing Military Areas With Authority to Exclude and Relocate "Any and All Persons," and Act of March 21, 1942

Executive Order 9066—February 19, 1942—Issued by President
Franklin Roosevelt

. . .

NOW, THEREFORE, by virtue of the authority vested in me as President of the United States, and Commander in Chief of the Army and Navy, I hereby authorize and direct the Secretary of War, and the Military commanders whom he may from time to time designate, whenever he or any designated Commander deems such action necessary or desirable, to prescribe military areas in such places and of such extent as he or the appropriate Military Commander may determine, from which any and all persons may be excluded, and with respect to which, the right of any person to enter, remain in, or leave shall be subject to whatever restrictions the Secretary of War or the appropriate Military Commander may impose in his discretion. The Secretary of War is hereby authorized to provide for residents of any such area who are excluded therefrom, such transportation, food, shelter, and other accommodations as may be necessary, in the judgment of the Secretary of War, of the said Military Commander, and until other arrangements are made, to accomplish the purpose of this order. The designation of military areas in any region or locality shall supersede designations of prohibited or restricted areas by the Attorney General under the proclamations of December 7 and 8, 1941, and shall supersede the responsibility and authority of the Attorney General under the said Proclamation in respect of such prohibited and restricted areas.

I hereby further authorize and direct the Secretary of War and the said Military Commanders to take such other steps as he or the appropriate Military Commander may deem advisable to enforce compliance with the restrictions applicable to each Military area hereinabove authorized to be designated, including the use of Federal troops and other Federal Agencies, with authority to accept assistance of state and local agencies.

I hereby further authorize and direct all Executive commanders in carrying out this Executive Order, including the furnishing of medical aid, hospitalization, food, clothing, transportation, use of land, shelter, and other supplies, equipment, utilities, facilities, and services.

This order shall not be construed as modifying or limiting in any way the authority granted under Executive Order 8972, dated December 12, 1941, nor shall it be construed as limiting or modifying the duty and responsibility of the Federal Bureau of Investigation, with respect to the investigation of alleged acts of sabotage or the duty and responsibility of the Attorney General and the Department of Justice under the Proclamations of December 7, and 8, 1941, prescribing regulations for the conduct and control of alien enemies, except as such duty and responsibility is superseded by the designation of military areas hereunder.

Act of March 21, 1942 (56 Stat. 173)

Be it enacted by the Senate and House of Representatives of the United States of America in Congress assembled, That whoever shall enter, remain in, leave, or commit any act in any military area or military zone prescribed under the authority of Executive Order of the President, by the Secretary of War, or by any military commander designated by the Secretary of War, contrary to the restrictions applicable to any such area or zone or contrary to the order of the Secretary of War or any such military commander, shall, if it appears that he knew or should have known of the existence and extent of the regulations or order and that his act was in violation thereof, be guilty of a misdemeanor and upon conviction shall be liable to a fine of not to exceed $5,000 or to imprisonment for not more than one year, or both, for each offense.

Sources: Executive Order No. 9066 of February 19, 1942, and Act of March 21, 1942 (56 Stat. 173).

* * *

The legality and constitutionality of Executive Order 9066 and the curfews, evacuation and internment programs resulting from those orders and regulations were challenged by some native-born American citizens of Japanese ancestry as unconstitutional infringements of their equal protection and especially due process rights. The United States Supreme Court ruled against them in three cases (Hirabayashi, Yasui, and Korematsu). Document 106 presents a summary of the ruling in the Gordon Hirabayashi decision.

DOCUMENT 106: *Hirabayashi v. United States* (June 21, 1943)

Mr. Chief Justice Stone delivered the opinion of the Court:

Appellant, an American citizen of Japanese ancestry, was convicted in the district court of violating the Act of Congress of March 21, 1942 . . . which makes it a misdemeanor knowingly to disregard restrictions made applicable by a military commander to persons in a military area prescribed by him as such, all as authorized by an Executive Order of the President.

The questions for our decision are whether the particular restriction violated, namely that all persons of Japanese ancestry residing in such an area be within their place of residence daily between the hours of 8:00 p.m. and 6:00 a.m., was adopted by the military command in the exercise of an unconstitutional delegation by Congress of its legislative power, and whether the restriction unconstitutionally discriminated between citizens of Japanese ancestry and those of other ancestries in violation of the Fifth Amendment.

The evidence showed that appellant had failed to report to the Civil Control Station on May 11 or May 12, 1942, as directed, to register for evacuation from the military area. He admitted failure to do so, and stated it had at all times been his belief that he would be waiving his rights as an American citizen by so [registering]. . . .

. . . [O]n March 22, 1942, General DeWitt issued Public Proclamation No. 3, 7 Federal Register 2543. After referring to the previous designation of military areas . . . it recited that "the present situation within these Military Areas and Zones requires as a matter of military necessity the establishment of certain regulations pertaining to all enemy aliens and

all persons of Japanese ancestry within said Military Areas and Zones.
. . . It accordingly declared and established that from and after March 27,
1942, "all alien Japanese . . . and all persons of Japanese ancestry residing
or being within the geographic limits of Military Zone 1 . . . shall be
within their place of residence between the hours of 8:00 p.m. and 6:00
a.m., which period is hereinafter referred to as the hours of curfew." . . .

The Chairman of the Senate Military Affairs Committee explained on
the floor of the Senate that the purpose of the proposed legislation was
to provide a means of enforcement of curfew orders and other military
orders made pursuant to Executive Order 9066. . . . He also stated to the
Senate that "reasons for suspected widespread fifth-column activity
among Japanese" were to be found in the system of dual citizenship
which Japan deemed applicable to American-born Japanese, and in the
propaganda disseminated by Japanese consuls, Buddhist priests and
other leaders among American-born children of Japanese. Such was
stated to be the explanation of the contemplated evacuation from the
Pacific Coast area of persons of Japanese ancestry, citizens as well as
aliens.

The conclusion is inescapable that Congress, by the Act of March 21,
1942, ratified and confirmed Executive Order 9066. . . . The question then
is not one of congressional power to delegate to the President the prom-
ulgation of the Executive Order, but whether, acting in cooperation, Congress and the Executive have constitutional authority to impose the
curfew restrictions here complained of. . . .

. . . In the critical days of March, 1942, the danger to our war production by sabotage and espionage in this area [from Washington State to
California] seems obvious. . . . The military commander's appraisal of
facts in the light of the authorized standard, and the inferences which
he drew from those facts, involved the exercise of his informed judgment. But as we have seen, those facts, and the inferences drawn from
them, support the judgment of the military commander, that the danger
of espionage and sabotage to our military resources was imminent, and
that the curfew order was an appropriate measure to meet it. . . .

The Constitution as a continuously operating charter of government
does not demand the impossible or the impractical. The essentials of the
legislative function are preserved when Congress authorizes a statutory
command to be operative, upon ascertainment of a basic conclusion of
fact by a designated representative of the government. . . . The present
statute, which authorized curfew orders made pursuant to Executive Order No. 9066 for the protection of war resources from espionage and
sabotage, satisfies those requirements. Under the Executive Order the
basic facts, determined by the military commander in light of knowledge
then available, were whether that danger existed and whether a curfew
order was an appropriate means of minimizing the danger. Since his

findings to that effect were, as we have said, not without adequate support, the legislative function was performed and the sanction of the statute attached to violations of the curfew order. It is unnecessary to consider whether or to what extent such findings would support orders differing from the curfew order.

The conviction under the second count is without constitutional infirmity. Hence we have no occasion to review the conviction on the first count, since, as already stated, the sentences on the two counts are to run concurrently and conviction on the second is to sustain the sentence. For this reason also it is unnecessary to consider the Government's argument that compliance with the order to report at the Civilian Station did not necessarily entail confinement in a relocation center. Affirmed.

Source: 320 U.S. 81 (June 21, 1943).

* * *

In December 1943, in recognition of our alliance with China in the war against Japan, the Congress repealed all of the various Chinese Exclusion Acts, authorized a small quota for immigration from China, and allowed for their naturalization. Two months later, President Roosevelt officially added a quota of 105 to the immigration provisions.

DOCUMENT 107: Act of December 17, 1943: To Repeal the Chinese Exclusion Acts

Be it enacted by the Senate and House of Representatives of the United States of America in Congress assembled, That the following Acts or parts of Acts relating to the exclusion or deportation of persons of the Chinese race are hereby repealed: [The Act then lists every Act or part of an Act passed since 1882.] *Provided,* That all charges for the maintenance or return of Chinese persons applying for admission to the United States shall hereafter be paid or reimbursed to the United States by the person, company, partnership, or corporation bringing such Chinese to a port of the United States as applicants for admission. . . .

Sec. 2. With the exception of Chinese wives of American citizens and those Chinese aliens coming under subsections (b), (d), (e) and (f) of section 4, Immigration Act of 1924 . . . all Chinese persons entering the United States annually as immigrants shall be allocated to the quota for the Chinese computed under the provisions of section 11 of the said Act.

A preference up to 75 per centum of the quota shall be given to Chinese born and resident in China.

Source: 57 Stat. 600; 8 U.S.C. 212(a).

* * *

In the continuing need for agricultural workers during the war years, Congress acted to fund additional temporary farm workers by appropriating funds for the program in 1944.

DOCUMENT 108: Act of February 14, 1944: Supply and Distribution of Farm Labor

Resolved by the Senate and House of Representatives of the United States of America in Congress assembled, That there is appropriated, out of any money in the Treasury not otherwise appropriated, the following sums, namely:

Title I.—Department of Agriculture

War Food Administration

For assisting in providing an adequate supply of workers for the production, harvesting, and preparation for markets of agricultural commodities essential to the prosecution of the war, $30,000,000, which sum, together with the amount appropriated in the Act of April 29, 1943 . . . shall be merged into one fund, to remain available until December 31, 1944, and to be expended by the War Food Administrator . . . appointed pursuant to Executive Order 9334, dated April 19, 1943, as follows:

Sec. 2. (a) For the purpose of assisting in providing adequate supply of workers in the production and harvesting of agricultural commodities within the several States, on the basis of need, not less than $14,000,000 and not more than $18,500,000 of the sum appropriated in section 1 . . . and the sums so apportioned shall be available for payment to such States for expenditure by the agricultural extension services of the land-grant colleges in such States in accordance with such agreements as may be entered into by the Administrator and such extension services. . . . The purposes for which such funds may be expended by such extension services shall include among other things, (1) the recruiting, placement (including the placement of such workers as sharecroppers), and training of such workers; (2) transportation, supervision, subsistence, protection, health and medical and burial services, and shelter for such workers and their families and necessary personal property. . . .

Title II—Executive Office of the President—Office of Emergency
Management

War Manpower Commission

Migration of workers: To enable the War Manpower Commission to
provide, in accordance with regulations prescribed by the Chairman of
said Commission, for the temporary migration of workers from foreign
countries within the Western Hemisphere . . . for employment in the continental United States with industries and service essential to the preservation, marketing, or distribution of agricultural products, including
the timber and lumber industries, and including the transportation of
such workers from points outside the United States to ports of entry of
the United States and return (including transportation from the place of
employment in the United States to port of entry of the United States in
any case of default by an employer to provide such transportation to a
worker, in which event the employer shall be liable to the United States
for the cost thereof), cost of temporary maintenance of the workers in
reception centers in foreign countries and in the United States, when
necessary, reasonable subsistence and emergency medical care of such
workers from the time of reporting for transportation to the United States
or return to the country of origin until arrival at the destination.

Source: 58 Stat. 11; 50 U.S.C., App. 1351.

* * *

In 1944 the U.S. Supreme Court upheld the constitutionality of the
executive order excluding Japanese American citizens from remaining
in certain "excluded zones." Document 109 summarizes the majority
opinion in the case.

DOCUMENT 109: *Korematsu v. United States* (December 18, 1944)

Mr. Justice Black delivered the opinion of the Court:

The petitioner, an American citizen of Japanese descent, was convicted
in a Federal district court for remaining in San Leandro, California, a
"Military Area," contrary to Civilian Exclusion Order No. 34 of the Commanding General of the Western Command, U.S. Army, which directed
that after May 9, 1942, all persons of Japanese ancestry should be excluded from that area. No question was raised as to petitioner's loyalty
to the United States. The Circuit Court of Appeals reaffirmed, and the

importance of the constitutional question involved caused us to grant certiorari . . . .

In the light of the principles we announced in the Hirabayashi Case [see Document 106] we are unable to conclude that it was beyond the war power of Congress and the Executive to exclude those of Japanese ancestry from the West Coast war area at the time they did. . . .

Like curfew, exclusion of those of Japanese origin was deemed necessary because of the presence of an un-ascertained number of disloyal members of the group, most of whom we have no doubt were loyal to this country. It was because we could not reject the finding of the military authorities that it was impossible to bring about the immediate segregation of the disloyal from the loyal that we sustained the validity of the curfew order as applying to the whole group. In the instant case, temporary exclusion of the entire group was rested by the military on the same ground. The judgment that exclusion of the whole group was for the same reason a military imperative answers the contention that the exclusion was in the nature of a group punishment based on antagonism to those of Japanese ancestry. . . .

We uphold the exclusion order as of the time it was made and when the petitioner violated it. . . . In doing so, we are not unmindful of the hardships imposed on a large group of American citizens. . . . But hardships are part of war, and war is an aggregation of hardships. All citizens alike, both in and out of uniform, feel the impact of the war in greater or lesser measure. Citizenship has its responsibilities as well as its privileges, and in time of war the burden is always heavier. Compulsory exclusion of large groups of citizens from their homes, except under circumstances of the direst emergency and peril, is inconsistent with our basic governmental institutions, But when under conditions of modern warfare our shores are threatened by hostile forces, the power to protect must be commensurate with the threatened danger. . . .

We are thus being asked to pass at this time upon the whole subsequent detention program in both assembly and relocation centers, although the only issues framed at the trial [related] to petitioner's remaining in the prohibited area in violation of the exclusion order. . . .

It is said that we are dealing here with the case of imprisonment of a citizen in a concentration camp solely because of his ancestry, without evidence or inquiry concerning his loyalty towards the United States. Our task would be simple, our duty clear, were this a case involving the imprisonment of a loyal citizen in a concentration camp because of racial prejudice. Regardless of the true nature of the assembly and relocation centers—and we deem it unjustifiable to call them concentration camps with all the ugly connotations that term implies—we are dealing specifically with nothing but an exclusion order. To cast this case into outlines of racial prejudice, without reference to the real military dangers which were presented, merely confuses the issue. Korematsu was not excluded from the Military Area because of hostility to him or his race. He was excluded because we are at war with the Japanese Empire, because competent military authorities feared an invasion of our West Coast and felt constrained to take proper security measures, because they decided that the military urgency of the situation demanded that all citizens of Japanese ancestry be segregated from the West Coast temporarily, and finally, because Congress, reposing its confidence in this time of war in our military leaders—as inevitably it must—determined that they should have the power to do just this. There was evidence of disloyalty on the part of some, the military authorities considered that the need for action was great, and time was short. We cannot—by availing ourselves of the calm perspective of hindsight—now say that at the time these actions were unjustified.

Affirmed.

Source: 323 U.S. 214 (1994).

* * *

In 1944 the Supreme Court decided the case of *Ex parte Mitsuye Endo*, which challenged the leave procedure of the War Relocation Authority. The appellant, Miss Endo, was evacuated from Sacramento, California, to the Tule Lake Relocation Center and later transferred to the Central Utah Relocation Center in Topaz, Utah, where she was detained at the time of the Court's decision. Justice Douglas delivered the unanimous decision of the Court, with Justices Murphy and Roberts filing separate concurring opinions. These opinions are excerpted in Document 110. The Court ruled that a citizen who was loyal could not be presumed a spy or saboteur based solely on that person's ancestry and, therefore could not automatically be said to present any threat related to sabotage or espionage. Since the law passed to authorize detention was to protect war efforts against sabotage and espionage, "detention which has no relationship to that objective is unauthorized." Justice Roberts was of the opinion that a loyal citizen had been deprived of her liberty for a period of years. Justice Murphy was of the opinion that detention was not authorized by either Congress or the Executive. In his view, "detention was another example of the unconstitutional resort to racism inherent in the entire evacuation program."

DOCUMENT 110: *Ex parte Mitsuye Endo* (December 18, 1944)

Certificate from the United States Circuit Court of Appeals for the Ninth Circuit, for the opinion of the Supreme Court of the United States on questions of law arising upon an appeal from a denial of the writ of habeas corpus by the District Court of the United States for the Northern District of California. Reversed.

[Attorney for the appellant argued that] Power to imprison without charge, trial, or any other process should be based on more than the implication from presidential orders and congressional statutes, the constitutionality of which orders and statutes themselves must be defended by far-fetched implication from definite powers given by the Constitution. . . .

Mr. Justice Douglas delivered the opinion of the Court . . . .

Mitsuye Endo, hereinafter designated as the appellant, is an American citizen of Japanese ancestry. She was evacuated from Sacramento, California, in 1942, pursuant to certain military orders which we will presently discuss, and was removed to the Tule Lake War Relocation Center located at Newell, Modoc County, California. In July, 1942 she filed a petition for a writ of habeas corpus in the District Court of the United States for the Northern District of California, asking that she be discharged and restored to liberty. That petition was denied by the District Court in July, 1943, and an appeal was perfected to the Circuit Court of Appeals in August, 1943. Shortly thereafter appellant was transferred from the Tule Lake Relocation Center to the Central Utah Relocation Center located at Topaz, Utah, where she is presently detained. The certificate of questions of law was filed here on April 22, 1944, and on May 8, 1944, we ordered the entire record to be certified to this Court. It does not appear that any respondent was ever served with process or appeared in the proceedings. But the United States Attorney for the Northern District of California argued before the District Court that the petition should not be granted. . . .

The Act of March 21, 1942, was a war measure . . . [The House report . . . stated,] "The necessity for this legislation arose from the fact that the safe conduct of the war requires the fullest possible protection against either espionage or sabotage to national defense material, national defense premises, and national defense utilities."

Moreover, unlike the case of curfew regulations (*Hirabayashi v. United States*, 320 U.S. 81, supra), the legislative history of the Act of March 21, 1942, is silent on detention. And that silence may have special significance in view of the fact that detention in Relocation Centers was no part of the original program of evacuation but developed later to meet what seemed to [be the administrative needs of officials who assumed] for the purposes of this case that initial detention was authorized.

But we stress the silence of the legislative history and of the Act and the Executive Orders on the power to detain to emphasize that such authority which exists must be implied. If there is to be the greatest possible accommodation to the liberties of the citizen with this war measure, any such implied power must be narrowly confined to the precise purpose of the evacuation program.

A citizen who is concededly loyal presents no problem of espionage or sabotage. Loyalty is a matter of heart and mind, not of race, creed, or color. He who is loyal is by definition not a spy or a saboteur. When the power to detain is derived from the power to protect the war effort against espionage and sabotage, detention which has no relationship to that objective is unauthorized.

Nor may the power to detain an admittedly loyal citizen or to grant him a conditional release be implied as a useful or convenient step in the evacuation program, whatever authority might be implied in case of those whose loyalty was not conceded or established . . .

The Act of March 21, 1942, was a war measure . . . That was the precise purpose of Executive Order No. 9066, for, as we have seen, it gave as the reason for the exclusion of persons from prescribed military areas the protection of such property "against espionage and against sabotage." And Executive Order No. 9102, which established the War Relocation Authority did so, as we have noted, "in order to provide for the removal from designated areas of persons whose removal is necessary in the interests of national security." The purpose and objective of the Act and of these orders are plain. Their single aim was the protection of the war effort against espionage and sabotage. It is in light of that one objective the powers conferred by the order must be construed . . . .

As the President has said of these loyal citizens:

"Americans of Japanese ancestry, like those of many other ancestries, have shown that they can, and want to, accept our institutions and work loyally with the rest of us, making their own valuable contribution to the national wealth and well-being. In vindication of the very ideals for which we are fighting this war it is important for us to maintain a high standard of fair, considerate, and equal treatment for the people of this minority as of all other minorities."

Mitsuye Endo is entitled to an unconditional release by the War Authority. . . . The judgment is reversed and the cause is remanded to the District Court for proceedings in conformity with this opinion. Reversed.

Mr. Justice Murphy, concurring:

I join in the opinion of the Court, but I am of the view that detention in Relocation Centers of persons of Japanese ancestry regardless of loyalty is not only unauthorized by Congress or the Executive but is another example of the unconstitutional resort to racism inherent in the entire evacuation program. As stated more fully in my dissenting opinion in Korematsu v. United States, decided this day [323 U.S. 233, ante, 208, 65 S Ct 193] racial discrimination of this nature bears no reasonable relation to military necessity and is utterly foreign to the ideals and traditions of the American people.

Moreover, the Court holds that Mitsuye Endo is entitled to an unconditional release by the War Relocation Authority. It appears that Miss Endo desires to return to Sacramento, California, from which Public Proclamations Nos. 7 and 11, as well as Civilian Exclusion Order No. 52, still exclude her. And it would seem to me that the "unconditional" release to be given Miss Endo necessarily implies "the right to pass freely from state to state," including the right to move freely into California. . . . If, as I believe, the military orders excluding her from California were invalid at the time they were issued, they are increasingly objectionable at this late date, when the threat of invasion of the Pacific Coast and the fears of sabotage and espionage are greatly diminished. For the Government to suggest under these circumstances that the presence of Japanese blood in a loyal American citizen might be enough to warrant her exclusion from a place where she would otherwise have the right to go is a position I cannot sanction.

Mr. Justice Roberts:

I concur in the result but I cannot agree with the reasons stated in the opinion of the Court for reaching that result. . . .

I conclude, therefore, that the court is squarely faced with a serious constitutional question—whether the relator's detention violated the guarantees of the Bill of Rights of the federal Constitution and especially the guarantee of due process of law. There can be but one answer to that question. An admittedly loyal citizen has been deprived of her liberty for a period of years. Under the Constitution she should be free to come and go as she pleases. Instead, her liberty of motion and other innocent activities have been prohibited and conditioned. She should be discharged.

Source: 323 U.S. 283–310.

* * *

At the end of World War II, Europe was trying to cope with literally millions of refugees and displaced persons, and this situation placed an immediate and dramatic pressure upon the immigration quotas of the United States for those countries. The paucity of quotas available were clearly evident given the millions of refugees. President Harry S. Truman issued a statement concerning the problem which contained a directive of how the government would deal with displaced persons and refugees.

DOCUMENT 111: Statement and Directive by the President [Truman] on Immigration to the United States of Certain Displaced Persons and Refugees in Europe, December 22, 1945

The war has brought in its wake an appalling dislocation of populations in Europe. Many humanitarian organizations, including the United Nations Relief and Rehabilitation Administration are doing their utmost to solve the multitude of problems arising in connection with this dislocation of hundreds of thousands of persons. Every effort is being made to return the displaced persons and refugees in the various countries of Europe to their former homes. The great difficulty is that so many of these persons have no homes to which they may return. The immensity of the problem of displaced persons and refugees is almost beyond comprehension.

A number of countries in Europe, including Switzerland, Sweden, France, and England, are working toward its solution. The United States shares the responsibility to relieve the suffering. To the extent that our present immigration laws permit, everything possible should be done at once to facilitate the entrance of some of these displaced persons and refugees into the United States.

In this way we may do something to relieve human misery, and set an example to the other countries of the world which are able to receive some of these war sufferers. I feel that it is essential that we do this ourselves to show our good faith in requesting other nations to open their doors for this purpose.

Most of these persons are natives of Central and Eastern Europe and the Balkans. The immediate quotas for all those countries for one year total approximately 39,000, two-thirds of which are allotted to Germany. Under the law, in any single month the number of visas issued cannot exceed ten percent of the annual quota. This means that from now on only about 3,900 visas can be issued each month to persons who are natives of these countries.

Very few persons from Europe have migrated to the United States during the war years. In fiscal year 1942 only ten per cent of the immigration quotas was used; in 1943, five per cent; in 1944, six per cent; and in 1945, seven per cent. As of November 30, 1945, the end of the fifth month of the current fiscal year, only about ten per cent of the quotas for the European countries has been used. These unused quotas however do not accumulate through the years, and I do not intend to ask the Congress to change this rule. . . .

I consider that common decency and fundamental comradeship of all human beings require us to do what lies within our power to see that our established immigration quotas are used in order to reduce human suffering. I am taking the necessary steps to see that this is done as quickly as possible. . . .

I am informed that there are various measures now pending before the Congress which would either prohibit or severely reduce further immigration. I hope that such legislation will not be passed. This period of unspeakable human distress is not the time for us to close or to narrow our gates. I wish to emphasize, however, that any effort to bring relief to these displaced persons and refugees must and will be strictly within the limits of the present quotas as imposed by law.

Upon the basis of a careful survey by the Department of State and the Immigration and Naturalization Service, it has been determined that if these persons were now applying for admission to the United States most of them would be admissible under the immigration laws. In the circumstances, it would be inhumane and wasteful to require these people to go all the way back to Europe merely for the purpose of applying there for immigration visas and returning to the United States. Many of them have close relatives, including sons and daughters, who are citizens of the United States and who have served and are serving honorably in the armed forces of our country. I am therefore directing the Secretary of State and the Attorney General to adjust the immigration status of the members of this group who may wish to remain here, in strict accordance with existing laws and regulations. . . .

The attached directive has been issued by me to the responsible government agencies to carry out this policy. I wish to emphasize, above all, that nothing in the directive will deprive a single American soldier or his wife or children of a berth on a vessel homeward bound, or delay their return. This is the opportunity for America to set an example for the rest of the world in cooperation towards alleviating human misery.

Source: Public Papers of the Presidents (December 22, 1945), 572–78.

* * *

Also in 1945, Congress responded with a novel piece of legislation to the war-generated spouses and children of members of the armed forces desiring to immigrate to be reunited with their family.

DOCUMENT 112: Act of December 28, 1945: Admission of Alien Spouses and Alien Minor Children of Citizen Members of the United States Armed Forces ("War Brides Act")

Be it enacted by the Senate and House of Representatives of the United States of America in Congress assembled, That notwithstanding any of the several clauses of section 3 of the Act of February 5, 1917, excluding physical and mentally defective aliens, and notwithstanding the documentary requirements of any of the immigration laws or regulations, Executive Orders, or Presidential proclamations issued thereunder, alien spouses, or alien children of United States citizens serving in, or having an honorable discharge certificate from the armed forces of the United States during the Second World War shall, if otherwise admissible under the immigration laws and if application for admission is made within three years of the effective date of this Act, be admitted to the United States: *Provided,* That every alien of the foregoing description shall be medically examined at the time of arrival in accordance with the provisions of section 16 of the Act of February 5, 1917, and if found suffering from any disability which would be the basis for a ground of exclusion except for the provision of this Act, the Immigration and Naturalization Service shall forthwith notify the appropriate public medical officers of the local community to which the alien is destined: *Provided further,* That the provisions of this Act shall not affect the duties of the United States Public Health Service so far as they relate to quarantinable diseases.

Sec. 2. Regardless of section 9 of the Immigration Act of 1924, any alien admitted under section 1 of this Act shall be deemed to be a nonquota immigrant as defined in section 4(a) of the Immigration Act of 1924....

Sec. 4. No fine or penalty shall be imposed under the Act of February 5, 1917, except those arising under section 14, because of the transportation to the United States of any alien admitted under this Act.

Sec. 5. For the purpose of this Act, the Second World War shall be deemed to have commenced on December 7, 1941, and to have ceased upon the termination of hostilities as declared by the President or by a joint resolution of Congress.

Sec. 6.* The alien spouse of an American citizen by marriage occurring before thirty days after the enactment of this Act, shall not be considered as inadmissible because of race, if otherwise admissible under this Act.

Source: 59 Stat. 659; 8 U.S.C. 232–236.

* * *

In 1946 the U.S. Supreme Court agreed to hear a case that would require it to reconsider the Schwimmer case decided in 1929 [Document 90]. The question at issue was whether an applicant for admission to citizenship could be naturalized if the individual was a conscientious objector to military service. The Court in this case did indeed reverse itself and ruled in favor of the applicant to be admitted despite his objector status. Document 113 presents an excerpt of the majority opinion in the Girouard decision, wherein the Court voted 7 to 1, with one Justice not participating, in favor of overturning the Schwimmer decision.

DOCUMENT 113: *Girouard v. United States* (April 22, 1946)

Mr. Justice Douglas delivered the opinion of the Court.

In 1943 petitioner, a native of Canada, filed his petition for naturalization in the District Court of Massachusetts. He stated in his application that he understood the principles of the government of the United States, believed in its form of government, and was willing to take the oath of allegiance which reads as follows:

"I hereby declare, on oath, that I absolutely and entirely renounce and abjure all allegiance and fidelity to any foreign prince, potentate, state, or sovereignty of whom or which I have heretofore been a subject or citizen; that I will support and defend the Constitution and laws of the United States of America against all enemies, foreign and domestic; that I will bear true faith and allegiance to the same; and that I take this oath freely without any mental reservations or purposes of evasion; So help me God."

To the question in the application "If necessary, are you willing to take up arms in defense of this country," he replied, "No (Noncombatant) Seventh Day Adventist." He explained that answer before the examiner by saying "it is a purely religious matter with me, I have no political or personal reason other than that." He did not claim before

*Sec. 6 added by Act of July 22, 1947 (61 Stat. 401).

his Selective Service board exemption from all military service, but only from combatant military duty. At the hearing in the District Court petitioner testified that he was a member of the Seventh Day Adventist denomination, of whom approximately 10,000 were then serving in the armed forces of the United States as noncombatants, especially in the medical corps; and that he was willing to serve in the army but would not bear arms. The District Court admitted him to citizenship. The Circuit Court of Appeals reversed, one judge dissenting. It took the action on the authority of *United States v. Schwimmer, . . . Macintosh, . . . and Bland*, saying that the facts of the case brought it squarely within the principles of those cases. The case is here on a petition for a writ of certiorari which we granted so that those authorities might be re-examined. . . .

It is to be found in the Nationality Act of 1940, 54 Stat. 1137 . . . 707 (a) provides that no person shall be naturalized unless he has been for stated periods and still is "a person of good moral character, attached to the principles of the Constitution of the United States, and well disposed to the good order and happiness of the United States."

While there are some factual distinctions between this case and the Schwimmer and Macintosh cases, the Bland case on its facts is indistinguishable. But the principle emerging from the three cases obliterates any factual distinction among them. As we recognized in *In re Summers*, 325 U.S. 561 . . . they stand for the same general rule—that an alien who refuses to bear arms will not be admitted to citizenship. As an original proposition, we could not agree with that rule. The fallacies underlying it were, we think, demonstrated in the dissents of Mr. Justice Holmes in the Schwimmer case and of Mr. Chief Justice Hughes in the Macintosh case.

The oath required of aliens does not in terms require that they promise to bear arms. Nor has Congress expressly made any such finding a prerequisite to citizenship. To hold that it is required is to read it into the Act by implication. But we could not assume that Congress intended to make such an abrupt and radical departure from our traditions unless it spoke in unequivocal terms.

The bearing of arms, important as it is, is not the only way in which our institutions may be supported and defended, even in times of great peril. Total war in its modern form dramatizes as never before the great cooperative effort necessary for victory. The nuclear physicists who developed the atomic bomb, the worker at his lathe, the seamen on cargo vessels, construction battalions, nurses, engineers, litter bearers, doctors, chaplains—these, too, made essential contributions. And many of them made the supreme sacrifice. . . . And the annals of the recent war show that many whose religious scruples prevented them from bearing arms, nevertheless were unselfish participants in the war effort. Refusal to bear arms is not necessarily a sign of disloyalty or a lack of attachment to our institutions. One may serve his country faithfully and devotedly, though his religious scruples make it impossible for him to shoulder a rifle. Devotion to one's country can be as real and as enduring among non-combatants as among combatants. One may adhere to what he deems to be his obligation to God and yet assume all military risks to secure victory. The effort of war is indivisible; and those whose religious scruples prevent them from killing are no less patriots than those whose special traits or handicaps result in their assignment to duties far behind the fighting front. Each is making the utmost contribution according to his capacity. The fact that his role may be limited by religious convictions rather than by physical characteristics has no necessary bearing on his attachment to his country or his willingness to support and defend it to his utmost. Petitioner's religious scruples would not disqualify him from becoming a member of Congress or holding other public office. . . .

There is not the slightest suggestion that Congress set a stricter standard for aliens seeking admission to citizenship than it did for officials who make and enforce the laws of the nation and administer its affairs. It is hard to believe that one need forsake his religious scruples to become a citizen but not to sit in the high councils of state. . . . Yet it is clear that these new provisions cover non-combatants as well as combatants. If petitioner had served as a non-combatant (as he was willing to do) he could have been admitted to citizenship by taking the identical oath which he is willing to take. Can it be that the oath means one thing to one who has served to the extent permitted by his religious scruples and another thing to one equally willing to serve but who has not had the opportunity? It is not enough to say that the petitioner is not entitled to the benefits of the new Act since he did not serve in the armed forces? He is not seeking the benefit of the expedited procedure and the relaxed requirements. The oath which he must take is identical with the oath which both non-combatants and combatants must take. It would, indeed, be a strange construction to say that "support and defend the Constitution and laws of the United States against all enemies, foreign and domestic" demands something more from some than it does from others. That oath can hardly be adequate for one who is unwilling to bear arms because of religious scruples and yet exact for another a promise to bear arms despite religious scruples. . . .

We do not think under the circumstances of this legislative history that we can properly place on the shoulders of Congress the burden of the Court's own error. The history of the 1940 Act is at most equivocal. It contains no affirmative recognition of the rule of the Schwimmer, Macintosh and Bland cases. The silence of Congress and its inaction are as consistent with a desire to leave the problem fluid as they are with an adoption by silence of the rule of those cases. But, for us, it is enough to say that since the date of those cases Congress never acted affirmatively on this question but once and that was in 1942. At that time, as we have noted, Congress specifically granted naturalization privileges to non-combatants who like the petitioner were prevented from bearing arms by their religious scruples. That was affirmative recognition that one could be attached to the principles of our government and could support and defend it even though his religious convictions prevented him from bearing arms. And, as we have said, we cannot believe that the oath was designed to exact something more from one person than from another. Thus the affirmative action taken by Congress in 1942 negatives [*sic*] any inference that otherwise might be drawn from its silence when it reenacted the oath in 1940. Reversed.

Source: 328 U.S. 61, April 22, 1946.

* * *

The Congress, with Cold War foreign policy considerations underlying the desire to stabilize conditions in Western Europe, began to modify the immigration quota law by enacting exceptions by other status to enable a greater number of immigrants to come to the United States. An example of such modification was the Displaced Persons Act of 1948. The act, which comprises twenty-three pages in the statutes, is only briefly excerpted in Document 114.

DOCUMENT 114: Act of June 25, 1948: Displaced Persons Act of 1948

Be it enacted by the Senate and House of Representatives of the United States of America in Congress assembled, That this Act may be cited as the Displaced Persons Act of 1948.

Sec. 2. [Defines all the key terms used, including "Commission," "Displaced Person," "Eligible displaced person," "eligible displaced orphan," and elaborately defines the areas in Europe in which the camps hold displaced persons who are eligible (e.g., England, France, free sector of Berlin, West Germany, and so on).]

(f).* A special non-quota immigrant visa may be issued to any alien who—

(1) [lists all the geographic areas from which the displaced person may come]

(2) is an orphan because of the death or disappearance of both parents, or because of abandonment or desertion by, or separation from or loss of both parents, or who only has one parent ... [who] agrees to release him for emigration. ...

(3)** has assurances submitted in his behalf for admission to the

*Subsection f added by Act of June 16, 1950 (64 Stat. 219).
**As amended by Act of June 28, 1951 (65 Stat. 96).

United States for permanent residence with a father or mother by adoption, or permanent residence with a near relative or with a person who is a citizen of the United States or an alien admitted to the United States for permanent residence, or is seeking to enter ... to come to a public or private agency approved by the Commission, and such relative, person, or agency gives assurances satisfactory to the Commission, that adoption or guardianship proceedings will be initiated with respect to such alien ... and

(5) is, at the time of the issuance of a visa, under the age of ten years. Not to exceed five thousand such special non-quota immigration visas shall be issued until July 1, 1952. ...

[The act gives a long list of various camps in Europe in which refugees or displaced persons are being held, and assigns a number of non-quota visas that may be given per place, e.g., Venezia Giulia, Yugoslavia, two thousand, etc.]

Sec. 3.* (a) II. During the three fiscal years beginning July 1, 1948 eligible displaced orphans defined in subdivisions (2), (3), and (4) of subsection (b) of this section seeking to enter the United States may be issued visas without regard to quota limitations for those years provided by subsection (c) of this section; *Provided*, That not more than three hundred and forty-one thousand such visas shall be issued under this Act, as amended, including such visas shall be issued under the Displaced Persons Act of 1948 and it shall be the duty of the Secretary of State to procure the cooperation of other nations, particularly the members of the International Refugee Organization, in the solution of the displaced persons problem by their accepting for resettlement a relative number of displaced persons, and to expedite the closing of the camps and terminate the emergency. [The original law provided for up to 202,000.]

[Subsequent subsections list the number of thousands of non-quota immigration visas to be issued for displaced persons from various regions: China, Poland, Greece, etc.]

(d) The selection of eligible displaced persons shall be made without discrimination in favor of or against a race, religion, or national origin of such eligible displaced persons, and the Commission shall insure that equitable opportunity for resettlement under the terms of this Act, as amended, shall be afforded to eligible displaced persons of all races, religions, and national origins. ...

Sec. 6. The preferences provided within the quotas by section 6 of the Immigration Act of 1924 ... shall not be applicable in the case of any eligible displaced person receiving an immigration visa under this Act, but in lieu of such preferences the following preferences, without priority in time of issuance of visas between such preferences shall be granted

*As amended June 28, 1951 (65 Stat. 96), following amendment by Act of June 16, 1950 (64 Stat. 219).

to eligible displaced persons and their family dependents who are the spouse or the unmarried dependent child or children under twenty-one years of age in the consideration of visa applications:

(a) First. Eligible displaced persons who have been previously engaged in agricultural pursuits and who will be employed in the United States in agricultural pursuits: . . .

(b) Second. Eligible displaced persons who are household, construction, clothing, and garment workers, and other workers needed in the locality in the United States in which such persons propose to reside, or eligible displaced persons possessing special educational, scientific, technological or professional qualifications.

(c) Third. Eligible displaced persons who are the blood relatives of citizens or lawfully admitted alien residents of the United States, such relationship in either case being within the third degree of consanguinity computed according to the rules of common law. . . .

Sec. 8. There be created a Commission to be known as the Displaced Persons Commission, consisting of three members to be appointed by the President, by and with the advice and consent of the Senate, for a term ending June 30, 1951, and one member of the Commission shall be designated by him as chairman. [Their salaries, the budget of the commission, etc., are thereafter specified, and their duties in guiding the resettlement, along with reports to be given by them to the President and Congress are spelled out. The commission is given the power to investigate the eligibility of persons applying, with the burden of proof of their eligibility being placed on the person seeking admission.]

[Subsequent subsections specify the numbers; for example, no more than 54,744 may be issued to persons of Germanic ethnic origin who were born in Czechoslovakia, Estonia, Hungary, Latvia, Lithuania, Poland, Rumania, Russia, or Yugoslavia. The act exempts them all from the head tax and other fees associated with the issuance of an immigration visa. The commission is empowered to make the necessary arrangements to transfer persons eligible for emigration to their places of embarkation and from that port to the port of entry in the United States. A Reconstruction Finance Corporation is authorized and directed to make appropriations of the monies to finance this transfer.]

Sec. 13. No visas shall be issued under the provisions of this Act to any person who is or has been a member of, or participated in, any movement which is or has been hostile to the United States or the form of government of the United States.

[Several subsections are then given regarding penalties—in fines and imprisonment—for violations of the act.]

Sec. 17. All transportation by ships or planes of aliens under this Act, to the United States, the cost of which is defrayed in whole or in part by the Government of the United States, shall be by ships or planes registered under the United States flag, or by ships owned by the United States.

Source: 62 Stat. 1009.

* * *

In the 1948 presidential campaign, the Progressive party issued a campaign handbook in which it stated the party's position on immigration and naturalization laws. The party called for the complete revision of the quota laws and the Displaced Persons Act away from what it termed was their racially biased perspective, for their repeal, and for granting an indemnity to Japanese American citizens who suffered losses during the internment of World War II. Document 115, which contains that statement in full, summarizes many issues the country was struggling with in the late 1940s as it began to reconsider the racially based approach of the national origins quota system.

DOCUMENT 115: Statement of the Progressive Party on Citizenship, Naturalization, and Immigration Policy, 1948

The laws of the United States still deny the rights of citizenship on the basis of race and national origin. Changes in the laws in recent years have won Chinese, East Indians, and Filipinos the rights of immigration and naturalization. But persons born in Japan, Korea, and certain Asiatic countries and Pacific Island areas are still denied the right of citizenship, though they may have lived in this country for decades and are devoted to American principles.

Persons denied the right of citizenship are singled out for further discrimination in the law. Eight states forbid or restrict land ownership by ineligible aliens. In California, they may not engage in commercial fishing, or receive old age pensions or state relief. Many states bar all but citizens to the bar and medical, teaching and other professions, meaning that ineligible aliens can never enter these professions. The California alien land law is so stringent that it forbids American citizens of Japanese origin to support ineligible alien parents with money derived from the use of land. The Report of the President's Commission on Civil Rights cites the case of Japanese American soldiers killed in the service of the U.S. who made battlefield wills deeding their land to their parents. The parents could not under the law receive the land, and it reverted to the state.

During the war all persons of Japanese descent were evacuated or excluded from the West Coast. This meant the mass evacuation of 110,000 people, two-thirds of whom were American citizens, without trial or hearing of any sort. Ground for this action was military security. It involved the concept of guilt by heredity or association which is contrary to American law and democracy. The evacuation was a mass quarantine measure and has been called "the most striking mass interference since slavery with the right to physical freedom." Hundreds of evacuees, furthermore, suffered business and property losses. Their just claims for indemnity must be honored.

In the postwar period, discrimination—not written into the law—has been practiced against those seeking citizenship. From all over the country have come authenticated reports of open racial and anti-democratic prejudice displayed by naturalization examiners. Yugoslav Americans who have applied for citizenship have been told that they cannot become citizens until they stop supporting relief for Yugoslavia or until they openly attack the Yugoslav government. In Boston and San Francisco, applicants for citizenship have been subjected to illegal and unwarranted difficulties and questioning because of their membership in the International Workers Order, a fraternal organization. In the Southwest, Mexican Americans have been refused citizenship on equally flimsy grounds.

The intensity of the drive against the foreign born is reflected in the fact that citizens who have already been naturalized have been threatened with revocation of citizenship. Several naturalized Yugoslav Americans were so threatened in Pennsylvania recently.

Immigration

U.S. immigration laws discriminate against the non Anglo-Saxon. The Immigration Act of 1924 fixes quotas by national origin. The annual quota for Great Britain and other countries of northern and western Europe amounted to 80 percent of the total world quota, while that of eastern and southern Europe was fixed at 13 percent. Quotas for Great Britain and northern and western Europe have rarely been filled. Quotas for countries from eastern and southern Europe have rarely been open, the waiting period being from two to five years.

The Report of the Commissioner General of Immigration for 1923 summed up the attitude of Congress and the administration in adopting this law:

While, the lawmakers were deeply concerned with the mental, moral, and physical quality of immigrants, there developed as time went on an even greater concern as to the fundamental racial character of the constantly increasing numbers who came. The record of arrivals year by year have shown the gradual falling off in the immigration of northwest European peoples representing racial stocks which were common to America even in colonial days and a rapid and remarkably large increase in the movement from southern and eastern European countries and Asiatic Turkey.

The Act of 1924 was pushed by racists, the American Legion, and other groups. Their racial theories were exemplified by Madison Grant, author of *The Passing of the Great Race*, who proclaimed:

These immigrants adopted the language of the native Americans, they wear his clothes, they steal his name, and they are beginning to take his women, but they seldom adopt his religion or understand his ideals.

Rabbi Stephen S. Wise, arguing against restrictions of immigration, declared:

I know something of America and I do not think it at all fair to assume as you gentlemen do . . . that the country is clamoring for the restriction of immigration, for the abolition of immigration. I tell you that America is still under this post-war hysteria. It is rapidly emerging. But that post-war hysteria which still remains continues to work in America, and I tell you that you are inflicting a great wrong upon thousands . . . of citizens of America.

The Act, which is based on racial theories no different from Hitler's, was passed. It drastically cut Jewish immigration into the United States. From 135,000 in 1921, Jewish immigration fell to about 40,000 after 1924. During the ten years of Nazi terror in Germany, only about 16,000 Jewish immigrants a year were admitted to the United States.

The racist immigration law remains on the statute books. Another discriminatory immigration law was passed in 1948. The Displaced Persons Act discriminates against Jews, Catholics and anti-fascists. The State Department has developed a new concept since the war in refusing entry here on any basis to persons who are or who may be suspected to be Communists.

The intensity and character of the "anti-foreign" drive in this country is shown up dramatically in the accusations directed against the UN and its personnel, not only by irresponsible Congressmen but by officers of the State Department and the Foreign Service. This is the kind of action which shocked most Americans a decade ago when it was taken by Nazi Germany. The intensification of the prejudice against the foreign born, against non Anglo-Saxons, with official sanction and instigation, is a measure of the speed with which the bipartisans are hastening us down the road to fascism. Only the Progressive Party can stop this drive to fascism and war. The Progressive Party fights with the understanding that the diversity of America's different peoples and cultures is the source of its democratic strength.

—The Progressive Party advocates the right of the foreign born to obtain citizenship without discrimination.

—The Progressive Party advocates the repeal of discriminatory immigration laws based upon race, national origin, religion, or political belief.

—The Progressive Party recognizes the just claims of the Japanese Americans for indemnity for the losses suffered during their wartime internment, which was an outrageous violation of our fundamental concepts of justice.

—The Progressive Party supports legislation facilitating naturalization of Filipinos, Koreans, Japanese, Chinese, and other national groups now discriminated against by law.

—The Progressive Party supports legislation facilitating naturalization of merchant seamen with a record of war service.

Source: Campaign Handbook of the Progressive Party, National Headquarters, Progressive Party, 39 Park Avenue, New York, New York, 1948, 140–44.

* * *

In 1949 President Truman issued a proclamation setting immigration quotas for a number of countries for whom the quota Act of 1924 needed revision because of changed boundaries and because some had just been established as independent nations.

DOCUMENT 116: President's Proclamation, No. 2846, July 27, 1949: Immigration Quotas

... NOW, THEREFORE, I, HARRY S. TRUMAN, President of the United States of America, acting under and by virtue of the authority vested in me. . . . do hereby proclaim and make known that the annual quotas of the nationalities indicated for the remainder of the fiscal year ending June 30, 1950, and for each fiscal year thereafter have been determined in accordance with the law to be, and shall be, as follows:

Country	Quota
Greece	310
Italy	5,799
Rumania	291
Union of Soviet Socialist Republics	2,798
Israel	100
Jordan (formerly Transjordan)	100
Syria	100
Lebanon	100

Source: President's Proclamation No. 2846 of July 27, 1949.

* * *

In October 1949 Congress enacted the Agricultural Act of 1949, which codified prior laws and provisions for temporary agriculture workers and established (until 1964) the "Bracero program" that permitted the legal immigration, of temporary agricultural workers. The law, which comprises some ten pages in the code, is excerpted briefly in Document 117.

DOCUMENT 117: Act of October 31, 1949: Agricultural Act of 1949 ("Bracero Program")

Be it enacted by the Senate and House of Representatives of the United States of America in Congress assembled, That this Act may be cited as the "Agricultural Act of 1949."

Sec. 501. For the purpose of assisting in such production of agricultural commodities and products as the Secretary of Agriculture deems necessary, by supplying agricultural workers from the Republic of Mexico ... the Secretary of Labor is authorized—

(1) to recruit workers ...

(2) to establish and operate reception centers at or near places of actual entry of such workers into the continental United States for the purpose of receiving and housing such workers for their employment in, or departure from, the continental United States;

(3) to provide transportation for such workers from recruitment centers ... to such reception centers and transportation from [them] ... to such recruitment centers after termination of employment;

(4) to provide workers with such subsistence ... while ... at reception centers;

(5) to assist such workers and employers in negotiating contracts for agricultural employment ...

(6) to guarantee the performance by employers of provisions of such contracts. ...

Sec. 502. No workers shall be made available under this title to any employer unless such employer enters into an agreement with the United States—

(1) to indemnify the United States against loss ...

(2) to reimburse the United States for essential expenses ...

(3) to pay to the United States, in any case in which a worker is not returned [essentially the costs incurred]. ...

Sec. 503. [Requires that the secretary of labor certify the lack of domestic workers who are able, willing, and qualified for the work and thus justify the need to import immigrant labor.]

Sec. 505.* Workers recruited under this title who are not citizens of the United States shall be admitted to the United States subject to the immigration laws . . . .

Sec. 506.(c) Workers recruited under the provisions of this title shall not be subject to the head tax levied under section 2 of the Immigration Act of 1917. . . .

Sec. 510. No workers will be made available under this title [after December 31, 1964, as amended by the act of December 13, 1963 (77 Stat. 363)].

Source: 63 Stat. 1051.

* * *

In June 1952 Congress enacted the Immigration and Nationality Act of 1952, also known as the McCarran-Walter Act. This massive comprehensive omnibus law, which comprises 200 pages in the Code of Statutes, codifies all the previous immigration and naturalization laws into one comprehensive statute. Although it mostly reenacted the various quota laws and the 1917 law provisions, as amended, up through 1952, it did detail some revisions in those laws as well. It maintained the basic quota system but did allow for some new immigration quotas for a revised Asia-Pacific Triangle." More importantly, this act has remained the basic law for nearly fifty years; most immigration legislation passed since then, such as those acts in 1965, 1976, 1986, and 1990, actually amend this act. Consequently, an outline of the principal sections of the law will first be given, followed by excerpts of some of the key revisions and provisions of the act—most sections of the law simply repeated provisions already presented in prior documents. The act illustrates, however, the gradual chipping away from the severe restrictionism of the era.

The act reflects the impact of Cold War–related foreign policy considerations upon U.S. immigration policy in its special considerations for the entrance of "refugees" and "anti-communist freedom fighters." The following is a basic outline of the act and its more important sections.

TITLE I—GENERAL

Sections 101–106, Definitions and powers of certain officials

*Sections 505–510 renumbered by Act of October 3, 1961 (75 Stat. 761).

TITLE II—IMMIGRATION

Chapter 1—Quota System

Sections 201–202, Numerical limitations and chargeability

Section 203, Allocation of visas

Sections 204–207, Immigrant and nonquota statuses

Chapter 2—Qualifications for Admission of Aliens

Sections 211–215, Documents, travel control requirements, and so on

Chapter 3—Issuance of Entry Documents

Sections 221–224, Visas for immigrants, nonquota immigrants, reentry permits

Chapter 4—Provisions Relating to Entry and Exclusion

Sections 231–240, Lists, detentions, physical exams, inspections, exclusions, records

Chapter 5—Deportation, Adjustment of Status

Sections 241–250, Classes of deportable aliens, apprehensions, suspension of deportation, adjustment of status, change of nonimmigrant status

Chapter 6—Special Provisions Relating to Alien Crewmen

Sections 251–257, Lists, conditional landing permits, discharges, and so on

Chapter 7—Registration of Aliens

Sections 261–266, Forms, procedures, notices, penalties

Chapter 8—General Penalty Provisions

Sections 271–280, Prevention, harboring, reentry of deported aliens, court jurisdiction, collection of penalties

Chapter 9—Miscellaneous

Sections 281–293, Nonimmigrant visa fees, members of armed forces, immigration stations, local jurisdiction, American Indians born in Canada, and so on

TITLE III—NATIONALITY AND NATURALIZATION

Chapter 1—Nationality at Birth and by Collective Naturalization

Sections 301–309, By birth, areas—Puerto Rico, Alaska, Hawaii, Virgin Islands, Guam, Children born out of wedlock, and so on

Chapter 2—Nationality through Naturalization

Sections 310–348:311, Eligibility

312, Requirements regarding English language
313, Prohibitions upon naturalization for persons opposed to government or law or who favor totalitarianism
316, Requirements to residence, good moral character, and attachments to principles of the Constitution, favorable disposition to the United States
318, Prerequisites to naturalization—burden of proof
324, Former citizens regaining U.S. citizenship

Chapter 3—Loss of Nationality

Chapter 4—Miscellaneous

TITLE IV—MISCELLANEOUS

DOCUMENT 118: Act of June 27, 1952: The Immigration and Nationality Act ("McCarran-Walter Act")

Title II—Immigration

Chapter 1—Selection System/Numerical Limitations

Sec. 201. (a) The annual quota of any quota area shall be one-sixth of 1 per centum of the number of inhabitants in the continental United States in 1920, which number, except for the purpose of computing quotas for the quota areas within the Asia-Pacific triangle, shall be the same number heretofore determined under the provisions of section 11 of the Immigration Act of 1924, attributable by national origin to such quota area: *Provided*, That the quota existing for Chinese persons prior to the date of enactment of this Act shall be continued, and, except for as otherwise provided in section 202 (e), the minimum quota for any quota area shall be one hundred. . . .

201. (c) There shall be issued to quota immigrants chargeable to any quota (1) no more immigrant visas in any fiscal year than the quota for such year, and (2) in any calendar month of any fiscal year, no more immigrant visas than 10 per centum of the quota of such year; except that during the last two months of any fiscal year immigrant visas may be issued without regard to the 10 per centum limitation contained herein. . . .

201. (e) The quota numbers available under the annual quotas of each quota area proclaimed under this Act shall be reduced by the number of quota numbers which have been ordered to be deducted from annual quotas authorized prior to the effective date of the annual quotas proclaimed under this Act under—

(1) section 19(c) of the Immigration Act of 1917, as amended;

(2) the Displaced Persons Act of 1948, as amended; and

(3) any other Act of Congress enacted prior to the effective date of the quotas [herein]. . . .

Sec. 202. (b) With reference to determination of the quota to which shall be chargeable an immigrant who is attributable by as much as one-half of his ancestry to a people or peoples indigenous to the Asia-Pacific triangle comprising all quota areas and colonies and other dependent areas situate wholly east of the meridian sixty degrees east of Greenwich, wholly west of the meridian one hundred and sixty-five degrees west, and wholly north of the parallel twenty-five degrees south latitude—

(1) there is hereby established, in addition to quotas for separate quota areas comprising independent countries, self-governing dominions, and territories under the international trusteeship of the United Nations situate wholly within said Asia-Pacific triangle, an Asia-Pacific quota of one hundred annually, which shall not be subject to the provisions of subsection (e);

(2) such immigrant born within a separate quota area situated wholly within such Asian-Pacific triangle shall not be chargeable to the Asia-Pacific quota, but shall be chargeable to the quota for the separate quota area in which he was born;

(3) such immigrant born within a colony or other dependent area situate wholly within said Asia-Pacific triangle shall be chargeable to the Asia-Pacific quota;

(4) such immigrant born outside the Asia-Pacific triangle who is attributable by as much as one-half of his ancestry to a people or peoples indigenous to not more than one separate quota area, situate wholly within the Asia-Pacific triangle, shall be chargeable to the quota of that quota area;

(5) such immigrant born outside the . . . triangle who is attributable to one-half of his ancestry to a people or peoples indigenous . . . to one or more colonies or other dependent areas situate [sic] wholly within the . . . triangle, shall be chargeable to the Asia-Pacific quota. . . .

(c) Any immigrant born in a colony or other component or dependent area of a governing country for which no separate or specific quota has been established, unless a nonquota immigrant as provided in section 101(a)(27) of this Act, shall be chargeable to the quota of the governing country . . . except that (1) not more than one hundred persons . . . shall be chargeable to the quota . . . in any one year. . . .

Sec. 203. (a) Immigrant visas to quota immigrants shall be allotted in each fiscal year as follows:

(1) The first 50 per centum of the quota of each quota area for such year, plus any portion of such quota not required for the issuance of immigrant visas to the classes specified in paragraphs (2) and (3), shall be made available for the issuance of immigrant visas (A) to qualified quota immigrants whose services are determined by the Attorney Gen-

eral to be needed urgently in the United States because of the high education, technical training, specialized experience, or exceptional ability of such immigrants and to be substantially beneficial prospectively to the national economy, cultural interests, or welfare of the United States, and (B) to qualified quota immigrants who are the spouse or children of any immigrant described in clause (A) if accompanying him.

(2) The next 30 per centum of the quota for each quota area for such year ... shall be made available for the issuance of immigrant visas to qualified immigrants who are the parents of citizens of the United States, such citizens being at least twenty-one years of age or who are unmarried. ...

(3) The remaining 20 per centum of the quota ... shall be made available ... to qualified immigrants who are the spouses or unmarried sons or daughters of aliens lawfully admitted for permanent residence. ...

(e) Every immigrant shall be presumed to be a quota immigrant until he establishes to the satisfaction of the consular officer, at the time of application for a visa, and to the immigrant officers, at the time of application for admission, that he is a nonquota immigrant. Every quota immigrant shall be presumed to be a nonpreference quota immigrant until he establishes to the satisfaction of the consular officer ... that he is entitled to a preference status under paragraph (1), (2), or (3) of subsection (a) or to a preference under paragraph (4) of such subsection.

Sec. 205. (a) In the case of any alien claiming in his application for an immigrant visa to be entitled to a nonquota immigrant status under section 101(a)(27)(A), or to a quota immigrant status under section 203(a)(2) or 203(a)(3), or to a preference under section 203(a)(4), the consular officer shall not grant such status or preference until he has been authorized to do so as provided in this section. [This continues for several subsections: (b) through (d) basically covers details for spouses and children, attorney general and secretary of state authorization of consular officer to grant nonquota status, and so on.] ...

[Section 212 reiterates all of the excluded classes of prior laws.]

Sec. 212. (d)(5) The Attorney General may in his discretion parole into the United States temporarily under such conditions as he may prescribe for emergent reasons or reasons deemed strictly in the public interest any alien applying for admission to the United States, but such parole of such alien shall not be regarded as an admission of the alien and when the purposes of such parole shall, in the opinion of the Attorney General, have been served the alien shall forthwith return or be returned to the custody from which he was paroled and thereafter his case shall continue to be dealt with in the same manner as that of any other applicant for admission to the United States. ...

Sec. 215. (a) When the United States is at war or during the existence of any national emergency proclaimed by the President, or, as to aliens, whenever there exists a state of war between or among two or more states, and the President shall find that the interests of the United States require that restrictions and prohibitions in addition to those provided otherwise by this section be imposed upon the departure of persons from and their entry into the United States, and shall make public proclamation thereof, it shall, until otherwise ordered by the President or the Congress be unlawful—[the act then lists seven subdivisions of various restrictions and prohibitions].

Chapter 2—Nationality and Naturalization

Chapter 2—Nationality through Naturalization

Sec. 311. The right of a person to become a naturalized citizen of the United States shall not be denied or abridged because of race or sex or because such a person is married. Notwithstanding section 405(b), this section shall apply to any person whose petition for naturalization shall hereafter be filed, or shall have been pending on the effective date of this Act.

Sec. 312. No person except as otherwise provided in this title shall hereafter be naturalized as a citizen of the United States upon his own petition who cannot demonstrate—

(1) an understanding of the English language, including the ability to read, write, and speak words in ordinary usage in the English language. . . .

(2) a knowledge and understanding of the fundamentals of the history, and of the principles and form of government, of the United States.

Sec. 313. (a) Notwithstanding the provisions of section 405(b), no person shall be naturalized as a citizen of the United States—[the act lists subsections (1) through (6) which prohibit the naturalization of anarchists, communists, totalitarians, and those who believe or publish such, etc.]. . . .

Sec. 316. (a) No person, except as otherwise provided for in this title, shall be naturalized unless such petitioner, (1) immediately preceding the date of filing his petition for naturalization has resided continuously, after being lawfully admitted for permanent residence, within the United States for at least five years and during the five years . . . has been physically present therein for periods totaling at least half of that time, and who has resided within the State in which petition is filed for at least six months, (2) has resided continuously within the United States from the date of the petition up to the time of admission to citizenship, and (3) during all the periods referred to in this subsection has been and still is a person of good moral character, attached to the principles of the Constitution of the United States, and well disposed to the good order and happiness of the United States. [The subsection then specifies when and how absences are accepted as exceptions to the "continuous" residing provision.] . . .

Sec. 337. (a) A person who has petitioned for naturalization shall, in order to be and before being admitted to citizenship, take in open court an oath (1) to support the Constitution of the United States; (2) to renounce and abjure absolutely and entirely all allegiance and fidelity to any foreign prince, potentate, state, or sovereignty of whom or which the petitioner was before a subject or citizen; (3) to support and defend the Constitution and laws of the United States against all enemies, foreign and domestic; (4) to bear true faith and allegiance the same; and (5) (A) to bear arms on behalf of the United States when required by law, or (B) to perform non-combatant service in the Armed Forces of the United States when required by law, or (C) to perform work of national importance under civilian direction when required by law. . . .

Sec. 349. (a) From and after the effective date of this Act a person who is a national of the United States whether by birth or naturalization, shall lose his nationality by—

(1) obtaining naturalization in a foreign state upon his own application, upon an application filed in his behalf by a parent, guardian, or duly authorized agent, or through the naturalization of a parent having legal custody of such person. . . .

(2) taking an oath or making an affirmation or other formal declaration of allegiance to a foreign state or a political subdivision thereof, or

(3) entering, or serving in, the armed forces of a foreign state . . . unless [prior to doing so] authorized by the Secretary of State and the Secretary of Defense . . . or

(4) accepting, serving in, or performing the duties of any office, post, or employment under the government of a foreign state or a political subdivision thereof . . . or

(5) voting in a political election in a foreign state . . . or

(6) making a formal renunciation of nationality before a diplomatic or consular officer of the United States in a foreign state, in such form as may be prescribed by the Secretary of State; or

(7) making in the United States a formal written renunciation of nationality in such form as may be prescribed by . . . the Attorney General . . . or

(8) deserting the military, air, or naval forces of the United States in a time of war, if and when he is convicted thereof by court martial and as the result of such conviction is dismissed or dishonorably discharged from the service . . . or

(9) committing any act of treason against, or attempting to overthrow, or bearing arms against, the United States . . . or

(10) departing from or remaining outside of the jurisdiction of the United States in time of war . . . for the purpose of evading or avoiding . . . service in the military. . . .

Sec. 352. [Lists how a person who has become a citizen by naturalization may lose citizenship.]

Sec. 353. [Lists the exceptions to the residency stipulations that may result in loss of citizenship obtained by naturalization as specified in sec. 352.]

Source: 66 Stat. 163.

* * *

President Harry Truman's veto message of the McCarran-Walter Act, which shows his position on immigration policy, is presented in Document 119. His view had little impact, however, as the Congress overrode his veto and passed the Immigration Act of 1952 over his objections.

DOCUMENT 119: President Harry S. Truman's Veto Message of the Immigration and Nationality Bill, June 25, 1952

I return herewith, without my approval . . . the proposed Immigration and Nationality Act.

In outlining my objections to this bill, I want to make it clear that it contains certain provisions that meet with my approval. This is a long and complex piece of legislation. It has 164 separate sections, some with more than 40 subdivisions. It presents a difficult problem of weighing the good against the bad, and arriving at a judgment on the whole.

H.R. 5678 is an omnibus bill which would revise and codify all of our laws relating to immigration, naturalization, and nationality.

A general revision and modernization of these law unquestionably is needed and long overdue, particularly with respect to immigration. But this bill would not provide us with an immigration policy adequate for the present world situation. Indeed, the bill, taking all its provisions together, would be a step backward and not a step forward. In view of the crying need for reform in the field of immigration, I deeply regret that I am unable to approve H.R. 5678. . . .

   . . .

I have long urged that racial or national barriers to naturalization be abolished. This was one of the recommendations in my civil rights message to the Congress on February 2, 1948. On February 19, 1951, the House of Representatives unanimously passed a bill to carry it out.

But now this most desirable provision comes before me embedded in a mass of legislation which would perpetuate injustices of long standing against many other nations of the world, hamper the efforts we are making to rally the men of the East and West alike to the cause of freedom, and intensify the repressive and inhumane aspects of our immigration procedures. The price is too high, and in good conscience I cannot agree to pay it.

I want our residents of Japanese ancestry, and all our friends throughout the Far East, to understand this point clearly. I cannot take the step I would like to take, and strike down the bars that prejudice has erected against them, without, at the same time, establishing new discriminations against the peoples of Asia and approving harsh and repressive measures directed at all who seek a new life within our boundaries. I am sure that with a little more time and a little more discussion in this country the public conscience and the good sense of the American people will assert themselves, and we shall be in a position to enact an immigration and naturalization policy that will be fair to all. . . . The bill would continue, practically without change, the national origins quota system, which was enacted into law in 1924, and put into effect in 1929. This quota system—always based upon assumptions at variance with our American ideals—is long since out of date and more than ever unrealistic in the face of present world conditions. . . .

The overall quota limitation, under the law of 1924, restricted annual immigration to approximately 150,000. This was about one-seventh of one percent of our total population in 1920. Taking into account the growth in population since 1920, the law now allows us but one-tenth of one percent of our total population. And since the largest national quotas are only partly used, the number actually coming in has been in the neighborhood of one-fifteenth of one percent. This is far less than we must have in the years ahead to keep up with the growing needs of the Nation for manpower to maintain the strength and vigor of our economy.

The greatest vice of the present quota system, however, is that it discriminates, deliberately and intentionally, against many of the peoples of the world. The purpose behind it was to cut down and virtually eliminate immigration to this country from Southern and Eastern Europe. A theory was invented to rationalize this objective. The theory was that in order to be readily assimilable, European immigrants should be admitted in proportion to the numbers of persons of their respective national stocks already here as shown by the census of 1920. Since Americans with English, Irish and German descent were most numerous, immigrants from those three nationalities got the lion's share—more than two-thirds—of the total quota. The remaining third was divided up among all the other nations given quotas.

The desired effect was obtained. Immigration from Eastern Europe was reduced to a trickle. The quotas allotted to England and Ireland remained largely unused, as was intended. Total quota immigration fell to half or a third—and sometimes even less—of the annual limit of

154,000. People from such countries as Greece, or Spain, or Latvia were virtually deprived of any opportunity to come here at all, simply because Greeks or Spaniards or Latvians had not come here before 1920 in any substantial numbers.

The idea behind this discriminatory policy was, to put it baldly, that Americans with English or Irish names were better people and better citizens than Americans with Italian or Greek or Polish names. It was thought that people of West European origin made better citizens than Rumanians or Balts or Austrians. Such a concept is utterly unworthy of our traditions and ideals. It violates the great political doctrine of the Declaration of Independence that "all men are created equal." It denies the humanitarian creed inscribed beneath the Statue of Liberty proclaiming to all nations, "Give me your tired, your poor, your huddled masses yearning to breathe free."

It repudiates our basic religious concepts, our belief in the brotherhood of man, and in the words of St. Paul that "there is neither Jew nor Greek, there is neither bond nor free . . . for ye are all one in Christ Jesus."

The basis of this quota system was false and unworthy in 1924. It is even worse now. At the present time, this quota system keeps out the very people we want to bring in. It is incredible to me that, in this year of 1952, we should again be enacting into law such a slur on the patriotism, the capacity, and the decency of a large part of our citizenry.

Today, we have entered into an alliance, the North Atlantic Treaty, with Italy, Greece, and Turkey against one of the most terrible threats mankind has ever faced. We are asking them to join with us in protecting the peace of the world. We are helping them to rebuild their defenses, and train their men, in common cause. But, through this bill we say to their people: You are less worthy to come to this country than Englishmen or Irishmen; you Italians, who need to find homes abroad in the hundreds of thousands—you shall have a quota of 5,645; you Greeks, struggling to assist the helpless victims of a communist civil war—you shall have a quota of 308; and you Turks, you are brave defenders of the Eastern flank, but you shall have a quota of only 225!

Today we are "protecting" ourselves, as we were in 1924, against being flooded by immigrants from Eastern Europe. This is fantastic. The countries of Eastern Europe have fallen under the communist yoke—they are silenced, fenced off by barbed wire and minefields—no one passes their borders but at the risk of his life. We do not need to be protected from immigrants from these countries—on the contrary we want to stretch out a helping hand, to save those who have managed to flee into Western Europe, to succor those who are brave enough to escape from barbarism, to welcome and restore them against the day when their countries will, as we hope, be free again. But this we cannot do, as we would like to do, because the quota for Poland is only 6,500, as against the 138,000 exiled Poles, all over Europe; because the quota for the now subjugated Baltic countries is little more than 700—against the 23,000 Baltic refugees imploring us to admit them to a new life here; because the quota for Rumania is only 289, and some 30,000 Rumanians, who have managed to escape the labor camps and the mass deportations of their Soviet masters, have asked for our help. These are only a few examples of the absurdity, the cruelty of carrying over into this year of 1952 the isolationist limitations of our 1924 law.

In no other realm of our national life are we so hampered and stultified by the dead hand of the past, as we are in this field of immigration. We do not limit our cities to their 1920 boundaries—we do not hold our corporations to their 1920 capitalizations—we welcome progress and change to meet changing conditions in every sphere of life, except in the field of immigration.

The time to shake off this dead weight of past mistakes is now. The time to develop a decent policy of immigration—a fitting instrument of our foreign policy, and a true reflection of the ideals we stand for, at home and abroad—is now. In my earlier message on immigration, I tried to explain to the Congress that the situation we face in immigration is an emergency—that it must be met promptly. I have pointed out that in the last few years, we have blazed a new trail in immigration, through our Displaced Persons Program. Through the combined efforts of the Government and private agencies, working together not to keep people out, but to bring qualified people in, we summoned our resources of good will and human feeling to meet the task. In this program, we have found better techniques to meet the immigration problems of the 1950's.

None of this fruitful experience of the last three years is reflected in this bill before me. None of the crying human needs of this time of trouble is recognized in this bill. But it is not too late. The Congress can remedy these defects, and it can adopt legislation to meet the most critical problems before adjournment.

The only consequential change in the 1924 quota system which the bill would make is to extend a small quota to each of the countries of Asia. But most of the beneficial effects of this gesture are offset by other provisions in the bill. The countries of Asia are told in one breath that they shall have quotas for their nationals, and in the next, that the nationals of the other countries, if their ancestry is as much as 50 percent Asian, shall be charged to these quotas.

It is only with respect to persons of oriental ancestry that this invidious discrimination applies. All other persons are charged to the country of their birth. But persons with Asian ancestry are charged to the countries of Asia, wherever they may have been born, or however long their ancestors have made their homes outside the land of their origin. These provisions are without justification.

I now wish to turn to other provisions of the bill, those dealing with the qualifications of aliens and immigrants for admission, with the administration of the laws, and with problems of naturalization and nationality. In these provisions, too, I find objections that preclude my signing this bill.

The bill would make it even more difficult to enter our country. Our resident aliens would be more easily separated from homes and families under grounds of deportation, both new and old, which would specifically be made retroactive. Admission to our citizenship would be made more difficult; expulsion from our citizenship would be made easier. Certain rights of native born, first generation Americans would be limited. All our citizens returning from abroad would be subjected to serious risks of unreasonable invasions of privacy. Seldom has a bill exhibited the distrust evidenced here for citizens and aliens alike—at a time when we need unity at home, and the confidence of our friends abroad. . . .

I am asked to approve the reenactment of highly objectionable provisions now contained in the Internal Security Act of 1950—a measure passed over my veto shortly after the invasion of South Korea. Some of these provisions would empower the Attorney General to deport any alien who has engaged in or has had a purpose to engage in activities "prejudicial to the public interest." No standards or definitions are provided to guide discretion in the exercise of power so sweeping. To punish undefined "activities" departs from traditional American insistence on established standards of guilt. To punish an undefined "purpose" is thought control.

These provisions are worse than the infamous Alien Act of 1798, passed in a time of national fear and distrust of foreigners, which gave the President power to deport any alien deemed "dangerous to the peace and safety of the United States." Alien residents were thoroughly frightened and citizens much disturbed by that threat to liberty.

Such powers are inconsistent with our democratic ideals. Conferring powers like that upon the Attorney General is unfair to him as well as to our alien residents. Once fully informed of such vast discretionary powers vested in the Attorney General, Americans now would and should be just as alarmed as Americans were in 1798 over less drastic powers vested in the President. . . .

Native-born American citizens who are dual nationals would be subjected to loss of citizenship on grounds not applicable to other native-born American citizens. This distinction is a slap at millions of Americans whose fathers were of alien birth. . . . Children would be subjected to additional risk of loss of citizenship. Naturalized citizens would be subjected to the risk of denaturalization by any procedure that can be found to be permitted under any State law or practice pertaining to minor civil law suits. Judicial review of administrative denials of citizenship would

be severely limited and impeded in many cases, and completely eliminated in others. I believe these provisions raise serious constitutional
questions. Constitutionality aside, I see no justification in national policy
for their adoption. . . .

In these and many other respects, the bill raises basic questions as to
our fundamental immigration and naturalization policy, and the laws
and practices for putting that policy into effect.

Many of the aspects of the bill which have been most widely criticized
in the public debate are reaffirmations or elaborations of existing statutes
or administrative procedures. Time and again, examination discloses that
the revisions of existing law that would be made by the bill are intended
to solidify some restrictive practice of our immigration authorities, or to
overrule or modify some ameliorative decision of the Supreme Court or
other Federal courts. By and large, the changes that would be made by
the bill do not depart from the basically restrictive spirit of our existing
laws—but intensify and reinforce it.

These conclusions point to an underlying condition which deserves
the most careful study. Should we not undertake a reassessment of our
immigration policies and practices in the light of the conditions we face
in the second half of the twentieth century? The great popular interest
which this bill has created, and the criticism which it has stirred up,
demand an affirmative answer. I hope the Congress will agree to a careful reexamination of this entire matter.

To assist in this complex task, I suggest the creation of a representative
commission of outstanding Americans to examine the basic assumptions
of our immigration policy, the quota system and all that goes with it,
the effect of our present immigration and nationality laws, their administration, and the ways in which they can be brought in line with our
national ideals and our foreign policy.

Such commission should, I believe, be established by the Congress. Its
membership should be bi-partisan and divided equally among persons
from private life and persons from public life. I suggest that four members be appointed by the President, four by the President of the Senate,
and four by the Speaker of the House of Representatives. The commission should be given sufficient funds to employ a staff and it should
have adequate powers to hold hearings, take testimony, and obtain information. It should make a report to the President and to the Congress
within a year from the time of its creation.

Pending the completion of studies by such a commission, and the consideration of its recommendations by the Congress, there are certain
steps which I believe it is most important for the Congress to take this
year.

First, I urge the Congress to enact legislation removing racial barriers
against Asians from our laws. Failure to take this step profits us nothing

and can only have serious consequences for our relations with the peoples of the Far East. A major contribution to this end would be the prompt enactment by the Senate of H.R. 403. That bill, already passed by the House of Representatives, would remove the racial bars to the naturalization of aliens.

Secondly, I strongly urge the Congress to enact the temporary, emergency immigration legislation which I recommended three months ago. In my message of March 24, 1952, I advised the Congress that one of the gravest problems arising from the present world crisis is created by the overpopulation in parts of Western Europe That condition is aggravated by the flight and expulsion of people from behind the iron curtain. In view of these serious problems, I asked the Congress to authorize the admission of 300,000 additional immigrants to the United States over a three year period. These immigrants would include Greek nationals, Dutch nationals, Italians from Italy and Trieste, Germans and persons of German ethnic origin, and religious and political refugees from communism in Eastern Europe. This temporary program is urgently needed. It is very important that the Congress act upon it this year. I urge the Congress to give prompt and favorable consideration to the bills introduced by Senator Hendrickson and Representative Celler (H.R. 3109 and H.R. 73765), which will implement the recommendations contained in my message of March 24.

I very much hope that the Congress will take early action on these recommendations. Legislation to carry them out will correct some of the unjust provisions of our laws, will strengthen us at home and abroad, and will serve to relieve a great deal of the suffering and tension existing in the world today. Harry S. Truman.

Source: Public Papers of the Presidents (June 25, 1952): 441–47. President Truman's Veto of the McCarran-Walter Act (June 25, 1952).

* * *

The U.S. Supreme Court reflected some of the fears dominating the Congress that were alluded to in President Truman's veto message [Document 119]. It handed down a decision in October 1952 concerning the procedures for dealing with aliens seeking admission who were detained at Ellis Island while their entry (or reentry in this case) was being examined. The Court affirmed sweeping powers to deny entry for national security concerns, as evidenced in Document 120, which provides a brief excerpt of the decision of *Shaughnessy v. United States.*

DOCUMENT 120: *Shaughnessy v. United States ex rel. Mezei* (March 16, 1953)

... But respondent's history here drastically differs from that discussed in Chew's Case. Unlike Chew who with full security clearance and documentation pursued his vocation for four months aboard an American ship, respondent apparently without authorization or reentry papers, simply left the United States and remained behind the Iron Curtain for 19 months. Moreover, while [Sec.] 307 of the 1940 Nationality Act regards maritime service such as Chew's to be continuous residence for naturalization purposes, that section deems protracted absence such as the respondent's clear break in an alien's continuous residence here. In such circumstances, we have no difficulty holding respondent an entrant alien or "assimilated to [that] status" for constitutional purposes. That being so, the Attorney General may lawfully exclude respondent without a hearing as authorized by the emergency regulations promulgated pursuant to the Passport Act. Nor need he disclose the evidence upon which that determination rests. ...

There remains the issue of respondent's continued exclusion on Ellis Island. Aliens seeking entry from contiguous lands obviously can be turned back at the border. ... While the Government might keep entrants by sea aboard the vessel pending determination of their admissibility, the resulting hardships to the alien and inconvenience to the carrier persuaded Congress to adopt a more generous course. By statute it authorized, in cases such as this, aliens' temporary removal from ship to shore. But such temporary harborage bestows no additional rights. Congress meticulously specified that such shelter ashore "shall not be considered a landing" nor relieve the vessel of the duty to transport back the alien if ultimately excluded. And this Court has long considered such temporary arrangements as not affecting the alien's status; he is treated as if stopped at the border. ... Thus we do not think that respondent's continued exclusion deprives him of any statutory or constitutional right. It is true that resident aliens temporarily detained pending expeditious consummation of deportation proceedings may be released on bond by the Attorney General whose discretion is subject to judicial review. ... By that procedure aliens uprooted from our midst may rejoin the community until the Government effects their leave. An exclusion proceeding grounded on danger to the national security, however, presents different considerations; neither the rationale nor the statutory authority for such release exists. Ordinarily to admit an alien barred from entry on security grounds nullifies the very purpose of the exclusion proceeding, Congress in 1950 declined to include such authority in the statute. That exclusion by the United States plus other nations' inhospitality results in present hardship cannot be ignored. But, the times being what they are, Congress may well have felt that other countries ought not shift the onus to us; that an alien in respondent's position is no more ours than theirs. Whatever our individual estimate of that policy and the fears on which it rests, respondent's right to enter the United States depends on the congressional will, and courts cannot substitute their judgment for the legislative mandate. . . . Reversed.

Source: 345 U.S. 206, March 16, 1953.

* * *

As authorized in the McCarran-Walter Act of 1952 [Document 118], President Truman established the President's Commission on Immigration and Naturalization, which issued its highly critical report, entitled *Whom Shall We Welcome,* in January 1953. The report discussed what it termed the insistent condemnation of the provisions of the 1952 act concerning enlarging the grounds for exclusion and deportation. It stressed the commission's view that U.S. immigration law is an essential part of the nation's foreign policy. It concluded that the national origins system had failed in its avowed purpose as a selection system, which it assessed as arbitrary, and that did not conform to the facts. It was highly critical of the naturalization processes and procedures. The report's conclusions and recommendations, excerpted below, became the basis for many of the later reforms and amendments to the 1952 act.

DOCUMENT 121: Recommendations of Presidential Commission on Immigration (January 1, 1953)

Conclusions

The immigration and nationality law embodies policies and principles that are unwise and injurious to the nation.

It rests upon an attitude of hostility and distrust against all aliens.

It applies discriminations against human beings on account of national origin, race, creed and color.

It ignores the needs of the United States and domestic affairs and foreign policies.

It contains unnecessary and unreasonable restrictions and penalties against individuals.

It is badly drafted, confusing and in some respects unworkable.

It should be reconsidered and revised from beginning to end.

Recommendations

Throughout this Report are various recommendations, appearing in the chapters in which particular subjects are discussed. The more important ones are briefly restated here, without reference to the order in which they appear elsewhere:

The Quota System

1. The national origins quota system should be abolished.

2. There should be a unified quota system, which would allocate visas without regard to national origin, race, creed, or color.

3. The maximum annual quota immigration should be one-sixth of 1 percent of the population of the United States, as determined by the most recent census. Under the 1950 census, quota immigration would be opened to 251, 162 immigrants annually, instead of the 154,657 now authorized.

4. All immigration and naturalization functions now in the Department of State and the Department of Justice should be consolidated into a new agency, to be headed by a Commission on Immigration and Naturalization whose members should be appointed by the President and confirmed by the Senate.

5. The maximum annual quota of visas should be distributed, as determined by the proposed Commission . . . on the basis of the following five categories:

   The Right of Asylum; Reunion of Families; Needs in the United States; Special Needs in the Free World; General Immigration.

6. For the next three years, within the maximum annual quota, there should be a statutory priority, implementing the Right of Asylum, for the admission annually of 100,000 refugees, expellees, escapees, and remaining displaced persons.

7. The allocation of visas within the maximum annual quota should be determined, once every three years, by the proposed Commission . . . subject to review by the President and Congress.

Fair Hearings and Procedure

8. Enforcement functions should be exercised, under the Commission's supervision and control, by an Administrator. Quasi-judicial functions should be exercised, under the Commission's supervision, by a statutory Board of Immigration and Visa Appeals.

9. The same officials should not be permitted to exercise both enforcement and judicial functions. Aliens should be accorded a fair hearing and procedure in exclusion and deportation cases. Hearings in deportation cases should conform with the requirements of the Administrative Procedure Act. Hearing

officers should be responsible only to the proposed Board of Immigration and Visa Appeals, which should have authority to exercise final administrative review of their decisions, subject to further review in limited cases by the Commission. Aliens should have a right of administrative review, before the Board of Immigration and Visa Appeals, from denials of visas; and have a clearly defined method of seeking court review of orders of deportation.

Admissions and Deportations

10. The conditions for admission of aliens into the United States should
    —bear a reasonable relationship to the national welfare and security;
    —be definite in their meaning and application;
    —include discretionary authority to waive specified grounds of inadmissibility, in meritorious cases;
    —provide for exclusions without hearing, for reasons of security, only upon direction of the Board of Immigration and Visa Appeals; and
    —not be based upon the so-called criminal judgments of totalitarian states.

11. The grounds for deportation of aliens already in the United States should
    —bear a reasonable relationship to the national welfare and security; not be technical or excessive;
    —not be retroactive so as to penalize aliens for acts which were not prohibited when committed; and
    —not require the deportation of aliens who entered the country at an early age, or those who have residents for such a long period as to become the responsibility of the United States.

12. In connection with the deportation of aliens, there should be discretionary authority to
    —allow them to depart voluntarily instead of deportation;
    —adjust their status within the United States if they are currently qualified to reenter;
    —suspend deportation under reasonable conditions; and
    —adjust the status of bona fide official defectors from totalitarianism.

13. A resident alien who is not otherwise deportable should not, by reason of a brief absence from the United States, be subject to exclusion or deportation.

14. Unless proceedings for deportation and denaturalization are brought within ten years, they should be barred.

15. Arrangements should be made to expedite the processing of visas for temporary visitors, including leaders in art, scientific and business fields, and the law should apply to such nonimmigrant aliens only such restrictions as are directly concerned with the health, safety, and security of the United States.

Security

16. The security of the United States should be protected by continuing to bar the entry of spies and saboteurs.
    Aliens who are present members or affiliates of any totalitarian party, including Communists, Nazis, and Fascists, should be denied admission to the United States except where their membership is involuntary; or affiliation is

not knowingly or willingly to further the aims and principles of such parties. They should be deported except where they entered the United States at an early age or have been residents for such a long period of time as to have become the responsibility of the United States.

Aliens who are former members or affiliates of any totalitarian party may be admitted provided they have repudiated and are now opposed to such totalitarian ideologies; and the responsible administrative officers make a finding that the admission of such aliens would not be contrary to the public interest.

They should be deported unless they have repudiated such doctrines for at least five years.

Citizenship

17. The law should not discriminate against naturalized citizens but should place them in the same status as native-born citizens, except where citizenship was procured by fraud or illegality. The law should minimize or remove restrictions which create statelessness, disrupt family unity, or impose unreasonable conditions or procedures upon the acquisition or retention of citizenship.

Source: Recommendations of Presidential Commission on Immigration, *Whom Shall We Welcome?*, January 1, 1953.

* * *

With the outbreak of the Korean War, President Truman issued a proclamation establishing the emergency powers aspects to control persons leaving or entering the United States. Document 122 presents a brief excerpt of the Proclamation, which was very similar in wording to those used during World War II.

DOCUMENT 122: President's Proclamation No. 3004, January 17, 1953: Control of Persons Leaving or Entering the United States

---

. . .

NOW, THEREFORE, I, HARRY S. TRUMAN, President of the United States, acting under and by virtue of the authority vested in me by section 215 of the Immigration and Nationality Act and by section 301 of title 3 of the United States Code, do hereby find and publicly proclaim that the interests of the United States require that restrictions and prohibitions, in addition to those provided by law, be imposed upon the departure of persons from, and their entry into, the United States; and I hereby proscribe and make the following rules, regulations, and orders with respect thereto: [the Proclamation then lists the rules and regulations as they were imposed in 1941, as above in Documents 99 and 100].

Source: President's Proclamation No. 3004 of January 17, 1953.

* * *

The refugee situation worldwide, including refugees still in Europe from World War II, and the foreign policy concerns of the Cold War contributed to a growing awareness in Congress that the quotas were too rigid, and it enacted the Refugee Relief Act of 1953, portions of which are provided in Document 123.

DOCUMENT 123: Act of August 7, 1953: Refugee Relief Act of 1953

Be it enacted by the Senate and House of Representatives of the United States of America in Congress assembled, That this Act may be cited as the "Refugee Relief Act of 1953."

Sec. 2. (a) "Refugee" means any person in a country or area which is neither Communist nor Communist-dominated, who because of persecution, fear of persecution, natural calamity or military operations is out of his usual place of abode and unable to return thereto, who has not been firmly resettled, and who is in urgent need of assistance for the essentials of life or for transportation.

(b) "Escapee" means any refugee who, because of persecution or fear of persecution on account of race, religion, or political opinion, fled from the Union of Soviet Socialist Republics or any other Communist, Communist-dominated, or Communist-occupied area of Europe including those parts of Germany under military occupation by the Union of Soviet Socialist Republics, and who cannot return thereto because of fear of persecution on account of race, religion, or political opinion.

(c)"German expellee" means any refugee of German ethnic origin residing in the area of the German Federal Republic, western sector of Berlin, or in Austria who was born in and was forcibly removed from or forced to flee from Albania, Bulgaria, Czechoslovakia, Estonia, Hungary, Latvia, Lithuania, Poland Rumania, Union of Soviet Socialist Republics, Yugoslavia, or areas provisionally under the administration or control or domination of any such countries, except the Soviet zone of military occupation of Germany.

(d)"Administrator" means the administrator of the Bureau of Security and Consular Affairs established in the Department of State pursuant to subsection (b) of section 104 of the Immigration and Nationality Act.

Sec. 3. There are hereby authorized to be issued two hundred five thousand special nonquota immigrant visas to aliens, specified in section 4 of this Act, seeking to enter the United States as immigrants and to their spouses and their unmarried sons or daughters under twenty-one years of age, including stepsons or stepdaughters and sons or daughters adopted prior to July 1, 1953, if accompanying them.

Sec. 4. (a) Special nonquota immigrant visas authorized to be issued . . . shall be allotted as follows:

(1) Not to exceed fifty-five thousand visas to German expellees. . . .

(2) Not to exceed thirty-five thousand visas to escapees residing in the area of the German Federal Republic or the western sectors of Berlin or in Austria.

(3) Not to exceed ten thousand visas to escapees residing within the European continental limits of the members of the North Atlantic Treaty Organization or in Turkey, Sweden, Iran or in the Free Territory of Trieste. . . .

(4) Not to exceed two thousand visas to refugees who (a) during WWII were members of the armed forces of the Republic of Poland, (b) were honorably discharged from such forces, (c) reside on the date of the enactment of this Act in the British Isles, and (d) have not acquired British citizenship.

(5) Not to exceed forty-five thousand visas to refugees of Italian ethnic origin, residing on the date of the enactment . . . in Italy or the Free Territory of Trieste. . . .

(6) Not to exceed fifteen thousand visas to persons of Italian ethnic origin . . . who qualify under any of the preferences specified in paragraph (2), (3) or (4) . . . of the Immigration and Nationality Act. . . .

(7) Not to exceed fifteen thousand refugees of Greek ethnic origin. . . .

(8) Not to exceed two thousand refugees of Greek ethnic origin . . . who qualify under any of the preferences . . . of the Immigration and Nationality Act. . . .

(9) Not to exceed fifteen thousand visas of refugees of Dutch ethnic origin. . . .

(10) Not to exceed two thousand . . . Dutch . . . under the preferences . . . of the Immigration and Nationality Act. . . .

(11) Not to exceed two thousand visas to refugees, residing within the district of an American consular office in the Far East. . . .

(12) Not to exceed three thousand visas to refugees, residing within the district of an American consular office in the Far East . . . under preferences . . . of the Immigration and Nationality Act. . . .

(13) Not to exceed two thousand visas to refugees of Chinese ethnic origin. . . .

(14) Not to exceed two thousand visas to refugees who on the date of the enactment of this Act are eligible to receive assistance of the United Nations Relief and Works Agency for Palestine Refugees and the Near East. . . .

Sec. 7. (a) Except as otherwise herein provided, no visa shall be issued to any alien under this Act unless assurance, in accordance with regulations promulgated pursuant to this Act, shall first have been given by a citizen or citizens of the United States that such alien, if admitted into the United States, will be suitably employed without displacing some other person from employment and that such alien and the members of such alien's family who shall accompany such alien . . . will not become public charges and will have housing without displacing some other person from housing. . . .

Sec. 11. (a) No alien shall be issued a visa under this Act or be admitted into the United States unless there shall have first been a thorough investigation and written report made and prepared by such investigative agency or agencies of the Government of the United States as the President shall designate, regarding such person's character, reputation, mental and physical health, history and eligibility under this Act, and such investigations in each case shall be conducted in a manner and in such time as the investigative agency or agencies shall determine to be necessary. . . .

Sec. 12. Priorities in the consideration of visa applications under this Act, except in the case of applications filed under paragraph (6), (8) or (10) of section 4 (a), without priority in time of issuance of visas as between such priorities or as between priority and nonpriority cases under this Act shall be given to—

(1) Persons whose services or skills are needed in the United States, if such need has been certified to the Administrator, at his request, by the United States Employment Service and who are employed in a capacity calling for such services or such skills; and

(2) Persons who are (A) the parents of citizens of the United States, such citizens being at least twenty-one years of age, or (B) spouses or unmarried sons or daughters under twenty-one years of age, including stepsons or stepdaughters and sons or daughters adopted prior to July 1, 1953, of aliens lawfully admitted for permanent residence, or (C) brothers, sisters, sons or daughters of citizens of the United States.

[The act also specifies treatment for orphans, adjustment of their status as bona fide nonimmigrants, and details the administrative processes for implementing the act including security measures of investigation and financial provisions to implement the act.]

Source: 67 Stat. 400.

* * *

Concerns over the process of revoking naturalization of persons suspected of being security risks were raised during the height of the Cold War era. In response to such fears, the attorney general issued a statement to allay those fears among the 7.5 million naturalized citizens. His statement is summarized in Document 124.

DOCUMENT 124: Attorney General Herbert Brownell, Jr., Affirms Equal Rights of Naturalized Citizens, 1954

Attorney General Herbert Brownell Jr., in a message to the 24th Annual Conference of the National Council of Naturalization and Citizenship meeting in New York City, declared that "the naturalized citizen is accepted by our people as a full and equal member in the fraternity of American citizenship," ... pointing out that the law-abiding naturalized citizens need have no fear of denaturalization proceedings. Proceedings of this kind, he said, are not aimed at the freedom of the naturalized citizen, but are a weapon against the lawless and corrupt.

"Our law provides that naturalization may be revoked through court proceedings in exceptional cases to protect our citizenship from those who would debase it by obtaining citizenship through deception. It relates only to misconduct in connection with the naturalization itself and is not aimed at any activity of the naturalized citizen after citizenship is granted.... Moreover, the Supreme Court repeatedly has emphasized the high value of American citizenship and has declared that naturalization can be revoked only upon evidence that it was improperly obtained...." "It is therefore unreal and untrue to assume that 7.5 million naturalized Americans live under the threat that their citizenship may be taken away...." "During the past few years a number of denaturalization proceedings have been brought against persons charged with subversive and criminal activities. But these suits have been brought against a small group of individuals whose naturalizations were tainted and whose activities have made them conspicuously undesirable...."

Source: Common Council for American Unity, Press Releases, No. 54–30, W-688, April 7, 1954.

* * *

In 1954 Congress amended the special quota for sheepherders by extending it another year, to September 1955; and in 1955, it amended the Agricultural Act of 1949 (the Bracero Program) by extending it to June 30, 1959. Another major event taking place in 1954 was the closing of Ellis Island as the nation's largest and primary immigration receiving and processing station. Document 125 contains a summary of an article written on the closing of Ellis Island, which characterizes and describes its significance.

DOCUMENT 125: Ellis Island Closes Down, November 1954

Ellis Island, gateway to America since 1892, has been retired from the nation's immigration service. The closing down of Ellis Island and five other seaport processing and detention centers at Boston, Seattle, San Francisco, San Pedro, and Honolulu was announced on November 11, 1954, by U.S. Attorney General Brownell. Ellis Island, situated in upper New York Bay, almost in the shadow of the Statue of Liberty, has served for sixty-two years as chief immigration station and port of entry to more than twenty million citizens-to-be. In the year 1907 alone, 1,200,000 immigrants were received and examined there.

The designation of Ellis Island as an immigration station followed the important U.S. Supreme Court ruling in 1890 which transferred jurisdiction over immigration from the states to the Federal Government. Two years later, with a hospital, detention quarters, hearing and inspection rooms, and a ferry house erected, Ellis Island began receiving the millions of hopeful immigrants who came seeking entry to these hospitable shores.

For these newcomers, representing over fifty different national backgrounds, speaking as many languages and several hundred dialects, and adhering to a dozen different religions, America was a refuge, a chance for a better life. They had come to find freedom from militarism and army service, from poverty, ghettos, and political oppression. They left Ellis Island to go into the cities, towns and villages of America, to work on farms or in factories and mills, in shops and stockyards, or on new bridges, roads and skyscrapers.

Ellis Island is a story often darkened, in the early years especially, by hardships and misunderstandings. This sombre legend of harsh treatment, cruel suspense, poor housing and worse food, was the product of an administrative task too vast for overworked officials and inadequate facilities.

"Three or four times a week, from nine o'clock in the morning to nine in the evening we were continuously examining aliens," is one inspector's recollection of 1907, the year of the heaviest immigration. "I thought it was a stream that would never end. Every twenty-four hours from three to five thousand people came before us, and I myself examined between four to five hundred a day. We were simply swamped by that human tide."

The tide of immigration sharply slackened with the beginning of World War I. A significant departure in immigration policy came in 1921 with the setting of quotas for each eligible nationality based on the numbers of such nationality resident in the United States, as determined by the census of 1910. After the Immigration Law of 1924, which made permanent and more stringent the numerical restrictions of the Quota Act of 1921, far fewer aliens were detained at Ellis Island for further examination. Immigrants were now inspected before embarking, given a second medical examination aboard ship and a final review of immigration papers before landing.

By the middle 1930's the Island's physical plant had been enlarged and modernized. Hospital space had been added, and the huge dormitories of the beleaguered past, with their collapsible iron bedsteads, three tiers high, gave way to clean, well-ventilated rooms. For those detained, there were recreation areas, a library and a reading room. These greater comforts made possible more considerate treatment of bewildered men and women. . . .

Originally the island comprised a scant three acres of grass, rock and sand. Today it covers twenty-one acres, a seven fold expansion made up of the soil and rock of many lands carried as ballast in foreign vessels and dumped over the years in the shallow waters surrounding the island. Though for the present, at least, it has seen its last immigrant, Ellis Island endures, physically, as an outpost of the European homeland.

Source: Common Council for American Unity, Press Releases, No. 55–1-W-830, January 4, 1955.

* * *

President Dwight D. Eisenhower favored a slightly more generous immigration policy than was embodied in the McCarran-Walter Act. In 1956 he presented a message stating his views on immigration. Document 126 presents an article summarizing his views in a column entitled "Letters from America."

DOCUMENT 126: President Dwight D. Eisenhower's Message on Immigration, February 8, 1956

The United States is, in a sense, a nation of immigrants. For that reason, among others, there has been great interest in President Eisenhower's February 8th message to Congress urging important changes in the country's immigration laws. And there can be little doubt that there is equally great interest on the part of those abroad who look to the United States as a future home for themselves and their children.

The President's message deals with four different aspects of our immigration policy. Of these, his recommendations regarding the national origin quota system will be of widest significance. Broadly, what President Eisenhower proposes is that Congress amend the present law to permit more persons to settle in the United States by increasing existing quotas and pooling unused quotas.

Under the present law—the Immigration and Nationality Act of 1952—commonly known as the McCarran-Walter Act—the number of quota immigrants who can settle in the United States is limited to a little less than 155,000. Mr. Eisenhower would increase that number to about 220,000, or one-seventh of one percent of the U.S. population in 1950. This increase of some 65,000 each year is justified, he said, by the gain in population as well as the economic growth of America over the past thirty years.

The president also proposes to pool unused quotas on a regional basis. In recent years such countries as Great Britain, Ireland, and France have used only a part of their quotas while there have been long waiting lists for quota numbers in other countries. In 1954, the most recent year for figures are available, only 94,000 quota immigrants arrived. About 60,000 quota numbers went unused.

Under President Eisenhower's proposal, a quota pool for each of four geographic regions—Europe, Asia, Africa, and Oceania—would be set up. Unused quota numbers from any country within a region would be assigned each year to the pool for that region. The quota numbers in each regional pool would then be available for one year to immigrants born anywhere in the region, if they qualified for a "preference" status under existing law. This pooling provision would benefit applicants from many countries, particularly in southern and southeastern Europe.

The President also asked Congress to end the so-called "mortgages" on future quotas. Under the Displaced Persons Act of 1948, many immigrant refugees entering the United States—mostly from central and eastern Europe—were charged against future immigration quotas. Fifty percent of the Greek quota, for example, has thus been mortgaged until the year 2017. . . .

"Throughout our history," the President said, "immigration to this land has contributed greatly to the strength and character of our republic." Americans recognize the truth of these words, as do our friends and relatives abroad. So in our letters we should tell them about President Eisenhower's message on immigration. At a time when immigration policy has been under sharp attack, it is surely in our best interest to show the world—should Congress approve—that once again we stand ready to open wider the gateway to America.

Source: Common Council for American Unity, "Letters from America" Index No. 56–13–750, February 27, 1956.

* * *

In 1957 Congress amended the Immigration and Nationality Act of 1952 to refine its definition and applicability to stepchildren, illegitimate children, and adopted minor-age children, as excerpted below in Document 127. The act illustrates the detail to which Congress refined the Immigration and Nationality Act in reaction to immigration pressures to reform the omnibus, often cumbersome, McCarran-Walter Act.

DOCUMENT 127: Act of September 11, 1957: To Amend the Immigration and Nationality Act and for Other Purposes (regarding refugees)

Be it enacted by the Senate and House of Representatives of the United States of America in Congress assembled, That subparagraph (B) of section 101 (b) (1) of the Immigration and Nationality Act is amended to read as follows:

"(B) a stepchild, whether or not born out of wedlock, provided the child has not reached the age of eighteen years at the time the marriage creating the status of stepchild occurred; or"

Sec. 2. Section 101 (b) (1) of the Immigration and Nationality Act is amended by adding at the end thereof the following new subparagraphs:

"(D) an illegitimate child, by, through whom, or on whose behalf a status, privilege, or benefit is sought by virtue of the relationship of the child to its natural mother;

"(E) a child adopted while under the age of fourteen years if the child has thereafter been in the legal custody of, and has resided with, the adopting parent or parents for at least two years: *Provided,* That no natural parent of any such adopted child shall thereafter, by virtue of such parentage, be accorded any right, privilege, or status under this Act."

Sec. 3. Section 203 (a) (1) of the Immigration and Nationality Act is amended by striking out "him" and inserting in lieu thereof the following: "or following to join him."

Sec. 4. (a) On or before June 30, 1959, special nonquota immigrant visas may be issued to eligible orphans as defined in this section who are under fourteen years of age at the time the visa is issued. Not more than two such special nonquota immigrant visas may be issued to eligible orphans adopted or to be adopted by any one United States citizen and spouse, unless necessary to prevent the separation of brothers and sisters.

(b) When used in this section, the term "eligible orphan" shall mean an alien child (1) who is an orphan because of the death or disappearance of both parents, or because of abandonment or desertion by, or separation or loss from, both parents, or who has only one parent due to the death or disappearance of, abandonment, or desertion by, or separation or loss from the other parent and the remaining parent is incapable of providing care for such orphan and has in writing irrevocably released him for emigration and adoption.

[The act then discusses the details for the issuance of visas, the exclusion from these provisions for such aliens afflicted with tuberculosis, the administrative power of the attorney general to authorize regulations to enforce the act, quota deduction procedures for the act as applied to "refugee-escapee," and the meaning of the term "general area of the Middle East."]

Source: 71 Stat. 639.

* * *

The failed Hungarian revolution in 1956 led to the foreign policy and Cold War need to do something to help assist and relocate the tens of thousands of Hungarian refugees, known as the "freedom fighters," who left Hungary after their revolt failed. In late 1956 President Eisenhower used the "parole" authority of the 1952 act to admit a group of over 15,000. Congress subsequently endorsed his novel use of parole (which previously had been applied only to individuals) by granting permanent residence to those already here by parole authority. Over 30,600 were ultimately admitted in this manner.

DOCUMENT 128: Act of July 25, 1958: To Authorize the Creation of a Record of the Admission for Permanent Residence in the Case of Certain Hungarian Refugees

Be it enacted by the Senate and House of Representatives of the United States of America in Congress assembled, That any alien who was paroled into the United States as a refugee from the Hungarian revolution under section

212 (d) (5) of the Immigration and Nationality Act subsequent to October 23, 1956, who has been in the United States for at least two years, and who has not acquired permanent residence, shall forthwith return or be returned to the custody of the Immigration and Naturalization Service, and shall thereupon be inspected and examined for admission into the United States, and his case dealt with, in accordance with the provisions of sections 235, 236, and 237 of that Act.

Sec. 2. Any such alien who, pursuant to section 1 of this Act, is found, upon inspection by an immigration officer or after hearing by a special inquiry officer, to have been and to be admissible as an immigrant at the time of his arrival in the United States and at the time of his inspection and examination, except for the fact that he was not and is not in possession of the document required by section 212 (a) (20) of the Immigration and Naturalization Act, shall be regarded as lawfully admitted to the United States for permanent residence as of the date of his arrival.

Sec. 3. Nothing contained in this Act shall be held to repeal, amend, alter, modify, affect, or restrict the powers, duties, functions, or authority of the Attorney General in the administration and enforcement of the Immigration and Nationality Act or any other law relating to immigration, nationality, or naturalization.

Source: 72 Stat. 419.

* * *

In September of 1959 Congress amended the Immigration and Nationality Act to again provide for the entry of certain relatives of citizens or resident aliens, as presented in Document 129.

DOCUMENT 129: Act of September 22, 1959: To Provide for the Entry of Certain Relatives of U.S. Citizens and Lawfully Resident Aliens

Be it enacted by the Senate and House of Representatives of the United States of America in Congress assembled, That section 203 (a) (2) of the Immigration and Nationality Act (66 Stat. 178) is hereby amended by striking out the period and adding the following: "or who are the unmarried sons or daughters of citizens of the United States."

Sec. 2. Section 203 (a) (3) of the Immigration and Nationality Act . . . is hereby amended by striking out the word "children" and substituting in lieu thereof "unmarried sons or daughters."

Sec. 3. The second sentence of paragraph 4 of section 203 (a) of the

Immigration and Nationality Act . . . is hereby amended to read: "Qualified quota immigrants of each quota area who are the brothers, sisters, married sons or married daughters of citizens of the United States shall be entitled to a preference of not exceeding 50 per centum of the immigrant visas available for issuance for each quota area under this paragraph, and such preference shall be available to the spouses and children of such qualified quota immigrants if accompanying them."

Sec. 4. Any alien who (1) is registered on a consular waiting list pursuant to section 203 (c) of the Immigration and Nationality Act . . . under a priority date earlier than December 31, 1953, and (2) is eligible for a quota immigrant status under the provisions of section 203 (a) (2), (3), or (4) of such Act on the basis of a petition approved by the Attorney General prior to January 1, 1959, and the spouse and the children of such alien, shall be held to be nonquota immigrants and, if otherwise admissible under the provisions of the Immigration and Nationality Act, shall be issued nonquota immigrant visas: *Provided*, That, upon his application for an immigrant visa, and for his admission into the United States, the alien is found to have retained his relationship to the petitioner, and status, as established in the approved petition.

Sec. 5. (a) Section 205 (b) of the Immigration and Nationality Act . . . is hereby amended to read:

"(b) Any citizen of the United States claiming that any immigrant is his spouse or child and that such immigrant is entitled to a nonquota immigrant status under section 101 (a) (27) (A) . . . or claiming than any immigrant is his parent or unmarried son or unmarried daughter . . . or any alien lawfully admitted for permanent residence claiming that any immigrant is his spouse or his unmarried son or unmarried daughter . . . or any citizen claiming that any immigrant is his brother or sister or his married son or his married daughter . . . may file a petition with the Attorney General. . . . The petition shall be in such form and shall contain such information and be supported by such documentary evidence as the Attorney General may by regulations prescribe. . . ."

(b) Section 205 (c) . . . is hereby amended by adding after the first sentence, the following: "Not more than two such petitions may be approved from one petitioner in behalf of a child as defined in section 101 (b) (1) (E), unless necessary to prevent the separation of brothers and sisters."

(c) Aliens who have been granted a preference under paragraph (4) of section 203 (a) . . . pursuant to petitions approved by the Attorney General on the ground that they are the adopted sons or adopted daughters of United States citizens shall remain in that status notwithstanding the provisions of section 1 of this Act, unless they acquire a different immigrant status pursuant to a petition hereafter approved by the Attorney General.

Sec. 6. Notwithstanding the provisions of sections 3 and 20 of the Refugee Relief Act of 1953, as amended, special nonquota immigrant visas may be issued to aliens eligible to enter the United States for permanent residence under all the applicable provisions of the Immigration and Nationality Act . . . *Provided*, That . . . the alien is found to have retained his relationship to the petitioner, and status, as established in the approved petition.

Source: 73 Stat. 644.

* * *

In July 1960, acting on the precedent set for the Hungarian freedom fighters, Congress passed a law to assist in the resettlement of certain "refugees-escapees" from Communist countries (such as Cuba) who had been paroled by the attorney general, which is excerpted in Document 130.

DOCUMENT 130: Act of July 14, 1960: To Enable the United States to Participate in the Resettlement of Certain Refugees and for Other Purposes

---

Resolved by the Senate and House of Representatives of the United States of America in Congress assembled, That under the terms of section 212 (d) (5) of the Immigration and Nationality Act the Attorney General may parole into the United States, pursuant to such regulations as he may prescribe, an alien refugee-escapee defined in section 15 (c). . . .

Sec. 2. (a) The Secretary of State is hereby directed to submit to the Attorney General, as soon as practicable following the date of enactment of this Act, an advisory report indicating the number of refugee-escapees, as specified in section 1 of this Act, who within the period beginning July 1, 1959, and ending June 30, 1960, have availed themselves of resettlement opportunities offered by nations other than the United States; and, thereafter, prior to January 1, and July 1 of each year to submit such an advisory report to the Attorney General indicating the number of such refugee-escapees who within the preceding six months have availed themselves of such resettlement opportunities. The Attorney General shall not parole into the United States pursuant to section 1 of this Act, in any six months period . . . a number of refugee-escapees exceeding twenty-five per centum of the number of such refugee-escapees indicated in such advisory report. . . .

(b) The Attorney General may, within the numerical limitation prescribed by subsection (a) of this section, parole into the United States ... not to exceed five-hundred refugee-escapees listed by the United Nations High Commissioner for Refugees as "difficult to resettle": *Provided,* That no refugee-escapee may be paroled into the United States pursuant to this subsection if he suffers conditions requiring institutionalization: *Provided further,* That in the case of each such refugee-escapee, the Attorney General receives and approves a finding by a voluntary relief agency or welfare organization recognized for this purpose by the Attorney General, that such refugee-escapee can, with some assistance, become self-supporting, or is a member of a family unit capable of becoming self-supporting. . . .

Sec. 4. Any alien who, pursuant to section 3 of this Act, is found, upon inspection by the immigration officer or after a hearing before a special inquiry officer, to be admissible as an immigrant under the Immigration and Nationality Act at the time of his inspection and examination, except for the fact that he is not in possession of the documents required by section 212 (a) (20) of the said Act, shall be regarded as lawfully admitted to the United States for permanent residence as of the date of his arrival. . . .

Sec. 10* (a) The status of an alien, other than an alien crewman, who was inspected and admitted or paroled into the United States may be adjusted by the Attorney General, in his discretion and under such regulations as he may prescribe, to that of an alien lawfully admitted for permanent residence if (1) the alien makes application for permanent residence, (2) the alien is eligible to receive an immigrant visa and is admissible to the United States for permanent residence, and (3) an immigrant visa is immediately available to him at the time his application is approved.

Source: 74 Stat. 504.

---

*Sec. 10 was amending Sec. 245 (a) of the Act of June 27, 1952 (66 Stat. 217).

Part IV

Immigration and Naturalization in an Age of Globalization— 1965 to 1996

Just as the quota approach to immigration and naturalization law reflected the racial ideas and concerns of that period, the new era ushered in with the Immigration Act of 1965 reflected the concerns of the civil rights era. The election of President John F. Kennedy in 1960 eased the way for a frontal attack on the quota system. While serving as U.S. senator, President Kennedy wrote *A Nation of Immigrants* (1958), in which he made obvious his favorable attitude toward more immigration. The civil rights movement was pushing the nation and its leadership, and indeed public opinion of the American population, to question and seriously reevaluate the racial bias of much of its laws. Immigration law did not escape that review. The post–World War II decades had chipped away at the quota system; the passage of special acts, nonquota immigration, and refugee-escapee enactments had all demonstrated that the national origin quota system was simply too inflexible and too biased to be continued.

The success of the first years of the Kennedy administration in basic economic policy, moreover, resulted in the ending of the recessions that had plagued much of the Eisenhower period and had worked to undercut opposition to immigration reform. The healthy economy of the early through mid-1960s enabled even organized labor to favor a more liberal immigration policy. By that time, the traditional supporters of the national origin quota system were unorganized and largely inactive. Senator Edward Kennedy, the youngest brother of the president, led the Senate forces seeking to change the law fundamentally. He met with leaders from the American Coalition, the American Legion, the Daughters of the American Revolution, and the National Association of Evangelicals. In his words, "No significant opposition to eliminating the national origins quota system was organized by any of their organizations" (LeMay 1987, 110). He argued persuasively for enactment of the bill that the Kennedy administration submitted to Congress in 1963 [Document 131].

The nation continued to struggle with the refugee problem, and Congress passed a law in 1966 which adjusted the status of Cuban refugees [Document 134]. In addition to dealing with the Cuban refugees, Congress responded to the Vietnam War, with its increasing involvement of U.S. soldiers, by enacting a law allowing for the easier naturalization of Vietnam war servicemen, as it had for virtually every other major war in which the United States had been involved during the preceding century. The president also responded to a refugee-flow problem, fed both by the continuation of a massive flow of Cuban refugees and by the exodus of Southeast Asians following the Communist victories in 1975, by issuing a proclamation in 1968 regarding the U.S. adherence to the UN Protocol on the Status of Refugees [Document 136]. Confronted with the fall of South Vietnam, Cambodia, and Laos to Communist forces and the hundreds of thousands of refugees, Congress further addressed the issue in a major revision of prior law concerning refugees by enacting the Refugee Act of 1980 [Document 139]. Besides making the regulation of refugees more systematic as well as increasing the number of such persons who could be admitted, the law recognized the new category of asylum seekers.

The changing composition of the flow of immigration, however, coupled with a troubled economy suffering from "stagflation" throughout the 1970s—a combination of high unemployment and high inflation due in part to the oil crisis of the decade—led to a growing political movement to again restrict immigration. The ending of the Bracero Program in 1964, one of the compromises that President Kennedy had agreed to in order to move the Congress to increase the overall immigration level, contributed to a dramatic increase in the number of illegal aliens crossing the nation's borders, mostly from Mexico. Added to this flow, simultaneous with the massive Mariel boatlift of Cubans in mid-1980, was an influx of "boat people" fleeing Haiti. This situation led to a strong political movement in the Congress to close the back door of immigration by dealing with the illegal immigration problem. President Ronald Reagan responded by setting up a special presidential task force in 1981 [Document 140]. Then, the Select Commission of Immigration and Refugee Policy (SCIRP) was established by Congress. Its recommendations advocated a new device and approach to control illegal immigration—an employers' sanctions approach. That was adopted in the Immigration Reform and Control Act (IRCA) of 1986 [Document 144], along with amnesty for illegal aliens and special provisions for Cuban and Haitians as well as for a special category of immigrants from countries adversely affected by the 1965 reforms.

IRCA had but a very temporary impact on the flow of illegal immigrants, however, and Congress felt continued pressure to deal with immigration reform. In 1990 it passed another major immigration act (IMMACT, 1990) [Document 145]. The continued flow of illegal immigration led to the state governments in the primary immigration receiving states (both legal and illegal flows) agitating for the federal government to do something about immigration.

Congress got the message. In 1996 it enacted two major pieces of legislation that responded to the political movement to restrict or control the illegal immigration flow. It passed a welfare reform act that included several provisions that essentially enacted some major portions of California's Proposition 187 [Document 148] and the immigration act of 1996 [Document 149], which was designed to address a variety of issues related to undocumented aliens, Central American refugees, the requirements for sponsoring immigrants, and the centralization and reform of naturalization procedures. The easing of concerns about immigration was matched by choruses of protest from various ethnic communities about the cuts in benefits for legal aliens, prompting Congress to restore some of them [Document 150]. Despite these shifts, the fluctuations of public sentiments regarding immigration leaves the future course of immigration policy somewhat uncertain, at best.

The Kennedy administration's proposal, which became the Immigration Act of 1965, in the spirit of the Civil Rights Act of 1964, was a reassertion and return to the nation's liberal tradition in immigration. It set up individual rather than group criteria for granting immigration visas. The debate in the U.S. Senate over the enactment of the bill reflected the full range of opinion on immigration policy. Senator Edward Kennedy, chief Senate sponsor of the measure, reflected the sentiments that the quota system approach was "un-American," and he argued that the bill achieved a sense of "fair play" in coping with immigration decisions as to who should be allowed to enter, and who should be restricted. Document 131 presents much of Senator Kennedy's comments, recorded in the *Congressional Record*, during the Senate debate over the bill.

DOCUMENT 131: Senator Edward Kennedy's Comments on the Kennedy Immigration Bill (1965)

Mr. President, the bill we are considering today accomplishes major reforms in our immigration policy. This bill is not concerned with increasing immigration to this country, nor will it lower any of the high standards we apply in selection of immigrants. The basic change it makes is the elimination of the national origins quota system in line with the recommendations of the last four Presidents of the United States and Members of Congress from both parties.

For forty-one years the immigration policy of our country has been crippled by this system. Because of it we have never been able to achieve the annual quota authorized by law. We have discriminated in favor of some people over others, contrary to our basic principles as a nation, simply on the basis of birth. We have separated families needlessly. We have been forced to forgo the talents of many professionals whose skills were needed to cure, to teach, and to enhance the lives of Americans.

The present law has caused thousands of instances of personal hardship, of which every senator is aware. Several times Congress has tried to correct the twisted results of the national origins system through emergency legislation. Six times between 1948 and 1962 laws were passed for the admission of refugees. Four times between 1957 and 1962 we have made special provisions for relatives of American citizens or orphans. In addition, each year we are called upon to consider thousands of private bills to accommodate persons caught in the backwash of this origins system.

These efforts to circumvent are further proof that the national origins system is in disrepute. We cannot continue to respect a law we constantly seek to circumvent. To continue with such a law brings discredit upon ourselves as legislators. The national origins system has even failed in the purpose for which it was intended: to keep the ethnic balance of our country forever as it was in 1920. In 1920, 79 percent of our white population was of northern and western European origin. During the first 30 years of the national origins system, only 39 percent of our total immigration came from such areas. Since 1952, some 3.5 million persons have been admitted to this country as immigrants. Two-thirds of them came outside the national origins quota. Since 1952, we have authorized 2.1 million national origins quota numbers. Only one-half of these numbers were used. From these figures it is obvious to the Judiciary Committee that the current system is as much a failure as a device as it is an embarrassment as a doctrine. The bill now before the Senate abolishes it altogether.

The new policy in the bill before us was developed under the administration of President Kennedy by experts both in Congress and the executive branch. Extensive hearings were held both last year and this, in the Senate and the House. The Senate Immigration Subcommittee has sat regularly since last February. We have heard over fifty witnesses. I can report, Mr. President, that opposition to this measure is minimal. Many of the private organizations who differed with us in the past now agree the national origins system must be eliminated.

The current bill phases out the national origins system over a three-year period. Beginning July 1, 1968, our immigration policy will be based on the concept of "first come, first served." We no longer will ask a man where he was born. Instead we will ask if he seeks to join his family, or if he can help meet the economic and social needs of the Nation. Favoritism based on nationality will disappear. Favoritism on individual worth and qualifications will take its place.

There have been, however, certain questions raised in the course of our hearings that indicate certain fears or concerns in the minds of some interested people. I would like to set them straight.

First was the fear that this legislation would result in a significant increase in overall immigration. As I previously stated, the number of quotas authorized each year will not be substantially increased. The world total—exclusive of the Western Hemisphere—will be 170,000, an increase of approximately 11,500 over current authorization. But 10,200 of that increase is accounted for by the inclusion of refugees in our general law for the first time.

There will be some increase in total immigration to the United States—about 50,000 to 60,000 per year. This results from changing the law from an individual country quota system to a worldwide system. These are the numbers that go unused each year because quota numbers given to a country that are not utilized are wasted. By removing the obstacle to use, all numbers authorized will now be used, thus the increase in immigration will be about the same as the number of quotas now wasted. More specifically, the future use of numbers can be estimated as follows. Under this bill, we will use the 170,000 numbers given to the world, exclusive of the Western Hemisphere, and about 60,000 more for immediate relatives. Over the past 10 years we have averaged 110,000 per year from the Western Hemisphere. This should continue, along with approximately 15,000 immediate relatives. Thus we will admit an estimated total of 355,000. This is but a 60,000 increase in total immigration over our average total for the last decade.

We are talking about 60,000 people, in a population nearing 200 million that is growing, without immigration, at a rate of 3 million per year. The percentage increase that immigration will represent is infinitesimally small. This legislation opens no "floodgate." Rather, it admits about the same number of immigrants that current law would allow, but for the national origins restriction.

Another fear is that immigration from nations other than those in northern Europe will not assimilate into our society. The difficulty with this argument is that it comes 40 years too late. Hundreds of thousands of such immigrants have come here in recent years, and their adjustment has been notable. At my request, many voluntary agencies that assist new immigrants conducted lengthy surveys covering people who have arrived since the late 1940's. The results would be most gratifying to any American. I have only found five cases of criminal complaints involving immigrants in our studies of many thousands. Unemployment rates among these people are much lower than the national average; business ownership between 10 percent and 15 percent higher; home ownership as high as 80 percent in one city and averaging about 30 percent elsewhere. . . .

Finally, the fear is raised that under this bill immigrants will be taking jobs away from Americans at a time we find it difficult to lower our unemployment rate below 4 percent. Mr. President, I have already described the more stringent controls that this bill gives to the Secretary of Labor to insure against any adverse effects of immigration on American labor. I would also point out that this measure has the complete support of the AFL-CIO, support that would not be forthcoming if the fear of job loss for Americans were real.

Source: Congressional Record, 89th Cong. 1st sess., 1965. Vol. III, pt. 18: 24225–29.

* * *

The immigration reform bill was resubmitted by President Lyndon Johnson in January 1965 and was introduced into the House by Representative Emmanuel Celler, chairman of the House Judiciary Committee, and into the Senate by Senator Philip Hart of Michigan and by both Senators Edward and Robert Kennedy (of Massachusetts and New York, respectively). Cosponsored by thirty-two senators, it sought to balance a number of goals: (1) to preserve family unity and reunite separated families; (2) to meet the need for some highly skilled aliens; (3) to ease problems created by emergencies, such as political upheavals, Communist aggression, and natural disasters; (4) to assist cross-national exchange programs; (5) to bar from the United States aliens who might present problems of adjustment due to their physical or mental health, past criminal history, or dependency or for national security reasons, (6) to standardize admission procedures; and (7) to establish limits for the Americas. It replaced the national origins quota system with a seven-category system of preference. Thus, the new law not only abolished the national origins system but also emphasized other terms than quota and non-quota immigrants. Prospective immigrants were non-preference, or met one of the preferences, or were not subject to new per country limits because they were immediate relatives of United States citizens or were special immigrants, including persons born in the Western Hemisphere, former U.S. citizens seeking to resume their citizenship, ministers, and former (or current) employees of the U.S. government abroad. Those seeking admission under the third or sixth employment preferences would now have to meet more stringent labor certification rules. The law, which comprises some twenty-pages in the Code of Statutes, is excerpted [in Document 132] with respect to its major provisions.

DOCUMENT 132: Act of October 3, 1965: Immigration and Nationality Act of October 3, 1965 (Re: Amending the Act of June 27, 1952)

Be it enacted by the Senate and House of Representatives of the United States of America in Congress assembled, That section 201 of the Immigration and Nationality Act . . . be amended to read as follows:

Sec. 201. (a) Exclusive of special immigrants defined in section 101 (a) (27), and of the immediate relatives of United States citizens specified in subsection (b) of this section, the number of aliens who may be issued immigrant visas or who may otherwise acquire the status of an alien lawfully admitted to the United States for permanent residence, or who may, pursuant to section 203 (a) (7) enter conditionally, (i) shall not in any of the first three quarters of any fiscal year exceed a total of 45,000 and (ii) shall not in any fiscal year exceed a total of 170,000.

(b) The 'immediate relatives' referred to in subsection (a) of this section will mean the children, spouses, and parents of a citizen of the United States: *Provided,* That in the case of parents, such citizen must be at least twenty-one years of age. . . .

(c) During the period from July 1, 1965, through June 30, 1968, the annual quota of any quota area shall be the same as that which existed for that area on June 30, 1965. . . .

(d) Quota numbers not issued or otherwise used during the previous fiscal year, as determined in accordance with subsection (c) hereof, shall be transferred to an immigration pool. Allocation of numbers from the pool and from national quotas shall not together exceed in any fiscal year the numerical limitations in subsection (a) of this section. The immigration pool shall be made available to immigrants otherwise admissible under the provisions of this Act who are unable to obtain prompt issuance of a preference visa due to oversubscription of their quotas, or subquotas as determined by the Secretary of State. . . .

(e) The immigration pool and the quota areas shall terminate June 30, 1968. Thereafter immigrants admitted under the provisions of this Act who are subject to the numerical limitations of subsection (a) of this Act will be admitted in accordance with the percentage limitations and in the order of priority specified in section 203.

Sec. 2. Section 202 of the Immigration and Nationality Act . . . is amended to read as follows:

"(a) No person shall receive any preference or priority or be discriminated against in the issuance of an immigrant visa because of his race, sex, nationality, place of birth, or place of residence, except as specifically provided in section 101 (a) (27), section 201 (b), and section 203: *Provided,* That the total number of immigrant visas and the number of conditional entries made available to natives of any single foreign state . . . shall not exceed 20,000 in any fiscal year. . . .

"(b) Each independent country, self-governing dominion, mandated territory, and territory under the international trusteeship of the United Nations, other than the United States and its outlying possessions, shall be treated as a separate foreign state for the purposes of the numerical limitation set forth in the proviso to subsection (a) of this section when approved by the Secretary of State. All other inhabited lands shall be attributed to a foreign state specified by the Secretary of State. For the purposes of this Act the foreign state to which an immigrant is chargeable shall be determined by birth within such foreign state." . . .

Sec. 3. Sec. 203 of the Immigration and Nationality Act . . . is amended as follows:

"Sec. 203. (a) Aliens who are subject to the numerical limitations . . . shall be allotted visas or their conditional entry authorized, as the case may be, as follows:

"(1) Visas shall be first made available, in a number not to exceed 20 per centum of the number specified in section 201 (a) (ii), to qualified immigrants who are the unmarried sons or daughters of citizens of the United States.

"(2) Visas shall next be made available, in a number not to exceed 20 per centum of the number specified in section 201 (a) (ii), plus visas not required to be classes specified in paragraph (1), to qualified immigrants who are spouses, unmarried sons or unmarried daughters of an alien admitted for permanent residence.

"(3) Visas shall next be made available, in a number not to exceed 10 per centum . . . to qualified immigrants who are members of the professions, or who because of their exceptional ability in the sciences or arts will substantially benefit prospectively the national economy, cultural interests, or welfare of the United States.

"(4) Visas shall next be made available, in a number not to exceed 10 per centum . . . to qualified immigrants who are the married sons or married daughters of citizens of the United States.

"(5) Visas shall next be made available, in a number not to exceed 24 per centum . . . to qualified immigrants who are the brothers or sisters of citizens of the United States.

"(6) Visas shall next be made available, in a number not to exceed 10 per centum of the number specified . . . to qualified immigrants who are capable of performing specified skilled or unskilled labor, not of a temporary or seasonal nature, for which a shortage of employable and willing persons exists in the United States.

"(7) Conditional entries shall next be made available by the Attorney General, pursuant to such regulations as he may prescribe and in a number not to exceed 6 per centum . . . to aliens who satisfy an Immigration and Naturalization Service officer at an examination in any non-Communist or non-Communist-dominated country, (A) that (i) because of persecution or fear of persecution on account of race, religion, or political opinion they have fled (I) from any Communist or Communist-dominated country or area, or (II) from any country within the general area of the Middle East, and (ii) are unable or unwilling to return to such country or area on account of race, religion, or political opinion, and (iii) are not nationals of the countries or areas in which their application for conditional entry is made; or (B) that they are persons uprooted by catastrophic natural calamity as defined by the President who are unable to return to their usual place of abode. For the purposes of the foregoing the term 'general area of the Middle East' means the area between and including (1) Libya on the west, (2) Turkey on the north, (3) Pakistan on the east, and (4) Saudi Arabia and Ethiopia on the south. . . .

"(8) Visas authorized in any fiscal year, less those required for issuance to the classes specified in paragraphs (1) through (6) and less the conditional entries and visas made available pursuant to paragraph (7), shall be made available to other qualified immigrants strictly in the chronological order in which they qualify. Waiting lists of applicants shall be maintained in accordance with regulations prescribed by the Secretary of State. No immigrant visa shall be issued to a nonpreference immigrant under this paragraph, or to an immigrant with a preference under paragraph (3) or (6) of this subsection, until the consular officer is in receipt of a determination made by the Secretary of Labor in pursuant to the provisions of section 212 (a) (14).

"(9) A spouse or child as defined in section 101 (b) (1) (A), (B), (C), (D), or (E) shall, if not otherwise entitled to an immigrant status and the immediate issuance of a visa, or to conditional entry under paragraph

(1) through (8), be entitled to the same status, and the same order of consideration provided in subsection (b), if accompanying, or following ... his spouse or parent. ...

"(d) Every immigrant shall be presumed to be a nonpreference immigrant until he establishes to the satisfaction of the consular officer and the immigration officer that he is entitled to a preference status." ...

Sec. 8. Section 101 of the Immigration and Nationality Act ... is amended as follows:

(a) Paragraph (27) of subsection (a) is amended to read as follows:

"(27) The term 'special immigrant' means—

"(A) an immigrant who was born in any independent foreign country of the Western Hemisphere or in the Canal Zone and the spouse and children of any such immigrant, if accompanying, or following to join him ...

"(B) an immigrant, lawfully admitted for permanent residence, who is returning from a temporary visit abroad;

"(C) an immigrant who was a citizen of the United States and may, under section 324 (a) or 327 of title III, apply for reacquisition of citizenship;

"(D) (i) an immigrant who continuously for at least two years immediately preceding the time of his application for admission ... has been, and who seeks to enter the United States solely for the purpose of carrying on the vocation of minister of a religious denomination, and whose services are needed by such religious denomination having a bona fide organization in the United States; and (ii) the spouse or the child of any such immigrant, if accompanying or following to join him; or

"(E) an immigrant who is an employee, or an honorably retired former employee, of the United States Government abroad, and who has performed faithful service for a total of fifteen years or more, and his accompanying spouse and children. ... "

Sec. 10. Section 212 (a) of the Immigration and Nationality Act ... is amended as follows: (a) Paragraph (14) is amended to read as follows: "Aliens seeking to enter the United States, for the purpose of performing skilled or unskilled labor, unless the Secretary of Labor has determined and certified to the Secretary of State and to the Attorney General that (A) there are not sufficient workers in the United States who are able, willing, qualified, and available at the time of the application for a visa and admission to the United States and at the place to which the alien is destined to perform such skilled or unskilled labor, and (B) the employment of such aliens will not adversely affect the wages and working conditions of the workers in the United States similarly employed. ..."

Sec. 11 (a) Section 221 (a) is amended by deleting the words "the particular nonquota category in which the immigrant is classified, if a nonquota immigrant," and substituting in lieu thereof the words "the preference, nonpreference, immediate relative, or special immigration classification to which the alien is charged." ...

Sec. 20. This Act shall become effective on the first day of the first month after the expiration of thirty days following the date of its enactment except as provided herein.

Sec. 21. (a) There is hereby established a Select Commission of Western Hemisphere Immigration (hereinafter referred to as the "Commission") to be composed of fifteen members. The President shall appoint the Chairman of the Commission and four other members thereof. The President of the Senate, with the approval of the majority and minority leaders of the Senate, shall appoint five members from the membership of the Senate. The Speaker of the House of Representatives, with the approval of the majority and minority leaders of the House, shall appoint five members from the membership of the House. Not more than three members appointed by the President of the Senate and the Speaker of the House of Representatives, respectively, shall be members of the same political party. A vacancy in the membership of the Commission shall be filled in the same manner as the original designation and appointment.

(b) The Commission shall study the following matters:

(1) Prevailing and projected demographic, technological, and economic trends as they pertain to the Western Hemisphere;

(2) Present and projected unemployment in the United States, by occupations, industries, geographic areas, and other factors in relation to immigration from the Western Hemisphere;

(3) The interrelationships between immigration, present and future, and existing and contemplated national and international programs and projects of Western Hemisphere nations, including programs and projects for economic and social development;

(4) The operation of immigration laws of the United States as they pertain to Western Hemisphere nations, including adjustment of status for Cuban refugees ... ;

(5) The implications of the foregoing with respect to the security and international relations of Western Hemisphere nations; and

(6) Any other matters which the Commission believes to be germane to the purposes for which it was established.

Source: 79 Stat. 911.

* * *

President Lyndon Johnson gave an address at the foot of the Statue of Liberty on October 3, 1965, while signing the Immigration Act of 1965 into law. That address is summarized in Document 133.

DOCUMENT 133: President Lyndon Baines Johnson's Statement at the Signing of the 1965 Immigration and Nationality Bill, Liberty Island, New York, October 3, 1965

. . . This bill that we will sign today is not a revolutionary bill. It does not affect the lives of millions. It will not reshape the structure of our daily lives, or really add importantly to either our wealth or our power.

Yet it is still one of the most important acts of this Congress and of this administration. For it does repair a very deep and painful flaw in the fabric of American justice. It corrects a cruel and enduring wrong in the conduct of the American Nation. . . .

. . . This bill says simply that from this day forth those wishing to immigrate to America shall be admitted on the basis of their skills and their close relationship to those already here.

The fairness of this standard is so self-evident that we may well wonder that it has not always been applied. Yet the fact is that for over four decades the immigration policy of the United States has been distorted by the harsh injustice of the national origins system.

This system violated the basic principle of American democracy—the principle that values and rewards each man on the basis of his merit as a man.

It has been un-American in the highest sense, because it has been untrue to the faith that brought thousands to these shores even before we were a country.

Today, with my signature, this system is abolished.

Asylum for Cuban Refugees

So it is in that spirit that I declare this afternoon to the people of Cuba that those who seek refuge here in America will find it. The dedication of America to our traditions as an asylum for the oppressed is going to be upheld.

I have directed the Departments of State and Justice and Health, Education, and Welfare to immediately make all the necessary arrangements to permit those in Cuba who seek freedom to make an orderly entry into the United States of America.

Our first concern will be with those Cubans who have been separated from their children and parents and their husbands and their wives and that are now in this country. Our next concern is with those who are imprisoned for political reasons. . . .

And I will send to the Congress tomorrow a request for supplementary funds of $12,600,000 to carry forth the commitment that I am making today. . . .

And so we Americans will welcome these Cuban people. For the tides of history run strong, and in another day they can return to their home-land to find it cleansed of terror and free from fear. . . .

And today we can all believe that the lamp of this grand old lady is brighter today—and the golden door that she guards gleams more bril-liantly in the light of an increased liberty for the people from all the countries of the globe. Thank you very much.

Source: The Papers of the Presidents, Lyndon B. Johnson, 1965, Vol. II (Washington, D.C.: Government Printing Office, 1966), 1037–1040.

* * *

As President Johnson alluded to above, the plight of the Cuban refugees was recognized and responded to by the Congress as well. In Novem-ber 1966 Congress passed a special act to adjust their status to per-manent residence.

DOCUMENT 134: Act of November 2, 1966: To Adjust the Status of Cuban Refugees to That of Lawful Permanent Residents of the United States, and for Other Purposes

Be it enacted by the Senate and House of Representatives of the United States of America in Congress assembled, That, notwithstanding the provisions of section 245 (c) of the Immigration and Nationality Act, the status of any alien who is a native or citizen of Cuba and who has been inspected and admitted or paroled into the United States subsequent to January 1, 1959 and has been physically present in the United States for at least two years may be adjusted by the Attorney General, in his discretion and under such regulations as he may prescribe, to that of an alien lawfully ad-mitted for permanent residence if the alien makes application for such adjustment, and the alien is eligible to receive an immigrant visa and is admissible to the United States for permanent residence. Upon approval of such application for adjustment of status, the Attorney General shall create a record of the alien's admission for permanent residence as of the date thirty months prior to the filing of such an application or the date of his last arrival into the United States, whichever date is later. The provisions of this Act shall be applicable to the spouse and child of any alien described in this subsection, regardless of their citizenship and place of birth, who are residing with such alien in the United States.

Source: 80 Stat. 1161.

* * *

The question of how one may lose one's citizenship was at issue again in 1967 in an important Supreme Court decision on the matter, *Afroyim v. Rusk*. In this case, the Court decided that a citizen who held dual citizenship with Israel did not lose his citizenship merely by the act of voting in an election of the country in which he held the other citizenship. The case is particularly significant in the strong language used by the justices in stipulating how limited is the government in "taking away" citizenship once granted by birthright or by naturalization.

DOCUMENT 135: *Afroyim v. Rusk* (May 29, 1967)

Mr. Justice Black delivered the opinion of the Court.

Petitioner, born in Poland in 1893, immigrated to this country in 1912 and became a naturalized American citizen in 1926. He went to Israel in 1950, and in 1951 he voluntarily voted in an election for the Israeli Knesset, the legislative body of Israel. In 1960, when he applied for renewal of his United States passport, the Department of State refused to grant it on the sole ground that he had lost his American citizenship by virtue of 401(e) of the Nationality Act of 1940, which provides that a United States citizen shall "lose" his citizenship if he votes "in a political election in a foreign state." . . . Because neither the Fourteenth Amendment nor any other provision of the Constitution expressly grants Congress the power to take away that citizenship once it has been acquired, petitioner contended that the only way he could lose his citizenship was by his own voluntary renunciation of it. . . .

The fundamental issue before this Court here, as it was in [*Perez v. Brownell*, 1946] is whether Congress can consistently with the Fourteenth Amendment enact a law stripping an American of his citizenship which he has never voluntarily renounced or given up. The majority in Perez held that Congress could do this because withdrawal of citizenship is "reasonably calculated to effect the end that is within the power of Congress to achieve." That conclusion was reached by this chain of reasoning: Congress has an implied power to deal with foreign affairs as an indispensable attribute of sovereignty. This implied power, plus the Necessary and Proper Clause, empowers Congress to regulate voting by American citizens in foreign elections; involuntary expatriation is within the "ample scope" of "appropriate modes" Congress can adopt to effectuate its general regulatory power. Then, upon summarily concluding that "there is nothing in the ... Fourteenth Amendment to warrant drawing from it a restriction upon the power otherwise possessed by Congress to withdraw citizenship" ... the majority specifically rejected the "notion that the power of Congress to terminate citizenship depends upon the citizen's assent."

First we reject the idea expressed in Perez that, aside from the Fourteenth Amendment, Congress has any general power, express or implied, to take away an American's citizenship without his assent. This power cannot, as Perez indicated, be sustained as an implied attribute of sovereignty possessed by all nations. Other nations are governed by their own constitutions, if any, and we can draw no support from theirs. In our country the people are sovereign and the Government cannot sever its relationship to the people by taking away their citizenship. Our Constitution governs us and we must never forget that our Constitution limits the Government to those powers specifically granted or those that are necessary and proper to carry out the specifically granted ones. The Constitution, of course, grants Congress no express power to strip people of their citizenship, whether in the exercise of the implied power to regulate foreign affairs or in the exercise of any specifically granted power....

... [A]ny doubt as to whether prior to the passage of the Fourteenth Amendment Congress had the power to deprive a person against his will of citizenship once obtained should have been removed by the unequivocal terms of the Amendment itself. It provides its own constitutional rule in language calculated completely to control the status of citizenship: "All persons born or naturalized in the United States ... are citizens of the United States. ..." There is no indication in these words of a fleeting citizenship, good at the moment it is acquired but subject to destruction by the Government at any time. Rather the Amendment can most reasonably be read as defining a citizenship which a citizen keeps unless he voluntarily relinquishes it....

[The] undeniable purpose of the Fourteenth Amendment to make citizenship of Negroes permanent and secure would be frustrated by holding that the Government can rob a citizen of his citizenship without his consent by simply proceeding to act under an implied power to regulate foreign affairs or some other power generally granted....

To uphold Congress' power to take away a man's citizenship because he voted in a foreign election in violation of 401(e) would be equivalent to holding that Congress has the power to "abridge," "affect," "restrict the effect of," and "take ... away" citizenship. Because the Fourteenth Amendment prevents Congress from doing any of these things, we agree with THE CHIEF JUSTICE's dissent in the Perez case that the Government is without power to rob a citizen of his citizenship under 402(e). . . .

Our holding is the only one that can stand in view of the language and the purpose of the Fourteenth Amendment, and our construction of that Amendment, we believe, comports more nearly than Perez with the principles of liberty and equal justice to all that the entire Fourteenth Amendment was adopted to guarantee. Citizenship is no light trifle to be jeopardized any moment Congress decides to do so under the name of one of its general or implied grants of power. In some instances, loss of citizenship can mean that a man is left without the protection of citizenship in any country in the world—as a man without a country. Citizenship in this Nation is part of a cooperative affair. Its citizenry is the country and the country is its citizenry. The very nature of our free government makes it completely incongruous to have a rule of law under which a group of citizens temporarily in office can deprive another group of citizens of their citizenship. We hold that the Fourteenth Amendment was designed to, and does, protect every citizen of this Nation against a congressional forcible destruction of his citizenship, whatever his creed, color, or race. Our holding does no more than to give to this citizen that which is his own, a constitutional right to remain a citizen in a free country unless he voluntarily relinquishes that citizenship. *Perez v. Brownell* is overruled. The judgment is Reversed.

Source: 387 U.S. 253, May 29, 1967.

* * *

The continuing problem of mass movements involving tens of thousands of refugees generated by war or natural disasters influenced the United Nations to revise its protocols relating to the status of refugees. The United States, as a nation which was a state party to the agreement and the protocols, was in essence agreeing to changes in its law dealing with the status of refugees as well. This was accomplished by President Lyndon Johnson when he issued a presidential proclamation regarding the UN protocols. Document 136 presents excerpts of some of the major provisions of the protocols as amended in 1967 and contained in the Presidential Proclamation of 1968.

DOCUMENT 136: Proclamation of the President of the United States [Lyndon Baines Johnson] November 6, 1968: Multilateral Protocol and Convention Relating to the Status of Refugees

The States Parties to the present Protocol,

Considering that the Convention relating to the Status of Refugees done at Geneva on 28 July 1951 (hereinafter referred to as the Convention) covers only those persons who have become refugees as a result of events occurring before 1 January 1951,

Considering that new refugee situations have arisen since the Convention was adopted and that the refugees concerned may therefore not fall within the scope of the Convention,

Considering that it is desirable that equal status should be enjoyed by all refugees covered by the definition in the Convention irrespective of the dateline 1 January 1951,

Have agreed as follows:

Article I—General Provisions

1. The States Parties to the present Protocol undertake to apply articles 2 to 34 inclusive of the Convention to refugees as hereinafter defined.

2. For the purpose of the present Protocol, the term "refugee" shall, except as regards the application of paragraph 3 of this article, mean any person within the definition of Article I of the Convention as if the words "As a result of events occurring before 1 January 1951 and ..." and the words "... as a result of such events," in article I A (2) were omitted.

3. The present Protocol shall be applied by the States Parties hereto without any geographic limitation, save that existing declarations made by the States already Parties to the Convention in accordance with Article 1 B (1) (a) of the Convention shall, unless extended under article 1 B (2) thereof, apply also under the present Protocol.

Article II—Co-operation of the National Authorities with the United Nations

1. The States Parties to the present Protocol undertake to co-operate with the Office of the United Nations High Commissioner for Refugees, or any other agency of the United Nations which may succeed it, in the exercise of its functions, and shall in particular facilitate its duty of supervising the application of the provisions of the present Protocol. . . .

Convention

Article 3—Non-discrimination

The Contracting States shall apply the provisions of this Convention to refugees without discrimination as to race, religion, or country of origin.

Article 7—Exemption from Reciprocity

1. Except where this Convention contains more favourable provisions, a Contracting State shall accord to refugees the same treatment as is accorded to aliens generally.

2. After a period of three years' residence, all refugees shall enjoy exemption from legislative reciprocity in the territory of the Contracting States.

3. Each Contracting State shall continue to accord to refugees the rights and benefits to which they were already entitled, in the absence of reciprocity, at the date of entry into force of this Convention for that State.

Chapter III, Gainful Employment

Article 17—Wage Earning Employment

1. The Contracting States shall accord to refugees lawfully staying in their territory the most favorable treatment accorded to nationals of a foreign country in the same circumstances, as regards to engage in wage-earning employment.

Chapter V, Administrative Measures

Article 27—Identity Papers

The Contracting States shall issue identity papers to any refugee in their territory who does not possess a valid travel document.

Article 32—Expulsion

1. The Contracting State shall not expel a refugee lawfully in their territory save on grounds of national security or public order.

2. The expulsion of such a refugee shall only be in pursuance of a decision in accordance with due process of law. . . .

3. The Contracting States shall allow such a refugee a reasonable period within which to seek legal admission into another country. The Contracting States reserve the right to apply during that period such internal measures as they may deem necessary.

Article 33—Prohibition of Expulsion or Return ("Refoulement")

1. No Contracting State shall expel or return ("refouler") a refugee in any manner whatsoever to the frontiers of territories where his life or freedom would be threatened on account of his race, religion, nationality, membership of a particular social group or political opinion.

2. The benefit of the present provision may not, however, be claimed by a refugee whom there are reasonable grounds for regarding as a danger to the security of the country in which he is, or who, having been convicted by a final judgment of a particularly serious crime, constitutes a danger to the community of that country.

Article 34—Naturalization

The Contracting States shall as far as possible facilitate the assimilation and naturalization of refugees. They shall in particular make every effort to expedite naturalization proceedings and to reduce as far as possible the charges and costs of such proceedings.

Source: (Avery, Pt. II), Orders, Proclamations, and Treaties 1208.233–1208.263.

* * *

Resident aliens who were cut off from medicare supplemental benefits of the Social Security Act sued the federal government in a class action case heard in Florida. The U.S. Supreme Court, which heard the case on appeal, upheld the constitutionality of the congressional act amending the Social Security law. Document 137 summarizes the decision.

DOCUMENT 137: *Mathews v. Diaz* (June 1, 1976)

Certain resident aliens instituted a class action in the United States District Court for the Southern District of Florida, challenging the constitutionality of the provisions of the Social Security Act (42 USCS 1395o(2)) which grant eligibility for the Medicare supplemental medical insurance program to resident citizens who are 65 or older, but which deny eligibility to aliens, 65 or older, unless they have been admitted for permanent residence and have resided in the county for at least five years. The three-judge District Court entered judgment for the plaintiffs, holding that the residency requirement violated the due process clause of the Fifth Amendment, and that since it could not be severed from the requirement of admission for permanent residence, the alien eligibility provisions were entirely unenforceable (361 F. Supp. 1).

On direct appeal, the United States Supreme Court reversed. In an opinion by Stevens, J., expressing the unanimous view of the court, it was held that (1) Congress had no constitutional duty to provide all aliens with benefits provided to citizens, and (2) the alien eligibility provisions of 1395 (2) did not deprive aliens who did not meet the eligibility requirements of liberty or property without due process of law under the Fifth Amendment, since (a) it was reasonable for Congress to make an alien's eligibility depend on both the character and duration of his residence, (b) the statutory classification drew a line qualifying those aliens who might reasonably be presumed to have a greater affinity to

270 U.S. Immigration & Naturalization Laws & Issues

the United States, and (c) the court would not substitute its judgment
for that of Congress.

Source: U.S. Supreme Court Reports, Briefs of Counsel, 48 L Ed 2nd. p. 964, infra:
478.

* * *

During the final weeks of the congressional session of 1976, the Congress passed a law to amend the Immigration Act of 1965 to deal with
a perceived problem created by that law. The result of the 1965 law
was that all would-be immigrants from the Western Hemisphere were
required to apply for visas on a first-come first-served basis, including
those who were close relatives of U.S. citizens and skilled foreign workers, groups who received preferences if from the Eastern Hemisphere.
By the mid-1970s the waiting period for immigrant visas in the Western
Hemisphere stretched in excess of two years. This waiting period
caused hardships for those who otherwise would have qualified for a
preferred status and have gained much faster entry into the United
States. To rectify these problems, the 1976 amendment law extended
the preference system to the Western Hemisphere nations. It was expected that the amendment would cut the waiting period for immigrants from Mexico, for example, in half. Document 138 presents the
1976 Congressional Quarterly Almanac's summary of the law's key
provisions.

DOCUMENT 138: Act of October 20, 1976, to Amend the
Immigration and Nationality Act of 1965

As signed into law, HR 14535:
1. Retained the annual hemispheric immigration ceilings of 170,000 for
the Eastern Hemisphere and 120,000 for the Western Hemisphere.
2. Extended the seven-point immigration preference system to visa
applicants from the Western Hemisphere, as follows: first preference,
unmarried sons and daughters under 21 years of age of U.S. citizens, 20
per cent of the hemispheric limitation; second preference, spouses and
unmarried sons and daughters of aliens with permanent resident status,
20 per cent plus any visas not required for the first preference; third
preference, professionals whose services are sought by U.S. employers,
10 per cent of the limitation; fourth preference, married children of U.S.
citizens, 10 per cent of the limitation plus any visas not required for the
first three categories; fifth preference, brothers and sisters of U.S. citizens,

21 years or older, 24 per cent of the limitation plus any visas not required for the previous categories; sixth preference, skilled and unskilled workers in short supply, 10 per cent of the limitation; seventh preference, refugees, 6 per cent of the limitation; nonpreference, others, any numbers not used by the seven preference categories.

3. Established a 20,000 per-country limit on immigrants from the Western Hemisphere.

4. Raised the visa allocations for colonies and other dependent areas from an annual limit of 200 to 600.

5. Required that visa allocations for colonies and dependent areas be charged against both the 20,000 limit for the mother country and the respective ceiling for the hemisphere where the colony or dependent area is located.

6. Set up a country-by-country triggering mechanism whereby the hemispheric visa percentage allotments for the various preference categories would become applicable within a given country whenever immigration from that country reaches its 20,000 limit in a preceding year, in order to assure that visas in lower preference categories would be available.

7. Retained the labor certification requirement for all third, sixth and nonpreference immigrants who intended to work in the United States. Under this procedure, prospective immigrants may be excluded unless the Secretary of Labor certifies that there is a shortage of U.S. workers in the immigrant's occupational category and that the alien's employment will not adversely affect wages and working conditions of American workers in similar occupations.

8. Required the Secretary of Labor to certify that equally qualified American professionals are available before denying labor certification for teachers or other immigrants with exceptional skills in the arts and sciences.

9. Recommended the establishment of a special advisory group of experts to advise the Secretary of Labor in difficult cases involving visa applicants with exceptional professional skills.

10. Provided that Cuban refugees present in the U.S. prior to the enactment of the bill who change their status to permanent resident will not be charged to the annual ceiling for Western Hemisphere visas. This provision would make an estimated 20,000 to 25,000 extra visas available each year to immigrants from other countries in the Western Hemisphere.

11. Allowed natives of the Western Hemisphere to adjust their status from nonimmigrant to permanent resident without first returning to their home countries. This provision had formerly applied only to the Eastern Hemisphere.

12. Prohibited aliens who are not immediate relatives of either U.S.

citizens or permanent residents from receiving an adjustment in status to permanent resident after accepting unauthorized employment in the U.S.

13. Prohibited aliens who were admitted to the U.S. in transit without visas from receiving an adjustment in status to permanent resident.

Source: 1976 Congressional Quarterly Almanac, vol. 32 (Washington, D.C.: Congressional Quarterly, 1977), 413–14.

* * *

In 1980 Congress dealt most specifically with the problem of refugee admissions. Older refugee laws tended to deal with the refugee as a single individual "escaping" communism, for example. But the 1960s and 1970s evidenced flows in which refugees arrived in mass asylum movements: 400,000 from Cuba, 340,000 from Vietnam, 110,000 from Laos, nearly 70,000 from the Soviet Union and a like number from Kampuchea (formerly Cambodia), 30,000 from Yugoslavia, nearly 25,000 from mainland China and Taiwan, nearly 20,000 each from Rumania and Poland, and about 10,000 each from Czechoslovakia, Spain, and Hungary. Such events strained the 20,000 per-country limit of the 1965 act. The Refugee Act of 1980, in an effort to systematize refugee policy, incorporated the UN definition of a refugee—one had a "well-founded fear of persecution" owing to race, religion, nationality, or membership in a social group or political movement—and initially allowed for 50,000 persons annually to enter as refugees. The president could notify Congress if he determined that events warranted an increase in the number and, after fiscal year 1982, he would have the responsibility of presenting Congress with a recommended total annual figure. Thus, for example, 72,000 were authorized for 1984 and 67,750 actually arrived. Another 11,600 were granted asylum (LeMay 1987, 123).

DOCUMENT 139: Act of March 17, 1980: The Refugee Act

Be it enacted by the Senate and House of Representatives of the United States of America in Congress assembled, That this Act may be cited as the "Refugee Act of 1980."

Sec. 101. (a) The Congress declares that it is the historic policy of the United States to respond to the urgent needs of persons subject to persecution in their homelands, including, where appropriate, humanitarian assistance for their care and maintenance in asylum areas, efforts to promote opportunities for resettlement or voluntary repatriation, aid for necessary transportation and processing, admission to this country of refugees for special humanitarian concern to the United States, and transitional assistance to refugees in the United States. The Congress further declares that it is the policy of the United States to encourage all nations to provide assistance and resettlement opportunities to refugees to the fullest extent possible.

(b) The objectives of this Act are to provide permanent and systematic procedures for the admission to this country of refugees of special humanitarian concern to the United States, and to provide comprehensive and uniform provisions for the effective resettlement and absorption of those refugees who are admitted.

Sec. 201 (a) Section 101 (a) of the Immigration and Nationality Act . . . is amended by adding after paragraph (41) the following new paragraph:

(42) The term 'refugee' means (A) any person who is outside any country of such person's nationality or, in the case of a person having no nationality, is outside any country in which such person last habitually resided, and who is unable or unwilling to return to, and is unable or unwilling to avail himself or herself of the protection of, that country because of persecution or a well-founded fear of persecution on account of race, religion, nationality, membership in a particular social group, or political opinion, or (B) in such special circumstances as the President after appropriate consultation . . . may specify. . . . The term 'refugee' does not include any person who ordered, incited, assisted, or otherwise participated in the persecution of any person on account of race, religion, nationality, membership in a particular social group, or political opinion.

(b) Chapter I or Title II of such Act is amended by adding after section 206 (8 U.S.C. 1156) the following new sections [207–209]:

Sec. 207. (a) (1) Except as provided in subsection (b), the number of refugees who may be admitted under this section in fiscal year 1980, 1981, or 1982, may not exceed fifty thousand unless the President determines, before the beginning of the fiscal year and after appropriate consultation. . . , that admission of a specific number of refugees in excess of such number is justified by humanitarian concerns or is otherwise in the national interest.

(2) Except as provided in subsection (b), the number of refugees who may be admitted under this section in any fiscal year after fiscal year 1982 shall be such number as the President determines, before the beginning of the fiscal year and after appropriate consultation, is justified by humanitarian concerns or is otherwise in the national interest.

(3) Admissions under this subsection shall be allocated among refugees of special humanitarian concern to the United States in accordance with a determination made by the President after appropriate consultation.

(b) If the President determines, after appropriate consultation, that (1) an unforeseen emergency refugee situation exists, (2) the admission of certain refugees in response to the emergency refugee situation is justified by grave humanitarian concern or is otherwise in the national interest, and (3) the admission to the United States of these refugees cannot be accomplished under subsection (a), the President may fix a number of refugees to be admitted to the United States during the succeeding period (not to exceed twelve months) in response to the emergency refugee situation and such admissions shall be allocated among refugees of special humanitarian concern to the United States in accordance with a determination made by the President after the appropriate consultation provided under this subsection. . . .

(4) The refugee status of any alien (and of the spouse or child of the alien) may be terminated by the Attorney General pursuant to such regulations as the Attorney General may prescribe if the Attorney General determines that alien was not in fact a refugee within the meaning of subsection 101 (a) (42) at the time of the alien's admission. . . .

(d)(1) Before the start of each fiscal year the President shall report to the Committees of the Judiciary of the House of Representatives and of the Senate regarding the foreseeable number of refugees who will be in need of resettlement during the fiscal year and the anticipated allocation of refugee admissions during the fiscal year. . . .

(3)(B) After the President initiates appropriate consultation prior to making a determination, under subsection (b), that the number of refugee admissions should be increased because of an unforeseen emergency refugee situation, to the extent that time and the nature of the emergency refugee situation permit, a hearing to review the proposal to increase refugee admissions shall be held unless public disclosure of the details of the proposal would jeopardize the lives or safety of individuals . . .

Sec. 208. (a) The Attorney General shall establish a procedure for an alien physically present in the United States or at a land border or port of entry, irrespective of such alien's status, to apply for asylum, and the alien may be granted asylum at the discretion of the Attorney General if the Attorney General determines that such alien is a refugee within the meaning of section 101(a)(42)(a). . . .

Sec. 209. (b) Not more than five thousand of the refugee admissions authorized under section 207(a) in any fiscal year may be made available by the Attorney General, in the Attorney General's discretion and under such regulations as the Attorney General may prescribe, to adjust to the status of an alien lawfully permitted for permanent residence the status of any alien granted asylum who—(1) applies for such adjustment;

(2) has been physically present in the U.S. for at least one year after being granted asylum,

(3) continues to be a refugee in the meaning of section 101(a)(42)(a) or a spouse or child of such refugee,

(4) is not firmly resettled in any foreign country, and

(5) is admissible (except as otherwise provided for under subsection (c) as an immigrant under this Act at the time of examination for adjustment of such alien. . . .

Sec. 203. (a) Subsection (a) of section 201 of the Immigration and Nationality Act . . . is amended to read as follows:

(a) Exclusive of special immigrants in section 101(a)(27), immediate relatives specified in subsection (b) of this section, and aliens who are admitted or granted asylum under section 207 or 208, the number of aliens born in any foreign country or dependent area who may be issued immigrant visas or who may otherwise acquire the status of an alien lawfully admitted to the United States for permanent residence, shall not in any of the first three quarters of any fiscal year exceed a total of seventy-two thousand and shall not in any fiscal year exceed two hundred and seventy thousand. . . .

(h)(1) The Attorney General shall not deport or return any alien (other than an alien described in section 241(a)(19) to a country if the Attorney General determines that such alien's life or freedom would be threatened in such country on account of race, religion, nationality, membership in a particular social group, or political opinion. . . .

Sec. 204. (2) The Attorney General shall establish the asylum procedure referred to in section 208(a) of the Immigration and Nationality Act (as added by section 201(b) of this title) not later than June 1, 1980. . . .

Sec. 301. (a) The President shall appoint, by and with the advice and consent of the Senate, a United States Coordinator for Refugee Affairs (hereinafter referred to as the "Coordinator"). The Coordinator shall have the rank of Ambassador-at-Large.

Source: 94 Stat. 102.

* * *

In 1981 the nation continued to debate and discuss both refugee and immigration policy, especially as it might deal with the increasing problem of mass refugee movements (some of which quickly outstripped the Refugee Act of 1980 in numbers seeking admission) and the growing number of illegal aliens entering annually. President Ronald Reagan appointed a special task force within his administration to study these problems and recommend policy alternatives. Document 140 presents President Reagan's statement on these issues.

DOCUMENT 140: President Ronald Reagan's Statement on U.S. Immigration and Refugee Policy (July 30, 1981)

Our nation is a nation of immigrants. More than any other country, our strength comes from our own immigrant heritage and our capacity to welcome those from other lands. No free and prosperous nation can by itself accommodate all those who seek a better life or flee persecution. We must share this responsibility with other countries.

The bipartisan select commission which reported this spring concluded that the Cuban influx to Florida made the United States sharply aware of the need for more effective immigration policies and the need for legislation to support those policies.

For these reasons, I asked the Attorney General last March to chair a Task Force on Immigration and Refugee Policy. We discussed the matter when President Lopez Portillo visited me last month, and we have carefully considered the views of our Mexican friends. In addition, the Attorney General has consulted with those concerned in Congress and in affected States and localities and with interested members of the public.

—The Attorney General is undertaking administrative actions and submitting to Congress, on behalf of the administration, a legislative package, based on eight principles. These principles are designed to preserve our tradition of accepting foreigners to our shores, but to accept them in a controlled and orderly fashion.

—We shall continue America's tradition as a land that welcomes peoples from other countries. We shall also, with other countries, continue to share in the responsibility of welcoming and resettling those who flee oppression.

—At the same time, we must ensure adequate legal authority to establish control over immigration: to enable us, when sudden influxes of foreigners occur, to decide to whom we grant the status of refugee or asylee; to improve our border control; to expedite (consistent with fair procedures and our Constitution) return of those coming here illegally; to strengthen enforcement of our fair labor standards and laws; and to penalize those who would knowingly encourage violation of our laws. The steps we take to further these objectives, however, must be consistent with our values of individual privacy and freedom.

—We have a special relationship with our closest neighbors, Canada and Mexico. Our immigration policy should reflect this relationship.

—We must also recognize that both the United States and Mexico have historically benefited from Mexicans obtaining employment in the United States. A number of our States have special labor needs, and we should take these into account.

—Illegal immigrants in considerable numbers have become productive members of our work force. Those who have established equities in the United States should be recognized and accorded legal status. At the same time, in doing so, we must not encourage illegal immigration.

—We shall strive to distribute fairly, among the various localities of this country, the impacts of our national immigration and refugee policy, and we shall improve the capability of those agencies of the Federal Government which deal with these matters.

—We shall seek new ways to integrate refugees into our society without nurturing their dependence on welfare.

—Finally, we recognize that immigration and refugee problems require international solutions. We will seek greater international cooperation in the resettlement of refugees, and, in the Caribbean Basin, international cooperation to assist accelerated economic development to reduce motivations for illegal immigration.

Immigration and refugee policy is an important part of our past and fundamental to our national interest. With the help of the Congress and of the American people, we will work towards a new and realistic immigration policy, a policy that will be fair to our own citizens while it opens the door of opportunity for those who seek a new life in America.

Source: *The Papers of the Presidents, Ronald Reagan, 1981*, Vol. I (Washington, D.C.: Government Printing Office, 1982), 676–77.

* * *

Of even greater importance than the views of the task force and of the Reagan administration was the report of the Select Commission on Immigration and Refugee Policy. Begun in the final days of the Carter administration, the commission was a joint presidential and congressionally appointed commission that began its work in 1979. It thoroughly studied immigration law and more particularly the problem of illegal immigration and issued a final report in 1981. Its recommendations formed the basis of subsequent legislative action by the Congress throughout the 1980s and even into the 1990s. Document 141 presents some of the major recommendations of the commission's final report.

DOCUMENT 141: Executive Summary Recommendations of the Select Commission on Immigration and Refugee Policy (1981)

The Select Commission recommends that:

1. The United States work with other nations and principal international organizations to collect information and research on migratory flows and treatment of international migration.

2. The United States expand bilateral consultation with other governments, especially Mexico and other regional neighbors regarding migration.

3. Border patrol funding levels be raised to provide for a substantial increase in the number and training of personnel, replacement sensor systems . . . and other needed equipment.

4. That regional border enforcement posts be established to coordinate work with the INS, the U.S. Customs Service, the DEA, and the U.S. Coast Guard in the interdiction of both undocumented/illegal migrants and illicit goods, specifically narcotics.

5. That high priority be given to the training of INS officers to familiarize them with the rights of aliens and U.S. citizens and to help them deal with persons of other cultural backgrounds.

6. That legislation be passed making it illegal for employers to hire undocumented workers.

7. That a program to legalize illegal/undocumented aliens now in the U.S. be adopted.

8. That eligibility for legalization be determined by interrelated measurements of residence—date of entry and length of continuous residence—and by specified groups of excludability that are appropriate to the legalization program.

9. That voluntary agencies and community organizations be given a significant role in the legalization program.

10. An annual ceiling of 350,000 numerically limited immigrant visas with an additional 100,000 visas available for the first five years to . . . allow backlogs to be cleared.

11. That a substantial number of visas be set aside for reunifying spouses and unmarried sons and daughters and it should be given top priority in the numerically limited family reunification. . . .

12. That country ceilings apply to all numerically limited family reunification preferences. . . .

13. That "special" immigrants remain a numerically exempt group but be placed within the independent category.

14. Creating a small, numerically limited subcategory within the independent category to provide for the immigration of certain investors.

15. That specific labor market criteria should be established by the selection of independent immigrants. . . .

16. A fixed-percentage limit to the independent immigration from any one country.

17. That U.S. allocation of refugee numbers include both geographic considerations and specific refugee characteristics. . . .

18. That state and local governments be involved in planning for initial refugee resettlement and that . . . a federal program of impact aid [be established] to minimize the financial impact of refugees on local services.

19. That refugee achievement of self-sufficiency and adjustment to living in the U.S. be reaffirmed as the goal of resettlement.

Source: The Select Commission on Immigration and Refuge Policy *Final Report* (Washington, D.C.: U.S. Government Printing Office), March 1, 1981: xv–xxxii.

* * *

In 1983 the U.S. Supreme Court rendered a decision in an immigration case that had importance beyond the immediate issue of immigration law. In *INS v. Chadha et al.*, a class action suit was filed against the INS over its deportation proceedings. The Court ruled that a House of Representative's use of the "legislative veto" of the executive branch's rules and regulations (that is, those of the INS) was unconstitutional. Document 142 is a summary of that decision.

DOCUMENT 142: *INS v. Chadha et al.* (June 23, 1983)

Decision: One-house congressional veto provision in 244(c)(2) of Immigration and Nationality Act held unconstitutional.

Summary:

An immigration judge suspended an alien's deportation pursuant to 244(c)(1) of the Immigration and Nationality Act (8 U.S.C.S. 1254(c)(1)). The United States House of Representatives passed a resolution vetoing the suspension pursuant to 244(c)(2) of the Act (8 U.S.C.S 1254(c)(2), which authorizes one House of Congress to invalidate the decision of the executive branch to allow a particular deportable alien to remain in the United States. The immigration judge reopened the deportation proceedings to implement the House order, and the alien was ordered deported. The Board of Immigration Appeals dismissed the alien's appeal, holding that it had no power to declare unconstitutional an Act of Congress. The United States Court of Appeals for the Ninth Circuit held that the House was without constitutional authority to order the alien's deportation and that 244(c)(2) violated the constitutional doctrine of separation of powers (634 F2nd 408).

On appeal, the United States Supreme Court affirmed. In an opinion by Chief Justice Burger, joined by Justices Brennan, Marshall, Blackmun, Stevens, and O'Connor, it was held that the legislative veto provision in 244(c)(2) was unconstitutional since the one-house veto was legislative in purpose and effect and subject to the procedures set out in Article I of the Constitution requiring passage by a majority of both Houses and presentment to the President.

Justice Powell, concurring in the judgment, expressed the view that the case should be decided on a narrower ground and declared that when Congress finds that a particular person does not satisfy the statutory criteria for permanent residence it has assumed a judicial function in violation of the principle of separation of powers.

Justice White dissented, expressing the view that the legislative veto is an important if not indispensable political invention and that neither Article I nor the doctrine of separation of powers is violated by this mechanism.

Justice Rehnquist joined by Justice White, dissenting, expressed the view that 244(c)(2) was not severable from the rest of the statute.

Source: 462 U.S. 919.

* * *

In 1985 another class action suit brought against the INS reached the Supreme Court. This case, *Jean et al. v. Nelson*, concerned denial of parole by the INS to undocumented Haitian aliens who were ruled as "economic refugees" and therefore excluded from parole status. A federal district court ruled in favor of the Haitians on the basis that the INS decision to detain the aliens without parole was made on the basis of race and national origin and was thus in violation of the equal protection clause in the Fifth Amendment to the Constitution. The Supreme Court affirmed the judgment of the appeals court, which although rejecting the constitutional claim accorded relief on the basis of INS regulation, remanding the case to the district court to ensure that the INS exercised its discretion in parole decisions in a nondiscriminatory manner. Document 143 presents a summary of the case and decision of the Supreme Court.

DOCUMENT 143: *Jean v. Nelson* (June 26, 1986)

Decision: Court of Appeals held to have improperly reached constitutional issue in deciding case challenging INS' denial of parole to undocumented Haitian aliens.

Summary:

The named representatives of a class of undocumented and unadmitted aliens from Haiti brought suit against the Commissioner of the Immigration and Naturalization Service (INS) in a Federal District Court, alleging in part that they had been detained without parole by INS officials on the basis of race and national origin, in violation of the equal protection guarantee of the Fifth Amendment to the United States Constitution. The District Court rejected the constitutional claim (544 F Supp 973), but a panel of the United States Court of Appeals for the Eleventh Circuit held that the Fifth Amendment's equal protection guarantee applied to the parole of unadmitted aliens (711 F2nd 1455). After a rehearing en banc, the Court of Appeals held that the Fifth Amendment did not apply to the consideration of unadmitted aliens for parole. Although rejecting the constitutional claim, the Court of Appeals accorded relief based on the applicable INS regulation (8 CFR 212.5), remanding to the District Court to ensure that the INS exercised its discretion in making parole decisions in an individualized and nondiscriminatory manner (727 F2d 957).

On certiorari, the United States Supreme Court affirmed the judgment remanding the case to the District Court. In the opinion of Justice Rehnquist, and joined by Justices White, Blackmun, Powell, Stevens, and O'Connor, it was held that the Court of Appeals should not have reached and decided the parole question on constitutional grounds, since the applicable statute and regulations were factually neutral and since the INS' parole discretion thereunder did not extend to considerations of race or national origin.

Justice Marshall, joined by Justice Brennan, dissented, expressing the view that there was no principled way to avoid reaching the constitutional issue and that aliens have a Fifth Amendment right to parole decisions free from invidious discrimination based on race or national origin.

Source: 472 U.S. 846.

* * *

The Immigration Reform and Control Act of 1986, commonly known as the IRCA, had a rather lengthy and tangled history. The Selected Commission of Immigration and Refugee Policy issued its report in 1981 calling for extensive legislative reform aimed mostly at closing the back door to control illegal immigration. It advocated an attempt to "demagnify" the draw or pull of the U.S. economy to illegal immigration by enacting a control device referred to as employer sanctions—making it illegal knowingly to hire an undocumented alien worker. It also suggested an amnesty program to provide legalization—permanent resident alien status—to an estimated 3 million illegal aliens then in the country. After Congress struggled for four years attempting to pass legislation to cope with the illegal alien problem, in 1986 a joint conference committee finally agreed on a package that could be enacted into law. Document 144 offers portions of the major provisions of IRCA.

DOCUMENT 144: Act of November 6, 1986: The Immigration Reform and Control Act (IRCA)

Title I—Control of Illegal Immigration

Sec. 101. Control of Unlawful Employment of Aliens

(a) In General

(1) In General—It is unlawful for a person or other entity to hire, or to recruit or refer for a fee, for employment in the United States—

(A) an alien knowing the alien is an unauthorized alien (as defined in subsection (h)(3) . . .

(B) an individual without complying with the requirements of subsection (b).

(2) Continuing employment—It is unlawful for a person or other entity, after hiring an alien for employment in accordance with paragraph (1), to continue to employ the alien in the United States knowing the alien is (or has become) an unauthorized alien with respect to such employment.

(3) Defense—A person or entity that establishes that it has complied in good faith with the requirements of subsection (b) with respect to the hiring, recruiting, or referral for employment of an alien in the United States who has established an affirmative defense that the person or entity has not violated paragraph (1)(A) with respect to such hiring, recruiting, or referral.

(4) Use of Labor Through Contract—For the purposes of this section, a person or other entity who uses a contract, subcontract, or exchange, entered into, renegotiated, or extended after the date of the enactment of this section, to obtain the labor of an alien in the United States knowing that the alien is an unauthorized alien . . . with respect to performing such labor, shall be considered to have hired the alien for employment in the United States in violation of paragraph (1)(A).

(5) Use of State Employment Agency Documentation—For the purposes of paragraph (1)(B) and (3), a person or entity shall be deemed to have complied with the requirements of subsection (b) with respect to the hiring of an individual who was referred for such employment by a State employment agency. . . .

(b) Employment Verification System—The requirements referred to in paragraphs (1)(B) and (3) are, in the case of a person or other entity hiring, recruiting, or referring an individual for employment in the United States, the requirements specified in the following three paragraphs:

(1) Attestation After Examination of Documentation—

(A) In General—The person or entity must attest, under penalty of perjury and on a form designated or established by the Attorney General by regulation, that it has verified that the individual is not an unauthorized alien by examining—

(i) a document described in subparagraph (B), or

(ii) a document described in subparagraph (C) and (D).

(B) Documents Establishing Both Employment Authorization and Identity—A document described in this subparagraph is an individual's—

(i) United States passport;

(ii) certificate of United States Citizenship;

(iii) certificate of naturalization;

(iv) unexpired foreign passport, if the passport has an appropriate, unexpired endorsement of the Attorney General authorizing the individual's employment in the United States; or

(v) resident alien card or other alien registration, if the card—

(I)　contains a photograph of the individual . . .

(II)　is evidence of authorization of employment in the United States

(C) Documents Evidencing Employment Authorization—A document described . . . is [a]

(i) social security account number card . . .

(ii) certificate of birth in the United States or establishing United States nationality at birth;

(iii) other documents evidencing authorization of employment in the United States which Attorney General finds, by regulation, to be acceptable for the purposes of this section.

(D) Documents establishing identity of an individual—A document described in this subparagraph is an individual's

(i) driver's license or similar document issued for the purpose of identification by a State, if it contains a photograph of the individual . . .

(ii) in the case of individuals under 16 years of age or in a State which does not provide for issuance of an identification document . . . referred to in clause (i), documentation of personal identity of such type as the Attorney General finds, by regulation, provides a reliable means of identification. . . .

(3) Definition of Unauthorized Alien—As used in this section, the term 'unauthorized alien' means, with respect to the employment of an alien at a particular time, that the alien is not at that time either (A) an alien lawfully admitted for permanent residence, or (B) authorized to be so employed by this Act or by the Attorney General. . . .

Deferral of Enforcement with Respect to Seasonal Agricultural Services—

(A) In General—Except as provided in subparagraph (B), before the end of the application period, it is unlawful for a person or entity (including a farm labor contractor) or an agent of such a person or entity, to recruit an unauthorized alien (other than an alien described in clause (ii) who is outside the United States to enter the United States to perform seasonal agricultural services.

(ii) Exception—Clause (i) shall not apply to an alien who the person or entity reasonably believes to meet the requirements of section 210(a)(2) of this Act (relating to the performance of seasonal agricultural services).

(j) General Accounting Office Reports—

(1) In General—Beginning one year after the date of enactment of this Act, and at intervals of one year thereafter for a period of three years after such date, the Comptroller General of the United States shall prepare and transmit to the Congress and to the taskforce established under subsection (k) a report describing the results of a review of the implementation and enforcement of this section during the preceding twelve-month period, for the purpose of determining if—

(A) such provisions have been carried out satisfactorily;

(B) a pattern of discrimination has resulted against citizens or nationals of the United States or against eligible workers seeking employment; and

(C) an unnecessary regulatory burden has been created for employers hiring such workers.

(k) Review by the Taskforce—

(1) Establishment of Taskforce—The Attorney General, jointly with the Chairman of the Commission on Civil Rights and the Chairman of the Equal Employment Opportunity Commission, shall establish a taskforce to review each report of the Comptroller General transmitted under subsection (j)(1).

(2) Recommendations to Congress—If the report transmitted includes a determination that the implementation of this section has resulted in a pattern

of discrimination in employment (against other than unauthorized aliens) on the basis of national origin, the taskforce shall, taking into consideration any recommendations in the report, report to Congress recommendations for such legislation as may be appropriate to deter or remedy such discrimination. . . .

(1) Termination Date for Employer Sanctions—

(1) If Report of Widespread Discrimination and Congressional Approval— The provisions of this section shall terminate 30 days after receipt of the last report required to be transmitted under subsection (j), if—

(A) the Comptroller General determines, and so reports . . . that a widespread pattern of discrimination has resulted against citizens or nationals of the United States or against eligible workers seeking employment solely from the implementation of this section; and

(B) there is enacted, within such period of 30 calendar days, a joint resolution stating in substance that the Congress approves the findings of the Comptroller General contained in such report.

(2) Senate Procedures for Consideration—Any joint resolution referred to in clause (B) of paragraph (1) shall be considered in the Senate in accordance with subsection (n). . . .

Sec. 111.(b) Increased Authorization of Appropriations for INS and EOIR—In addition to any other amounts authorized to be appropriated, in order to carry out this Act, there are authorized to be appropriated to the Department of Justice—

(1) for the Immigration and Naturalization Service, for fiscal year 1987, $12,000,000, and for fiscal year 1988, $15,000,000 . . . to provide for an increase in the border patrol personnel of the INS so that the average level of such personnel in each fiscal year 1987 and 1988 is at least 50 per cent higher than such level for fiscal year 1986. . . .

Title II—Legalization

Sec. 201. Legalization of Status. . . .

Sec. 245A. (a) Temporary Resident Status—The Attorney General shall adjust the status of an alien to that of an alien lawfully admitted for temporary residence if the alien meets the following requirements:

(1) Timely Application—

(A) During Application Period—Except as provided in subparagraph (B), the alien must apply for such adjustment during the 12-month period beginning on a date (not later than 180 days after the date of enactment of this section) designated by the Attorney General. . . .

(2) Continuous Lawful Residence Since 1982—

(A) In General—The alien must establish that he entered the United States before January 1, 1982, and that he has resided continuously in the United States in an unlawful status since such date and through the date the application is filed under this subsection.

(B) Non-immigrants—In the case of an alien who entered the United

States as a non-immigrant before January 1, 1982, the alien must establish that the alien's period of authorized stay as a non-immigrant expired before such date through the passage of time or the alien's unlawful status was known to the Government as of such date. . . .

(4) Admissible as Immigrant—

For the purposes of this subsection, an alien in the status of a Cuban and Haitian entrant described in paragraph (1) or (2)(A) of section 501(e) of Public Law 96–422 shall be considered to have entered the United States and to be in an unlawful status in the United States.

(b) Subsequent Adjustment to Permanent Residence and Nature of Temporary Resident Status—

(1) Adjustment to Permanent Residence—The Attorney General shall adjust the status of any alien provided lawful temporary resident status under subsection (a) to that of an alien lawfully admitted for permanent residence if the alien meets the following requirements:

(A) Timely Application After One Year's Residence—The alien must apply for such adjustment during the one-year period beginning with the nineteenth month that begins after the date the alien was granted such temporary status.

(B) Continuous Residence—The alien must establish that he has continuously resided in the United States since the date the alien was granted such temporary resident status.

(C) Admissible as Immigrant—The alien must establish that he—

(i)   is admissible to the United States as an immigrant, except as otherwise provided under subsection (d)(2), and

(ii)   has not been convicted of any felony or three or more misdemeanors committed in the United States.

(D) Basic Citizenship Skills—The alien must demonstrate that he either—

(I) meets the requirements of section 312 (relating to minimal understanding of ordinary English and a knowledge and understanding of the history and government of the United States. . . .

(II) is satisfactorily pursuing a course of study (recognized by the Attorney General) to achieve an understanding of English and such knowledge and understanding of the history and government of the United States. . . .

(h) Temporary Disqualification of Newly Legalized Aliens from Receiving Certain Public Welfare Assistance—

(1) In General—During the five year period beginning on the date an alien was granted lawful temporary resident status under subsection (a), and notwithstanding any other provision of law—

(A) except as provided in paragraphs (2) and (3), the alien is not eligible for—

(i) many programs of financial assistance furnished under Federal law . . .

(ii) medical assistance under a State plan approved under Title XIX of the Social Security Act; and

(iii) assistance under the Food Stamp Act of 1977; and

(B) a State or political subdivision therein may, to the extent consistent with paragraph (A) and paragraphs (2) and (3), provide that an alien is not eligible for the programs of financial assistance or for medical assistance described in subparagraph (A) (ii) furnished under the law of that State or political subdivision . . .

Unless otherwise specifically provided by this section or other law, an alien in temporary lawful residence status granted under subsection (a) shall not be considered (for purposes of any law of a State or political subdivision providing for a program of financial assistance) to be permanently residing in the United States under color of law.

(2) Exceptions.—Paragraph (1) shall not apply—

(A) to a Cuban and Haitian entrant (as defined in paragraph (1) or (2)(A) of section 501(e) of Public Law 96–422, as in effect on April 1, 1983) . . .

Title III—Reform of Legal Immigration, Part A—Temporary Agricultural Workers

Sec. 301. H-2A Agricultural Workers

(a) Providing New 'H-2A' Nonimmigrant Classification for Temporary Agricultural Labor—Paragraph (15)(H) of section 101 (a) (8 U.S.C. 1101(a)) is amended by striking out "to perform temporary services or labor," in clause (ii) and inserting in lieu thereof, "(a) to perform agricultural labor or services, as defined by the Secretary of Labor in regulations and including agricultural labor defined in section 3121(g) of the Internal Revenue Code of 1954 and agriculture as defined in section 3(f) of the Fair Labor Standards Act of 1938 . . . or a temporary or seasonal nature, or (b) to perform other temporary service or labor."

(b) Involvement of Departments of Labor and Agriculture in H-2A Program—Section 214(c) (8 U.S.C. 1184(c)) is amended by adding to the end the following: "For purposes of this subsection with respect to non-immigrants described in section 101(a)(15)(H)(ii)(a), the term 'appropriate agencies of Government' means the Department of Labor and includes the Department of Agriculture. The provisions of section 216 shall apply to the question of importing any alien as nonimmigrant under section 101(a)(15)(H)(ii)(a)."

(c) Admission of H-2A Workers—Chapter 2 of Title II is amended by adding after section 215 the following new section:

"Sec. 216(a) Conditions for Approval of H-2A Petitions—(1)

A petition to import an alien as an H-2A worker . . . may not be approved by the Attorney General unless the petitioner has applied to the Secretary of Labor for a certification that—

"(A) there are not sufficient workers who are able, willing, and qualified, and who will be available at the time and place needed, to perform the labor or services involved in the petition, and

"(B) the employment of the alien in such labor or services will not adversely affect the wages and working conditions of workers in the United States similarly employed."

[Title IV of the act specifies various reports to Congress over the next three years dealing with comprehensive reports on immigration, unauthorized alien employment, the H-2A program, the legalization program, evidence of discrimination, and the visa waiver pilot program.]

Source: 100 Stat. 3360.

* * *

In 1990 the Congress moved to enact reforms of the legal immigration law and process. In doing so it also modified or clarified certain provisions within IRCA. The major piece of legislation set new ceilings for a worldwide level of immigration, especially as related to the reunification of immediate family members. It redefined the preference system with respect to family reunification and to employment, and it made permanent a new category of preference called "diversity immigrants," introduced in IRCA as a temporary measure. It also established a Commission on Legal Immigration Reform and provided for a temporary stay of deportation for certain aliens for family unity and temporary protected status. Key provisions in the rather lengthy act are excerpted in Document 145.

DOCUMENT 145: Act of November 29, 1990: The Immigration Act of 1990

Sec. 201. (a) In General—Exclusive of aliens described in subsection (b), aliens born in a foreign state or dependent area who may be issued immigrant visas or who may otherwise acquire the status of an alien lawfully admitted to the United States for permanent residence are limited to

(1) family-sponsored immigrants described in section 203(a) . . . in a number not to exceed in any fiscal year the number specified in subsection (c) for that year, and not to exceed in any of the first three quarters of any fiscal year 27 percent of the worldwide level under such subsection for all such fiscal year;

(2) employment-based immigrants described in subsection 203(b) . . . in a number not to exceed in any fiscal year the number specified in subsection (d) for

that year, and not exceed in any of the first 3 quarters of any fiscal year 27 percent of the worldwide level under such subsection for all of such fiscal year; and

(3) for fiscal years beginning with fiscal year 1995, diversity immigrants described in section 203(c) . . . in a number not to exceed in any fiscal year the number specified in subsection (e) for that year, and not to exceed in any of the first three quarters of any fiscal year 27 percent of the worldwide level under such subsection for all such fiscal year.

(2)(A)(i) Immediate Relatives—For purposes of this subsection, the term 'immediate relatives' means the children, spouses, and parents of a citizen of the United States, except that, in the case of parents, such citizens be at least 21 years of age. In the case of an alien who was the spouse of a citizen of the United States for at least 2 years at the time of the citizen's death and was not legally separated from the citizen at the time of the citizen's death, the alien shall be considered, for the purpose of this subsection, to remain an immediate relative after the date of the citizen's death but only if the spouse files a petition under section 204(a)(1)(A) within 2 years after such date and only until the date the spouse remarries.

(c) Worldwide Level of Family-Sponsored Immigrants—(1)(A) The worldwide level of family-sponsored immigrants under this subsection for a fiscal year is, subject to subparagraph (B) equal to—

(i) 480,000 minus

(ii) the number computed under paragraph (2), plus

(iii) the number (if any) computed under paragraph (3).

(B)(i) For each of fiscal years 1992, 1993, and 1994, 465,000 shall be substituted for 480,000 in subparagraph (A)(i).

(ii) In no case shall the number computed under subparagraph (A) be less than 226,000 . . .

(d) Worldwide Level of Employment-Based Immigrants—(1) The worldwide level of employment-based immigrants under this subsection for a fiscal year is equal to—

(A) 140,000 plus

(B) the number computed under paragraph (2).

(2) The number computed under this paragraph for a fiscal year is the difference (if any) between the maximum number of visas which may be issued in section 203(a) . . . during the previous fiscal year and the number of visas issued under that section during that year.

(e) Worldwide Level of Diversity Immigrants—The worldwide level of diversity immigrants is equal to 55,000 for each fiscal year.

Sec. 102. Per Country Levels.

Sec. 202 (8 U.S.C. 1152) is amended—(1) by amending subsection (a) to read as follows:

(a) Per Country Level—

(1) Nondiscrimination—Except as specifically provided in paragraph (2)

and in sections 101(a)(27), 201(b)(2)(A)(i), and 203, no person shall receive any preference or priority or be discriminated against in the issuance of an immigrant visa because of a person's race, sex, nationality, place of birth, or place of residence.

(2) Per Country Levels for Family-Sponsored and Employment-Based Immigrants—Subject to paragraphs (3) and (4), the total number of immigrant visas made available to natives of any single foreign state or dependent area under subsections (a) and (b) of section 203 in any fiscal year may not exceed 7 percent (in the case of a single foreign state) or 2 percent (in the case of a dependent area) of the total number of such visas made available under such subsection in that fiscal year.

Subtitle B—Preference System

Part I—Family-Sponsored Immigrants

Sec. 111. Family-Sponsored Immigrants

Sec. 203 (8 U.S.C. 1153) is amended—

(1) by redesignating subsections (b) and (e) as subsections (d) through (g), respectively, and

(2) by striking subsection (a) and inserting the following:

(a) Preference Allocation for Family-Sponsored Immigrants—Aliens subject to the worldwide level specified in section 201(c) for family-sponsored immigrants shall be allotted visas as follows:

(1) Unmarried sons and daughters of citizens . . . in a number not to exceed 23,400 plus any visas required for the class specified in paragraph (4).

(2) Spouses and unmarried sons and unmarried daughters of permanent resident aliens . . . shall be allocated visas in a number not to exceed 114,200 plus the number (if any) by which such worldwide level exceeds 226,000 plus any visas not required for the class specified in paragraph (1); except that not less than 77 percent of such visa numbers shall be allocated to aliens described in subparagraph (A).

(3) Married sons and married daughters of immigrants—in a number not to exceed 23,400, plus any visas not required for the classes specified in paragraphs (1) and (2).

(4) Brothers and sisters of citizens—in a number not to exceed 65,000, plus any visas not required for the classes specified in paragraphs (1) through (3) . . .

(c) Legalized Alien Defined—In this section, the term 'legalized alien' means an alien lawfully admitted for temporary or permanent residence who was provided—

(1) temporary or permanent residence status under section 210 of the Immigration and Nationality Act,

(2) temporary or permanent residence status under section 245A of the Immigration and Nationality Act, or

(3) permanent residence status under section 202 of the Immigration Reform and Control Act of 1986.

Part 2-Employment-Based Immigrants

Sec. 121. Employment-Based Immigrants.

(a) In General—Section 203 (8 U.S.C. 1153) is amended by inserting after subsection (a), as inserted by section 111, the following new subsection:

(b) Preference Allocation for Employment-Based Immigrants—Aliens subject to the worldwide level specified in section 201(d) for employment-based immigrants in a fiscal year shall be allocated visas as follows:

(1) Priority Workers—Visas shall first be made available in a number not to exceed 40,000, plus any visas not required for the classes specified in paragraphs (4) and (5), to qualified immigrants who are aliens described in any of the following subparagraphs (A) through (C):

(A) Aliens with extraordinary ability—in sciences, arts, education, business, or athletics which has been demonstrated by sustained national or international acclaim and whose achievements have been recognized in the field through extensive documentation.

(B) Outstanding Professors and Researchers. . . .

(C) Certain Multinational Executives and Managers. . . .

(2) Alien members of Professions holding advanced degrees or aliens of exceptional ability. . . .

(3) Skilled workers, professionals, and other workers. . . .

(4) Certain special immigrants—Visas shall be made available, in a number not to exceed 10,000 to qualified special immigrants described in section 101 (a)(27) . . . of which not more than 5,000 may be made available in any fiscal year to special immigrants described in subclause (II) or (III) of section 101(a)(27)(C)(ii).

(5) Employment Creation—

(A) In General—Visas shall be made available, in a number not to exceed 10,000, to qualified immigrants seeking to enter the United States for the purpose of engaging in a new commercial enterprise—

(i) which the alien has established,

(ii) in which such alien has invested . . . or is actively in the process of investing, capital in an amount not less than the amount specified in subparagraph (C), and

(iii) which will benefit the United States economy and create full-time employment for not fewer than 10 United States citizens or aliens lawfully admitted for permanent residence or other immigrants lawfully authorized to be employed in the United States (other than the immigrant and the immigrant's spouse, sons, or daughters).

292 U.S. Immigration & Naturalization Laws & Issues

Part 3—Diversity Immigrants

Sec. 131. Diversity Immigrants

Sec. 203, as amended by sections 111 and 121 of this Act, is further amended by inserting after subsection (b) the following new subsection:

(c) Diversity Immigrants—

(1) In General—Except as provided in paragraph (2), aliens subject to the worldwide level specified in section 201(e) for diversity immigrants shall be allotted visas each fiscal year as follows:

(A) Determination of Preference Immigration—The Attorney General shall determine for the most recent previous 5-year period for which data are available, the total number of aliens who are natives of each foreign state and who (i) were admitted or otherwise provided lawful permanent resident status ... and (ii) were subject to the numerical limitations of section 201(a) ... or who were admitted or otherwise provided lawful permanent resident status as an immediate relative or other alien described in section 201(b)(2) ... (iv) Redistribution of Unused Visa Numbers—If the Secretary of State estimates that the number of immigrant visas to be issued to natives in any region for the fiscal year under this paragraph is less than the number of immigrant visas made available to such natives under this paragraph for the fiscal year, subject to clause (v), the excess visa numbers shall be made available to natives (other than the natives of a high-admission state) of the other regions in proportion to the percentages otherwise specified in clauses (ii) and (iii).

Subtitle C—Commission and Information

Sec. 141. Commission of Legal Immigration Reform.

(a) Establishment and Composition of Commission—(1) Effective October 1, 1991, there is established a Commission on Legal Immigration Reform ... which shall be composed of 9 members to be appointed as follows:

(A) One member who shall serve as Chairman, to be appointed by the President.

(B) Two members to be appointed by the Speaker of the House of Representatives who shall select such members from a list of nominees provided by the Chairman of the Subcommittee on Immigration ... of the Committee on the Judiciary of the House of Representatives.

(C) Two members to be appointed by the Minority Leader of the House ... who shall select such members from a list of nominees provided by the ranking minority member of the Subcommittee on Immigration ... of the Committee on the Judiciary of the House. ...

(D) Two members to be appointed by the Majority Leader of the Senate ... from a list provided by the Chairman of the Subcommittee of Immigration and Refugee Affairs of the Committee on the Judiciary of the Senate.

(E) Two members appointed by the Minority Leader of the Senate. ...

Title III—Family Unity and Temporary Protected Status

Sec. 301. Family Unity.

(a) Temporary Stay of Deportation and Work Authorization for Certain Eligible Immigrants—

The Attorney General shall provide that in the case of an alien who is an eligible immigrant . . . who has entered the United States before [May 5, 1988], who has resided in the United States on such date, and who is not lawfully admitted for permanent residence, the alien—. . . .

(2) The term 'legalized alien' means an alien lawfully admitted for temporary or permanent residence who was provided—

(A) such under section 210 of the Immigration and Nationality Act;

(B) temporary or permanent residence status under section 245A of the Immigration and Nationality Act, or

(C) permanent residence status under section 202 of the Immigration Reform and Control Act of 1986. . . .

Sec. 302. Temporary Protected Status.

(a) In General—The Immigration and Nationality Act is amended by inserting after section 244 the following new section:

"Sec. 244 A. (a) Granting of Status—

"(1) In General—In the case of an alien who is a national of a foreign state . . . under subsection (b) and who meets the requirements of subsection (c), the Attorney General—

"(A) may grant the alien temporary protected status in the U.S. and shall not deport the alien from the U.S. during the period in which such status is in effect, and

"(B) shall authorize the alien to engage in employment in the U.S. and to provide the alien with an 'employment authorized' endorsement or other appropriate work permit.

(b) Designations—

"(1) In General—The Attorney General, after consultation with appropriate agencies . . . may designate any foreign state . . . under this subsection only if—

"(A) the Attorney General finds that there is an ongoing armed conflict within the state, and, due to such conflict, requiring the return of aliens who are nationals of that state . . . would pose a serious threat to their personal safety.

"(B) the Attorney General finds that—

(i) there has been an earthquake, flood, drought, epidemic, or other environmental disaster in the state resulting in a substantial, but temporary, disruption of living conditions in the area affected,

(ii) the foreign state is unable, temporarily, to handle adequately the return to the state of aliens who are nationals of the state, and

(iii) the foreign state officially has requested designation under this paragraph; or

"(C) the Attorney General finds that there exists extraordinary and temporary conditions in a foreign state that prevent aliens who are nationals from the state from returning to the state safely. . . . "

(c) No effect on Executive Order 12711—Nothwithstanding subsection (g) of section 244 A of the Immigration and Nationality Act . . . such section shall not supercede or affect Executive Order 12711 (April 11, 1990), relating to policy implementation with respect to nationals of the People's Republic of China.

Sec. 303. Special Temporary Protected Status for Salvadorans.

(a) Designation—

(1) In General. El Salvador is hereby designated under section 244(b) of the Immigration and Nationality Act, subject to the provisions of this section.

(2) Period of Designation—Such designation shall take effect on the date of the enactment of this section and shall remain in effect until the end of the 18-month period beginning January 1, 1991.

Title IV—Naturalization

Sec. 401. Administrative Naturalization.

(a) Naturalization Authority.—Section 310 (8 U.S.C. 1421) is amended to read as follows: "Sec. 310. (a) Authority in Attorney General—The sole authority to naturalize persons as citizens of the United States is conferred upon the Attorney General.

"(b) Administration of Oaths.—An applicant for naturalization may choose to have the oath of allegiance under section 337 (a) administered by the Attorney General or by any District Court of the United States for any State or by any court of record in any State having a seal, clerk, and jurisdiction in actions in law or equity, or law and equity, in which the amount in controversy is unlimited. . . .

Sec. 402. Substituting 3 Months residence in INS District or State for 6 months residence in a State.

Section 316(a)(1) (8 U.S.C. 1427(a)(1) is amended by striking "and who has resided within the State in which the petitioner filed the petition for at least six months" and inserting "and who has resided within the State or within the district of the Service in the United States in which the applicant filed the application for at least three months."

Sec. 403. Waiver of English Language Requirement for Naturalization.

Section 312(1) (8 U.S.C. 1423(1) is amended by striking "is over fifty years of age and has been living in the United States for periods totaling at least twenty years subsequent to a lawful admission for permanent residence" and inserting "either (A) is over fifty years of age and has been living in the United States for periods totaling at least 20 years subsequent to a lawful admission for permanent residence, or (B) is over 55 years of age and has been living in the U.S. for periods totaling at least 15 years subsequent to a lawful admission for permanent residence."

Sec. 405. Naturalization of Natives of the Philippines Through Certain Active-Duty Service During World War II.

(a) Waiver of Certain Requirements.—(1) Clauses (1) and (2) of section 329(a) of the Immigration and Nationality Act . . . shall not apply to the naturalization of any person—

(A) who was born in the Philippines and who was residing in the Philippines before the service described in subparagraph (B);

(B) who served honorably—

(i) in an active-duty status under the command of the United States Armed Forces in the Far East, or

(ii) within the Philippine Army, the Philippine Scouts, or recognized guerilla units, at any time during the period beginning September 1, 1939, and ending December 31, 1946;

(C) who is otherwise eligible for naturalization under section 329 of such Act; and

(D) who applies for naturalization during the 2-year period beginning on the date of the enactment of this Act.

Sec. 406. Public Education regarding naturalization benefits. Section 332 (8 U.S.C. 1443) is amended by adding at the end the following subsection:

"(h) In order to promote the opportunities and responsibilities of United States citizenship, the Attorney General shall broadly distribute information concerning the benefits which persons may receive under this title and the requirements to obtain such benefits. In carrying out this subsection, the Attorney General shall seek the assistance of appropriate community groups, private voluntary agencies, and other relevant organizations. . . ."

Sec. 407. Conforming Amendments.

(d) Substituting Appropriate Administrative Authority for Naturalization Court.—(1) Section 316 (8 U.S.C. 1427) is amended—

(A) in subsection (b), by striking "the court" each place it appears and inserting "the Attorney General",

(B) in subsection (b), by striking "date of final hearing" and inserting "date of any hearing under section 336(a),"

(C) in subsection (e), by striking "the court" and inserting "the Attorney General". . . .

(E) in subsection (g)(1), by amending the first sentence to read as follows: "An applicant for naturalization under this subsection may be administered the oath of allegiance under section 337(a) by any district court of the United States, without regard to the residence of the applicant."

Source: 104 Stat. 4981.

* * *

Despite the national legislation intended to curb illegal immigration, the size and flow seemed unabated and the political pressure to do more increased during the 1990s. States that received the largest numbers of both legal and illegal immigrants, such as California, Florida, and Texas, sued the federal government in their respective federal district courts for the estimated billions of dollars they were having to bear for costs related to illegal immigrants and their children. In 1994 California attempted legislatively to reduce the draw of its economy and services and to send a message to Congress by passing an anti-immigration measure—Proposition 187.

DOCUMENT 146: California's Proposition 187, November 1994: The "Save Our State" Initiative

Section 1. Findings and Declaration

The People of California find and declare as follows:

That they have suffered and are suffering economic hardship by the presence of illegal aliens in the state. That they have suffered and are suffering personal injury and damage by the criminal conduct of illegal aliens in the state. That they have a right to the protection of their government from any person or persons entering this country unlawfully.

Therefore, the People of California declare their intention to provide for cooperation between their agencies of state and local government with the federal government, and to establish a system of required notification by and between such agencies to prevent illegal aliens in the United States from receiving benefits or public services in the State of California.

Section 2. Manufacture, Distribution or Sale of False Citizenship or Resident Alien Documents: Crime and Punishment.

Section 113. Is added to the Penal Code, to read:

Section 113. Any person who manufactures, distributes or sells false documents to conceal the true citizenship or resident alien status of another is guilty of a felony and shall be punished by imprisonment in the state prison for five years or by a fine of seventy-five thousand dollars.

Section 3. Use of False Citizenship or Resident Alien Documents: Crime and Punishment.

Section 114. Is added to the Penal Code, to read:

Section 114. Any person who uses false documents to conceal his or her true citizenship or resident alien status is guilty of a felony, and shall be punished by imprisonment in a state prison for five years or by a fine of twenty-five thousand dollars.

Section 4. Law Enforcement Cooperation with INS.

Section 834b is added to the Penal Code, to read:

Section 834b. (a) Every law enforcement agency in California shall fully cooperate with the United States Immigration and Naturalization Service regarding any person who is arrested if he or she is suspected of being present in the United States in violation of federal immigration laws.

(b) With respect to any such person who is arrested, and suspected of being present in the United States in violation of federal immigration laws, every law enforcement agency shall do the following:

(1). Attempt to verify the legal status of such person as a citizen of the United States, an alien lawfully admitted as a permanent resident, an alien lawfully admitted for a temporary period of time or as an alien who is present in the United States in violation of immigration laws. The verification process may include, but shall not be limited to, questioning the person regarding his or her date and place of birth and entry into the United States, and demanding documentation to indicate his or her legal status.

(2). Notify the person of his or her apparent status as an alien who is present in the United States in violation of federal immigration laws and inform him or her that, apart from any criminal justice precedings [sic], he or she must obtain legal status or leave the United States.

(3). Notify the Attorney General of California and the United States Immigration and Naturalization Service of the apparent illegal status and provide any additional information that may be requested by any other public entity.

(c) Any legislative, administrative, or other action by a city, county, or other legally authorized local governmental entity with jurisdictional boundaries, or by a law enforcement agency, to prevent or limit the cooperation required by subdivision (a) is expressly prohibited.

Section 5. Exclusion of Illegal Aliens from Public Social Services.

Section 10001.5. is added to the Welfare and Institutions Code, to read:

Section 10001.5 (a) In order to carry out the intention of the People of California that only citizens of the United States and aliens lawfully admitted to the United States may receive the benefits of public social services and to ensure that all persons employed in the providing of those services shall diligently protect public funds from misuse, the provisions of this section are adopted.

(b) A person shall not receive any public social services to which he or she may not otherwise be entitled until the legal status of that person has been verified as one of the following:

(1) A citizen of the United States.

(2) An alien lawfully admitted as a permanent resident.

(3) An alien lawfully admitted for a temporary period of time.

(c) If any public entity in this state to whom a person has applied for public social services determines or reasonably suspects, based upon the information provided to it, that the person is an alien in the United States in violation of federal law. . . . [services will not be provided and the INS will be notified]

Section 6. Exclusion of Illegal Aliens from Publicly Funded Health Care.

Chapter 1.3 (commencing with Section 130) is added to Part 1 of Division 1 of the Health and Safety Code to read:

Chapter 1.3. Publicly-Funded Health Care Services.

Section 130. (a) In order to carry out the intention of the People of California that, excepting emergency medical care as required by federal law, only citizens of the United States and aliens lawfully admitted to the United States may receive the benefits of publicly-funded health care, and to ensure that all persons employed in the providing of those services shall diligently protect public funds from misuse, the provisions of this section are adopted. . . .

(c) If any publicly-funded health care facility in this state from whom a person seeks health care services, other than emergency medical care as required by federal law, determines or reasonably suspects, based on the information provided it, that the person is an alien in the United States in violation of the federal law. . . . [services will not be provided and the INS will be notified]

Section 7. Exclusion of Illegal Aliens from Public Elementary and Secondary Schools.

Section 48215. Is added to the Education Code to read:

Section 48215. (a) No public elementary or secondary school shall admit, or permit the attendance of, any child who is not a citizen of the United States, an alien lawfully admitted as a permanent resident, or a person who is otherwise authorized under federal law to be present. . . .

(b) Commencing January 1, 1995, each school district shall verify the legal status of each child enrolling in the school district for the first time. . . .

(d) By January 1, 1996, each school district shall also have verified the legal status of each parent or guardian of each child referred to. . . .

(e) Each school district shall provide information to the State Superintendent of Public Instruction, the Attorney General of California and the United States Immigration and Naturalization Service regarding any enrollee or pupil, or parent or guardian, attending a public elementary or secondary school in the school district determined or reasonably suspected to be in violation of federal immigration laws within forty-five days after becoming aware of an apparent violation. . . .

(f) For each child who cannot establish legal status in the United States, each school district shall continue to provide education for a period of ninety days from the date of the notice. . . .

Section 8. Exclusion of Illegal Aliens from Public Postsecondary Educational Institutions.

Section 66010.8. is added to the Education Code to read:

Section 66010.8. (a) No public institution of postsecondary education shall admit, enroll, or permit the attendance of any person who is not a citizen of the United States, an alien lawfully admitted as a permanent resident, in the United States, or a person who is otherwise authorized under federal law to be present in the United States.

(c) Commencing with the first term or semester that begins after January 1, 1996, and at the end of each term or semester thereafter, each public postsecondary educational institution shall verify the status of each person enrolled or in attendance at that institution. . . .

Section 9. Attorney General Cooperation with the INS.

Section 53609.65. Is added to the Government Code, to read:

Section 53609.65. Whenever the state or a city, or a county, or any other legally authorized local government entity with jurisdictional boundaries reports the presence of a person who is suspected of being present in the United States in violation of federal immigration laws to the Attorney General of California, that report shall be transmitted to the United States Immigration and Naturalization Service. The Attorney General shall be responsible for maintaining on-going and accurate records of such reports, and shall provide any additional information that may be requested by any other government entity.

Section 10. Amendment and Severability.

. . . In the event that any portion of this act or the application thereof to any person or circumstances is held invalid, that invalidity shall not affect any other provision or application of the act, which can be given effect without the invalid provision or application, and to that end the provisions of this act are severable.

Source: *Lulac et al. v. Wilson et al.* 908 F.Supp. 755 (C.D.Cal. 1995): 787–91.

* * *

The last provision of Proposition 187 anticipated a federal court challenge as to the law's constitutionality. It was, of course, immediately brought to court by the League of United Latin American Citizens (LU-LAC). The federal district court did, indeed, rule that most of the law

was unconstitutional. California Governor Pete Wilson had cam-
paigned for his office running on a strongly pro–Proposition 187 stand,
and was comfortably reelected; the proposition was approved by 59
percent of the California voters. During his campaign he asserted that
passage of Proposition 187 would send a message to Congress to enact
tougher anti-illegal alien measures. Document 147 presents the summary judgment of the federal court decision on the initiative measure
which granted an injunction to bar the state from enforcing Proposition
187.

DOCUMENT 147: *LULAC et al. v. Wilson et al.* (November 20, 1995)

Summary:

    Public interest groups and individual citizens, in consolidated actions,
brought suit for declaratory and injunctive relief to bar California Governor, Attorney General and other state actors from enforcing provisions
of the voter-approved California initiative measure requiring state personnel to verify immigration status of persons with whom they come
into contact, report persons in United States unlawfully to state and federal officials, and deny those persons social services, health care, and
education benefits. On plaintiff's motions for summary judgment, the
District Court, Pfaelzer, J., held that: (1) classification, notification, cooperation and reporting provisions of the measure had direct and substantial effect on immigration, so as to be preempted by federal
immigration law; (2) initiative's denial of public benefits based on federal
determinations of immigration status was not impermissible regulation
of immigration; (3) provision excluding illegal aliens from public elementary and secondary schools was preempted by federal law as being
prohibited by equal protection clause of Fourteenth Amendment; (4) verification components of measure prohibiting public postsecondary education to persons not authorized under federal law to be in the United
States were permissible; (5) provisions of measure criminalizing making
and using false documents to conceal true citizenship or resident alien
status were legitimate exercise of state's police power; (6) provisions denying public social services to illegal immigrants as applied to federally
funded programs administered by the state that awarded benefits regardless of immigration status conflicted with and was preempted by
federal law; (7) provisions of measure prohibiting public postsecondary
educational institutions from admitting, enrolling or permitting attendance of persons not authorized under federal law to be present in the
United States were not preempted by federal law; and (8) criminal pen-

alties contemplated by provision criminalizing the manufacture, distribution, sale or use of false documents to conceal immigration status were not preempted by federal law.

Motions granted in part and denied in part.

Source: 908 F.Supp. 755 (C.D.Cal. 1995).

* * *

The highly popular voter approval of Proposition 187 and Governor Pete Wilson's easy margin of victory in his reelection bid did not go unnoticed by the U.S. Congress. Even though much of Proposition 187 was overturned by the federal district court decision, the Congress moved to enact national legislation that essentially enforced those portions of 187 that were ruled unconstitutional as state infringements of the national government's sole authority to enact immigration law or were state actions preempted by existing federal law. In 1996 the Congress passed and President Clinton signed into law two measures that essentially enacted the provisions of Proposition 187. Congress enacted a welfare reform act which contained several immigrant-related provisions (concerning both legal and illegal immigrants) that had aspects similar to those contained in Proposition 187. These immigrant-related provisions are summarized in Document 148 (H.R. 3734, P.L. 104–193). In addition, from 1994 through 1996, the Congress grappled with bills that would reform immigration law more generally—not just dealing with problems of illegal immigration. A sufficient consensus to enact broad-scale legal immigration reform could not be reached, and many issues concerning legal immigration were separated from those regarding illegal immigration. Congress cleared a measure dealing with illegal immigration and some aspects of legal immigration only after folding its provisions into the omnibus fiscal 1997 spending bill (H.R. 3610, P.L. 104–208), which President Clinton signed into law on September 30, 1996. Because the full measure covers more than two hundred pages, Document 149 includes only portions of the immigration section of the omnibus spending bill.

DOCUMENT 148: The Personal Responsibility and Work Opportunity Act of August 22, 1996: The Immigration-Related Provisions

The new welfare law imposed new restrictions on both legal and illegal immigrants, including provisions to:

Illegal Aliens

1. Restrictions. Restrict the federal benefits for which illegal aliens and legal non-immigrants, such as travelers and students, could qualify. The benefits denied were those provided by a federal agency or federal funds for:

—Any grant, contract, loan, professional license or commercial license.

—Any retirement, welfare, health, disability, food assistance or unemployment benefit.

2. Exceptions. Allow illegal aliens and legal non-immigrants to receive:

—Emergency medical services under Medicaid, but denied coverage for pre-natal or delivery assistance that was not an emergency.

—Short-term, non-cash emergency disaster relief.

—Immunizations and testing for treatment for the symptoms of communicable diseases.

—Non-cash programs identified by the attorney general that were delivered by community agencies such as soup kitchens, counseling, and short-term shelter, that were not conditioned on the individual's income or resources and were necessary for the protection of life and safety.

—Certain housing benefits (for existing recipients only).

—Licenses and benefits directly related to work for which a non-immigrant had been authorized to enter the United States.

—Certain Social Security retirement benefits protected by treaty or statute.

3. State and local programs. Prohibit states from providing state or local benefits to most illegal aliens, unless a state law was enacted after August 22, 1996, the day the bill was enacted, that explicitly made illegal aliens eligible for the aid. However, illegal aliens were entitled to receive a school lunch and/or breakfast if they were eligible for a free public education under state or local law. A state could also opt to provide certain other benefits related to child nutrition and emergency food assistance.

Legal Immigrants

4. Current immigrants. Make most legal immigrants, including those already in the United States, ineligible for SSI and food stamps until they became citizens; existing recipients to have an eligibility review by August, 1997. This ban was exempt for:

—Refugees, those granted asylum and aliens whose deportation was being withheld.

—Those who had worked in the United States for ten years.

—Veterans and those on active military duty, as well as their spouses and un-married children.

5. Future immigrants. Bar legal immigrants who arrived in the United States after August 22, 1996 from receiving most low-income federal benefits for five years after their arrival. Individuals exempt from this ban were:

—Refugees and those granted asylum and aliens whose deportation had been withheld, as well as Cuban and Haitian entrants.

—Veterans and those on active military duty, their spouses and minor children.

—Programs exempt from this ban were:

—Emergency medical service under Medicaid.

—Short-term, non-cash emergency disaster relief.

—Child nutrition, including school lunch programs, WIC [Women, Infant, and Children program], etc.

—Immunization and testing for treatment of symptoms of communicable diseases.

—Foster care and adoption assistance.

—Non-cash programs identified by Attorney General [soup kitchens, etc.].

—Loans and grants for higher education.

—Elementary and secondary education.

—Head Start program for pre-school children.

—Assistance from the Job Training Partnership Act.

6. State options. Allow states to deny benefits from the welfare block grant, Medicaid and social service block grants to most legal immigrants, with exemptions the same as for SSI and Food Stamps; future immigrants subject to the five-year ban noted above.

—Existing recipients to be continued until January 1, 1997.

—Exemptions granted to refugees, those granted asylum, etc.; those who worked in U.S. for ten years; veterans and those on active military duty, their spouses and minor children.

7. Sponsors. Expand circumstances under which an immigrant's sponsor would be financially responsible for that individual, generally affecting those entering the United States sponsored by a member of their immediate family. Affidavits of support would be legally enforceable for up to ten years after the immigrant last received benefits. Programs exempted were the same as those exempted from the five-year ban on benefits to future immigrants.

8. Reporting and verifying. Requires agencies that administer SSI, hous-

ing assistance or the welfare block grant to report quarterly to the INS the names and addresses of people they knew were unlawfully in the United States. Charged the Attorney General to issue regulations requiring within 18 months that anyone applying for federal benefits be in the United States legally and that States administering federal benefits would have to comply with the verification system within 24 months after they were issued.

Source: 1996 Congressional Quarterly Almanac, vol. 52 (Washington, D.C.: Congressional Quarterly, 1997), 6–17–6–18.

DOCUMENT 149: Illegal Immigration Reform and Immigrant Responsibility Act, September 30, 1996: Immigration Provisions of the Omnibus Spending Bill

1. Border agents. Authorize funding to increase the number of Border Patrol agents by 1,000 per year through fiscal 2001, doubling the total force from 5,000 to 10,000. The bill also authorized funds to increase the number of clerical workers and other support personnel at the border by 300 per year through fiscal 2001.

   The bill ordered the INS to relocate as many agents as possible to border areas with the largest number of illegal immigrants and to coordinate relocation plans with local law enforcement agencies. The INS was required to report to Congress on these activities within six months of enactment.

2. Other INS employees. Authorize funding of 900 additional INS agents to investigate and prosecute cases of smuggling, harboring or employing illegal aliens and 300 new agents to investigate people who overstay their visas.

3. Border fence. Authorize $12 million for the second and third tiers of a triple fence along a 14-mile strip at the U.S.–Mexico border south of San Diego, and for roads surrounding the fence. The project was exempt from the strictures of the 1973 Endangered Species Act and the 1969 Environmental Policy Act if either would prevent expeditious construction. It allowed the Attorney General to acquire land through condemnation for the fence.

4. Border Crossing Cards. Require the INS to develop alien identification cards that include a biometric identifier, such as a fingerprint, that could be read by machine, and for future cards that could use such devices as retina scanners.

5. Fleeing through checkpoints. Create a penalty up to five years in prison for fleeing through an INS checkpoint and deportation of those convicted.

6. Entry-Exit system. Order the Attorney General, within two years of enactment, to create a data base of information gathered from the documents people filled out as they legally entered and left the country which would allow the INS to match entry and exit records to identify people who overstayed their visas.

7. Pre-inspection. Require the INS to establish "pre-inspection" stations at five of the 10 foreign airports that were the departure points for the largest number of inadmissible immigrants to screen people who did not have proper documents.

8. State-federal cooperation. Allow the INS to enter into agreements with state and local governments for help in investigating, arresting, detaining and transporting illegal immigrants.

Document Fraud and Alien Smuggling

9. Wiretaps. Grant wiretap authority to the criminal division of the Justice Department for investigating cases of immigration document fraud.

10. Penalties for alien smuggling. Create felonies for alien smuggling for up to 10 years in prison for the first and second offenses, and 15 years for subsequent offenses; and make it a crime with up to five years in prison for employers who knowingly hired 10 people or more who were smuggled into the United States.

11. Prosecutors. Create 25 positions for Assistant United States Attorneys to prosecute cases of alien smuggling and document fraud.

12. Undercover operations. Grant broad authority for the INS to conduct undercover operations to track organized illegal immigration rings, including allowing the INS to establish or acquire companies, deposit funds in bank accounts without regard to federal regulations, and use profits from such front companies to offset expenses.

13. Document fraud. Increase penalty for document fraud from 5 years to 10 or 15 years in most cases; and, if fraud was used in facilitating a drug trafficking crime, a new penalty of 20 years in prison, and if involving terrorism, the penalty is 25 years.

14. Assisting in document fraud. Create a civil penalty for hiring someone to make a false application for public benefits such as food stamps. It further created a criminal penalty for "knowingly and willfully" failing to disclose it. This offense is punishable by up to 15 years.

15. False attestation of citizenship. Create a criminal penalty of up to five years in prison for falsely claiming U.S. citizenship.

16. Illegal voting. Create a criminal penalty for up to one year in prison for unlawfully voting in a federal election.

17. Seizure of assets. Allow courts in imposing sentences against violators of immigration statutes, to seize vehicles, boats, airplanes, and real estate if they were used in the commission of a crime or profit from the proceeds of a crime.

18. Involuntary servitude. Increase the penalty from five years in prison to 10 years for employers who kept workers in a state of involuntary servitude.

19. Subpoenas and evidence. Allow INS agents to subpoena witnesses and to videotape testimony at deportation proceedings.

Detention and Deportation

20. Readmission of deported aliens. Bar any alien who had been deported from re-entry into the United States for five years; and up to 10 years if the alien left while deportation proceedings were in progress or attempted to re-enter the country unlawfully; and bar repeat offenders for two years, as well as people convicted of aggravated felonies.

21. Status of illegal aliens. Deny legal status to anyone who resided in the United States unlawfully for at least 180 days; and persons so convicted could not gain legal status for three years. People in the country illegally for a year or more could not become legal for ten years, except for minors or persons with a pending application for asylum, or were battered women and children, or were people granted protection under the family unity provision of the 1990 Act, or spouses and minor children granted amnesty under the Immigration Reform and Control Act of 1986 to stay in the United States even if they entered illegally, while their application for legal status was pending.

22. Inadmissibility of arriving aliens. Allow people who arrived in the United States without legitimate documentation to be detained and deported without hearing unless they could demonstrate a credible fear of persecution back home. An asylum officer was to screen each case. An officer who decided there was no credible fear could deport the applicant. The applicant could request a review by an immigration judge within seven days, during which time the applicant had to remain in detention. The review could take place by telephone or tele-conference.

23. Detention of certain aliens. Require the detention of most illegal aliens serving criminal sentences after their prison terms were completed. The attorney general could release certain illegal immigrants from detention centers if there was insufficient space if he determined their release did not pose a security risk or a risk of fleeing, or who came from countries that would not take them back.

24. Deportation proceeding. Streamline deportation by replacing multiple proceedings with one, allowing proceedings by telephone or teleconference, and after 10 day notice of a hearing.

25. Departure. Require aliens be deported within 90 days of a deportation order, with mandatory detention during that period. Violent criminals would have to complete their prison terms before being deported; some non-violent criminal aliens could be deported before their term was up.

26. Deportation appeals. Limit judicial review of deportation orders. The state department could discontinue all visas for countries that declined to take back their deported nationals.

27. Criminal alien tracking. Authorize $5 million for a criminal alien tracking center using criminal alien data base authorized in the 1994 crime law (PL 103–322) to be used to assist local governments in identifying criminals who might be deportable.

28. Prisoner transfer treaties. Advise the president to negotiate bilateral prisoner transfer treaties to allow criminals to serve their terms in their home coun-

tries; and for the Secretary of State and Attorney General to report to Congress by April 1, 1997 on the potential for such treaties.

29. Vaccinations. Make a potential immigrant who did not have proof of proper vaccinations inadmissible to the United States.

30. Stalking. Add stalking, domestic violence and child abuse to the list of crimes that made someone deportable.

31. Benedict Arnold's language. Permanently bar from entry anyone who renounced his or her citizenship to avoid taxes.

32. Delegation of authority. Allow the attorney general to authorize local law enforcement officials to perform the duties of an immigration officer in the event of a mass influx of immigrants.

33. Judicial deportation. Broaden authority of judges to issue deportation orders, allowing someone deported as part of probation or a plea agreement.

34. Military bases. Create a pilot program on the use of closed military bases as INS detention centers.

Employee Verification

35. Employment verification programs. Order the attorney general to create three pilot programs—a basic pilot program, a Citizen Attestation Program, and the so-called Machine-Readable Document Pilot Program—to test the effectiveness of workplace verification systems, participation in which by employers would be voluntary; and the attorney general was to choose the states where each program would be tested, though in some cases employers in non-selected states could participate. All federal departments and agencies within the chosen states were required to participate in the program.

36. Basic pilot program. Allow participating employers to contact the INS via telephone, fax, or e-mail, to check job applicant's immigration status. INS to maintain a data base of names, Social Security numbers, and other information useful to verify an applicant's eligibility to work; and the INS to respond to inquiries within 3 days, and if the tentative response was that the person was not legal, the INS to have 10 days to confirm that determination. The program was to be tested in five of the seven states with the largest number of illegal immigrants.

37. Citizen attestation program. Create a similar program that would allow applicants to bypass the check if they attested that they were U.S. citizens; the penalty for false claims set at up to five years in prison being presumed sufficient to prevent widespread abuse.

38. Machine-readable documentation program. Allow employers to scan a card into a machine, which would verify the owner's Social Security number with the INS data base; to be placed in states selected by the attorney general in which driver's licenses or other state documents included Social Security numbers that could be read by machine.

39. Non-discrimination. Make it harder for the government to sue employers who used immigration laws to discriminate against certain workers, job applicants or other individuals by placing the burden on the government to

show that the employer "acted for the purpose, or with the intent to discriminate" against the individual.

Public Benefits

40. Public charges. Allow any consular agent to deny an immigrant visa on the basis that the person was likely to become a public charge.

41. Income requirement. Require sponsors of legal immigrants to earn at least 25 per cent more than the federal poverty level and to sign an affidavit that they would be financially responsible for the people they sponsored.

42. Driver's license pilot program. Allow states to create pilot programs to explore the feasibility of denying driver's licenses to illegal immigrants; the attorney general to report to Congress on these programs after three years.

43. Social Security. Clarify that Social Security benefits were not to be paid to illegal immigrants.

44. Student aid. Order the General Accounting Office to study the use of student aid by illegal immigrants and to report on such to Congress within one year of enactment.

45. Welfare. Require the GAO to report to Congress within 180 days on the unlawful use of means-tested benefits—such as food stamps and cash welfare—by illegal immigrants.

46. Battered women and children. Amend the new welfare law to permit certain illegal immigrants who were victims of domestic violence to qualify for public benefits.

47. Nonprofit organizations. Amend the welfare law so that non-profit charitable organizations were no longer required to verify the immigration status of applicants to determine their eligibility for benefits.

48. Food stamps. Allow legal immigrants who were receiving food stamps, and who would lose them under provisions of the new welfare law, to continue receiving them until April 1, 1997, and as long as August 22, 1997—when the process of certifying people for food stamps was complete.

49. Falsely applying for benefits. Allow judges to double the monetary penalty and triple the prison terms for anyone who forged or counterfeited any United States seal to make a false application for public benefits.

50. Reimbursement for medical care. Allow reimbursement to states and localities for emergency medical care of illegal immigrants, if the care was not already reimbursed via existing federal programs in an amount subject to appropriations.

51. Assisted housing. Require the Secretary of Housing and Urban Development to deny financial assistance through subsidized housing programs to families in which all members were illegal immigrants. If families were split between legal and illegal immigrants, HUD could adjust the size of the benefit to match the percentage of family members who were in the United States legally.

Other Provisions

52. Forced population control. Stipulate that anyone who had been forced to undergo sterilization or an abortion, or who had been persecuted for failure to do so, could be eligible for asylum or refugee status—up to 1,000 persons per year to be admitted to the United States under the program.

53. Parole. Limit the ability of the INS to use parole of detainees to facilitate mass immigration [as it did with Cubans in 1994 when some 20,000 were paroled, for example]. When the government did use parole to facilitate immigration, the parolees would count toward caps on legal immigration.

54. Asylum. Require that asylum applications from people already in the United States be filed no later than one year after entry; asylum interviews to take place within 45 days of application; a ruling within 180 days, and an appeal to be filed within 30 days of the ruling. The provision allowed asylum to be denied for many reasons, and asylum could be rescinded if the circumstances changed, such as if a new government came to power in the home country of the person granted asylum.

55. Public education. Deny visas to immigrants whose intention was to attend a public elementary or secondary school for more than one year.

56. Visas. Clarify that a short-term visa was void as soon as the person stayed longer than its term; requiring a new visa to be issued in the home country of the applicant. [Previously, anyone could obtain visas in nearby countries, such as Canada and Mexico.]

57. Buddhist monks. Allow the State Department unlimited authority to determine the procedures and locations for processing immigrant visa applications—allowing them to require Vietnamese monks and nuns of the An Quang Buddhist sect in Thailand to return to Vietnam to apply for visas to the United States. [This provision was in response to a Court of Appeals decision ruling such requirement was discrimination based on nationality. The U.S. Supreme Court was expected to rule on the case in 1997.]

58. Genital mutilation. Create a crime punishable by prison for performing female genital mutilation.

59. Mail-order brides. Require "international matchmaking organizations" to disseminate to their clients information about U.S. immigration laws under penalty of a $20,000 fine for failure to do so; and require the Attorney General to prepare a report to Congress on the mail-order bride business within a year of enactment.

60. Temporary agriculture workers. Require the INS to report by the end of 1996 whether or not the United States had an adequate number of temporary agricultural workers.

61. State issued documents. Set national standards for birth certificates, driver's licenses and other identification documents. The Department of Transportation was to set standards for IDs which had to include Social Security numbers, and agencies issuing them had to keep these numbers on file and confirm their accuracy with the Social Security Administration. The

standards were intended to make such documents more tamper-resistant; were to be issued within one year; and to be complied with by October 1, 2000.

62. Tamper-proof Social Security cards. Require the Social Security Administration to develop a prototype tamper-proof identity card.

Source: 1996 Congressional Quarterly Almanac, vol. 52 (Washington, D.C.: Congressional Quarterly, 1997), 5–8–5–10.

* * *

The 1996 welfare reform act and its provisions targeting legal aliens provoked a strong reaction among many ethnic groups and others that surfaced once the anti-immigrant fervor eased and the economy improved. Document 150 presents an excerpt from a *New York Times* article summarizing recent developments by the Clinton administration and the Congress.

DOCUMENT 150: "Legal Immigrants Would Regain Aid in Clinton Plan" (January 25, 1999)

Reflecting the shift away from the anti-immigrant sentiments of the early 1990s and responding to intense criticisms that budget reforms in 1996 had been made at the expense of immigrants, Congress and the president modified some of the drastic welfare cuts enacted in 1996 which had targeted the foreign born. The Balanced Budget Act of 1997 restarted Supplemental Security Income for the disabled as well as Medicaid benefits for 420,000 legal immigrants who were present in the country on August 22, 1996. The Agricultural Research Act of 1998 once again provided food stamps for 225,000 legal immigrant children, senior citizens, and persons with disabilities who had entered the country by August 22, 1996. Budget proposals for Year 2000 budget include provisions for:

a) restoring medical benefits for immigrants who have arrived after August 22, 1996, are then present in the country for five years and subsequently become disabled;

b) making food stamps available to immigrants who had been in the country on August 22, 1996, and subsequently reached the age of 65 and qualified for the food stamp program;

c) providing health coverage for legal immigrant children who entered the country after August 22, 1996; and

d) giving the states the option of providing Medicaid coverage for pre-
natal care to legal immigrant women who arrived after August 22, 1996.

Source: Michael Janofsky, "Legal Immigrants Would Regain Aid in Clinton Plan,"
New York Times, January 25, 1999, pp. 1, 19.

Glossary

Adjustment to Immigrant Status. A procedure whereby a nonimmigrant may apply for a change of status to a lawful permanent resident if an immigrant visa is available for his or her country. The alien is counted as an immigrant as of the date of the adjustment.

Alien. A person who is not a citizen or national of the United States.

Amicus curiae. A "friend of the court" legal brief submitted by a state or an interest group that is not a party to a case but which has an interest in the outcome of the case in which it argues its position on the case.

Amnesty. The granting of legal relief or pardon; in the Immigration Reform and Control Act, granting legal temporary resident status to a previously illegal (undocumented) alien.

Asia-Pacific Triangle. An area encompassing countries and colonies from Afghanistan to Japan and south to Indonesia and the Pacific Islands. Immigration from this area was severely limited to small quotas established in the McCarran-Walter Act (1952). The Asia-Pacific Triangle replaced the Asiatic Barred Zone.

Asiatic Barred Zone. Established by the Immigration Act of 1917, it designated a region from which few natives could enter the United States.

Asylee. A person in the United States who is unable or unwilling to return to his or her country of origin because of persecution or a well-founded fear of persecution. The person is eligible to become a permanent resident after one year of continuous residence in the United States.

Asylum. The granting of temporary legal entrance to an individual who is an asylee.

Border card. A card allowing a person living within a certain zone of the U.S. border to cross back and forth legally for employment purposes without a passport or visa.

Border patrol. The law enforcement arm of the Immigration and Naturalization Service.

Bracero program. A temporary farm worker program that allowed, from 1942 to 1964, migrant farm workers to come to the United States for up to nine months annually to work in agriculture.

Certiorari. A writ issued by the U.S. Supreme Court to send up for its review upon appeal the records of a lower court case.

Cuban/Haitian Entrant. Status accorded Cubans who entered the United States illegally between April 15, 1980, and October 10, 1980, and Haitians who entered the country illegally before January 1, 1981. Those qualified who were in residence continuously for one year were allowed to adjust their status to legal immigrants by the Immigration Reform and Control Act of 1986.

Debarkation. Leaving a ship or airplane to enter the United States.

Deportation. A legal process by which a nation sends an individual back to his or her country of origin after refusing them legal residence in the United States.

Diversity immigrants. A special category of immigrants established by the Immigration Act of 1990 to allow a certain number of visas to be issued to immigrants from countries which previously had low admission numbers. Initially established by the Immigration Reform and Control Act (1986), they were then referred to as persons from countries "adversely affected" by the 1965 immigration legislation. At least 40 percent of the visas were reserved for natives of Ireland.

Due process of law. The constitutional limitation on governmental behavior to deal with an individual according to prescribed rules and procedures.

Emigrant. An individual who voluntarily leaves his or her country of birth for permanent resettlement elsewhere.

Emigration. The act of leaving one's place of origin or birth for permanent resettlement.

Employer sanctions. A restrictive provision of the Immigration Reform and Control Act which imposes civil fines or criminal penalties, when there is a pattern or practice of violation, for knowingly hiring an illegal immigrant.

Equal protection of the law. The constitutional guaranteed right that all persons be treated the same before the law.

Escapee. An individual fleeing persecution from a (Communist or Communist-dominated) government usually for racial, religious, ethnic, social organization, or political opinion reasons.

Eugenics. A pseudo-scientific theory of racial genetics.

Excluded categories. A listing in immigration law of those persons specifically denied entrance to the United States for stated reasons for the purpose of permanent settlement.

Exclusion. The denial of legal entrance to a sovereign territory.

Exempt. An individual or class or category of individuals to whom the provision of the flexible numerical cap set by the 1990 act do not apply.

Expulsion. The decision of a sovereign nation legally to compel an individual to leave its territory permanently.

Green card. A document issued by the INS that certifies an individual as a legal immigrant entitled to work in the United States. The term is still used, but the identification card is no longer green.

Guest worker program. A program enabling the legal importation of workers for temporary labor in specified occupations.

Identity papers. Legal documents recognized by the government as establishing a person's identity.

Illegal alien. An individual who is in a territory without documentation permitting permanent residence.

Immediate relatives. In recent immigration law, spouses, minor children, parents (of a citizen or resident alien over twenty-one years of age), and brothers or sisters of a U.S. citizen or permanent resident alien who are exempt from the numerical limitations imposed on immigration to the United States.

Immigrant. An alien admitted to the United States as a lawful permanent resident.

Investor immigrant. Established by the 1990 act, an individual permitted to immigrate based on a promise to invest $1 million in an urban area or $500,000 in a rural area to create at least ten new jobs.

Legalized alien. An alien lawfully admitted for temporary or permanent residence under the Immigration and Nationality Act of 1965 or under the Immigration Reform and Control Act of 1986.

Literacy test. A device imposed upon immigrants by the 1917 Immigration Act to restrict immigration to persons able to read and write. Never effective in reducing immigration numbers dramatically, it was eliminated in 1924.

Mortgaging. The legal device to "borrow" against future fiscal year immigration quotas to allow entrance of immigrants, for refugee or humanitarian purposes, after their national origin fiscal quota had been filled. It was used during the 1950s.

Naturalization. The conferring, by any means, of citizenship upon a person after birth.

Nonimmigrant. An alien seeking temporary entry into the United States for a specific purpose other than permanent settlement—such as a foreign government official, tourist, student, temporary worker, or cultural exchange visitor. Between 1965 and 1990, such persons were referred to "as those exempt from numerical limitations" and since then as those "not subject to the numerical cap." There are a number of categories for such "special immigrants."

Nonpreference. A category of immigrant visas apart from family and employment-based preferences that was available primarily between 1966 and 1978. This category was eliminated by the Immigration Act of 1990.

Nonquota immigrant. A person allowed entrance by specific reason who was not charged against a nation's annual quota.

Parolee. An alien, appearing to be inadmissible to the inspecting officer, allowed to enter the United States under urgent humanitarian reasons or when that alien's entry is determined to be for significant public benefit.

Passport. A legal identification document issued by a sovereign nation-state attesting to the nationality of an individual for international travel purposes.

Permanent resident. A noncitizen who is allowed to live permanently in the United States and who can travel in and out of the country without a visa and can work without restriction. This person also is permitted to accumulate time toward becoming a citizen.

Preference system. A device used in immigration law primarily since 1928 to establish rules and procedures to determine the order in which the limited number of immigration visas were to be issued.

Preferences. Specific categories of individuals to be awarded visas for permanent immigration, mostly either family or employment based.

Protocol. An international agreement governing the understanding and procedures that member states who are parties to a treaty agree upon for a given purpose; for example, the UN protocols regarding the status and treatment of refugees.

Pull factor. Characteristics of a country that attract immigrants for permanent resettlement.

Push factor. A reason that compels an individual to emigrate from his or her nation of origin and seek permanent resettlement elsewhere.

Quota immigrant. Prior to 1965, an individual seeking entrance to the United States or coming under the system which fixed an annual number of visas to be awarded to persons from a particular nation or territory. This system was phased out in 1968.

Refugee-parolee. A qualified applicant for conditional entry between 1970 and 1980 whose application for admission could not be approved because of inadequate numbers of seventh preference visas. The applicant was paroled into the United States under the parole authority granted to the attorney general.

Relocation camps. Places established by executive order for holding Japanese aliens or Japanese American citizens during World War II on their way to ten permanent internment camps used until they were closed in 1946. They are often referred to as concentration camps.

Special Agricultural Workers. Aliens who performed labor in perishable agricultural commodities for a specified period of time and were admitted for temporary and then permanent residence under the Immigration Reform and Control Act.

Transit alien. An alien in immediate and continuous transit through the United States, with or without a visa. Transit aliens are principally aliens and their families serving at the UN headquarters and foreign government officials and their family members.

Unauthorized alien. An individual who is in a territory without documentation—an illegal immigrant.

Undocumented alien. An individual in a sovereign territory without legal authorization to be there—an illegal alien.

Visa. A legal document issued by a consular or similar State Department official allowing a person to travel to the United States for either permanent or temporary reasons—such as immigrant, student, tourist, government representative, business, or cultural exchange.

Withdrawal. An alien's voluntary removal of an application for admission in lieu of an exclusion hearing before an immigration judge.

Xenophobia. An unfounded or exaggerated fear of resident foreigners.

Selected Bibliography

Adamic, Louis. *Nation of Nations.* New York: Harper and Brothers, 1945.

Alienkoff, Thomas A. *Immigration and Nationality Laws of the United States.* St. Paul, Minn.: West Publishing, 1990.

Anbinder, Tyler. *Nativism and Slavery: The Northern Know Nothings and the Politics of the 1850's.* New York: Oxford University Press, 1992.

Archdeacon, Thomas. *Becoming American: An Ethnic History.* New York: Free Press, 1983.

Auerbach, Frank L. *Immigration Laws of the United States.* 2d ed. New York: Bobbs Merrill, 1961.

Balderrama, Francisco E. *In Defense of La Raza: The Los Angeles Mexican Consulate and the Mexican Community, 1929–1936.* Tuscon: University of Arizona Press, 1982.

Balderrama, Francisco E., and Raymond Rodriguez. *Decade of Betrayal: Mexican Repatriation in the 1930's.* Albuquerque: University of New Mexico Press, 1995.

Baldwin, Carl R. *Immigration Questions and Answers.* New York: Allworth Press, 1995.

Barbour, Scott, ed. *Immigration Policy.* San Diegos: Greenhaven Press, 1995.

Barkan, Elliott Robert. *And Still They Come: Immigrants and American Society, 1920–1990s.* Wheeling, Ill.: Harlan Davidson, 1996.

———. *Asian and Pacific Islander Migration to the United States: A Model of New Global Patterns.* Westport, Conn.; Greenwood Press, 1992.

———. *A Nation of Peoples: A Sourcebook on America's Multicultural Heritage.* Westport, Conn.: Greenwood Press, 1999.

Baum, Dale. "Know Nothingism and the Republican Majority in Massachusetts: The Political Realignment of the 1850's." *Journal of American History* 64, no. 4 (1978): 959–86.

Beals, Carleton. *Brass Knuckle Crusade.* New York: Hastings House, 1960.

Bean, Frank D., Barry Edmonston, and Jeffrey S. Passel, eds. *Undocumented Mi-*

gration to the United States: IRCA and the Experience of the 1980s. Santa Monica, Calif.: Rand Corporation, 1990.

Beck, Roy H. *The Case Against Immigration.* New York: Norton, 1996.

Bennett, David. *The Party of Fear: From Nativist Movements to the New Right in American History.* Chapel Hill: University of North Carolina Press, 1988.

Bennett, Marion. *American Immigration Policies: A History.* Washington, D.C.: Public Affairs Press, 1963.

Bernard, William S., ed. *Immigration Policy: A Reappraisal.* New York: Harper, 1950.

Betten, Neil. "Nativism and the Klan in Town and City: Valparaiso and Gary, Indiana." *Studies in History and Sociology* 4, no. 2 (1973): 3–16.

Billington, Ray A. *The Origins of Nativism in the United States, 1800–1844.* New York: Arno Press, 1974.

Bodnar, John E. "The Procurement of Immigrant Labor: Selected Documents." *Pennsylvania History* 4, no. 2 (1974) 189–206.

Borjas, George. *Friends and Strangers: The Effect of Immigration on the U.S. Economy.* New York: Basic Books, 1997.

Breitman, Richard, and Alan M. Kraut. *American Refugee Policy and European Jewry, 1933–1945.* Bloomington: Indiana University Press, 1987.

Briggs, Vernon M., Jr. *Mass Immigration and the National Interest.* 2d ed. Armonk, N.Y.: M. E. Sharpe, 1996.

Briggs, Vernon M. Jr., and Stephen Moore. *Still an Open Door?: U.S. Immigration Policy and the American Economy.* Washington, D.C.: American University Press, 1994.

Bryce-LaPorte, R. S., ed. *A Sourcebook on the New Immigration.* New Brunswick, N.J.: Transaction Books, 1981.

Calavita, Kitty. *Inside the State: The Bracero Program, Immigration, and the INS.* New York: Routledge, 1992.

Chan, Sucheng, ed. *Entry Denied: Exclusion and the Chinese Community in America, 1882–1943.* Philadelphia: Temple University Press, 1991.

Chiswick, Barry R., ed. *The Gateway: U.S. Immigration and Policies.* Washington, D.C.: American Enterprise Institute, 1982.

Clark, Malcolm, Jr. "The Bigot Disclosed: 90 Years of Nativism." *Oregon Historical Quarterly* 75, no. 2 (1974) 108–90.

Commission on the Wartime Internment and Relocation of Civilians. *Personal Justice Denied.* Washington, D.C.: U.S. Government Printing Office, 1982.

Cornelius, Wayne, and Ricardo Montoya. *America's New Immigration Law: Origins, Rationales, and Potential Consequences.* San Diego: Center for U.S.–Mexican Studies, 1983.

Craig, Richard. *The Bracero Program: Interest Groups and Foreign Policy.* Austin: University of Texas Press, 1971.

Crewdson, John. *The Tarnished Door.* New York: N.Y. Times Books, 1983.

Curran, Thomas. *Xenophobia and Immigration, 1820–1930.* Boston, Twayne, 1975.

Daniels, Roger. *Coming to America: A History of Immigration and Ethnicity in American Life.* New York: Harper, 1990.

———. "No Lamps Were Lit for Them: Angel Island and the Histography of Asian-American Immigration." *Journal of American Ethnic History* 17, no. 1 (Fall 1997): 3–18.

————. *Not Like Us: Immigrants and Minorities in America, 1890–1924.* Chicago: Ivan R. Dee, 1997.

————. *The Politics of Prejudice: The Anti-Japanese Movement in California and the Struggle for Japanese Exclusion.* 2d ed. Berkeley: University of California Press, 1977.

DeLeon, Arnoldo. *They Called Them Greasers: Anglo-American Attitudes Towards Mexicans in Texas, 1821–1900.* Austin: University of Texas Press, 1983.

"Developments in the Law—Immigration Policy and the Rights of Aliens." *Harvard Law Review* 96, no. 6 (1983): 1268–1465.

Dinnerstein, Leonard. *America and the Survivors of the Holocaust.* New York: Columbia University Press, 1982.

————. *Anti-Semitism in America.* New York: Oxford University Press, 1994.

Dinnerstein, Leonard, and Frederick Jaher. *Uncertain Americans: Readings in Ethnic History.* New York: Oxford University Press, 1977.

Dinnerstein, Leonard, and David Reimers. *Ethnic Americans.* New York: Harper and Row, 1975.

Divine, Robert A. *American Immigration Policy: 1924–1952.* New Haven: Yale University Press, 1957.

Duleep, Harriot O., and Wunnava Phanindra. *Immigrants and Immigration Policy.* Greenwich, Conn.: JAI Press, 1996.

Dunlevy, James A., and Henry Gemery. "Economic Opportunity and the Response of 'Old' and 'New' Migrants to the United States." *Journal of Economic History* 38, no. 4 (1978): 901–17.

Edmonston, Barry, and Jeffrey S. Passel, eds. *Immigration and Ethnicity: The Integration of America's Newest Arrivals.* Washington, D.C.: Urban Institute, 1994.

Eisinger, Peter K. "Ethnic Political Transition in Boston: 1884–1933: Some Lessons for Contemporary Cities." *Political Science Quarterly* 93, no. 2 (1978): 217–39.

Emberson, Edward Proper. "Colonial Immigration Laws," Ph.D. Dissertation. New York: Columbia University, 1900.

Fairchild, Henry Pratt. *The Melting Pot Mistake.* New York: Arno Press, 1977.

Fawcett, James T., and Benjamin Carino, eds. *Pacific Bridges: The New Immigration from Asia and the Pacific Islands.* Staten Island, N.Y.: Center for Migration Studies, 1987.

Feingold, Henry. *The Politics of Rescue: The Roosevelt Administration and the Holocaust, 1938–1945.* New Brunswick: Rutgers University Press, 1970.

Feldstein, Stanley, and Lawrence Costello, eds. *The Ordeal of Assimilation: A Documentary History of the White Working Class, 1830–1970.* Garden City, N.Y.: Doubleday, 1974.

Fitzgerald, Keith. *The Face of the Nation: Immigration, the State, and the National Identity.* Stanford, Calif.: Stanford University Press, 1996.

Fix, Michael. *Immigration and Immigrants: Setting the Record Straight.* Washington, D.C.: Urban Institute, 1994.

Fix, Michael, and Jeffrey S. Passel. *The Door Remains Open: Recent Immigration to the United States and a Preliminary Analysis of the Immigration Act of 1990.* Washington, D.C.: Urban Institute, 1991.

Franklin, Frank G. *The Legislative History of Naturalization in the United States*. New
    York: Arno Press, 1969.
Gavit, John. *Americans by Choice*. New York: Harper, 1922.
Gibson, William. *Aliens and the Law*. Chapel Hill: University of North Carolina
    Press, 1940.
Gjerde, Jon, ed. *Major Problems in American Immigration and Ethnic History*. Boston:
    Houghton Mifflin, 1998.
Goldstein, Robert J. "The Anarchist Scare of 1908: A Sign of Tensions in the
    Progressive Era." *American Studies* 15, no. 2 (1974): 55–78.
Gordon, Charles. "The Alien and the Constitution." *California Western Law Review*
    9 (Fall 1971): 1–36.
Gordon, Charles E., and Harry Rosenfield. *Immigration Law and Procedure*. New
    York: Matthew Bender, 1980.
Gordon, Michael. "Labor Boycott in New York City: 1880–1886." *Labor History*
    16, no. 2 (1975): 184–229.
Gotanda, Neil. "A Critique of 'Our Constitution is Colorblind.' " *Stanford Law
    Review* 44, no. 1 (November 1991): 1–68.
Guerin-Gonzales, Camille. *Mexican Workers and the American Dream: Immigration,
    Repatriation, and California Farm Labor, 1900–1939*. New Brunswick: Rutgers
    University Press, 1994.
Hammamoto, Darrell Y., and Rodolfo Torres, eds. *New American Destinies: A
    Reader in Contemporary Asian and Latino Immigration*. New York: Routledge,
    1997.
Handlin, Oscar. *Boston's Immigrants*. Cambridge: Harvard University Press, 1979.
Handlin, Oscar, ed. *Immigration as a Factor in American History*. Englewood Cliffs,
    N.J.: Prentice-Hall, 1959.
———. *The Uprooted*. 2d ed. Boston: Little, Brown, 1973.
Hansen, Marcus Lee. *Atlantic Migration, 1601–1860*. New York: Harper Torch-
    books, 1961.
Harper, Elizabeth. *Immigration Laws of the United States*. 3d ed. Indianapolis:
    Bobbs Merrill, 1975.
Higham, John. *Send These to Me*. New York: Atheneum, 1975.
———. *Strangers in the Land: Patterns of American Nativism, 1860–1925*. New
    Brunswick: Rutgers University Press, 1955.
Hing, Bill Ong. *Making and Remaking Asian America Through Immigration Policy,
    1850–1990*. Stanford, Calif.: Stanford University Press, 1993.
Hoerder, Dirk, ed. *American Labor and Immigration History: 1877–1920*. Urbana:
    University of Illinois Press, 1982.
Hofstadler, Richard, ed. *U.S. Immigration Policy*. Durham, N.C.: Duke Press Policy
    Studies, 1984.
Hofstadler, Richard, and Michael Wallace. *American Violence*. New York: Knopf,
    1971.
Holt, Michael. "The Politics of Impatience: The Origins of Know-Nothingism."
    Journal of American History 60, no. 2 (1973): 309–33.
Hosokawa, William. *The Quiet Americans*. New York: William Morrow, 1969.
Howe, Irving. *World of Our Fathers*. New York: Simon and Schuster, 1976.
Hundley, Norris, ed. *The Asian-American: The Historical Experience*. Santa Barbara,
    Calif.: American Bibliography Center, CLIO Press, 1976.

Hutchinson, Edward. *Legislative History of American Immigration Policy, 1798–1965*. New Brunswick: Rutgers University Press, 1981.

Isbister, John. *The Immigration Debate: Remaking America*. West Hartford, Conn.: Kumarian Press, 1996.

Jones, Maldwyn Allen. *American Immigration*. 2d ed. Chicago: University of Chicago Press, 1992.

Karst, Kenneth L. *Belonging to America: Equal Citizenship and the Constitution*. New Haven: Yale University Press, 1989.

Keely, Charles. *U.S. Immigration: A Policy Analysis*. New York: Population Council, 1979.

Kettner, James H. *The Development of American Citizenship: 1608–1870*. Chapel Hill: University of North Carolina Press, 1978.

Kim, Hyung-Chan. *Asian Americans and Congress: A Documentary History*. Westport, Conn.: Greenwood Press, 1996.

Kim, Hyung Chan, ed. *Asian Americans in Congress: A Documentary History*. Westport, Conn.: Greenwood Press, 1995.

———. *A Legal History of Asian Americans, 1790–1990*. Westport, Conn.: Greenwood Press, 1994.

Kinzer, Donald. *An Episode in Anti-Catholicism: The American Protective Movement*. Seattle: University of Washington Press, 1963.

Kiser, George, and David Silverman. "Mexican Repatriation During the Great Depression." *Journal of Mexican American History* 3, no. 1 (1973): 139–64.

Knobel, Dale. *"America for the Americans": The Nativist Movement in the United States*. New York: Twayne, 1996.

Konvitz, Milton R. *The Alien and the Asiatic in American Law*. Ithaca, N.Y.: Cornell University Press, 1946.

Kraut, Alan. *Silent Travelers: Germs, Genes and the "Immigrant Menace."* Baltimore: Johns Hopkins University Press, 1994.

Kritz, Mary M. *U.S. Immigration and Refugee Policy: Global and Domestic Issues*. Lexington, Ky.: Lexington Books, 1983.

Lai, Him Mark, Genny Lim, and Judy Yung. *Island: Poetry and History of Chinese Immigrants on Angel Island, 1910–1940*. San Francisco: Hoc Doi—Chinese Culture Foundation, 1980.

Lane, A. "American Labor and European Immigrants in the Late Nineteenth Century." *Journal of American Studies* 11, no. 2 (1977): 241–60.

Laws Applicable to Immigration and Nationality. Compiled by Carl B. Hyatt and edited by Edwina Austin Avery. Washington, D.C.: Government Printing Office, 1953.

Lee, Erika. "Immigrants and Immigration Law: A State of the Field Assessment." *Journal of American Ethnic History*. Forthcoming.

Leibowitz, A. "Refugee Act of 1980: Problems and Concerns." *Annals of the American Academy of Political and Social Science* 1 (1983): 163–71.

LeMay, Michael. *Anatomy of a Public Policy*. New York: Praeger, 1994.

———. *From Open Door to Dutch Door: An Analysis of U.S. Immigration Policy Since 1820*. New York: Praeger, 1987.

———. *The Struggle for Influence*. Lanham, Md.: University Press of America, 1985.

Levine, Daniel B., Kenneth Hill, and Robert Warren, eds. *Immigration Statistics: A Story of Neglect*. Washington, D.C.: National Academy Press, 1985.

Lieberson, Stanley. *A Piece of the Pie: Blacks and White Immigrants Since 1880*. Berkeley: University of California Press, 1980.

Linkh, Richard M. *American Catholicism and European Migration*. New York: Center for Migration Studies, 1975.

Litt, Edgar. *Ethnic Politics in America*. Glenview, Ill.: Scott, Foresman, 1970.

Loesher, Gil, and John A. Scanlan. *Calculated Kindness: Refugees and America's Half Open Door, 1945 to Present*. New York: Free Press, 1986.

Lopez, Ian F. Haney. *White Law: The Legal Construction of Race*. New York: New York University Press, 1996.

Lowe, Lisa. *Immigrant Acts: On Asian American Cultural Politics*. Durham, N.C.: Duke University Press, 1997.

Lutton, Wayne, and John Tanton. *The Immigration Invasion*. Petosky, Mich.: Social Contract Press, 1994.

Maharidge, Dale. *The Coming White Minority: California's Eruptions and America's Future*. New York: Random House, 1996.

Martinez, Oscar J. *Border People: Life and Society in US–Mexico Borderlands*. Tucson: University of Arizona Press, 1994.

McCarthy, Kevin F., and George Vernez. *Immigration in a Changing Economy: California's Experience*. Santa Monica, Calif.: Rand, 1997.

McClain, Charles J. *In Search of Equity: The Chinese Struggle Against Discrimination in Nineteenth Century America*. Berkeley: University of California Press, 1994.

McClellan, Grant S., ed. *Immigrants, Refugees and U.S. Policy*. New York: H. W. Wilson, 1981.

McClymer, John F. "The Federal Government and the Americanization Movement, 1915–1924." *Prologue* 10, no. 1 (1978): 23–41.

McDowell, Lorraine, and Paul T. Hill. *Newcomers in American Schools*. Santa Monica, Calif.: Rand, 1993.

McGouldrick, Paul F., and Michael Tannen. "Did American Manufacturers Discriminate Against Immigrants Before 1914?" *Journal of Economic History* 37, no. 3 (1977): 723–46.

Miller, Stuart C. *The Unwelcome Immigrant: The American Image of the Chinese, 1785–1882*. Berkeley: University of California Press, 1969.

Morris, Milton. *Immigration—The Beleaguered Bureaucracy*. Washington, D.C.: Brookings Institution, 1985.

Neuman, Gerald L. "The Lost Century of American Immigration Law, 1776–1875." *Columbia Law Review* 93, no. 8 (December 1993): 1834, 1837–38.

North, David. *Immigration and Income Transfer Policies in the United States: An Analysis of a Non-Relationship*. Washington, D.C.: New Trans-Century Foundation, 1980.

Novak, Michael. *The Rise of the Unmeltable Ethnics*. New York: Macmillan, 1972.

O'Neill, Terry. *Immigration: Opposing Viewpoints*. San Diego: Greenhaven Press, 1992.

Overdyke, W. Darrell. *The Know-Nothing Party in the South*. Gloucester, Mass.: Peter Smith, 1968.

Papadetriou, Demetrious, and Mark Miller, eds. *The Unavoidable Issue*. Philadelphia: Institute for the Study of Human Issues, 1984.

Peffer, George A. "Forbidden Families: Emigration Experiences of Chinese Women Under the Page Laws, 1875–1882." *Journal of American Ethnic History* 6, no. 1 (1986): 28–46.

Perea, Juan F. *Immigrants Out!: The New Nativism and the Anti-Immigrant Impulses in the United States*. New York: New York University Press, 1997.

Pickus, Noah M. J. *Becoming American/America Becoming: Duke University Workshop on Immigration and Citizenship*. *Final Report*. Durham, N.C.: Duke University, 1998.

Piore, Michael. *Birds of Passage: Migrant Labor and Industrial Societies*. New York: Cambridge University Press, 1979.

Pitkin, Thomas. *Keepers of the Gate: A History of Ellis Island*. New York: New York University Press, 1975.

Portes, Alejandro, and Ruben G. Rumbaut. *Immigrant America: A Portrait*. 2d ed. Berkeley: University of California Press, 1996.

Post, Louis F. *The Deportation Delirium of Nineteen-Twenty*. Chicago: Charles H. Kerr, 1923.

Preston, William, Jr. *Aliens and Dissenters: Federal Suppression of Radicals, 1903–1963*. Cambridge, Mass.: Harvard University Press, 1963.

Proper, Emberson Edward. "Colonial Immigration Laws: A Study of the Regulation of Immigration by the English Colonies in America." Ph.D. diss., Columbia University, 1900.

Pypic, George. *South Slavic Immigration in America*. Boston: Twayne, 1978.

Rak, Mary Kidder. *Border Patrol*. Boston: Houghton Mifflin, 1983.

Reimers, David M. *Still the Golden Door: The Third World Comes to America*. 2d ed. New York: Columbia University Press, 1992.

———. *Unwelcome Strangers: American Identity and the Turn Against Immigration*. New York: Columbia University Press, 1998.

Ringer, Benjamin B. *We the People and Others*. New York: Tavistock Publishers, 1983.

Rischin, Moses, ed. *Immigration and the American Tradition*. Indianapolis: Bobbs-Merrill, 1976.

Rosenblum, Gerald. *Immigrant Workers: Their Impact on American Labor Radicalism*. New York: Basic Books, 1973.

Rumbaut, Ruben G. *Immigrant Children in California Public Schools: A Summary of Current Knowledge*. Baltimore: Johns Hopkins University Center for Research on Effective Schooling for Disadvantaged Students, 1990.

Salyer, Lucy E. *Laws Harsh as Tigers: Chinese Immigrants and the Shaping of Modern Immigration Law*. Chapel Hill: University of North Carolina Press, 1995.

Samuel, Joseph. *Jewish Immigration to the U.S., 1881–1910*. New York: Arno Press, 1969.

Sarna, Jonathan, and David Dalin, eds. *Religion and State in American Jewish Experience*. Notre Dame, Indiana: University of Notre Dame Press, 1994.

Saveth, Edward. *American Historians and European Immigrants, 1875–1925*. New York: Free Press, 1938.

Saxton, Alexander. *The Indispensable Enemy: Labor and the Anti-Chinese Movement in California*. Berkeley: University of California Press, 1971.

Schlesinger, Arthur M. *The Disuniting of America: Reflections on a Multicultural Society.* New York: Norton, 1992.

Select Commission on Immigration and Refugee Policy. *Final Report.* Washington, D.C.: U.S. Government Printing Office, 1981.

Severance, Frank H., ed. *Millard Fillmore Papers.* New York: Kraus Reprint, 1970.

Shumsky, Neil L. *The Evolution of Political Protest and the Workingmen's Party of California.* Columbus: Ohio State University Press, 1991.

Sibley, Mulford Q. *The Transformation of American Politics, 1840–1860.* Englewood Cliffs, N.J.: Prentice-Hall, 1967.

Simon, Julian. *The Economic Consequences of Immigration.* Cambridge, Mass.: Basil Blackwell, 1990.

Simon, Rita J., and Susan Alexander. *The Ambivalent Welcome: Print Media, Public Opinion and Immigration.* Westport, Conn.: Praeger, 1993.

Smith, Darrell Hevenor, and H. Guy Herring. *Bureau of Immigration: Its History, Activities, and Organization.* Baltimore: Johns Hopkins University Press, 1924.

Smith, James. *Freedom's Fetters: Alien and Sedition Laws.* Ithaca, N.Y.: Cornell University Press, 1956, 1963.

Sowell, Thomas, *Ethnic America: A History.* New York: Basic Books, 1981.

Sowell, Thomas, ed. *Essays and Data on American Ethnic Groups.* Washington, D.C.: Urban Institute Press, 1978.

Steiner, Edward. *On the Trail of the Immigrant.* New York: Fleming H. Revell, 1906.

Szumski, Bonnie, ed. *Interracial America Opposing Viewpoints.* San Diego: Greenhaven Press, 1996.

Takaki, Ronald. *Chinese America: History and Perspectives, 1990.* Brisbane, Calif.: Chinese Historical Society of America, 1990.

———. *Strangers from a Distant Shore: A History of Asian Americans.* Boston: Little, Brown, 1989.

Taylor, Philip. *The Distant Magnet: European Emigration to the U.S.A.* New York: Harper and Row, 1971.

Teitelbaum, M. "Rights Versus Rights: Immigration and Refugee Policy in the United States." *Foreign Affairs* 59 (1980): 21–59.

Teitelbaum, Michael S., and Myron Weiner. *Threatened Peoples, Threatened Borders: World Migration and United States Policy.* New York: W. W. Norton, 1995.

Thernstrom, Stephen. *Harvard Encyclopedia of America Ethnic Groups.* Cambridge, Mass.: Harvard University Press, 1980.

Ueda, Reed. *Postwar Immigrant America: A Social History.* Boston: Bedford Books, St. Martin's Press, 1994.

United States General Accounting Office. *Illegal Aliens: Extent of Welfare Benefits Received on Behalf of U.S. Citizen Children.* Washington, D.C.: U.S. Government Printing Office, 1997.

United States Immigration and Naturalization Service. *An Immigrant Nation: United States Regulation of Immigration, 1798–1991.* Washington, D.C.: Immigration and Naturalization Service, 1991.

Vecoli, Rudolph, and Joy Lintelman. *A Century of American Immigration, 1884–1984.* Minneapolis: University of Minnesota Continuing Education and Extension, 1984.

Wareing, J. "The Changing Pattern of Immigration into the United States, 1956–1975." *Geography* 63, no. 3 (1978): 220–24.

Warren, Robert, and Ellen P. Kraly. *The Elusive Exodus: Emigration from the United States.* Washington, D.C.: National Academy Press, 1985.

Weiss, Richard. "Ethnicity and Reform: Minorities and the Ambience of the Depression Years." *Journal of American History* 66, no. 3 (1979): 566–85.

Weissbrodt, David. *Immigration Law and Procedure.* St. Paul, Minn.: West Publishing, 1984.

White, Jerry C. "A Statistical History of Immigration." *Immigration and Naturalization Reporter* 25 (Summer 1976).

Whittke, Carl. *We Who Built America.* Akron, Ohio: Case Western Reserve University Press, 1967.

Williamson, Charlton Jr. *The Immigration Mystique: America's False Conscience.* New York: Basic Books, 1996.

Williamson, Jeffrey G. "Migration to the New World: Long-Term Influence and Impact." *Explorations in Economic History* 11, no. 4 (1974): 357–89.

Wyman, David. *The Abandonment of the Jews: America and the Holocaust, 1941–1945.* New York: Pantheon Books, 1984.

———. *Paper Walls: America and the Refugee Crisis.* Amherst: University of Massachusetts Press, 1968.

Wyman, Mark. *Round-Trip to America: The Immigrants Return to Europe, 1880–1930.* Ithaca, N.Y.: Cornell University Press, 1993.

Yang, Philip Q. *Post-1965 Immigration to the United States: Structural Determinants.* Westport, Conn.: Praeger, 1995.

Yans-McLaughlin, Virginia, ed. *Immigration Reconsidered: History, Sociology, and Politics.* New York: Oxford University Press, 1990.

Ziegler, Benjamin. *Immigration: An American Dilemma.* Lexington, Mass.: D.C. Heath, 1953.

Index

ABOUT THE EDITORS

MICHAEL LEMAY is Professor of Political Science at California State University, San Bernardino. He also teaches in the Ethnic Studies Program. He is the author of six journal articles, several book chapters, and seven books, including several specifically concerning immigration policy: *From Open Door to Dutch Door* (1987), *The Gatekeepers: Comparative Immigration Policy* (1989), and *Anatomy of a Public Policy* (1994). He serves as a regular reviewer and has published in the *International Migration Review*, the *Journal of American Ethnic History*, and the *Social Science Quarterly*.

ELLIOTT ROBERT BARKAN is Professor of History and Ethnic Studies at California State University, San Bernardino. He is a specialist in immigration history, having authored some two dozen articles on the topic, and is the author of two recent volumes: *Asian and Pacific Islander Migration to the United States* (1992) and *And Still They Come: Immigrants and American Society, 1920–1990s* (1996). He edited another volume for Greenwood Press, *A Nation of Peoples: A Sourcebook on America's Multicultural Heritage* (1999). He serves as the book review editor for the *Journal of American Ethnic History* and, until recently, was a member of the executive board of the Immigration and Ethnic History Society.

DEMCO